PRAISE FOR THE FILMS OF SAM RAIMI

THE EVIL DEAD

"I'd wandered in [to a theater] one afternoon, not knowing anything, and seeing the first *Evil Dead* movie. And I thought it was an absolute knockout ... you very rarely get the chance to see any film, especially by a young filmmaker with no money, where you can see the imprint of his style so strongly."

— Simon Moore, screenwriter, *The Quick and the Dead*

SPIDER-MAN

"... a geek orgasm..."

— Brian Michael Bendis, writer, quoted in *Entertainment Weekly*

"... Maguire's understated presence and Raimi's off-kilter sensibility are what make *Spider-Man* both a successful adaptation and an enjoyable film in its own right."

— Ethan Alter, *Film Journal International*

DARKMAN

"Raimi works from inside the cheerfully violent adolescent-male sensibility of superhero comics, as if there were no higher style for a filmmaker to aspire to, and the absence of condescension is refreshing."

— Terrence Rafferty, *The New Yorker*

ARMY OF DARKNESS

"Raimi builds awareness of movie technique into our responses, he makes us laugh at our own connoisseurship because, after all, it's really a connoisseurship of schlock."

— Peter Rainer, *The Los Angeles Times*

A SIMPLE PLAN

"Raimi turns the screws of the relentless plot with quiet precision, aiming for queasily escalating suspense ..."

— David Ansen, *Newsweek*

ALSO BY JOHN KENNETH MUIR

FROM APPLAUSE:

An Askew View: The Films of Kevin Smith (2002)

FROM POWYS MEDIA:

Space: 1999 — The Forsaken (2003)

FROM MCFARLAND:

The Encyclopedia of Superheroes on Film and Television (2003)

Eaten Alive at a Chainsaw Massacre: The Films of Tobe Hooper (2002)

Horror Films of the 1970s (2002)

Terror Television (2001)

An Analytical Guide to TV's One Step Beyond, the 1959–61 Paranormal Anthology (2001)

The Films of John Carpenter (2000)

A History and Critical Analysis of Blake's 7 (1999)

A Critical History of Dr. Who on Television (1999)

Wes Craven: The Art of Horror (1998)

An Analytical Guide to TV's Battlestar Galactica (1998)

Exploring Space: 1999 (1997)

THE UNSEEN FORCE

THE FILMS OF SAM RAIMI

JOHN KENNETH MUIR

The Unseen Force: The Films of Sam Raimi
by John Kenneth Muir

Library of Congress Cataloging-in-Publication Data:
Muir, John Kenneth, 1969–
The unseen force : the films of Sam Raimi /
by John Kenneth Muir.
p. cm.
Includes bibliographical references.
1. Raimi, Sam — Criticism and interpretation. I. Title.
PN1998.3.R365M85 2004
791.4302'33'092 — dc22
2003021353

British Library Cataloging-in-Publication Data
A catalog record of this book is available from the British Library

APPLAUSE THEATRE & CINEMA BOOKS
151 West 46th Street, 8th Floor
New York, NY 10036
Phone: (212) 575-9265
Fax: (646) 562-5852
Email: info@applausepub.com
Internet: www.applausepub.com
Applause books are available through your local bookstore, or you may order at http://www.applausepub.com or call Music Dispatch at 800-637-2852

Sales & Distribution
NORTH AMERICA:
Hal Leonard Corp.
7777 West Bluemound Road
P.O. Box 13819
Milwaukee, WI 53213
Phone: (414) 774-3630
Fax: (414) 774-3259
Email: halinfo@halleonard.com
Internet: www.halleonard.com

EUROPE:
Roundhouse Publishing Ltd.
Millstone, Limers Lane
Northam, North Devon
Ex 39 2RG
Phone: 01237-474474
Fax: 01237-474774
roundhouse.group@ukgateway.net

To my Lulu, who passed in 2003 while this book was in preparation, and to the 1973 Oldsmobile Delta 88 — both of 'em classics.

And for Bob Vesterman, my own Bruce Campbell

CONTENTS

ACKNOWLEDGMENTS

Despite the fact that it's my name emblazoned out there on the spine of this book, several important individuals contributed to this text.

First and foremost, I'd like to thank the two Junes in my life. June Clark, my agent and friend, who went above and beyond the call of duty to make this project a reality — all while I recovered from acute appendicitis. And the other "June," my wife Kathryn, who spent long weekends proofing the text, offering input and debate.

Also, I'd like to acknowledge the talented and all-around good folk in Michigan and California who contributed their insights on Raimi cinema to this study of the director. In alphabetical order, this group consists of Ian Abercrombie, Betsy Baker, Douglas Beswick, Brent Briscoe, Gary Cole, Kevin Conway, Willem Dafoe, Peter Deming, Chris Doyle, Phil Gillis, Daniel Goldin, Richard Grove, Lance Henriksen, Joe LoDuca, William Mesa, Simon Moore, Verne Nobles, Tim Philo, Robert Primes A.S.C., Thell Reed, Cliff Robertson, Amy Robinson, Chelcie Ross, Ellen Sandweiss, Randy Ser, Thomas Smith, Dana Stevens, Tom Sullivan, Theresa Tilly, Sheree J. Wilson, and Christopher Young. Also, special thanks to Karen Eide.

I'd also like to highlight the cooperation and generosity of makeup artist Tom Sullivan at Dark Age Productions, who provided many of the photographs included here and was an exceptional resource and asset throughout the text's preparation. Thanks, Tom — you're the best!

Last but not least, my admiration goes to the book's humble subject, director Sam Raimi — an artist who inspired not only this text, but a new generation of independent filmmakers across America.

INTRODUCTION

AS LONG AS I LIVE, I'LL NEVER FORGET my sister's retelling of the pivotal demonic ambush in *The Evil Dead*, the film she had just survived on a Friday night, tax day in 1983. In enthusiastic, if revolted, detail she recounted how an unfortunate character dashed from an isolated forest cabin into the darkened woods only to be tied down by invasive vines and then, chillingly, laid spread-eagle before a particularly substantial branch with, well, a woody.

I listened with fearful attention, not yet having developed my sister's fascination with the horror genre, but even at that young age, I suspected that *where* my sister had seen the film had as much impact as the drama itself.

The Wellmont, a grand old theater in Montclair, New Jersey, had once played host to comedians Abbott and Costello, but was no longer a thriving venue when it showed *The Evil Dead* in the early eighties. This was the dawn of the multiplex, and the Wellmont's once-expansive auditorium had been parceled into three tiny screens. Accordingly, contemporary fare was often more Deadite than Jerseyite, *Zombie Island Massacre* (1984) and its ilk having supplanted more typical Hollywood fare.

It turns out, I was flat wrong to dismiss my sister's verve for *The Evil Dead*, as I discovered when I first saw it on home video (a new market at the time) a year or so later, accompanied by a cadre of horror-loving high school buddies. By then, I was fully indoctrinated in the horror movie ethos, baptized by fire during a showing of Tobe Hooper's intense *The Funhouse* (1981), and understood that *The Evil Dead* went way beyond anything I'd seen, so much so that a first viewing left me weak in the knees. As connoisseurs of such things are aware, that's a rarified condition reserved only for the best of the best, the most harrowing of horror masterpieces, like Hooper's *The Texas Chain Saw Massacre* (1974), John Carpenter's *Halloween* (1978), and George Romero's *Dawn of the Dead* (1979).

The Evil Dead saw characters dismembered, chopped to bits, splattered with bodily fluids of bright primary colors, and generally violated in a most visceral manner. The ads termed the unrated film a "grueling" experience in terror and were right on the money. Among my circle of friends, the name of Sam Raimi, *The Evil Dead*'s young director, became *legend*. It was a legend that grew with the release of *Evil Dead 2*, a film as funny and thrilling as its predecessor was terrifying, in no small part because of Raimi's unique style of in-your-face, gonzo camera work.

Lest anyone forget, this was the sequel that witnessed a zombie's detached eyeball (with stalk...) fly across a room and land flatly in the open mouth of a screaming heroine, who promptly gagged on the offending body part. Much of that memorable ocular flight, from popping eye socket to yawning esophagus, was recorded from the perspective of the severed eye itself.

On an average Saturday night, in your parents' basement surrounded by teenage friends, that is precisely the sort of thing that merits a cheer, and even hardened critics, who usually have, at most, a grudging admiration for horror, took notice. Mark Horowitz wrote in *Film Comment* that the flying eyeball shot was nothing less than "startlingly magnificent."[1]

In at least one sense, it is the legacy of that flying eyeball that explains the existence of this book, an in-depth, behind-the-scenes review of the two-decade long career of Sam Raimi. Certainly, it was an audacious shot, a unique way to approach what might have been a routine gore sequence. More succinctly, it remains a metaphor for Raimi's approach to filmmaking: his unwavering ability to garner a laugh amidst screams and, in the process, reveal things the audience has not witnessed before, or at least not in that fashion.

Not coincidentally, such an approach mirrors the definition of genius established by Raimi's favorite director, the late John Huston (1906–1987). Huston once described a genius as "someone who sees things in a way that illuminates them and enables you to see things in a different way."[2] Or to put it in another, perhaps less grandiose manner, "How can you hate a director this flamboyant?"[3] Critic David Denby asked that question in *New York* magazine, his interrogative capturing the essence of early Raimi, a director willing to take "outrageous chances"[4] all for the sake of audience approval. Even if his early movies are somehow deemed silly today, the director's dedicated and innovative approach to forging memorable entertainment won him the admiration of many, including actress Sharon Stone who demanded he direct her postmodern Western, *The Quick and the Dead* (1995).

Everybody remembers the old adage that there's nothing new under the sun, as well as its show business corollary, that there are really only seven types of stories to vet. Yet Raimi's enthusiasm and innovation, particularly in the realm of the visual, successfully expresses familiar stories in fresh ways, whether he toils on a Western (*The Quick and the Dead*), a Sinbad/Ray Harryhausen–style fantasy-adventure (*Army of Darkness*), a sports bio-pic (*For Love of the Game*), or the superhero origin myth (*Darkman, Spider-Man*).

As a result of Raimi's energy and innovation, the audience feels exhilarated and drawn into the tale. Film critic Kevin Thomas of the *Los Angeles Times* noted in 1987 that Raimi is a "dynamo who knows how to make a movie as cinematic as possible,"[5] and in the age of interchangeable, over-edited, all-hype, no-substance entertainment, that's a quality worth championing.

Weaned on a diet of movies while growing up in suburban Michigan, Raimi actually trained himself to become not a latter-day horror maestro, as some reviewers have attempted to pigeonhole him, but rather a consummate entertainer; a storyteller who could hold his audience rapt. "I just wanted to entertain the audience," he famously commented once, "give them surprises and fun — an all-out show."[6]

"He has a couple of things in his background that are telling," reveals Tim Philo, the cameraman and lighting expert who collaborated with Raimi on *The Evil Dead* in 1979. "One is that he was a magician as a teenager. He would give magic shows and sometimes [on *The Evil Dead*] he would say 'I want to do this because it's a twist on a magic trick,' or 'I want to do this just because they'll wonder how we did it.'

"And sometimes we would say, 'But why do we care? *Tell the story!*' And he would say, 'No, you've gotta trick the audience. You've gotta leave 'em wondering how you did it.' He had great instincts that way."

The other characteristic that serves Raimi well in forging entertaining, involving motion pictures, according to Philo, is his long history and experience making super 8mm "amateur" movies as an adolescent. "He refined his instincts," Philo explains. "When you make super 8mm films, you sit at the projector with your hand on the control, trying to keep the sound in synch, kind of doing a mix on the spot.

"So he sat there projecting all of his films for almost every showing of them. Which means he's there watching the movie *with* the audience. His experience is that if the audience gets bored for a second, you take those reels off and you cut those shots out. He was constantly paring down. There were times on *The Evil Dead* when I'd say 'Sam, this is a good idea, but it's going to come off as comical,' and he would say, 'That doesn't matter, as long as the audience isn't bored. Whether they're frightened, freaked out, or laughing, those are all good reactions.'"

What this story uncovers is Raimi's overwhelming desire, some might say *compulsion*, to entertain, as well as his uncanny ability to understand how to entertain. Consequently, Anthony Lane, film critic in the *New Yorker*, described him as a director "enthusiastic to the point of lunacy."[7] But why was it so important for Raimi to entertain? Ellen Sandweiss, co-star of *The Evil Dead*, reveals that this drive is born of his very personality: the need to play and perhaps, to direct play.

"His boyishness is so important to understanding his character, his Peter Pan kind of personality," she reports. "I mean, he always has been and always will be a big kid. He gets a twinkle in his eye and tells a story just like he's a little boy." Thus, entertaining an audience is an extension of boyhood play, of holding the attention of the nearest grown up or, in this case, a movie theater filled with people. As David Chute astutely wrote of Raimi for *Film Comment*:

> Nobody working seems to love the movie-ness of movies more than he does, reveling in the fun stunts that can be pulled with cranes and dolly tracks and wide-angle lenses. From the flying eyeball POV shot in *The Evil Dead* to the shaft of sunlight beaming through a perforated torso in *The Quick and the Dead*, he's happily assumed the role of everybody's movie-mad kid brother, tickled pink at his own baroque ingenuity.[8]

Perhaps in recognition of the fact that even enthusiasm gets old after a while, Raimi has adapted his style over time, developing a deep flair with actors and subtle storytelling abilities that match those camera acrobatics. His 1998 film, *A Simple Plan* is low key and haunting, a modern-day cautionary tale about greed that merits comparisons with John Huston's essay on like-minded material, *The Treasure of the Sierra Madre* (1948). Similarly, Raimi's 2000 effort, *The Gift*, is the emotional story of a mother disconnected from her children, but one wrapped in genre packaging.

And, of course, in 2002, Raimi directed a little film called *Spider-Man*, which earned more money in its opening weekend than any film in history.

The reason for its success? Raimi felt as enthusiastic and enamored of the comic book material as any dyed-in-the-wool Marvel Comics fan and approached it respectfully, with faith to what had been established on the page.

Considering Raimi's ascension to the top tier of critically successful and commercially profitable filmmakers, this is an appropriate time to study the director and his history; to see where he's been and how he's gotten to this point. Certainly his influence on other filmmakers continues to be enormous, from the "shaky cam" shots in the Coen brothers' canon to the early oeuvre of *Lord of the Rings* director Peter Jackson, which have, on occasion, been termed the "direct progeny"[9] of Raimi's works. In 2003, *Pirates of the Caribbean: Curse of the Black Pearl* struck box-office gold with sword-wielding, joke-cracking skeleton minions and a daffy sense of humor, characteristics and tone right in tune with Raimi's own — and underrated — period fantasy, *Army of Darkness* (1993).

Historically, Raimi remains an interesting director because his films evidence a complete mastery of each succeeding generation of special effects. His films span from the so-called classic era featuring stop-motion animation (*The Evil Dead*, *Evil Dead 2*), to the next generation utilizing optical combinations of highly detailed miniatures and live actors (the Introvision process, as in *Darkman* and *Army of Darkness*), right up to the digital age, of which *Spider-Man* is a watershed. Raimi's understanding of the camera, both its limitations *and* potential, integrates each of these effects approaches into his stories in a manner most singular. His individuality has managed to survive not just in the more naturalistic "old style" effects (like the bullet hole in the gunfighter's head in *The Quick and the Dead*), but in the computer realm as well. His Spider-Man swings with grace, a comic book character brought to joyous life.

On a personal note, Raimi is a director worthy of admiration not merely for his technical ingenuity and inventive visuals, but because of his determination and loyalty. He often works with his old buddies from Detroit, including Bruce Campbell, an underrated physical comedian and actor with old-fashioned, larger-than-life Hollywood screen presence; and Robert Tapert, a savvy producer who has reached the top of his game too, shepherding popular series like *Hercules: the Legendary Journeys* and *Xena: Warrior Princess* through multiple seasons in television syndication.

For some reason, independent directors choosing to make horror films are often saddled with the descriptor of "exploitation" filmmaker, but what Raimi and company accomplished over twenty years ago with *The Evil Dead* is actually a case study in filmmaking outside the studio system. His story is illuminating in that regard alone. Also, as the interviewees in this book gladly and forcefully testify, Raimi seems to be a genuinely nice guy.

"We hear and read of the legendary tyrannical directors and some of the ones that were flawed," Academy Award–winning actor Cliff Robertson confided in this author, "but we don't hear enough, because I guess there aren't that many, about directors who have a benevolence not only among the cast, but the crew. So when you see Sam walking carefully and quietly amongst his cast and crew, you get the feeling of a director who is conscious of his responsibilities, but even more conscious of his sensitivities to the people around him. It's very rare. Some directors have huge egos and expect you to genuflect when they walk on the set, but he is a remarkable man."

In attempting to parse the tale of Raimi's films, this text highlights many first-person accounts and interviews from a number of eclectic sources, from the cinematographers who shot Raimi's early films to the producers, screenwriters, actors, special effects magicians and composers who collaborated to make his films the stuff of legend and the focus of obsessive cult followings. This distinguished group of over thirty film artists sheds light on everything from Raimi's first steps in the world of filmmaking to his work process as he became a Hollywood player, as well as the behind-the-scenes stories of each and every film he's directed.

So crank up the shaky cam and watch out for low-flying eyeballs.

1

GROWING UP "WITHIN THE WOODS" OF MICHIGAN

BY 1959, THE YEAR DIRECTOR SAM RAIMI arrived on this mortal coil, the television set had already become a permanent resident in 90 percent of American households.[1] That historical factoid is probably as pertinent to a good understanding of this contemporary filmmaker's genesis as is any revelation from his personal family history.

Arriving in Royal Oak, Michigan, approximately a week shy of Halloween in late October of 1959, Sam Raimi was born a full decade after fellow movie brats Steven Spielberg, George Lucas, and John Carpenter. However, like those other contemporary filmmakers, Raimi grew up in a comfortable middle-class environment where entertainment, courtesy of television, was ubiquitous.

The primetime television of Raimi's youth, the mid-to-late sixties, bulged with Westerns and comedies, and local Michigan stations had hours upon hours to fill in their weekend and late night schedules. More often than not, showings of older movies like *King Kong* (1933), *Pride of the Yankees* (1942), and *The Treasure of the Sierra Madre*, the last of which Raimi saw for the first time at age ten, plugged the gaps. Similarly, the popular comedy teams of earlier eras, including Laurel and Hardy, the Little Rascals, Abbott and Costello and, significantly, the prolific Three Stooges, were granted a second hearing thanks to television's national growth spurt.

The new format exposed a new generation of enthusiastic fans to these acts and, not surprisingly, young Raimi was among the converted. "If there were a way to bring back Moe, Larry and Curly, I'd do it," he wished once. "It was really them I loved. They were the magic."[2]

"He was an encyclopedia of old comedies and had very specific tastes," says makeup and special effects artist Tom Sullivan, a collaborator with Raimi on *The Evil Dead*. "His knowledge of the history of the Stooges was impressive, and I'd swear he had all their episodes memorized. He saw Larry, Moe, Curly and Shemp as discounted geniuses and, with his detailed analysis, I came around to his opinion. Making the 'Stooge' connection goes a long way for me in understanding and enjoying his films."

With television proving an indelible influence, Raimi developed a love of filmed entertainment from an early age. Though some social critics argue that watching television or films represents a passive act in which the percipient simply "vegetates" or "zones out," for many filmmakers the act of absorbing entertainment is more akin to an apprenticeship, an independent film study of sorts, and the necessary precursor to practice with a camera. For young Raimi, the universe of film became nothing less than a second language, suffusing every aspect of his life.

As Robert Primes, ASC (American Society of Cinematographers), director of photography on Raimi's *Crimewave* (1985) describes it, "Sam had a very romantic view of life. I had the feeling that his wisdom was not from life, but from movies, and from doing movies. It was almost as if he'd grown up in a world that [consisted of] some huge percentage of cinema."

A so-called movie brat, Raimi apparently learned a sense of manners and etiquette from his early, observant, TV-watching days. The films of the 1950s, aired during his youth, affected him. "Sam is so proper," actress Sheree J. Wilson, his lead in *Crimewave*, notes with admiration. "He's really old fashioned. As a human being, well, I've said to him, 'You were born in the wrong era.' He's one of those guys who says '*swell*.'"

This sense of decorum, professionalism and courtesy later accounted for Raimi's consistent attire on film sets. His one-time mentor, director Verne Nobles explains the rationale of this formal gear. "If you notice on the set, he wears a tie. The old time directors that I worked with in my youth wore ties, wore jackets, wore sports coats. Sam does that." Raimi himself has noted that his fashion sense is an homage to master of suspense Alfred Hitchcock,[3] D.W. Griffith, and other legends of Hollywood history.

One could make the same notation about Raimi's film projects. Each film he's directed is a tribute to past productions. "Raimi and the newer generation have this great love of comic book sci-fi or horror," fellow director David Cronenberg (*Shivers* [1975], *Scanners* [1981], *The Fly* [1986]) noted recently. "They want to make films that they saw as kids — movies that are only about movies and pop culture. They're totally self-referential."[4]

However, there is a second important element of Raimi's genesis as a moviemaker that must be considered equally as important, if not more so, than his admiration for Hollywood history and the movie culture of his youth: *opportunity*.

Because his parents, Detroit suburbanites Leonard and Celia, were business owners and relatively well-off financially, they had the resources to bring an Eastman Kodak 8mm camera into their Franklin, Michigan, household, which granted young Raimi access to the very technology that could mimic the entertainment transmitted before his eyes on the cathode ray tube.

Inspired by his father's elaborately shot home movies, which he felt "captured reality" and could even alter the flow of time when playing reels out of order,[5] Sam Raimi realized *he* could be the one calling the shots and controlling space and time, the magical mechanisms of the universe. By age thirteen, Sam purchased his own camera with the money he made raking leaves for neighbors.[6]

But if television brought the world of Hollywood directly into Raimi's living room, and a super 8mm camera afforded him the opportunity to hone his skills, there were other influences too. The mass media of the 1960s brought not only movies and television programs into the family abode, but also televised baseball games, and Raimi became a devoted fan of the great American pastime. "I had friends and I played baseball and I watched the Three Stooges," said Raimi. "My parents were middle-class people who happened to be exceptionally supportive of what I wanted to do, even if I wanted to do something crazy like make movies."[7]

Similarly, Marvel Comics' stable of imperfect, angst-ridden superheroes — Daredevil, Spider-Man, the Hulk, the Fantastic Four and the X-Men among them — originated in the era of Raimi's youth, and the young man was introduced to the world of Stan Lee's *Amazing Spider-Man* by his brother Sander, six years his senior. When teenage Sander later died in a tragic accident, the event reportedly "colored everything he did for the rest of his life,"[8] including Raimi's interest in comic books.

When Raimi was twelve, his mother commissioned an artist to paint a depiction of Peter Parker's costumed alter ego in Sam's bedroom, and today, the director is famously known to possess a collection of comic books that tops out at 2,500 issues.[9]

So, gathering his influences, Raimi came out of a secure, entertainment-driven universe that he would later describe as consisting primarily of Three Stooges paraphernalia, comic books, and Fig Newtons.[10] Raimi's enduring romance with the movies blossomed and as an adult, he described the experience of watching them in the most obsessive, loving terms, objecting to FBI piracy warnings because they killed the "glow" of movie foreplay:

> When you sit in a theater, there's a great deal of expectation as you wait for the film to begin. You're in the darkness and the screen clears and that arc lamp comes on the projector and the screen is flooded with light. Then the logo comes up and it's brilliant. It calls to mind all the great classics that have come before.[11]

THEY CALL HIM BRUCE

Auteur theories notwithstanding, film is truly a collaborative art form. Regardless of any one director's vision or genius, by necessity, filmmaking requires a group effort. Actors, musicians, editors, producers, assistant directors, grips, special effects and makeup artists, lighting technicians, and cinematographers each make necessary contributions in the realization of any director's plan for a film. In this regard, Raimi has been a particularly blessed fellow. He not only had an older brother (Ivan) and younger brother (Ted) assist him with his super 8mm back yard epics, but also at a very young age became involved with a number of like-minded, dedicated individuals, all of whom wanted to pursue film not just as a hobby, but as a vocation.

Many of these cohorts from Detroit, including Josh Becker (*Thou Shall Not Kill ... Except* [1985], *Lunatics: A Love Story* [1991], *Running Time* [1997]) and Scott Spiegel (*From Dusk Till Dawn 2: Texas Blood Money* [1999]), have become successful, much-admired movie directors themselves.

One celebrated figure in Raimi's story is his frequent "star," cult actor and B-movie icon Bruce Campbell. A denizen of Bloomfield Township, Michigan, Campbell as a young man starred in amateur films with his friend Spiegel, films that featured Stooge-esque titles such as *Three Pests in a Mess*, *Three Smart Saps* and *Inspector Klutz Saves the Day*. The obsession with the Three Stooges, not unlike Raimi's, was definitely a "boy" thing according to Campbell, because girls "don't think pain is funny, but guys think that pain is funny."[12]

Campbell first met Raimi in eighth grade at West Maple Junior High School and, together with Spiegel and others, formed the Metropolitan Film Group, sometimes known as "the Michigan Mafia."[13] This group, which also included the late Bill Kirk and future assistant director/producer John Cameron, attended Wiley E. Groves High School in Birmingham and financed their own movies by raking leaves and shoveling snow, and then pooled their earnings to purchase super 8mm film rolls from the local five and dime.[14]

These early efforts, which often consisted of pie-throwing battles or crazy chase scenes, were directed by each member of the bunch, not merely Raimi, who sometimes performed as a villain. As Campbell recalled in the *Austin Chronicle*:

> In my neighborhood [in Royal Oak, Michigan], I was working with a couple of guys, and in Sam's neighborhood he was working with a couple of guys, and then in high school these neighborhoods sort of collided. We met in drama class — he was big in magic at that time — and I hung out with Sam being his magic show assistant at Bar Mitzvahs and stuff.[15]

When not shooting films like their comedy dealing with the disappearance of Jimmy Hoffa, Bruce and Sam spent snowy winters sledding in Franklin Hills, daring one another to top each other's runs. This was a very physical group of kids, but lest the Michigan Mafia sound like a boy's only club, another important contributor to the early works was Ellen Sandweiss, a young woman with a long-standing love of performing. "It started out really with playing cello when I was very young," Sandweiss explains, "I headed more and more toward acting and singing in my high school years, because I felt the classical music world was very lonely, and I didn't like sitting home practicing by myself. Basically, I was in plays with Sam and Bruce in high school and a couple of their super 8mm films. *Shemp Eats the Moon* — I'm sure you've heard of that one. One of my favorites."

Sandweiss quickly became indoctrinated into the slapstick, movie-crazed world of Raimi and Campbell and offers unique insights into their character at that age. "While we did projects together and I laughed at their jokes, they were both very shy with girls," she relates. "I wouldn't say we sat and had long intimate chats, but I thought then — and still think now — that Bruce and Sam are two of the funniest people I know. They weren't your typical high school geeks. I spent many of my high school years cracking up at their Three Stooges shtick and their pratfalls, and for that I'm very grateful."

On the flip side of that coin, Raimi and Campbell had found in Sandweiss nothing short of a kindred spirit, a performer willing to go that extra mile to achieve a good shot. "I think they knew I would not be wimpy," Sandweiss considers. "They knew I was a hearty soul and would run through swamps. How they knew that, I'm not sure, but somehow they sensed it in me."

"RIP" TAPERT, THE HAPPY VALLEY KID, AND IT'S MURDER!

After high school, there was a brief parting of the ways for the Michigan Mafia. Campbell departed to attend college at Western Michigan University, while Raimi attended Michigan State University with his older brother, Ivan. Together the brothers Raimi founded the Creative Filmmaking Society on campus and set about planning and executing new film ventures, which they screened to fellow students on Friday night and charged a nominal admission to recoup their production expenses.

It was at this point that another Raimi collaborator entered the fray, producer Robert G. Tapert, then a business major. Tom Sullivan, who contributed so many memorable props and effects to *The Evil Dead*, remembers how Tapert melded with the Michigan bunch. "As I recollect, Rob Tapert was Ivan Raimi's roommate at MSU and wanted to work in fish and game. I think he said he was going to count fish for a living. Rob had a natural enthusiasm and fit right in."

Like the brothers Raimi, Tapert had an interest in film and soon agreed to headline in their latest production. "Rob starred in the leading role in *The Happy Valley Kid* as a naïve, innocent college freshman pushed over the edge," Sullivan relates. "His chief tormenter was played by Sam. Sam stuck screwdrivers in Rob's ears, threw his bike into the river, and tortured Rob till the kid snaps.... By the time *Kid* hit the screen, Rob was credited as Rip Tapert. Rip kept up with Sam and Bruce in humor and high spirits."

The Happy Valley Kid also marked an important turning point for Raimi and friends: it was highly profitable, having cost less than a thousand dollars and eventually grossing five times its budget.

"Shows were on Friday evenings," Sullivan recalls, "and Sam would show his super 8mm comedies to students to make enough money to pay for the campus auditorium." And the nature of Raimi's other films at that time? "His films like *Six Months to Live* and *The Happy Valley Kid* told character-driven stories with comedic and tragic touches. Sure they were 'sappy' in the Three Stooges kind of way, but that was completely intentional."

The screenings at the college also provided Raimi with good feedback. He could assess how his films played with a crowd and, after a few efforts, was able to chart his evolution as a filmmaker from the off-the-cuff remarks of his audiences, who grew increasingly more receptive, or according to the self-deprecating Raimi, at least less put-off.

Sullivan also recollects meeting Bruce Campbell, who did not appear in

The Happy Valley Kid, but often came to visit Raimi at school. "Bruce seemed very shy and quiet. Not the party animal he is today. When Bruce started into his characters or doing shtick with Sam and Scott, he'd come alive. All of these guys were exceptionally funny. Their humor represented the history of humor. Vaudeville, the Stooges and every comedy ever made were constantly referenced. I remember a lot of admiration for Don Knotts and serious discussions of *The Ghost and Mr. Chicken* (1966). I bet Sam does a remake some day."

And Sullivan's thoughts on the Raimi of the mid-1970s? "From my experience as an artist inspired at an early age to learn to draw, paint and sculpt, etc., I've found that enthusiasm is more valuable than innate talent. Sam definitely had drive when I met and worked with him. He knew what he was going to be doing as a career — the only challenge was creating that opportunity."

Following *The Happy Valley Kid*, Raimi, Tapert and Campbell embarked on a follow-up project featuring comedic elements. "*It's Murder!* was Sam's most ambitious project to date," Sullivan explains of the venture. "It had a large cast, several car chases, fights, endless jokes and gags, not to mention the already standard soundtrack. Sam had bought a large super 8mm reel device, so a two-hour film could be shown without changing reels. Filming for *It's Murder!* only had a couple of weekends left to complete when I first met Sam. Its star, Scott Spiegel, was a riot, another filmmaker friend of Sam's from their early school days."

Sullivan contributed to the production by mimicking the sound of "pills splashing into a glass of water" and also created an inventive poster for the film's premiere.

And the plot? "*It's Murder!* tells the story of a private dick investigating the murder of a wealthy head of a peculiar family," Sullivan describes. Raimi played the villain, a wheelchair-bound foil for Campbell's hapless and clueless detective.

"It comes off as an homage to the Three Stooges with endless bad puns and prop humor," Sullivan states. "Hurt by bad lighting and its length, it still showcases some real treats. The action and violence is graphic and over the top, but best of all, twelve-year-old Ted Raimi steals the show as a devious offspring. It tends to go on and on, but it is strangely watchable especially if you know the participants."

Unfortunately, *It's Murder!* didn't meet with the same success as *The Happy Valley Kid*, even a $1.50 a ticket, failing to earn back the two grand it cost to produce. "When it premiered at the Creative Society's screening, it had a bunch of walk outs," Sullivan remembers. "I think Sam learned to make films that didn't demand such particular tastes from his audience."

LEARNING CURVE

After *It's Murder!* failed to connect with its collegiate audience, Sam Raimi and the Metropolitan Film Group adopted a different tack. Moviemaking was clearly in their blood and an enthusiastic Tapert in particular was convinced it could represent a profitable venture. But before the group could make a study of what stories they felt would sell to audiences in the latter half of the 1970s, Raimi and Campbell unexpectedly acquired a mentor who knew all too well the ropes — and pitfalls — of the industry.

In 1977, Bruce Campbell was hired as a production assistant by a director named Verne Nobles, an artist whose history in Detroit and Hollywood went back several decades. In the fifties, Nobles worked as a gofer for the legendary director George Stevens (1904–1975), who helmed Hollywood classics including *Gunga Din* (1939), *Shane* (1953), *Giant* (1956), *The Diary of Anne Frank* (1959) and *The Greatest Story Ever Told* (1965).

After successful writing stints for *Teen Life* and *Teen Post* magazines early in his career, Nobles also worked as a photographer for Warner Brothers Records in the formative days of that record company. His first assignment as a director involved a Cadillac commercial shot in Florida starring George Gobel (1919–1991). He recalls that he "generally got into the motion picture industry as a trainee ... to learn."

However, not very long after his stint in Hollywood had begun, Nobles left California because his wife decided she wanted to return home to Detroit. But Nobles had moviemaking in his veins. "I got the idea then how little people in the Midwest at that time understood the film business, or how to get into the film process, and that's when I first started a teaching process."

And it wasn't a moment too soon, as Nobles explains. "The film business in the Midwest was nil. There was only Dick Gagnon, who shot most of his stuff in California. There were no real schools at that time teaching film, so I created a company within a company, and Dick Gagnon certainly helped me a great deal, and I started doing Chevrolet and national and local commercials. Anything I could get. My producer at that time was Karen Lund. Karen and I both had the idea of helping young people. We started hiring kids who wanted to get into the film business, and we felt that if they had a chance to learn it from the pros, they would be taking the first step toward taking our place when we were gone."

Eager to learn, Campbell became Nobles' production assistant. "He learned very quickly that there are three important things to a *goomby*'s job, a production assistant," Nobles recollects. "One is: run everywhere. Don't hesitate, *go*. Don't walk, run. Also, carry a rag and a book in your pocket. Whenever you're not doing anything, take the book out and write something in it so you look busy, and if you run out of things to write, take the rag out of your pocket and wipe your hands off. George Stevens taught me that a thousand years before, and I always used that. That's exactly what Bruce did, but he made it funny. He actually became a very light side of our days when we were shooting two hundred days a year. I think it was because of him and a few other people at that time that I decided to start an acting and production school."

It wasn't long before Nobles found another enterprising student in his class. "Bruce brought his friend, this very shy but very interesting young man, Mr. Raimi," Nobles relates. "Sam was like a sponge. He asked a thousand questions and then asked another thousand questions. He always wanted to know something, but it was a two-sided street. They were also making me sharp, especially Bruce. On the set, Bruce would question me. Not many people question me as a director; they just don't, so whenever I find someone that actually questions me and they're right, I really have a great deal of respect for them, and Bruce would do that."

Nobles also recalls that he and his top students had a running dialogue about favorite movies. "We [Raimi and Nobles] talked about *The Treasure of the Sierra Madre*. It's a very interesting picture from a director's standpoint, and I think that's the reason Sam likes it. It's a very emotional picture. There are several things in that picture that tear at the emotions; that pull from your emotions. And the camera work is brilliant."

Raimi and Campbell also entertained Nobles' class with comedic impressions. "They studied the Three Stooges," he acknowledges. "They knew all of their bits and they would do them for the class."

But it wasn't all fun and games either. Nobles had several lessons to impart to the youngsters, and they were eager to learn. "They were so serious about their work. In class, when we got down to it, I said, 'If you're going to make films, there are some rules you have to follow. If you learn them, nothing else matters ... you can do whatever you want. Just learn the basics.'"

And what were these rules? "One rule in directing is *crossing the line*," Nobles elaborates. "In film, you can't cross the line, or if you do, it's obvious and stupid. When Sam did his first big film for Universal years later, *Darkman*, he commented to somebody, and it was in a newspaper, that he was scared to death that, when I saw the picture, I'd see him cross the line. He didn't, of course. But the screen is one dimensional, and that's the hardest thing to teach somebody. If you have somebody in a typical Western scene with a cowboy on the left and a cowboy on the right and they're coming toward each other [on a street] to draw and shoot, you have to stay on one side of them or the other. You cannot cross over to the other side because the characters will reverse themselves.

"That got them thinking, 'Wait a minute, what else is there about making a film that we should know?' Well, editing is a *bow tie*, and they were fascinated by that. If you look at any film, the normal process of shooting or editing is that you start at the widest end of the bow tie and move into close-up. Once you're on the close-up, you get out of it by going the other way on the bow tie. If you look at any film, you will see that 75 percent or more of them are built on the process where you start with a wide shot or a master and move into the close-up.

"That knowledge started getting into their heads," Nobles continues. "What they were shooting started to change because they really thought about it now. And they watched film after film and caught it. The light bulb went off and they knew there was a process, rules to making films. You cannot break those rules unless you're smart enough to know how to break them and get around them. One thing that Sam Raimi has accomplished in his career is his ability to break the rules, but have you [the audience] not realize or understand how he's done it. He broke rule after rule in *Spider-Man* and was making his own rules."

Yet even as Raimi and Campbell found guidance in Nobles' tutorials on the essentials of film grammar, there were other lessons to learn. They knew they could make a good movie, but could they sell one? What kind of independently produced movie would sustain itself in the market and not suffer the same fate as the idiosyncratic *It's Murder*?

The troika of hopefuls turned their eyes to the box office and discovered that in the world of low-budget, independently produced films, the horror genre was undisputed king.

LIKE CLOCKWORK

In the mid-to-late 1970s, films like *The Texas Chain Saw Massacre*, Wes Craven's *The Hills Have Eyes* (1977) and *Halloween* made a killing at the box office, showcasing the talents of their young directors and also filling theater seats. For the most part, these films were independently produced and well-reviewed, or at the very least, met with grudging admiration for their efficiency in getting the job done. For very little money, Hooper, Craven and Carpenter each made profitable calling cards to the industry. Outside the world of low budget, horror was a profitable gamble too: Friedkin's *The Exorcist* (1973) set off a mini "devil" boom that came to include successful pictures such as the Italian import *Beyond the Door* (1975), Richard Donner's *The Omen* (1976) and *Damien: Omen II* (1978). Scary movies definitely equaled big bucks.

The horror genre not only offered the Michigan Mafia an opportunity to strut its stuff with a stylish first effort, it offered a built-in audience, an appetite waiting to be fed. After studying the trend and watching many of the horror pictures of the day, the ambitious Tapert insisted that "we need to make something we can sell,"[16] and the focus quickly shifted to producing a horror film. The intrepid group, including Tom Sullivan, then began in autumn of 1978, what the artist remembers as several trips to drive-in theaters for "an on-the-spot analysis of low-budget film techniques, and to look for the things that worked and what did not."

But could Raimi, the director of madcap melodrama and slapstick comedy, direct a horror film? Would he even care to do it? "I like horror films," Raimi told interviewer Stanley Wiater about the genre he would soon become associated with. "Not only because they are scary and fun, but the world of horror offers to a filmmaker a great world in which to experiment with cinematic techniques and lighting and sound effects, because you're dealing with a world, not that we know, but the world that lies between the spaces."[17]

Even if Raimi believed he could accomplish something new and exciting within in the genre, would investors risk money on that belief? "The challenge for Sam, Rob and Bruce now was how to raise funds," Sullivan explains. "With no track record and looking like high schoolers, the plan took shape to make a super 8mm horror film that would demonstrate that Sam could tell a scary story and deliver the thrills."

Thus work promptly began on a short film that showcased Raimi's ability to terrorize audiences. The resulting seven-minute film, *Clockwork*, involved a young woman home alone late at night, a killer stalking her from outside, determined to break in. Sullivan outlines the project: "It starred Cheryl Guttridge and Scott Spiegel. Cheryl played a woman in her home being assaulted by a killer. My contribution was a title card for *Clockwork*. Not much of a part, but the film showed a different side of Sam and was easily the best photographed film yet."

Remembering further details, Sullivan observes that *Clockwork* was a "cornerstone in subject matter for Sam and had a distinctly humorless tone. During the climax, a lone woman with a large kitchen knife stabs her assaulter in the mouth, who stumbles around with a blade firmly lodged in his adams apple. Now that I think of it, *Clockwork* has elements of *Within the Woods*. The assault from outside. The violation that must be punished."

With *Clockwork* deemed a successful venture, it was time to produce a more dramatic and lengthier short, a "preview" or sales tool to impress potential investors. "At this point, I seem to recall the script for *Book of the Dead* was being developed by Sam after he'd heard the title in a class dealing with Egyptology," Sullivan remembers.

In interviews, Raimi has noted that his inspiration for the feature script, which concerned five college students confronting demonic forces in an isolated forest, was the climax of Shakespeare's *MacBeth*. As those familiar with the Bard's tragedy will recall, *MacBeth* featured Birnam Wood, a forest, coming to life — in a sense, anyway — around a human dwelling, Dunsinane Castle, rather than an isolated cabin.[18] But before Raimi's script, which he kept carefully secret, could come to life, it was time to make the necessary business preparations.

"When Sam and Rob got serious about doing a feature and started talking to a lawyer, they kept the story secret from me and others to protect their property," Sullivan recalls of *The Evil Dead* screenplay. "I would get questions from Sam that gave me some hints of what was to come. 'Can you do makeup on a girl so her face is on fire and she is still talking?' I talked about dummy heads and articulation through cables, and about a year or so later, that was how I designed the 'Shelly on Fire' sequence.

"Rob became the mediator between Sam and us on the film," Sullivan adds. "Sam wrote the script and then the plan was to determine what was needed to put together a 'package' for investors."

RENAISSANCE MEN

At this point, another legendary figure enters the story of the Michigan Mafia: Detroit lawyer Phillip A. Gillis. An attorney since 1949, Detroit Law School graduate Gillis worked at a small firm with three other lawyers in the late seventies when he received an urgent and most unusual plea for help from a close friend.

"Rob Tapert's father is a close friend of mine," Gillis relates, "and Rob was up at Michigan State. His father said to me, 'My crazy son wants to make a movie and he wants to raise some money and everything, and he needs legal advice, and I figured I'd send him to my friend Phil Gillis, who would talk some sense into him.'" But things didn't turn out quite the way the senior Tapert had hoped.

Gillis still recalls that first meeting with the Detroit trio. "The substance of it was that Sam, Robert and Bruce came up to my office. I had just moved into the Renaissance Center, which was a new set of office buildings in Detroit. The bookshelves weren't even up yet. They came in with a super 8mm film projector, and they had a five-minute movie [*Clockwork*].

"It had a lot of suspense in it, like shadows under the door and then suddenly the gal who was the principal actress in it was standing next to the door, and these hands come smashing through and grabbed her around the waist, and I jumped five feet into the air."

It's no accident that a similar "jolt" reappeared in the final version of

The Evil Dead, this time with a beleaguered Campbell leaning against the cabin's front door, accosted by the arms of an angry Deadite as the limbs burst through the wood-paneled door behind him. It worked once, it worked again.

"That type of movie is really not my favorite," Gillis observes, "but I was taken by the quality of it. I told them what had to be done to raise money, that they would need to prepare a private placement memorandum which could not be distributed to more than fifteen people within the state of Michigan, otherwise they would have to do what is called a registration. Anyway, I told them I would prepare it for them and quoted them a fee. They said, 'Where the hell are we gonna get that kind of money?' So I said, 'I'll take a piece of the action. You can give me two shares,' and I think they were selling shares for $10,000 a piece. So I got two shares for doing legal work, and afterward I was so impressed with their industry and talent that I bought another share and a half myself."

One might wonder if Gillis had assumed a big risk investing his own time and money in a bunch of neophyte filmmakers, but he persuasively insists not, and time has borne out his perspective. "Number one, I was satisfied with their integrity, and my judgment has been vindicated by the way they've treated us [the investors] ever since," Gillis states emphatically. "Let me tell you something about those kids. I got a check last year from them, and it's the second one. It's a six-figure check. With Hollywood accounting I could have just gotten my money back and that would have been it, but those kids are very honorable."

With the legal issues out of the way, Sam Raimi, Bruce Campbell and Rob Tapert became ensconced as the brain trust of an organization called Renaissance Pictures, general partners in a limited liability partnership. Now it was time to raise capital, but they still needed a product to wow the investors, something a bit more substantial than the impressive *Clockwork*. That's how a thirty-minute short film, *Within the Words*, came to life and the point where the story of *The Evil Dead* and the films of Sam Raimi really begins...

WITHIN THE WOODS

For the newest Michigan Mafia effort, makeup designer and special effects man Tom Sullivan was in his element, able to focus on a variety of impressive makeup effects and props. For Sullivan, horror movies like the one envisioned by Raimi were nothing less than a labor of love, a passion ever since he saw the original *King Kong* on a Saturday morning when he was five-years-old. When he was still just a kid, Sullivan acquired a book about dinosaurs and a set of dinosaur plastic toys and promptly began making his own dioramas with miniature trees as foliage, good practice, it turned out, for the movies he would some day work on.

Counting Willis O'Brien, Forrest Ackerman's *Famous Monsters*, and Ray Harryhausen among his influences, Sullivan in his junior year at Wheaton North High School purchased a super 8mm camera and produced his own stop-motion dinosaur movie entitled *Time Eater*. "Not a shred of plot," Sullivan recalls of the effort, which included foam rubber dinosaurs and miniature jungles, "but I put some animated dinosaurs on film." Previous to his work with Raimi, Sullivan had also completed some production illustrations for an unmade H. P. Lovecraft–inspired independent film entitled *The Cry of Cthulhu*. Following this experience, Sullivan was very enthusiastic to contribute to the then-titled *Book of the Dead*.

Another familiar face on *Within the Woods* was Raimi's high school friend Ellen Sandweiss, who portrayed the film's much-put-upon heroine named, appropriately enough, Ellen. In the short film, Campbell portrayed her boyfriend, Bruce, and that fact alone was a recruiting inducement for Sandweiss. "I was excited because I had a huge crush on Bruce, and I got to play his girlfriend in that," she remembers. "I had just started to forgive him [Bruce] for fake kissing me on stage during a play we were in during high school. I may still not have forgiven him yet. We were in a Neil Simon play or something, and I was so excited because finally I was going to get to kiss him, and he did a fake stage kiss, and I was really pissed."

When asked about the *Within the Woods* script, affable Sandweiss notes that she is not a horror movie fan, so it is difficult for her to assess. "You ask me if it was a good script? No, it sucked," she laughs affectionately. "We were all hitting each other over the head with axes and stuff. But what Sam was always so good at was being imaginative with so little money and resources. But I didn't know anything about horror movies at the time, or that he was breaking any new ground."

Sullivan recalls that *Within the Woods*, shot on the grounds of the Tapert family estate in Marshall, Michigan, was actually "a thirty-minute version of *Evil Dead*." In the film, the arrogant "Bruce" character revealed a distinct lack of respect for certain cursed Indian artifacts and was punished by supernatural forces for his transgression.

"This time Bruce is the possessed demon and Ellen Sandweiss is the one who struggles to survive," Sullivan explains. "Sam asked me to do the special effects and makeup and I was responsible for some special props like the Indian pottery fragments and knife. I also painted the unfired pottery that would be smashed over Bruce's head for a fight scene. Bruce ended up wearing my glasses to help create his character Bruce and Ellen wore my blue jacket as she splashed through the swamps south of Marshall, Michigan.

"The makeup was a real test of my skills and Bruce's tolerance of pain and patience," Sullivan reveals. "To achieve the effect of Bruce having been ravaged by an unseen force, I sculpted and cast an eyeball [with optic nerve] to be dangled from his torn and mutilated face. This was glued over his eye, and then scars and mud and fake blood were added. I had cast Bruce's arm to produce a foam rubber arm with a blood tube for a crowd-pleasing dismemberment.

"Makeup application on Bruce was done by applying spirit gum to the back of the prosthetic eye piece, and when tacky, it stuck into position and held until set," continues Sullivan. "Then I would paint latex rubber over the edges and dry it with a hair dryer. After Bruce was cooked, I would paint the makeup. Rubber mask grease paint was called for, but I'm pretty sure I didn't have any. It might have been anything from blemish cream to acrylic paint I used on him, probably both.

"The foam rubber arm that was to be cut off by a desperate Ellen was in the position of holding an implement. The fake arm had a tube running out of its elbow and was duct-taped to Bruce's elbow. His forearm was folded up to his chest and is laughably noticeable in a couple of shots," the artist recalls. "It adds to the charm."

But all did not go according to plan with the dramatic effects. "When we shot the foam hand dismemberment scene, Bruce saved the day with a memorable improvisation," says Sullivan. "I had never done any foam latex castings before, and I coated the mold with liquid latex prior to filling the mold with the cake-batterlike foam mixture and baking it. The result was a thick rubber skin over the foam filler.

"It looked okay," Sullivan notes of the skin, which was to fall off when Ellen sliced through it with a knife, but it "proved too tough to pull off, so Bruce bit right through it. When Sam yelled 'Cut,' the crew went crazy. That was the grossest thing I've ever seen."

Today, Sullivan can still describe the atmosphere of the set. "Filming was long and busy. It started early on a Friday and ran very late. I was there for all of the shooting and kept pretty busy trying to stay ahead of production. Bruce wore the makeup the whole weekend and reached what is now called 'the Latex Point,'" the point of frustration and pain beyond which wearing makeup drives one to madness (please see the Raimi lexicon).

"What impressed me most about *Within the Woods* was how Sam, Rob and Bruce worked together. The mood on the set was busy and focused, but also like a fun party. Rob kept everything moving and had a real gift as a go-between. He was great at relaying Sam's wishes and was supportive of my work."

Once the short film was completed, Sullivan knew that they'd achieved their goal of making a terrifying short film. "*Within the Woods* really packs a punch," says the artist. "The grainy and darkly lit ambience is disarming and helps deliver the shocks. There is a very real siege and struggle present and a build-up that lets you sense how bad things are going to get. Sure it's a cliché situation for the character, but Sam put the dark, grim comedy elements in."

After the premiere of *Within the Woods* at a crew member's home in Detroit, the next hurdle was getting the film seen by paying audiences and prospective investors. To that end, the Michigan Mafia's resident business major, Rip Tapert, succeeded again, cajoling a local theater owner into running *Within the Woods* before a showing of the midnight cult favorite, *The Rocky Horror Picture Show*[19] in the dog-days of summer, 1979.

That could have been the end of the story, but wasn't. At least one *Within the Woods* showing was attended by a member of the press, journalist Michael McWilliams of the *Detroit Free Press*. The writer not only interviewed Raimi and his friends, he also wrote a positive piece about the short, comparing it favorably with *Night of the Living Dead* (1968), *Carrie* (1976) and other popular horror enterprises of the era. The publicity not only brought in curious audiences, but like-minded aspiring filmmakers, including a talented young man named Tim Philo

Like Raimi, Philo had toiled to make super 8mm films with friends since he was a kid, producing a few James Bond rip-offs with titles like *Wilkinson Bond* and *A Little Help From My Friends*. He even shot a *Tonight Show* parody called *The Jack Bogie Show*. "Basically it [filmmaking] was just a chance to get out and have some chase scenes and then some fight scenes, except for *The Jack Bogie Show*, which we did as a class project and was somehow supposed to be for American Culture," he explains.

Philo remembers the moment he first met Raimi. "There was a write-up in the local paper about Sam, and his screening of *Within the Woods*, the super 8mm precursor to *Book of the Dead* and when I saw that, I knew immediately that I wanted to meet those guys. So I went to the midnight show at this theater on the edge of town. The show that was on before it was *Saturday Night Fever*. As soon as Sam hit the door of the theater and walked in — flanked by Rob and Bruce — he immediately said to me, 'You're here to see *Saturday Night Fever*?' And I said, 'No, I'm here to see *Within the Woods*,' and he said, 'Oh, good!'"

And Philo's thoughts on the short? "I had two thoughts about it. First, I was very impressed by it, and understood that these guys knew what they were doing in one sense, in that they knew how to tell a story and were making a really fun film. And second off, that technically they needed a lot of help. So I approached them right away and said, 'Whatever you guys are doing next, I want to be involved.' We chatted a little bit and we exchanged numbers and stayed in touch."

Still, all was not yet set to film a feature film. Philo could foresee one snag in terms of technology. "They said they were trying to expand this [*Within the Woods*] to a full-blown feature. And I said, 'Great! Naturally, you'll shoot it in 16mm," and they said they were test shooting it in super 8mm. I said, 'Okay, that's fine, but when you do shoot it, and it's in 16mm, get in touch."

After some time, and a failed experiment to blow-up to 16mm a short super 8mm production called *Terror at Lulu's* lensed at Mrs. Raimi's lingerie shop, the Renaissance Pictures boys did get back in touch with Philo. *Evil Dead* had its cinematographer, and the rest, as they say, is history.

THE EVIL DEAD (1982)

THE ULTIMATE EXPERIENCE IN GRUELING TERROR!

CAST AND CREW

RENAISSANCE PICTURES PRESENTS *THE EVIL DEAD*

WRITER AND DIRECTOR: Sam Raimi
PHOTOGRAPHY AND LIGHTING: Tim Philo
SPECIAL MAKEUP EFFECTS: Tom Sullivan
PHOTOGRAPHIC SPECIAL EFFECTS: Bart Pierce
MUSIC: Joe LoDuca
MUSIC ENGINEERED AT AUDIOGRAPHICS BY: Ed Wolfrum
FILM EDITOR: Edna Ruth Paul
ASSISTANT EDITOR: Joel Coen
SUPERVISING SOUND EDITOR: Joe Masefield
EXECUTIVE PRODUCERS: Robert Tapert, Bruce Campbell and Sam Raimi

STARRING

Bruce Campbell: Ash
Ellen Sandweiss: Cheryl
Hal Delrich: Scott
Betsy Baker: Linda
Sarah York: Shelly
Dorothy Tapert, Scott Spiegel, Ted Raimi and Ivan Raimi: False Shemps

Filmed in Morristown, Tennessee, and Detroit, Michigan.

THERE'S SOMETHING OUT THERE IN THE WOODS...

FIVE COLLEGE STUDENTS, Ashley, Linda, Scott, Shelly and Cheryl, vacation in a remote cabin in the Tennessee woods. Cheryl has a seizure and draws a strange object, a book emblazoned with an inhuman face on its cover. Later, a cellar door flies open of its own volition, and the group discovers in the basement a shotgun, a strange ceremonial knife, a tape recording, and a book like the one Cheryl imagined.

The group plays the tape and listens to the reports of a professor who excavated the ruins of an ancient Sumerian city called Kandar. There he discovered a volume of funerary incantations, the Book of the Dead, bound in human flesh and inked in blood. The professor warns that slumbering demons can be resurrected by reciting passages from the book.

As the professor reads aloud the incantations on the tape, the woods beyond the cabin awaken with a force of evil. What follows is a night of madness as each vacationer becomes possessed by inhuman forces. A lone hero emerges, the shell-shocked Ash, but faces difficult choices. The only way to kill a demon is to dismember it, but his girlfriend, Linda, is already possessed....

FIRST STEPS

As the 1970s wound down, Sam Raimi, Robert Tapert and Bruce Campbell drew closer to achieving their dream of professional moviemaking. What stood between them and their freshman feature-length effort was nothing less than the root of all evil: *money*. However, just as the Renaissance team had learned the ropes of shooting and editing films, so did it prove adept at fundraising.

"They went around hustling all their friends and relatives and sold eleven shares out of fifteen," attorney Phil Gillis explains. Each share of *The Evil Dead* (then entitled *Book of the Dead*) cost $10,000, and Gillis himself purchased the final two shares of eleven. "And because this wasn't a flim-flam thing, they had a provision that the money would go into escrow and that they would not break escrow until they had sold nine shares," Gillis reports. "When they had $90,000, they could say, 'Go! We'll make the movie,' but not before."

"We'd make them sick, then ask them to invest," is how Raimi described fundraising and *Within the Woods*' visceral impact on prospective cash cows. "I think they're a little horrified. As any normal person would be."[1] One of those investing was Brian Manoogian, a lawyer friend of Gillis' recently graduated from law school. Manoogian completed work on *The Evil Dead* legal prospectus and also signed a loan with a bank in Detroit. Along with Gillis' support, Manoogian's assistance carried the Renaissance men to their magic threshold of $90,000, and consequently, the privilege to break escrow.

"After a year of showing *Within the Woods* to lawyers, doctors, and friends and family, Sam, Rob and Bruce raised the capital needed to start filming," Tom Sullivan explains. After much waiting, *The Evil Dead* was officially a go.

DON'T LOOK IN THE BASEMENT

Now it was time to prep and cast the picture. On the latter front, there were already two acting certainties: Campbell and Sandweiss. Both performers had established their worth and enthusiasm on previous Raimi sets and became the only cast members not required to audition.

"When I run through a swamp, I run through a swamp," Sandweiss explains of her gamesmanship. "I fall and eat swamp water and give it my all. I guess I proved my ability to be tortured and withstand hardship, and somehow they wanted me to be in *Evil Dead.*" In particular, she would play Cheryl, Ash's sensitive sister.

The *Book of the Dead* also featured two additional female roles, the characters of Linda and Shelly. Betsy Baker, a Michigan State University graduate (in Theater Education and Classical Voice) who grew up in southwest Michigan, right on Lake Michigan, remembers how she found her way to the part of Linda.

"I actually went off and sang professionally in Florida for a year or so and then decided to move back to Detroit because I wanted to get experience in TV commercials and film, and surprisingly Detroit is huge in making local and regional TV commercials," says Baker. "It's a large source of industrial films, and I felt it would be a great opportunity to learn that craft. I was able to do a lot of films and TV commercials in Detroit as well as some stage and opera."

Then the call came from the Michigan Mafia, followed by an invitation to meet. "I met them at a restaurant, I think it was named Pasquales, on a street called Woodward in the suburbs of Detroit," Baker recalls.

"It was an Italian restaurant, and they called me to ask if I would meet them there. They sounded fairly young on the phone and not too dangerous, so I agreed to meet them, thinking that if they were dangerous I could run away or into the kitchen. As it turned out, they were not only *not* dangerous, but actually harmless. They basically said that they'd done a lot of little films together and were thinking of doing a scary movie. They asked me to read and audition."

That audition happened in the Raimi family basement with many onlookers. Theresa Tilly (really Theresa Mary Seyferth), likewise auditioned for a role after starring in many commercials, performing in children's theater for Henry Kilmartin's Trunk Company, and working in the Somerset Dinner Theater. Like Baker, Tilly eventually landed in the basement.

"I was a young woman being asked to come down to some unknown man's basement and do a reading of a sort of questionable script," Tilly considers. "It was disconcerting, but being in this type of business, every day is an adventure. You never know what you'll be asked to do. It wasn't that scary; it was daytime, and they did seem nice on the phone, and it was their parents' basement, which seemed to make it more legitimate. Basically they had some folding chairs set up, and they gave you some lines and asked you to repeat them. It was an oddball audition to say the least. I do remember them having me scream and do my idea of what a monster would be." Consequently, Tilly was cast as the ill-fated Shelly. She appears in *The Evil Dead* under the name Sarah York.

A young fellow named Hal Delrich (really Rich Demanicor) also won a role, that of Scotty, the smart aleck among the vacationers. "Rich is the nicest guy in the world," Tilly describes. "Rich was always very sweet, and I think a very good actor. He was just a natural. I think he was very athletic and had a background in competitive swimming."

With actors cast and production staff on board, *The Book of the Dead* began to coalesce. "I remember being at Sam's house and meeting his mother," Tilly notes. "We actually met at her lingerie place at one point, but I remember sitting in Sam's kitchen and his living room and meeting his family and having organizational meetings there."

It was at this point that a fateful decision was made. "They broke the news to us that we actually weren't shooting in Michigan, because it was getting to be later in the fall," Baker explains. "It was going to be extremely cold in Michigan, and they decided to go down South to a small town in Tennessee."

But things took a strange turn, as Sandweiss reveals. "They thought — foolishly — it was going to be warmer down there. And it turned out being the coldest winter that Morristown, Tennessee, had ever seen!"

"And ironically," Baker adds, "one of the mildest in the state of Michigan..."

With a start date set, production revved up. "I only had about two or three weeks with the *Book of the Dead* script before we left for Tennessee," Sullivan reports. "That left me time to analyze the special effects requirements and find the materials. I had a day to do castings of Ellen Sandweiss, Teresa Tilly, Betsy Baker and Hal Delrich. Some stuff I had shipped to Tennessee, like the R&D foam, a simple and reliable foam rubber mixture used for the Linda leg and Shelly arms."

And what was the script like for *Evil Dead* at this point in its preproduction history?

"The script changed quite a bit. It was only fourteen pages," Tilly remembers. "They kept saying, 'We're probably going to add things to it. The basic structure was the same, but you never really had any idea how these monsters were going to be created, or what specifically you were going to do as a monster. You just got the idea you'd go in a car and something would happen, and the rest was not very specific."

Baker's memories jibe with Tilly's recollection, although some sources list the script at a length of roughly sixty pages. "I think there were different editions and revisions. It was a very short script. Things were added, deleted, moved around, but all in all none of us were ever handed a two hundred–page script. The most was maybe fifteen to twenty pages."

"I liked the script," Sullivan recollects. "It was a little talky in areas, but Sam fixed that on his own. I thought it demanded a lot, and I had so little time for preproduction that specific effects and makeup designs were impossible. I recognized the Lovecraftian elements and most of all, saw the volume and variety of work as an astounding showcase of what I could do. I had worked hard to develop the skills. I finally had an opportunity to do my stuff."

And what stuff it was! Sullivan's designs and props for *Evil Dead* have become legendary, appearing even in unrelated films such as *Jason Goes to Hell: The Final Friday* (1993). His props have also been lovingly recreated by fans. Foremost among these items is the Book of the Dead itself, the Necronomicon ex Mortis. It is a design which appears in all the *Evil Dead* movies and was described on screen as being "bound in human flesh and inked in human blood."

Sullivan had time to create the prop, replete with blank pages, while still in East Lansing. "The script introduces the book differently than how I saw it," Sullivan observes. "'Beneath a dusty cloth, he finds a book which appears to be covered in some kind of animal hide, with an ancient form of writing on the cover,' quoted the script. I told Sam that if this is a book of evil then it should have a visceral and tactile, repulsive cover."

"One of the most disgusting and disturbing things I had ever read about Nazi atrocities were the lampshades and book covers, etc., made of human skin. That pretty much tops evil for me," the makeup artist explains, describing how he set out to create a volume that would appear hewn from real human facial features and organic tissue. "In order to make a recognizable piece of skin, I used a face. The idea of having to hold someone's face to read a book seemed to fit the lore of the book I was developing. Before we left for Tennessee, I had made molds of Hal and the ladies and I brushed about ten layers of mold rubber in Hal's mold and the others, and contact-cemented these "skins" into a piece of corrugated cardboard, and made the pages out of office store–bought parchment, bound together with paper from a grocery bag ... and instant movie history.

"I illustrated the book sitting at the kitchen table in Morristown," Sullivan recounts. "When I got my essential tasks finished and prepped for the next day, I wanted to fill the book with art just to satisfy myself and give the actors that much more to work with. I am an active artist and had to show off. I used elements of the script and extrapolation of mine." Among Sullivan's inventions were flying Deadites, beings who would not appear until the climax of *Evil Dead 2*.

Sullivan also designed and built another disturbing prop: a ceremonial knife that often finds its way into the soft flesh of unsuspecting victims. "The Kandarian dagger in the script is an 'ancient dagger' or 'Sumerian Dagger' with no description. As a sacrificial dagger and a tool of the Black Arts, my initial concept was to make the blade wrapped by a hilt of bones," Sullivan explains. "The actual creation was cleverly quick: I bought the widest flat stock of aluminum I could find at an East Lansing hardware store.

It wound up be being an unimpressive 1¼ inches wide. I cut it with a hack saw and ground the edge of the tip with a power tool.

"The hilt of bones was embarrassingly easy," Sullivan elaborates. "I took a handful or two of a papier-mâché product called Celluclay and shaped a thick, curved handle over the blade and stuck dried chicken bones and twelve-inch skeleton model kit parts into the papier-mâché, let it dry, and painted with some acrylic paint."

But the real coup de grâce on this prop was what the dagger could do. "I always tried to bring to the set more than what Sam requested," Sullivan reports. "In the dagger for example, I had drilled a hole through the miniature skull on the hilt, through the papier-mâché, so a blood tube could make the skull puke blood when it stabs people." On screen, as *Evil Dead* fans remember, this means the little skull on the blade handle, with yawning maw, processes the blood of the victim just stabbed like torrents of red sputum.

While Sullivan toiled to bring to life such gruesome props, cinematographer Philo also made plans. "I read the script and had a few meetings with Sam, Robert and Bruce about different things and different ways we were going to be able to technically do things," Philo explains.

"One of the key elements visually, as in *Within the Woods*, was going to be a wide-angle POV shot moving through the woods, occasionally knocking down trees, chasing people — what we called 'the force shots.' Those were planned to be achieved with a steadicam, which was just invented two or three years before we made the film. There weren't many of them around, and they assured me, yes, it was budgeted and that we were going to use a steadicam."

But that wasn't the case, as Philo remembers. "It was 'Oh, we *might* be able to use a steadicam for two weeks, so we may have to do all those shots during a concentrated time.'"

That didn't happen either...

"'Oh, *maybe* it's one week,' and then a few days before the shoot they said, 'Oh yeah, the steadicam is out,' and they wanted to know how we should do those shots. We talked, and it was a combination of the super–wide angle lens and the shaky-cam mechanism that I came up with. It was somewhat based on another idea that a friend gave me about using a long board and holding it from either end, and going through the woods that way," Philo describes. "But it didn't prove all that useful. Put a long board between two people, and you're always going to find a tree pretty quickly." The design was then modified to accommodate a shorter board and voilà: instant unsteadicam.

On other fronts, Philo's procured the equipment the production required. "The cameras I got from the University I had been going to and working for," he recounts. "They had a production facility that I was able to use equipment from. There was an Arriflex 16BL package and also an Arriflex S, just battery powered, with a variable speed motor.

"Just two cameras," Philo reports, "and we used prime lenses on basically every shot, and no filtration, because it was going to be blown up to 35mm, and I'd done some research on what we should be doing for that. As far as I was concerned, the approach to the film, and I think it was in line with what Sam had been doing on *Within the Woods*, is basically you compose and create a strong image that's going to come through. That way you don't have time to focus on the grain so much or a lot of things that might be wrong with a composition. The camera was always moving, or it was cutting every half second, so if you get a good strong composition and it's cut together quickly, nobody is bothered by the fact that it's got a little less resolution, or a little less color information."

Armed with cameras, script and an armful of inventive props and supplies, it came time for *The Evil Dead* crew to make the exodus from Michigan. "I think I was picked up and driven to Detroit," Sullivan remembers, "where I met cinematographer Tim Philo, sound recorder John Mason, who was a film teacher at a local college, and Josh Becker, the ambitious 'brains' of the Franklin[, Michigan,] gang, who was to prove an enduring production assistant and kept the only journal of the production." As for Sullivan, he lived by the Boy Scout motto: *be prepared*.

"For the shoot in Morristown, I brought about a gallon of liquid latex rubber, a bag of Hydrocal plaster, food coloring, some white clown grease paint, crepe hair, acrylic paints, brushes, buckets, bowls, an electric cake mixer, sketch pads, pencils, heavy-duty aluminum foil, modeling clay and all the issues of *Cinemagic*, (Don Dohler's super 8mm *Special Effects for Armatures* magazine) I had at the time.

"We left around noon and headed south on 75," Sullivan reports of the trek southward. "We talked film the whole time, and it was clear we were comfortable with each other and about Sam's project. We pulled into Morristown, Tennessee, in the early morning and called the local film commission and assistant producer Gary Holt to lead us to our cast and crew house."

COME FOR A DAY ... STAY FOREVER

Nestled in east Tennessee's Holston Valley (approx. population: 58,000) near Clinch Mountain, stands the little community of Morristown. First settled in 1782, this "crossroads of Dixie" is widely known as the region that raised pioneering American hero Davy Crockett.

Oddly enough, in light of *Evil Dead*'s production duration, Morristown's motto is actually "Come for a day ... stay forever." That's almost precisely what happened when Raimi set out in November of 1979 to direct his first feature film. The plan was to spend six short weeks in Morristown, but as is often the case with low-budget filmmaking, there were complications.

For one thing, as Tennessee Film Commission liaison Gary Holt informed the cast and crew, the original cabin they planned to feature was no longer available. Instead, Holt and Tapert searched for a replacement while the cast and crew spent the first few days shooting the film's opening scenes in and around Clinch Mountain, including the driving trip to the cabin in Sam's beloved car, the cream-colored 1973 Oldsmobile Delta 88, a vehicle he lovingly terms "the Classic."

Some of these scenes involved tricky stunt work on a perilous stretch of road near a river. Philo remembers hanging upside down from the car roof, looking through the camera while Raimi held on to him, all to capture shots of the car's interior. The crew also filmed on a bridge some fifteen miles away from the cabin that was eventually pressed into service. "It was something that our contact from the state, Gary Holt arranged for us," Philo notes, "*two* bridges actually. There was one they drive across and a slightly smaller one that got wrecked."

Elsewhere, a usable cabin was finally found, but there were major issues with the new "set" and its location. Sullivan sets the scene: "The cabin was a couple of miles from our residence, outside Morristown, well into a hilly, wooded area. We parked the cars at the road entrance to the tenth-of-a-mile dirt way to the cabin. This way we could shoot the Delta 88 driving down an overgrown, untrampled trail."

The location was so remote, in fact, the crew had concerns about the locals. Richard Grove, co-star in *Army of Darkness*, remembers hearing about it. "Bruce told me that when they were shooting *Evil Dead*, the people in the hills were just weirder than the movie. They always worried when they were out there, because people would come around and watch what they were doing, and they all looked very strange and very weird."

"They'd heard of us," notes Philo. "In the middle of the night, some of the local kids would come in and check on us and see what we were doing."

And the cabin itself? "It was a shell of a building," Sullivan reports. "Largely intact, it had no windows, doors, plumbing or electricity, and a three-inch carpet of cow manure."

As Theresa Tilly politely describes it, the cabin "needed a lot of work." Betsy Baker remembers that before filming could even begin, everybody on the cast and crew had to make the locale not just camera ready, but liveable. "It truly was a sight that you just walked upon and said, 'Oh my god, what have I done?' This was going to be a great adventure, but every single one of us had to pitch in cleaning, sweeping, nailing down things that were about to fall off, or making sure the floorboards were not going to come up. It was filthy dirty, and animals had been living there. It smelled pretty bad."

"I think there was a functional toilet and maybe some cold running water, and that was about it," Sandweiss explains, "and no electricity."

Because the cabin has become such a famous location and is no longer standing, following a fire in the 1980s, this author asked Sandweiss to provide the reader with a mini-tour of the edifice. "We spent a lot of time in it, and it was very small. You walk in the front door and you're right in the main room," she begins. "To the right of you is the window, where I was sketching on my pad, next to the fireplace. To the left of you is the spot where the girls were playing cards. That was the largest room in the house, but it was tiny. Then there was a little kitchen area, where we all had our little toast and Ash is mumbling inanely. I don't even remember if that was a real kitchen or not.

"I think that there were two bedrooms," she continues. "There was the one they put Betsy in after I stabbed her ankle, which was so tiny that there was just room to make a tiny, makeshift bed. Then I think the room I was in, when I foolishly went out to see who was in the woods, was the only actual bedroom. There was a small bathroom that was just horrible that we didn't use. It was pretty bad."

The production company's home base during this period and throughout the shoot wasn't much more luxurious than the "rustic" cabin. "I was personally more concerned about my living conditions," Tilly acknowledges. "I had no idea I was probably going to spend more time in the cabin than I ever would in my bedroom, because I had never done anything like this before."

"There was a house that we all stayed in," Philo picks up the thread. "The number [of occupants] changed a bit depending on how many actors were with us and whether people came to help out from Detroit, but there was a cast and crew of about thirteen people. The house was about two miles along back roads from the driveway of the cabin, just around the backside of a mountain. The sound man and I shared a room and all the actresses shared a room. These were pretty small rooms in a split-level suburban house. The living room was like a bunk room for about five people."

"There was no privacy," Baker explains. "It felt sometimes like we were intruding on a really bad fraternity house. The first few weeks were exciting and exhilarating, and we were making a movie. After about the fourth week, we were dirty, muddy, cranky and cold, and we had some delays. All of the sudden, stepping over people sleeping, and unrolled sleeping bags, and dirty clothes that hadn't been washed in weeks became kind of grating."

Still, the excitement was palpable. "I recall a lot of adrenaline that night," Sullivan notes of the beginning of production, "and sleeping on the floor in a sleeping bag was a great way to start out exhausted for a grueling schedule." He should know; he was there for a long while. "*The Evil Dead Companion* states I was only in Tennessee for three days. The author had mistaken my time in Tennessee with a visit by Bart Pierce, who only stayed three days, while I worked for seven weeks, except for the drive home and back for Christmas," he corrects.

Once shooting began, *The Evil Dead* began a rigorous routine. "Bruce was the alarm clock for everyone," Philo reveals. "He got up before everyone else and woke everybody up ... starting with me!"

CABIN FEVER

"We all lived in this house, but people were not living normal hours," Theresa Tilly remembers of *The Evil Dead*'s principal photography. "We'd be contacted at two in the morning, and they'd say 'Time to get up and start your filming day.' That was one crew, but there would be another crew that was just getting back at three in the morning, and they were working on something they would continue the following day."

"For the most part, we filmed at night and tried to sleep during the day," Sandweiss articulates. "We were constantly freezing since there was no heat in the cabin."

"It was cold," Philo repeats, "and I was the only one who knew how to load the film magazines. We tried to train someone else, but he deflected it by saying, 'No, I don't want the responsibility.' So going from shooting on a messy set to the back [of the cabin] to load the film magazines, I had to wash my hands with scalding coffee. There was no running water on the set, no way to get clean, so you would just go to the coffee pot and scald your hands and put 'em [the magazines] in the bag and load 'em up."

The low temperature was a difficulty, especially considering the shots Philo was meant to capture. "I think Sam has a sense, having done fight scenes before in super 8mm, that they ought to be hand-held. You get the camera in the right place and keep it hand-held, and it's going to have a good active feel to it. But because there was so much action in the film, that resulted in lots and lots of hand-held stuff, and I have to say that with the cold weather and hand-holding a metal camera hours and hours a day, basically, during my sleeping time, my hands were bent claws, like arthritis. We were too young for arthritis, but my hands would just ache all night while I was trying to sleep."

Considering the extreme cold and physical nature of the film, rehearsal was not a high priority. "We would rehearse a scene a few times before we did it, if you want to call that a rehearsal," Sandweiss explains with a good-natured laugh. "There's only so much screaming and grunting you can rehearse. Certainly we did almost no character work at all. All I knew was that I was the bitchy, hippie sister of Ash. And I was the outsider because the other four were coupled up. Which was funny for me, because here I was from the theater department of University of Michigan, and doing character analysis there, and I go do a movie and Sam just says, 'Can you grunt a little louder? When you're spitting that karo syrup out of your mouth, can you open your mouth a little wider?' That's the kind of direction I got."

"On the set, Sam had a straight ahead kind of style," reports Sullivan of principal photography, a process he was part of for seven weeks, for sixteen to eighteen hours a day — with no assistants. "I don't get the impression from talking to the cast that Sam shot master shots and then the close-ups and two shots. He had the sequence already cut in his head and so he would shoot the parts of the action, to the dismay of the actors. It was difficult to maintain the flow and continuity of emotions. As the makeup guy, I got the daily scoop on the shoot.

"Sam and Rob kept the film moving," reports Sullivan. "I'm not sure where 'Fish and Game' Tapert got it, but he has a definite gift for producing. *Evil Dead* was a trial by fire for everyone, but while Sam was the 'passion,' Rob was the 'calm.' Rob had a very well-organized set, and I remember the comradeship and mellow yet busy atmosphere. No ego clashes or tempers flaring. Everybody pitched in and saw it through. That does not happen for everyone in show business. There was — and still is — a lot of loyalty to the guys."

Though the physical hardships endured by Campbell have become widely known thanks to his best-selling memoir, *If Chins Could Kill: Confessions of a B Movie Actor*, there were plenty of endurance tests to go around. Lest one conclude Raimi is a sadist, one should remember that low-budget films, and in particular low-budget horror films, boast a long history of difficult shoots. *The Last House on the Left* (1972) and *The Texas Chain Saw Massacre* are just two examples, like *Evil Dead*, of productions where cast and crew gave it their all and then went beyond even that benchmark in an effort to make something unique and memorable.

For Sandweiss, the shooting of the infamous "rape by a tree" sequence rates high on her "difficult" meter. "It seems to me that it was probably one or two nights," she remembers. "One of the things that took so long about all the running and being chased by the 'force' was that they had to make it look like it was toppling trees, so they would cut trees off at the stump and then put them back on — *the tree back on its stump* — and then push it over as we were filming, so it would look like the force was knocking them down. That takes a lot of time.

"I was running," she remembers of those nights, "just running. There was no path. I just ran my ass off, and got scraped, bumped and bruised, and fell a lot. And it was freezing."

For this and other chase sequences, special camera rigs and tracks were constructed, an ambitious feat considering budget and time limitations. "One thing we did was set up a wheelchair track with four-by-eight plywood [sheets] going down the driveway," Philo remembers. "Right beside the driveway was the woods. We'd light a stretch of that, so that the actress could run through the woods, and we'd actually be traveling on the wheelchair [sitting] sideways, down this path. Then we'd try to get some speed up, and then try to stop. It wasn't very different when we did *Evil Dead 2*. It was the same thing."

After the chase came the notorious attack by vines and branches, a sequence filmed in reverse. "They would start out with the vines wrapped around me, and as they shot them, they would pull them off, then play it in reverse," Sandweiss explains.

"Vines were puppeted and ripped through a pre-cut costume and waxed back together," Sullivan reports. "I painted scars all over Ellen so when her clothing tore, a scratch could be seen."

Regarding the infamous sequence, Sandweiss has a healthy sense of perspective. "I knew in a broad sense that the trees were going to attack me, but I had no idea that it was going to be sexual in nature, and furthermore I didn't know until I saw it on the big screen myself how explicit it was going to be. That's not to say I didn't know what I was doing when I was doing it, but in some ways I thought the lighting was going to be such, or the camera angle was going to be such, that certain things wouldn't appear a certain way.

"And I certainly didn't know what sound effects would be added. Especially the final sound effect of that scene," [a moan of what sounds like sexual satisfaction], "which was the stupidest, most unnecessary thing.

"It went one step too far," Sandweiss considers. "And certainly it's the one thing that has been difficult for me, because I'm a normal person now and have children and a husband and a life. It's been difficult for me to come to terms with, but the good news is that I have, and I'm able to look at it with humor. It has provided me now with endless opportunity for humor in terms of when people ask me questions about it at conventions. I have numerous responses about the fun I had with "Bud," or the terrible case of Dutch Elm disease I had to get rid of. All sorts of quips, and in fact, Bruce Campbell helped me come up with a few."

In interviews over the years, Raimi has backed away from the intensity demonstrated in this sequence, saying he regrets it and that he wouldn't do it if he could go back and change things.[2]

Considering the scene's notoriety, Sandweiss takes the opportunity to set the record straight regarding her decision to leave acting after the film. "People misquote me by saying my experience on *Evil Dead* was so awful that it turned me away from acting forever. That's totally untrue. I just made a decision, for many reasons, not to, at least on a full-time basis."

Tilly also had an encounter with the exploitation side of low-budget horror filmmaking. "I do not remember a topless scene being in the script in the very beginning," she establishes. "What I recall is that when we got down there, Sam broached the subject, and I don't remember exactly how it was said. I guess it's like [if] some famous filmmaker, Francis Ford Coppola, hired me to do a shoot and [said,] 'Yes, you have to take your shirt off in this scene.' I'd think, 'Yeah, it's Coppola; I'll do it.' But these guys were just a bunch of stooges and the idea [was that] I would have to trust them with this, and who knew what it would turn into. I thought I could talk them out of it, but I do remember it was a horrible night; I dreaded it. In some ways, it ruined the whole trip for me because I had to constantly know what was going to happen."

Today, Tilly, like Sandweiss, has achieved a measure of peace about her brief on-screen nudity. "It's kind of a harmless scene," she comments. "You can't see much."

Betsy Baker's most difficult moments came during the shooting of the scene involving Linda's premature burial. "I knew I was going to be hit over the head with beams, but I was told that the beams they'd gotten from the Morristown Sears and Roebucks looked like wooden beams, but were actually nothing more than Styrofoam," she relates.

"To me, Styrofoam meant a little kick board for a swimming pool, but now I understand there are different grades. These beams were unbelievably painful, and I was being hit over the head. Rob was off camera and Bruce was on camera, and it was one of those things where I looked at the beam beforehand and thought it didn't look too bad. But when you get a nine-foot Styrofoam beam coming at you at a good velocity, it's going to hurt. We did that for six or seven takes and I was screaming. Anyone within thirty miles of the set knew that it was as much as they could do with me."

But the beam beating was just a precursor to the burial. "There was a hole," Baker explains, "and I was buried under dirt. Even the slightest amount of dirt becomes very heavy, to the point where it does become frightening. I didn't like the weight of it and did want to make sure they were going to take me out of there."

Tilly, too, had further demons to confront, namely her own claustrophobia during the sequence in which Ash dismembers Shelly and the camera reveals her severed body parts twitching on the floor. The effect was accomplished by digging under the cabin's floorboards and then cutting holes through the floor in which Tilly and Shelly Shemps (on-screen doubles; see Lexicon) could extend their various limbs, meant to appear severed, though still mobile. "Having to sit underneath the floor of this cabin, nailed to the floor, was pretty torturous and scary. But it wasn't just me, it was Rob and Bruce who were under there too. That was the other part of these horrible things — the boys did them too. They didn't just make us do it. We were all in the same boat ... except none of them had to go topless.

"I was really claustrophobic, probably more so than I am today. I didn't know if there were rats or snakes or bugs under there. It was literally the ground; we were under the ground. At one point, Tim and Sam both fell asleep. I just couldn't believe it, but they had fallen asleep at the camera! I was horrified that they were prolonging this torture any more than necessary."

"There were times when we were just beside ourselves with tiredness," Sandweiss notes. "You'd sit around for hours caked in sticky blood, not able to touch anything, and you're freezing and you can't see anything because you have the contacts in. It was physically uncomfortable a lot of the time, but it was also fun."

Philo remembers an occasion when exhaustion nearly led to hysteria. "There was one point on the set when Sam had been up for three days straight. We were trying to get finished with an actress. That was when we were shooting for fifty hours straight, but Sam had been up before that, doing storyboards. As we got finished laying out this big scene, Sam laid down on the couch for a moment and fell asleep, and we couldn't wake him up. The actress was getting panicky about it, so we started pulling him up and pulled his upper body off the couch just a bit. Well, Sam stayed in that position, half-risen, about six inches up, but still completely asleep. The actress was almost screaming, it was such an unnatural position. So we had to let Sam sleep through the filming of that."

"It was pretty serious," Baker adds. "Sam actually fell asleep to the point of such deep sleep that we couldn't wake him. We thought something had happened to him."

There were times, according to Philo, that fatigue actually shut things down. "There were two different times during the eight weeks that I was down there, that Rob Tapert, after about three hours of night shooting, came in and just said, 'I'm calling it. Everybody has to go home and go to bed.' Nobody can function without sleep. Sam would say, 'No, we're behind schedule,' but those were good decisions Rob made. We were grinding to a halt."

Far away from the exhausted moviemakers, back in the warmest Michigan winter in some time, Phil Gillis kept abreast of the movie's progress. "I heard from them every week. I made the mistake of telling Rob that I had some Wang Laboratory shares, and he checked the paper every day, and those shares were going up considerably at the time. 'I see Wang went up four points ... can you send us some money? We don't have enough to go to McDonalds.' So I'd send him a little."

The experience shooting *Evil Dead* lived up to the ad line conjured for the film — "the ultimate experience in grueling terror" — but a commonality among all the people interviewed for this book is that they loved doing it. It was a grand adventure and a time of their lives they recollect vividly.

"I'll always remember being out on the hillside while some prop was being reconstructed inside so we could throw Bruce into it again, and Sam and I were laying up on the hill," Philo describes the scene, a moment when both men were covered in caked blood and the production was severely understaffed. "It was freezing outside and it was the middle of the night — something like two in the morning — and we're just laying there looking at the stars, and Sam said to me 'Tim, it's never going to be this hard again, it's never going to be this bad again.'

"But then Sam paused and said, 'But it's never going to be this good again.' He really understood that when you make something with very little money, the investors were not coming down to Tennessee to look over your shoulders the way executives will when you have millions of dollars at stake. In this case, it was basically take as much money as possible, and with as much elbow grease as possible, make a flick."

THE FINAL CHAPTER OR A NEW BEGINNING?

By the end of December 1979, obligations in the real world, both familial and financial, forced many *Evil Dead* creators to return to more normal lives in Michigan. Sandweiss and Delrich were among those who departed around Christmas of 1979. Principal photography went over schedule, right into the new year, and money was running out.

"It was pretty clear from the beginning that we would be finishing the film back in Michigan, especially a lot of FX shots and inserts needed for editing," Sullivan explains. "I had given my word to the guys that I would see it through, and I am proud to say I did. At the end of six weeks, Rob asked — if not pleaded with — me to stay for a couple more weeks in Tennessee. I was desperately homesick, but when I tried to get the time off from work, I could only get another week. In my seventh week, I not only kept up the shooting requirements, but I prepped a couple of gags like the Scotty eye-gouging head, and Hal wore his makeup for two days after I had left. What a trooper!"

With cast and crew departing and work still to be completed, the act of "fake shemping" or doubling came into play, with those still on location often performing double and triple duty behind and in front of the camera.

Production assistant Josh Becker was one of the folks that remained in Tennessee until the bitter end, and later remarked in a interview with writer Amy Murphy that "not quitting during the production of the first *Evil Dead*" was the hardest thing he ever did in his life.[3]

Overall the group — bonded by their time together — still kept in touch, even after the trek home to Detroit. "I would actually call down to the set in Tennessee when I got home," Theresa Tilly reveals. "It was one of those love-hate things, like people who love their tormenters."

Others found that their services were still required. "We had a lot of insert shooting still to do," Philo acknowledges. "When push came to shove down in Tennessee, what got left behind were the inserts and close-ups. When we went back to Michigan, we shot all the basement sequences, a lot of inserts in Sam's garage, and also some scenes out in rural Michigan."

Among those recalled for duty during this stage of production (in Marshall, Michigan) was Betsy Baker. "I think we did some pick-up shots outside, which would mean it would be graveyard pick-ups; that was the only time Linda was really outside. Hands and head coming out of the ground again, that kind of thing."

For those who missed rural Tennessee, Raimi, Campbell and Tapert brought souvenirs of Morristown to Detroit. "When they packed out of Tennessee, they brought back in the van the camera equipment, but also pieces of the cabin. They took out a chunk of the wall, they took out some door pieces, a bit of the floor," says Philo. "This was done so that the additional footage shot in Michigan would match the footage already in the can."

"The FX shots of Shelly's dismemberment scene were shot in April and May of 1980 at Sam Raimi's parents' garage," Sullivan recalls of the next stage of shooting. "The shot of Shelly's hand being chopped off was done on a raised platform that represented the floor of the cabin. A slot was made in the floor and one of those fake Shemps, a young woman, fed her hand through the floor board, and I attached a foam rubber arm with a tube for blood blowing. Sam wanted the axe to cut near the wrist. In case of any possible criminality should the Shemp be injured, Sam would handle the axe, and it was a successful one-take wonder. Good thing; I only had one arm!"

In the spring, Raimi traveled to New York City with film canisters of *Evil Dead* in tow. His mission: to assemble the picture with film editor Edna Ruth Paul and her assistant Joel Coen. If the latter name sounds familiar, it should. Joel Coen is one half of the acclaimed writing/directing team, the Coen brothers, creators of such films as *Barton Fink* (1991), the Academy Award–winning *Fargo* (1996), and *O Brother, Where Art Thou?* (2000). Then bedecked in long hair, Joel Coen had left the University of Texas (at Austin) graduate program for practical industry experience in New York City, to work on films as a production assistant and assistant editor.[4]

"We got to see the first rough cut, the first assemblage of it on videotape in the spring of 1980," Philo remembers of his first peek at a cut-together *Evil Dead*. "Edna Paul was working in New York, and it was incredibly long and boring, but we had a lot of confidence that the shots were there."

One sequence that was still missing, however, was the special effects climax. As Raimi worked in New York, the effects team in Detroit prepared for another phase of "grueling" work.

I'M MELTING...

"Sam wanted whatever happened to be bigger and more disgusting than the rest of the film," Philo reports of the film's climactic confrontation between Ash and the Deadites. "And another dictate that Sam had was that it had to feature something new in the way of special effects, just so he could say this had special effects nobody had ever done before."

"Initially, Sam had a simple idea for the finale," Sullivan adds. "Fill the characters' clothes full of balloons and deflate them with smoke leaking out of their bodies. I thought that with all the violence we had shot, that would be disappointing. And if somebody in the audience blew raspberries during the Deadite deflation that would get the wrong response. In Morristown, I pitched Sam the idea of doing a stop-motion animation meltdown. I could build replicas of the characters in dyed modeling clay and emulate the Morlock stop-motion decomposition from George Pal's *The Time Machine* (1960). We could stretch out the sequence with interesting, gory cleverness.

"I quickly did a dozen storyboards outlining how Cheryl and Scotty could disintegrate into the puddle of bile we were leaving on the floor of the cabin in Tennessee," Sullivan describes. "Sam went for it and connected me with Bart [Pierce] after we had gotten back to Michigan. After some equipment discussions with Sam, we ended up with a fairly unique 16mm Mitchell camera. Known for their superb film registration and Mitchell's reputation as the maker of the cameras that shot *King Kong* and all of Harryhausen's films, we felt we were in film fantasy heaven."

The filmmakers had a plan, but stop-motion animation is anything but easy. Sullivan elaborates: "Stop-motion animation is a technique as old as motion pictures themselves. Film is made of thousands of "frames" or pictures on a strip of celluloid. The film can be shot running at twenty-four frames per second, and when projected at that speed will create the illusion of persistence of vision and movement. With many cameras, one picture or frame can be taken at a time, and the object being photographed can move a tiny distance, and a new frame photographed. Move and shoot. When projected, the object will appear to be moving. However, for animators, we take this to some depth. There is an unlimited range of styles in animation, as in any art, but for those of us interested in creating lifelike characters, animals and physical effects, the study of movement, motion, anatomy and the physics of the real world is essential.

"Bring along some patience as well," adds Sullivan. "As I mentioned, it takes twenty-four separate photographs and movements just to film one second of running time."

Sullivan, Philo and Pierce commenced this labor-intensive process. "The finale effects and several other FX shots were done in a final three-and-a-half-month shoot in Bart Pierce's basement," Sullivan recollects. "Bart and his wife had a two-week-old baby and a three-year-old boy. I slept on a cot in the basement for a month, until that started to affect my work."

"With no budget," Philo considers, "what you wind up with is the resource of people putting in their time. I worked months on that stop-motion stuff and none of that was paid. We went in on Friday night, started to work on it, shot all night, slept a few hours, shot through Sunday, and the film went to the lab Monday morning. Maybe you'd get a 1.8-second shot out of all that. But it was fun to be on our own, and my input was that I got to match the light to [the cabin interior; live action] to the extent I could."

The process represented an unusual variation on stop-motion photography. As many viewers of classic horror films and Sinbad fantasy pictures may recall, in some moments, stop-motion animation appears jerky, even robotic. Philo, Sullivan and Pierce were of one mind that they did not want that to be the case for the ferocious Deadites. "We had decided to double expose each frame of animation to smooth over any jerks or pops in the stop motion, to feel more like the live-action footage of facial bile and hair falling off," Sullivan says. "Bart had to shoot and reverse the camera to double expose each frame."

Another technique the special effects troika utilized was one that had not been attempted before: a total merging in individual shots of live-action physical effects like dripping blood with stop-motion photography of the model's degeneration. This effect was achieved with mattes. "In a few shots, we had a live-action side, with the fluid running, and — on the other side of a matte line — a claymation meltdown and disintegration of the character's heads," Philo specifies.

Sullivan credits the blending of photographic techniques to Pierce. "Bart employed a split screen matte process to combine the facial portions of the clay head I was animating with the live sections where we would blow bile out of the skull [with tubes], and pull the scored sections of wig down with fish line."

"Shooting that was just grueling hours," comments Philo. "Fortunately," Sullivan adds, "I found myself getting into that stop motion 'zone.' It's a very absorbing process and time. Pain and the outside world go away."

Just keeping track of which shots were in the 'can' took time and energy. "I had drawn thirty thumbnail storyboards of the sequence in full, and I would put a red check on a board when we had a successful shot back from the lab," Sullivan recalls.

Philo had a mission too. "I had the film clips over a little rewind spindle and viewer, so I would cut the thing together over on the side. What I was producing was called an *advisory cut*. That's what Sam asked for. He said, 'Shoot the shots and give us a cut so we know what we're looking for, because if we just get the footage, we're not going to know how it's cut together.'"

"We would send the footage off to Sam, and Sam would message back to keep sending more," Sullivan notes. "In total, after starting the film in October 1979 and finishing November 22, 1980, I had worked for seven months on *Evil Dead*!"

And so it went, until the nefarious Deadites, imagined on paper by Raimi and brought to life by cameramen, performers, and special effects magicians, met — in gory spotlight — their famous demise. One critic later made specific note of the finale, recommending "Tom Sullivan's amazing special makeup effects climax."[5]

CREATURES OF THE NIGHT, WHAT MUSIC THEY MAKE...

The Evil Dead still wasn't complete. "It was slow going for a couple of years because they had no money," Phil Gillis recalls. "They got the film in the can for under a hundred thousand dollars, but then there was post-production work. They ran out of money, and there was color correction they had to do, sound they had to add."

And an original musical score was needed to complement the action. According to legend, director and maverick John Carpenter screened his masterpiece, *Halloween* sans his pulse-pounding score to a test audience of studio executives, and not a one found the movie scary. However, when Carpenter added music to his cut, well, the rest is history. As this anecdote proves, mood music is an essential ingredient in a horror film, and Raimi hooked up with a young talent, Joe LoDuca, who could help him achieve success on this front.

Today Joe LoDuca is an Emmy Award–winning composer, a talent who has made a career scoring films, like Christophe Gans' fantasy *Brotherhood of the Wolf* (2002), and TV series, including *Xena: Warrior*

Princess. However, back in the seventies, he was new to the business and the very notion of scoring films. A Detroit native, LoDuca developed an interest in music at a young age and fell into the rock band scene as a teenager. Proficient in guitar, LoDuca graduated from De La Salle Collegiate and Wayne State University with a degree in composition and performance. Later, his music was heard nationally on Dennis Wholey's PBS program, *LateNight America*.[6]

It was shortly after his graduation that LoDuca met Raimi and Tapert through a friend who was raising capital for *The Evil Dead*. "I think the point at which I came in was when they'd finished principal photography in Tennessee, and I don't know that I'd seen much of it," LoDuca remembers.

"They were doing reshoots, and I was mostly hearing about all the practical jokes that had taken place during the shoot. I was just impressed by their chutzpah, their wackiness. There was something about their energy that was very attractive to me, and I wanted to be involved in whatever they were doing.

"We went to Sam's parents' den, had these huge bowls of popcorn, and went through the movie," LoDuca recounts. "To be honest with you, I was aboard just because of my own sensibilities. I wasn't a fan of horror movies, but I realized that I had to do some quick study. After knowing these guys, who were so likeable, and seeing these images, which were so totally violent, I tried to reconcile them in my own mind. And I got the idea that the way they were approaching the movie was like a big game. They're trying to scare you. It's a system of entertainment and, in some ways, pranks."

LoDuca remembers his indoctrination into scoring horror films. "I knew that there were certain things that had to happen; certain shots and surprises that would mean that the music would start off with a bang after the silence. That's part of the system of setting up the scares, and that was something Sam taught me. He taught me how to set up a false scare; the way you go silent. And it's funny, I was able to see another generation of horror films with my daughter and say, 'Watch, the music will go out here and there'll be a big scare,' and she'd say, 'How do you know that?'"

LoDuca also found the Renaissance boys extremely knowledgeable about movie scores. "They could hum *Patton*. They could hum all these great scores that I wasn't really aware of, other than being a moviegoer, and I think that was my jumping-off point too. There was a certain amount of tribute and honor [in the score], and it plays into my own sensibility of things like melody and harmony."

And what instruments and techniques did LoDuca utilize to create the jolting, moody and creepy *Evil Dead* score? "I knew we could overdub, but that the score was going to have an intimate sound because we couldn't afford an orchestra, even though Sam had even maybe wanted one. It turned out in our favor to have the string quartet because of the intimacy of the cabin. Some of the melodic instruments would then be strings.

"There's a certain sense of melodrama that Sam likes to go for in certain films," LoDuca considers, "and I think that to have a violin sweetly playing a love scene seems to fit in with that sensibility. It's always that combination of violence, sentimentality and humor that makes up his style.

"A piano was in there as well. We recorded in an attic studio of an engineer friend, and it was an upright piano that wasn't perfectly in tune, which is something that you might have found in the cabin. We didn't have a lot of rehearsal time, so the performance of the strings is less than perfect."

For LoDuca, the music reflected the film's visual style. "I knew that it [the movie] was crude, but its crudeness worked for it. The strangeness of that is that the music is equally crude, but it all sort of works together: the real garish lighting, the out-of-tuneness of the strings. What was painful was that since it was my first experience with film, I was literally calculating the hit points of the film with a calculator, entering frame numbers and doing the math. 'At such and such a tempo, and at such and such a beat, this will occur,' so it was pretty painful for me."

SHOWTIME

With a final cut at a duration of 85 minutes, *The Evil Dead* — still titled *Book of the Dead* — premiered in Detroit. "I remember the first public screening of it," Phil Gillis reminisces. "The place was packed. Sam, Bruce and Rob got all their friends and the investors, and hired klieg lights at the front of the Redford Theater, which is a high-class neighborhood theater in Detroit that seats about nine hundred people.

"I haven't seen it in twenty years, but I remember the meltdown scene," Gillis says, awed. "They spent a lot of money melting down a skeleton and there was green oatmeal, or Cream of Wheat — I don't know what the hell it was! It was green Cream of Wheat coming out of their sleeves, and then the crickets came crawling out. When the crickets came out, some guy in the audience shouted 'That's enough, already!'"

"I was amazed," says Sullivan, who attended the premiere with his wife Penny and both parents. "It worked. It had this charm. It was never boring. And once it got going, it was as intense as hell."

"I think all of us were stunned by it, because it's like being at war, and then somebody shows you war movies made during the battle," Philo remembers his initial reaction. "Each shot comes up and you think of the context and struggle related to it. The whole thing is a little hard to take in. The film has a strange pace too. I've sat with eager midnight shows watching the thing, and you get to the twenty-four-minute mark and the kids behind you are saying, 'This sucks, nothing's happening, when's there going to be some blood?' Then as soon as Betsy gets stabbed in the ankle with the pencil, you're off to the races and they're going, 'Arrgh, this is good.'"

"A lot of the time, mostly I was thinking, 'Oh my god, my parents are here!" Sandweiss remembers. "I was proud of it. I was in a movie and I was so young, and there were all of these people there, and people were making a big deal of it. But my parents and Sam's parents were there seeing me do these terrible things, so it was a little embarrassing. The story that I always tell is that when my mother was walking down the aisle after the Redford premiere, she saw a woman she knew, who maybe was a friend of Sam's mother. And the woman just came up and put her hand on my mother's shoulder and said, 'What we have to put up with from our children.'"

Although he didn't attend the premiere, old mentor and friend Nobles did get a special showing. "In 1981 or '82, I was at 20th Century Fox and I got a call they were in town, and 'Can they come over to the lot?' They sat in my office and handed me a three-quarter inch of *Evil Dead* and I played it. And I said, 'This is probably the best thing you guys have ever done.' It was still raw, but it was a thousand times better than *Blair Witch*, and I said, 'My god, these kids have done it! They've learned everything they needed to learn, and applied it over and over again, and were ready to make a hit.'"

BOOKING BOOK OF THE DEAD

Despite a successful world premiere and the approbation of a former mentor, *Book of the Dead* had a long journey to get playtime in theaters. It still needed a distributor and a catchier title. (On the latter front, Tom Sullivan suggested two colorful alternatives: *Sex Bad, Must Kill!* and *Lick the Blood Off My Shovel!*) In an effort to publicize the film, Sullivan developed promotional artwork, including a poster entitled "Beloved" which dramatized "a skeleton rushing out of a swampy grave, clutching the severed head of an attractive brunette." The poster hung in Tapert's office for a year, as the Renaissance team struggled to get their debut feature into theaters.

Then they met Irvin Shapiro (1906–1989), another quasi-mythic figure in film history. The late Shapiro has been described as a "great believer in the horror genre," and a man with a "nose for fresh talent."[7] He had worked in the film industry for generations, taking a hand in the publicity and selling of classic films such as Jean Renoir's *Grand Illusion* and Sergei Eisenstein's *Battleship Potemkin*.

In the horror genre, Shapiro had previously teamed with independent director George Romero after *Night of the Living Dead*, arranging distribution deals for that director's little-known follow-ups, *There's Always Vanilla*

(1971), *Jack's Wife* (1973; on video as *Season of the Witch*), and the brilliant *Knightriders* (1981). Richard Rubinstein, a talent who became Romero's producing partner at Laurel Entertainment, also served as Shapiro's administrative assistant, and noted that Shapiro "knew a tremendous amount" about the business, and served as his "godfather" in the industry.[8] A talent who had a significant hand in the formation the Cannes Film Festival, Shapiro, according to rumors, came into possession of some genuine Picasso artworks for the cost of a meal and a bottle of wine ... and not an extravagant bottle, either.

In December of 1981, Raimi, Campbell and Tapert screened *Book of the Dead* for Shapiro, at the time managing a company called Films Around the World. Shapiro liked the film and agreed to help. "Totally honest guy, good sense of humor," Campbell described the living legend. "When we met him he must have been about 80....He'd been around forever. We were fortunate ... he totally bought into it."[9]

Shapiro also "bought" into the project financially, providing funds to spearhead the photography of publicity stills,[10] and sending young Raimi to France, where the renamed *The Evil Dead* would play at Cannes. It was there the ball really began rolling for *Evil Dead*. Stephen King, best-selling horror author, happened to be at one of the screenings. In November 1982, he reviewed the film for Carol Serling's *Twilight Zone Magazine* and reported "standing ovations," but more importantly, he called the Renaissance Pictures debut "the most ferociously original horror film of the year 1982."[11]

From the Grand Guignol guru of *Carrie*, *Salem's Lot* and *Cujo*, there could be no higher compliment, and the accolade provided *The Evil Dead* crew a nice and enduring blurb to include on posters. In the same piece, King interviewed Raimi, who explained how the film had been financed and that several distributors, including Paramount, had turned the film down.

The increased publicity eventually brought a buyer to the table. In this case it was New Line, the House that Freddy Built, named so because of the success of the *Nightmare on Elm Street* franchise in the mid-to-late 1980s. But at the time, New Line was still in dodgy territory, Craven's first Krueger picture not yet released. New Line had re-released Hooper's seminal *The Texas Chain Saw Massacre*, but was floating with little funds and even less personnel.[12] But what mattered was that New Line could get *Evil Dead* into theaters, even though the film eventually went out unrated because the MPAA unceremoniously slapped it with an X, the kiss of death. "We really marketed it for drive-ins, which at the time made up something like 22 percent of the market," Tapert later reported of the distribution strategy.[13]

The unrated *Evil Dead* opened in America on April 15, 1983, the same day as Chuck Norris' *Lone Wolf McQuade*, the theatrical release of Steven

Spielberg's twelve-year-old TV-movie *Duel* (1971), and Adrian Lyne's breakthrough, *Flashdance*. It premiered in New York at the Rivoli and other houses, and it played at the Wellmont in Montclair, New Jersey. Willem Dafoe, Raimi's future Goblin in *Spider-Man* remembers seeing the movie on 42nd Street. "I remember a vivid film-going experience," he recalls. "It seemed quite extreme, quite fresh, and quite personal."

Though horror movies — even the best, like Friedkin's *The Exorcist* — usually meet with outright disdain, Raimi's debut picture scored some positive reviews. In the *Los Angeles Times* Kevin Thomas noted it was an "instant classic, probably the grisliest well-made movie ever" and credited it as being a "product of the vivid imagination of Samuel M. Raimi, for whom this film is clearly just the beginning."[14] Archer Winston wrote in the *New York Post* that "horror addicts" would "gobble up this dish of gore and disgust," and that it was the horror genre's "pièce de résistance."[15]

Film Comment recognized Raimi as one of the "new faces of 1982," alongside *The Road Warrior* director George Miller, special effects innovator Rob Bottin, and performers Amanda Plummer and Mickey Rourke. Writer David Chute noted in the same piece that Raimi specialized "in direction action, cattle-prod shock tactics, top-speed, ground-level tracking shots embellished with percussive sound effects."[16] *Monthly Film Bulletin*'s Kim Newman enthused that "Samuel M. Raimi has turned his mish-mash of horror-comic familiars, *Exorcist*-style levitation and possession and undigested chunks of Lovecraft lore into an enjoyable, catch-all roller-coaster ride through the splatter genre."[17]

But all was not sunshine and roses. *People* magazine quipped that "If there are any ancient Sumerians around, they ought to sue for defamation of character."[18] Similarly, David Sterritt reported for the *Christian Science Monitor* that the film consisted of "purposeless violence inflicted with clockwork regularity on one-dimensional characters."[19]

Overseas, particularly in England, *The Evil Dead* proved a smash, scoring high in Scotland, where it landed in second place at the box office, beaten only by Spielberg's *E.T.* The film survived close scrutiny by the BBFC (British Board of Film Censors) in England with a few cuts and premiered at the London Film Festival, where it was met with excitement and appreciation.

Simon Moore, screenwriter of *The Quick and the Dead* and an accomplished independent filmmaker in his own right, recalled to this author his surprise upon discovering the film. "I'd wandered in [to a theater] one afternoon, not knowing anything, and seeing the first *Evil Dead* movie. And I thought it was an absolute knockout. I think you very rarely get the chance to see any film, especially by a young filmmaker with no money, where you can see the imprint of his style so strongly."

Despite enthusiastic audiences, *The Evil Dead* soon had another problem with censors, especially overseas. Upon its release, videotapes of *The Evil Dead* were later confiscated in the UK on "the grounds that irresponsible parents made the tapes available to children."[20]

In particular, the Video Recordings Act of 1984 granted right-wing watchdog censors the lawful power to ban and confiscate films dubbed "video nasties" because of their perceived violent content and lack of socially redeeming qualities. Heading this campaign to censor and destroy horror films on video (including *The Texas Chain Saw Massacre*, *I Spit on Your Grave* and *Last House on the Left*) was the late Mary Whitehouse (1910–2001), a former art teacher and ultra-right-wing conservative Christian[21] who christened Raimi's *The Evil Dead* exhibit A, "the number one nasty."[22] Apparently, this pronouncement was made without Whitehouse ever having seen the film, or any of the others on her list. Despite the controversy, Raimi's first film topped the trade listing as the most widely viewed nasty on the infamous list.[23]

But while trouble brewed for Deadite fans in England, *The Evil Dead* continued to perform well in other regions. Raimi, Tapert, Sullivan and Ted Raimi attended Knokke Heist, a film festival in Belgium in 1983, where Sullivan demonstrated his makeup acumen on a willing Ted. Later, Sullivan was Renaissance's representative to the 1983 Saturn Awards in L.A. where *Evil Dead* was nominated as best genre film. In the final balloting, it lost that honor to Paul Bartel's cannibal comedy, *Eating Raoul*.

The Evil Dead made a tremendous splash with horror film fans, but the fact that it was unrated prevented it from becoming the box office bonanza it might have been, like the following year's *Nightmare on Elm Street*. The film grossed a little over a million dollars in theaters, still a huge number for a film that, with post-production and promotion factored in, cost approximately $350,000.

The Evil Dead did not burn itself into the general American consciousness until a new and more intimate secondary movie market blossomed: *home video*. Whereas in years past, fans had to wait for a theatrical re-release of their favorite films or, in the case of low-budget horror movies, until scheduled on late-night local TV, now it was possible, with just a few dollars in your pocket and a VCR in your den, to see your favorite movie any time you wished.

Wes Craven's *Swamp Thing* (1982), a failure during its run at the summer box office (because of competition that included *Star Trek II: The Wrath of Khan*, *E.T.*, *Poltergeist*, *The Road Warrior*, *Firefox*, *John Carpenter's The Thing* and *Annie*), was among the first "failed" films that found a receptive and large audience through VHS rentals. *The Evil Dead* was another movie that became popular in this manner, a whispered secret between teenage friends. "Have you seen *that* movie, the unrated one where the woman gets attacked by a tree?" high school kids asked, and *Evil Dead* got checked out from video stores again and again.

"It is a rite of passage for a form of entertainment that was non-existent twenty-five years ago," Baker says. "By being able to see this movie, they [teenage boys] became men," Theresa Tilly laughs, "which is funny..."

From there, *Evil Dead*'s popularity exploded. For Philo, it was not a total surprise. After all, one always hopes a movie is going to be remembered. "When we were doing *Evil Dead*, it was very funny to be working on this thing where the budget was like $90,000 to shoot it, and having so little resources, but still thinking that when this is seen, it's going to be talked about years from now, and they're going to be talking about Sam as a director. It was almost absurd to be thinking about this at that point, but we understood critics were going to look at what was being done and why. That was an interesting thing. I think it's great the film has had the run it has. I wish more people had seen it initally when it came out, but *Flashdance* opened the same day."

"I am amazed at the responses I have gotten from *Evil Dead* fans about my props," adds Sullivan. "Sam's film attracts very creative people. I have had professional artists tell me that the first thing they created and that inspired them to be artists was my Book of the Dead. I am collecting fan art replicas of my props for my Convention Museum. I am flattered and flabbergasted by what *Evil Dead* hath spawned."

For the women of the *Evil Dead*, who returned to normal lives after the premiere at the Redford, it was shocking when the film's popularity exploded. "Basically, all along the way, I really never thought that much was going to happen with it," Sandweiss admits. "When it first came out on drive-in screens, I thought that's where it would end.

"Then video was invented. I saw it in a few video stores and I thought 'Okay, this is where it will end.' And I just thought it died. I totally forgot about it and thought it was gone. I had young children, and it's really mostly just the woods scene [that bothers her]. It's not the fact I was in a B horror film that is sometimes lacking in taste.

"Then it really started getting more popular, and my kids became young teenagers and I started hearing about it from them and their friends. And that's when it started bothering me. The fact is that too many people let their kids watch these things way too young. Finally, I just couldn't keep it from them any longer. My thirteen-year-old still hasn't seen it. All their little boyfriends would grin at me, but yet my kids didn't know."

Two sequels came and went in 1987 and 1993, and it appeared *Evil Dead* fever was waning, but then Al Gore invented the Internet. With the ascension of the World Wide Web came a gathering of avid fans from around the globe interested in *The Evil Dead.* "It was a big surprise to us that there is this whole subculture that is so Internet based," explains Sandweiss. "First, it wouldn't have happened without video rental. Then it wouldn't have happened even further without Web sites. And we were absolutely amazed about the whole thing."

The easy communication venue of e-mail and proliferation of Raimi/*Evil Dead*–centric Web sites not only landed *Evil Dead* in the top three of *Billboard*'s video sales charts in late November 1998 (where it eclipsed *Austin Powers*),[24] it reunited Sandweiss, Baker and Tilly for the first time in twenty years.

"Betsy found me," Tilly remembers, "and we realized this movie had a cult following and that people loved it. We found Ellen and contacted her and had this sobbing phone call for about two hours. And we all talked about the embarrassment that went along with being in the movie, and how we didn't want our children to know about it, and how it was like this secret that we didn't tell people about."

But what Baker, Sandweiss and Tilly soon found out — from fans who loved the film — was that there was nothing to be embarrassed about. In its long journey to the Internet Age, *The Evil Dead* had become as revered as *Halloween* and *The Exorcist.*

Understanding that fact, this trio of former Deadites formed the "Ladies of *The Evil Dead*" Web site and began attending horror conventions. "When Theresa, Betsy and I decided to come out of the cellar, so to speak, about two years ago, what we really decided was that this whole thing is hysterical," Sandweiss says. "The three of us are these nice, middle-aged soccer moms with kids, and we were in this amazingly popular cult film where we did terrible things and played monsters. What a hoot it would be to come out and meet the fans and actually make a little money, which we never did at the beginning. Basically, what we really all decided was that this could be fun."

"We have fans who know every word verbatim," Baker reveals. Tilly agrees. "This is bigger than we had any idea. We discovered that we don't have to be embarrassed by it. It's a good thing for a lot of people."

Their return to the spotlight also paved the way for *Evil Dead* reunions. "Having the opportunity to spend time with these women, and Bruce and Rich and Tom and Sam has been like attending a high school reunion, going back and seeing the kids that you grew up with," Tilly remarks. "None of us ever disliked each other — there were only good feelings for everybody on the shoot. Talking about the movie is not painful, it's just fun and kind of cool."

Sullivan also established a Web site, Dark Age Productions, and interacts with fans. "I just saw the final showing of *Evil Dead! The Musical* in Chicago. Remastered picture and audio DVDs are available of *Evil Dead*; marketing and film offers are opening up to us more minor players in the films, and its popularity is growing around the world. I have done interviews for *Evil Dead* fan clubs around the world and even performed a cameo in a fan film homage to *Evil Dead* called *Return to the Woods*. And, *Evil Dead* has been referenced in films from *Splash* to *High Fidelity*. Sam's career went nowhere," Sullivan jokes, "but somebody wants *The Evil Dead* on the landscape of American culture."

"As a horror film, I think *Evil Dead* is one of the greatest of all time because of the story itself... and the way it was filmed," enthused Eric Levin, the director of the entertainment group at Solomon Friedman publishing, the Detroit publicist for Dreamworks, MGM, New Line Cinema, and a lifetime *Dead* fan, on the dawn of Anchor Bay's release of the digitally remastered version of the film. "It was the perfect mix of camp and just nasty gore. It was everything I could have wanted at the time in a horror film, and it still is."[25]

For Tim Philo, shooting *Evil Dead* remains a significant life event. "There is something about dedicating yourself to a product when you don't have a lot of other responsibilities. As young people, it wasn't that hard for us to walk away and work 110 hours a week, which is what we were doing on this film.

"There was a period when we shot for fifty hours straight and watched rushes that we hadn't been able to get to. We watched footage for two or three hours and conked out. Money wasn't a factor in it. I worked for months after the money had gone away. But when it is being approved by a lot of different levels and lots of different types of people, by bankers, executives, story editors and everything, you will tend to end up with homogenized products. That's one of the strong points of very independent cinema, when you get someone with a strong vision like Sam's, and someone with a lot of energy who just wants to go for it with both guns blazing, you get a less homogenized view of things."

RAIMI RAP

JACK-OF-ALL-TRADES: Tom Sullivan's multiple responsibilities behind the scenes of *Evil Dead* just grew and grew. "I was to create the props, makeup and special effects, and as I found out upon arrival [in Morristown], I was also going to be the uncredited and unpaid art director. Rob and Sam explained that if my name was credited for all the jobs I was doing, it would look like a low-budget film," Sullivan notes.

SECOND-HAND SMOKE: One of the creepiest moments in *The Evil Dead* involves the first view of the cabin's interior, as Scott enters the main entranceway. A wisp of smoke is immediately visible, as though a long-sealed crypt has been opened. "The door opens and you see not only dust in the air, but a little blue wisp," Philo clarifies. "That's from Sam's cigarette. He was the one inside the cabin with me, tossing dirt in the air so that we had a shaft of light come in. Not only was there dirt in the air, but his cigarette smoke is at the left edge of that."

MISSING SHEMP: "I was supposed to go down there to Tennessee," Phil Gillis laments of his missed opportunity at stardom. "They had a scene where I was supposed to be whittling wood or something on the side of the road. But the day they were going to shoot it, I had a professional commitment, a trial or something. At that time, I wasn't all that convinced it was going to be a smash hit. I'm sure if I'd known, I'd have demanded a speaking part."

GIGGLES GIRL: Baker's Linda becomes a terrifying Deadite in *Evil Dead*, projecting a strange, laughing evil. "I remember having long talks with Sam over the character of Linda," Baker relates. "We didn't know where she was going to go because she was so sweet and innocent and pure. That giggle and baby-doll character was not in the script. Sam and I improvised it. We were sitting in the living room, and I would say, 'What if we made her into this sick, sweet baby doll that you pull a string out of her back and she laughs?' And he wanted to hear a little. So we just played a bit, and he thought it was really sick and said, 'Let's do it.'"

Not surprisingly, considering its creepy tenor, that giggle has come back to haunt Baker. "People ask me to giggle like that all the time. But when I do it, they shriek and beg me to stop."

HANDY MAN: The terror of the Deadites becomes apparent when Cheryl, minding her own business with a sketch pad, is possessed by Kandarian demons. In a frightening scene, her hand acts of its own volition and draws the Book of the Dead. Although autonomous hands are a familiar element of the *Evil Dead* series, as Sandweiss notes, "I know Bruce's hand has tried to kill him a lot..." this is one occasion in which the possession is played as stark horror.

"What I don't remember is which hand I used," Sandweiss notes of her intense performance. "I do remember that I was gripping the pencil in my fist, like a clutched fist rather than the way you would hold a pencil, which is an easy way to make it look haphazard. But also, what you don't know is that Tom Sullivan had drawn a sketch of the book for the movie that I had hidden underneath the page that I was drawing on, so I could see through it a little bit. I was using that as a kind of guide to draw the book, since I'm not an artist."

"I did the finished drawing of the clock Cheryl is drawing," Sullivan adds. "For the possessed drawing I remember trying a couple of ways for Ellen to do the drawing, but I recall that she had the concept down pretty well and nailed it on her own in two or three takes. I still have the drawing pad, and it's in my museum."

SOMETHING'S AFOOT: One of the absolute goriest and hard-to-watch sequences in *Evil Dead* involves Cheryl stabbing a pencil into Linda's foot. Sullivan recalls how that moment was achieved. "I had made a mold of Betsy Baker's foot and leg as she held the kneeling position Linda is in when stabbed. A dowel was placed in the mold as the foam rubber mixture was poured in, and then baked in the kitchen oven till cured. I painted the foam casting with acrylic paints and hollowed out the far side of the fake ankle to make room for a blood balloon.

"On the set, I held the foot as Ellen stabbed the fake leg. She had a perfect strike, but the pencil blocked the hole, so Sam started yelling, 'Grind it around and make it hurt!' Ellen did, and in one take history was made."

SYRUP SHORTAGE: There was so much blood in *The Evil Dead* that its makers faced critical supply shortages. "We used up all the Karo syrup and red food coloring for about fifty miles around Morristown, Tennessee," Philo explains. This shortage required frequent treks to nearby retailers. "We had to drive out and inquire from all these places if they'd gotten any Karo syrup in..."

MAKE HIS DAY: During principal photography in Morristown, everybody was focused on making the best movie possible. That includes Tapert, who was nervous about certain aspects of the film.

"When we were down in Tennessee shooting, we had Rob as the money man," Philo relates. "He had gone to a couple of people for advice about how to make this movie. They told him to make sure that it's bright enough to be able to see it on a screen at a drive-in. 'If it's too dark, people get pissed off at a drive-in, so don't let that happen!'

The case in point was *Escape from Alcatraz*, a Clint Eastwood actioner. "The escape scene was almost all in the dark and people in the drive-in theaters were blowing their horns through the whole movie. So Robert was constantly at my shoulder saying, 'Is it bright enough? We don't have a problem with it being bright, do we?'

"When we were shooting the basement scenes, Rob came to my shoulder and said, 'Bruce goes into a shadow right there just before the scare.' I said, 'Yeah, that's right.' He said, 'I can't see his face!' And I said, 'Rob, we're forty-four minutes into the film, if we're still establishing what he looks like, forget about it.' He goes from being lit to being silhouetted to being lit, and it was okay, he could be silhouetted for a minute..."

HEAD GAMES: The makers of *The Evil Dead* carry a variety of battle scars. "I'm sure you've heard of the infamous contacts that we were wearing," Sandweiss begins. "We couldn't see through them, so in essence we were blind wearing those. The cellar had an opening, maybe four feet at most, I think, and the scene was that I had to get kicked in the face and fall backward into the cellar.

"Not having eyes in the back of my head, I was not able to see where I was going. I had to totally time the faking of being kicked in the face and trustingly fling myself backward into a hole. Of the eight takes that we did, I think six of those times I actually made it. Once in particular, I just flung myself a little too far over to the left and slammed my head into the side of the opening. It was your basic blunt trauma to the head feeling; headache material."

DUCT TAPE; NO PLASTIC: Baker had her own rendezvous with pain. "When I was dragged out [of the cabin] the very first time, it was extremely unpleasant in real life. I really did get dragged on the wooden floor and down the steps, and I was only in a nightgown. The first time we did it, I said I was in too much pain to do it two or three more times, so we grabbed a piece of carpet from the floor and we duct taped it to my back.

"It was a perfect solution so that my spine wouldn't get injured," Baker reports, "until we decided to rip off the duct tape and carpet at the end of the evening. That was *extremely* painful and a good lesson never to put duct tape on human skin. That was one of the most uncomfortable nights of shooting."

FINAL SHOT: *The Evil Dead* culminates with a visual and gut-busting bang. Believing himself victorious over the dastardly Deadites, Ash limps out of the cabin into the warm, safe glow of sunlight. That is, until, a rampaging demon smashes through the house behind him and attacks before an artful black-out.

"I have to say, I didn't do that shot," Philo notes of the signature "force" camera move that climaxes the picture. "I was eager to do it all along. I left the production after weeks down there, and they said they were going to shoot for another four or five days and then pack it up and come back. And I said I wanted to do that last shot, 'So call me and I'll come back down, because I really want to shoot Bruce all bloody in daylight.' Because every morning we'd finish up and he'd walk out of the cabin, and I'd go, 'This gorgeous deep blood all over that blue shirt, I want to shoot this.'

"It turned into a week, two weeks, three weeks. I don't know if they were getting that many shots, because they were short handed and having to fake the different actors with different crew people dressing up in different ways. They finally came back (to Michigan) and said, 'Yeah, we did it' [that shot]."

GOOD INVESTMENT: "They made these other movies later on and they'd always put in the small print, *Evil Dead III* or *Evil Dead IV* or something," Gillis reports. "And the only reason they did that was to be able to send us money. I bought a small Lexus, and then I got a check for $100,000. It came in out of the blue, so I called up Rob and said, 'Why the hell didn't you tell me? I would have bought the bigger Lexus...'"

THE MORE YOU KNOW: For more information on the background, stars and effects of *The Evil Dead*, there are great resources on the Web. Sullivan's official site is Dark Age Productions, located at www.darkageproductions.com. The Ladies of the Evil Dead (Sandweiss, Baker and Tilly) reside at www.ladiesoftheevildead.com. Campbell's official site is www.bruce-campbell.com and his funny autobiography from St. Martins, *If Chins Could Kill*, is also available.

"...PUTRID BON-BON ASSORTMENTS PAINTED BY SOME DEMENTED RENOIR..."

The passage quoted above comes from *Village Voice* critic Elliott Stein, who reviewed *The Evil Dead* in May 1983. Stein also observed that the movie's "palette is richer than you'd expect in a sleazoid horror film. Exteriors are in melancholic autumnal tones, corpses are awash in pastel red and greens," and that "Philo's camera is on the prowl during most of the film — these dogged, well-organized movements manage to impose some formal cohesion on the vacuous proceedings."[26]

That may not be a rave, true, but at the very least this review accords a grudging acknowledgment that Raimi's debut feature is artfully, if not tastefully, designed and executed.

Keeping the Stein quote in mind, it is prudent to remember that the most effective horror films are often those featuring the simplest of stories, yet expressing their rudimentary tales well, via either memorable and adroit visuals or a suspenseful pace, usually heightened by staccato editing. A masked killer stalks a babysitter on Halloween night; a creature from nightmares haunts a teenager's waking life; an isolated woman fears she's been impregnated by the Devil; a group of kids get lost in the woods and are pursued by Evil with a capital E; etc.

Whether the film is *Halloween*, *A Nightmare on Elm Street*, *Rosemary's Baby*, *The Blair Witch Project* or *The Evil Dead*, the narrative template for a good horror film need not be complicated. In this case, the Michigan boys studied the "classics" well and adopted the vacation- or road-trip-gone-wrong scenario utilized successfully in films as diverse as John Boorman's *Deliverance* (1972), *The Texas Chain Saw Massacre*, *The Hills Have Eyes*, *Tourist Trap* (1979), *Jeepers Creepers* (2001), and *Wrong Turn* (2003). Adorned with Michael Berryman's murderous glare, the poster for Craven's *Hills Have Eyes* appears briefly in the cabin's cellar in *The Evil Dead*, an acknowledgment of genre tradition.

The road trip/vacation gone wrong scenario is effective because viewers understand that a trip to an unfamiliar destination takes us out of our element, and therefore a vital sense of security and safety is sacrificed. Being a stranger in a strange land renders one alone, removing all links to the familiar and comforting. Untethered, characters, and thus viewers, cling to the simple things — a telephone, a car that probably won't start, even a flashlight with low batteries. These tools become lifelines, important survival implements if the fish-out-of-water characters are to survive their ordeals. *The Evil Dead* is a classic example of the scenario: a vacation in the mountains turned into a blood-curdling nightmare, thanks to some ancient Sumerian spirits. A sign with the legend "Travel at Own Risk" appears early on, and this warning sets the tone.

In more specific terms, *The Evil Dead* brings to mind a few other horror classics. Romero's 1968 *Night of the Living Dead* commenced with several shots of a lonely car traversing a twisted road, en route to an isolated cemetery. Romero's camera tracked the car's trajectory, and the winding road leading into a rural locale seemed ominous and foreboding. Here, Ash drives four friends up the winding roads of the mountains, unaware that all around him a dark force has gathered. "We were big fans of what Romero had done with a small budget ... and just one cabin,"[27] Raimi once noted, citing *Living Dead* as an influence. The winding road, the late 1960s to early 1970s car model, and the isolated, rural location all play into a feel reminiscent of *Living Dead*.

Then, just seconds later, there's a close encounter with an oncoming truck nicknamed "Lazy Mary," harking back to the Mack truck incident in the climax of Hooper's *Chain Saw* with a similarly christened "Black Maria." Yet if these narrative locales and elements play as tribute to the great horrors of earlier vintage, the opening scene also reveals Raimi's unique visual genius and ability to leap beyond convention.

From the get go, Raimi stacks events atop one another in *The Evil Dead*, front-loading the suspense. Conventional film wisdom advises the intrepid student that crosscutting is an effective tool to generate tension, but also, importantly, that crosscutting between more than two opposing forces will confuse audiences. Raimi hasn't even reached the five-minute point in his first feature film before shattering that convention. During the opening sequence, he crosscuts between *three* elements: the approaching truck, the demon Force point of view subjective shot, and the car carrying the kids to the cabin. Significantly, this happens before the characters are formally introduced, or even particularly recognizable.

"That's what Sam wanted," Philo remembers. "He wanted three elements there. He was told by various people, his editor included, I think, that crosscutting three things wasn't going to work, but Sam insisted, and he was right. Who cares if people are disoriented at the beginning of a film?"

The inclusion of a third perspective in the opening scene sets the film on its metaphorical edge, generating the feeling that something is amiss, off kilter. The film's visuals thus reflect content: that a deadly power is loose and influencing events, nearly killing Ash and friends when it assumes control of the car and almost causes a collision.

Much of *Evil Dead*'s value as a horror film arises from its surprising, unpredictable nature, particularly the manner in which it reveals information to the audience. The movie may not be surprising narratively — let's face it, everybody understands something bad is going to happen to these kids — but within those predictable confines of horror story telling, Raimi lets loose and deploys the camera to express terror in revolutionary ways.

This unsettling feeling is generated in even the smallest of details. As the Oldsmobile Delta first approaches the secluded cabin, a heartbeat sound effect reverberates on the soundtrack. It is revealed to be not a heartbeat at all, but rather a hanging porch swing banging against the front wall of the cabin. But just when the film has lulled the audience into a kind of trance with this metronome-like, repetitive banging sound, it abruptly stops. The swing comes ominously to a stand-still for no reason. Again, this unusual moment fosters the notion of something off, something uprooting expectations, perhaps even a master manipulator behind the scenes, whether it be the dark Force in the woods according to the script, or the mind of Raimi, who helms the picture.

Almost immediately, there is another little surprise. Scotty (Hal Delrich) enters the cabin and there is mist *inside* it, not outside. Later, protagonists such as Linda, Cheryl, Shelly and Scotty surprise us again by becoming antagonists. It is unsettling to cross these traditional lines of character orientation, and not something done lightly. In fact, Wes Craven avoids co-joining good guys and bad guys in one character, calling it a "very dangerous violation of a basic dramatic rule. You should have a clear-cut hero and villain and not mix the two together."[28] Again, Raimi breaks long-standing rules, generating discomfort in the process.

A feeling of imbalance, of unpredictability also plays out in the number of vacationers at the cabin: two couples and Cheryl. "It was asymmetrical; there was a fifth wheel from the beginning," notes Baker of the screenplay's character structure. "The fact that we let Cheryl intrude on this supposedly romantic weekend from the beginning makes it a little edgy. She's the one that screws up the entire weekend."

"Throughout the whole thing, I was thinking, 'What the hell am I doing here with these two couples?'" adds Sandweiss, shedding light on the issue. "I'm not even a nice person, why did they bother bringing me? Did I have one nice or pleasant thing to say in the movie?" Indeed, it is Cheryl, the sensitive, artistic member of the bunch, who first explicitly draws the presence of the Deadites into a human being. They possess her first, as if understanding that as the odd-man-out, she is the weak link. It is a very deliberate, artistic set up that, much like the three points of view in the opening driving sequence, contributes to a viewer's sense of uneasiness.

One must also note the effective, honest performances in the film. Without exception they are spare and believable, fostering a sense of identification. Some critics have categorized the characters in *The Evil Dead* as "one dimensional" or "cardboard," but it is probably more accurate to state that these are simply very physical roles that fulfill certain purposes within the script. "The best characters in horror films are nulls," Philo opines, "people that you don't know, so it is easier to relate to them because you don't know *too* many specific things. You don't know that someone is breaking up with a boyfriend, or that they are an orphan. You don't need to. You have somebody who is not so defined, and it is easier to relate to them.

"I look back to something like *Night of the Living Dead*," Philo continues. "Those people in the basement? You don't get their stories. You're just like, 'Hey, this is who you're left with. These are the survivors.' Some of the more interesting, creepier horror films, like *Night of the Living Dead* or *The Hills Have Eyes*, have these displaced people out in the backwoods where anything could happen. Where the rules were taken away, or they were fish out of water."

In any discussion of specific *Evil Dead* scenes, Cheryl's rape by the woods is certain to be addressed. It's probably *Evil Dead*'s most controversial sequence and another unexpected twist. Though Raimi apparently regrets the scene and Sandweiss herself feels it goes too far, one senses it is part and parcel of this "package of unpredictability" Raimi brings to the table. Philo and Sullivan have both stressed that Raimi's foremost purpose is to entertain an audience, elicit a reaction, and that their challenge on the finale was to do something bigger, better and gorier than what they had done in the film before, something new, to shock viewers. Joe LoDuca thinks that the film was a game for the makers, with Raimi attempting to scare people as a kind of prank.

"I don't like violence," Raimi likewise reported in 2001, buttressing this argument. "I will say, *The Evil Dead* and *Evil Dead 2*, those early horror movies I made, were about trying to show the supernatural as an outrageous, funny, bold, exciting and terrifying force."[29]

In light of these first-person insights about the director's motivation, one might deduce the tree attack was designed not to be misogynist, but rather an example of shock and awe to keep the audience on edge, and therefore engaged. This reading is not meant to suggest that the assault is not graphic or sexual in nature — it clearly is both — but merely that it works consistently within the film's framework. It remains a harrowing and trademark moment, probably because Sandweiss is a sincere performer, giving her all and seeming genuinely terrified of the circumstances, but also because, in the words of author Jake Horsely, the sequence has "the all-redeeming virtue of being genuinely imaginative, a borderline artistic-mythic concept. Those pagan roots have emerged again and dragged the maiden, like Persephone into Hades, back to the jungle."[30] Sure, a snake crawled up between Maren Jensen's legs in a bathtub in *Deadly Blessing* (1981), but where else had horror fans seen something like *this* before? The rape may qualify as "exploitation" by definition, but it also represents a taboo shattered, and therefore it is instantly memorable.

Some reviewers have interpreted the rape sequence and the fact that three women do most of the terrorizing in the film to symbolize that director Raimi is out to create a movie with a particular political or sexual agenda. This author believes no such thing is likely, firstly because Raimi tends not to work "preachy" messages into his films, which, after all, would spoil the pure entertainment factor.

Secondly, the grouping of three women and two men has a more basic function. It generates an edgy, off-kilter feel. And, the film is much more interesting to view not as some polemic about women-turned-she-bitches, but something more personal and human: *friends turned enemies*. What *The Evil Dead* truly depicts, at least if there is a subtext to be interpreted, is something akin to a personal apocalypse, a personal hell for the weak-willed and sensitive Ashley. Before fans get upset over this unflattering description of their heroic icon, they should recall that this was before Campbell was "Ash," the sarcastic, wisecracker of *Evil Dead 2* and *Army of Darkness*. Here he is just a stumbling, bumbling average guy, Ashley. He finds himself bullied and cajoled by the sarcastic Scotty, henpecked by his bothersome sister Cheryl, and consumed, one might even say "whipped," by his love for beautiful Linda.

"My visual sense, and having talked with Sam a little bit about it when we were shooting, I said, 'Basically we're shooting a nightmare — that's the whole visual style I'm going for,'" Tim Philo recalls, "and Sam said, 'Keep that stuff to yourself,'" preferring not to color performances in one direction or another.

"In relation to the film being shot in a nightmare way, the appropriateness of it is that it is a kind of paranoid fantasy of friends," Philo considers. "It's Bruce's paranoid fantasy of his friends all turning against him as they turn, one by one, into zombies and throttle him."

Within that context of a personal apocalypse, a nightmare in which ally turns into nemesis, *Evil Dead* also strives for and attains a genuine gothic texture. The film has been credited with the resurrection of the Lovecraftian cycle in film,[31] thus inspiring films such as *Re-Animator* and *From Beyond*, but more to the point, it utilizes core gothic conceits. Gothic literature, the Romantic response to the Enlightenment's sense of rationalism, often concerned the battle for control over a hero or heroine's soul. Stoker's Dracula was a gothic protagonist, simultaneously frightening and alluring, demonic and yet attractive and powerful.

Consider the Deadites of *Evil Dead*: they are two-faced creations as well; beautiful and inviting one moment, horrible and evil the next. This facet of the film's tapestry is especially pronounced when Ash carries out his beloved, Linda, to bury her. She is garbed in a flowing white nightgown, the preferred garb of the gothic heroine, and the general setting is a remote one, amongst nature, another tenet of the literature. "Linda comes out in this very sexy nightgown and is laid very gently to rest," Betsy Baker notes of the scene, "and then the evilness comes out of the ground."

It is that gothic yin and yang, that Linda can function as both object of desire *and* object of terror, that informs the scene of her resurrection. Visually, Raimi does something interesting and totally disgusting with this sequence: he makes her murder an example, like the rape in the woods, of something akin to sexual climax. Consider the events of the scene: Ash decapitates Linda with a shovel. Her headless corpse lands on his prone form, essentially mounting him, and what happens? Tons of deep black goop, blood perhaps, ejaculate into his face, dousing him in the fluid. In adult movie lingo this is a cum shot, folks.

Further deepening the sexual metaphor, Raimi cuts to a shot of Linda's bare legs straddling and crawling excitedly over Ash's lower body. On the soundtrack she moans with pleasure, even though her head is missing...

This is a beautifully orchestrated yet sickening perversion of sexual intercourse, an orgasmic gratification achieved through death and dismemberment. And, making it socially valuable, it is perfectly in keeping with a long-standing gothic tradition of attraction and repulsion finding embodiment inside one character. Like the other Deadites, Linda is both beauty and beast, attractive and repellant, a modern-day *Rappaccini's Daughter*. To love her is to die, to love death itself.

However, the factor making *The Evil Dead* an effective horror film of the highest caliber is not this undercurrent of gothic idealism. In attempting to engage the audience, Raimi adopts formalistic film techniques with a vengeance and then carries them to a new level. What is formalism? As film students recall, movies and directors tend to fall into two distinct camps.

Formalists like Alfred Hitchcock prefer to "play the audience like a piano," utilizing the camera to actively express things and make the viewer feel a particular emotion, usually fear or discomfort. Thus what the camera sees and *how* it sees things (film grammar, in other words) emotionally impacts the audience. For instance, the rapid-fire quick-cutting in Janet Leigh's *Psycho* shower scene raises the viewer's blood pressure with its very pace, an approach first adopted in early Russian silent films. Sometimes it is even called "shock cutting."

Oppositely, realists like Jean Renoir take a rather more subdued route, deploying the camera not to express events so much as record them. That's the reason why long shots and deep focus are the preferred modus operandi of the realist, so viewers can detect a wide tapestry in each composition and pick and choose what is actually "important" to a reading of the film.

There is no doubt Raimi is a formalist. In fact, one might term him a *hyper*-formalist. In *Evil Dead*, he wants the audience to feel every blow, experience every attack, and come away shell-shocked. To accomplish this affecting tone, he manipulates film in a singular way. Note for instance that the evil force is never seen in its non-human form. Of course, *Evil Dead* probably could not have afforded a convincing visible evil force on a production budget of $90,000, but how is the Force depicted in the movie? Always in the first-person subjective shot, the POV.

In other words, the audience *is* the rampaging force. It is the audience that barrels across a small lake in the opening shot, gliding over the placid water. It is the audience that pursues the characters relentlessly through the woods. It is the audience that rockets from the outbuildings through the cabin into Ash's screaming face.

The first-person subjective shot has been employed in sometimes controversial fashion in other horror movies. For instance, many critics objected to its use in the opening shots of *Halloween*, wherein young Michael Myers murdered his sister and the audience gazed through his mask-adorned eyes. The critics' primary complaint was that by adopting this technique John Carpenter had essentially made the audience an accomplice to murder, therefore subtracting any moral component from the movie, the judgment that "murder is bad."

Raimi travels further down this road in *The Evil Dead*. He rams the characters' discomfort right down the viewer's throat. We are carried on the wings of an invisible demon and spared no detail of the violence and terror. We are passengers trapped aboard a kamikaze jet, propelled without control into terror, always racing toward death and violence.

Raimi's extensive use of close-ups mirrors this "ambush" style of formalist filmmaking. Again, the standard rule posits that in comedies, directors should not deploy close-ups because this particular shot heightens audience identification with a character's pain. If Charlie Chaplin falls on a banana peel and the camera stands back at some distance, the pratfall is funny, not sad or disturbing, because we aren't close enough to feel his pain.

Notice that the last section of *Evil Dead*, during the horrific meltdown, is absolutely packed with close-ups of Bruce Campbell experiencing nothing less than mind-blowing fear and anguish. Again, the audience is there, in his face, every time a new chunk of flesh or a putrid dollop of bile slams into his face. The impact of such close shots is one of heightened identification. The audience is spared no impact, wet or otherwise.

Cockeyed angles, expressing how the world has gone off-kilter since the ascent of the Deadites, are also effectively marshaled during Ash's return from the cellar following the blood flood. And consider too the efficacy of intense, quick cutting in the film's final confrontation, as Scotty pulls on Ash's leg and Ash desperately reaches forward to hook the Book of the Dead with Linda's necklace. As in *Psycho*, the effect of the machine gun–style, staccato editing is an almost unconscious heightening of the adrenaline. The audience cannot help but feel involved.

Evil Dead's ad-line is right on the money; this is a grueling experience more than an old-fashioned horror movie with a sense of decorum and boundaries. The POV shots assure that the action happens to us, the numerous close-ups build identification with the expressive lead actor, and the film builds relentlessly, refusing to end or release its choke-hold. Surprise (three perspectives in the highway scene) builds on unanticipated horrors (Cheryl's rape by the trees), and Raimi's selections and deployment of these techniques has the audience reeling. Thank heavens this film was not filmed in 3-D or in Mike Todd Jr.'s "glorious Smell-O-Vision," lest the audience leave the theater with eyes poked, noses tweaked, clothes soaked in blood, and heads literally clubbed.

As my film study mentor from my college days would no doubt remind us at this juncture, all of this style in the service of what — *shlock?* Why champion such tactics? In this case, *The Evil Dead* remains remarkable because the director studied the form through examples like *The Hills Have Eyes* and *Night of the Living Dead* and understood not only how to apply the right techniques to his story and paid homage to the genre in the process, but then traveled far beyond the traditional application of those techniques to make his horror movie a harrowing, new kind of "hyper" experience. Like it or hate it, this film has visceral impact, and what higher compliment can be paid a horror movie? This is a film that reinvigorates the *form* of horror in cinema.

Raw, crude and powerful, *The Evil Dead* represents filmmaking on an emotional, basic and almost primeval level. Frankly, there is no better way to approach this particular genre. If *The Evil Dead* were a romance, these gut-punching techniques, like the unsteadicam, the roaming first-person subjective shot and the extreme close-ups would no doubt be woefully out of place, but in this venue, where the goal is to scare people, Raimi and his cohorts have succeeded brilliantly in applying the right techniques — and imagining new ones — to augment the tale of five kids under siege by horrible monsters. Underneath that level, there is an application of the gothic ethos and some kind of paranoid statement about personal betrayal, but none of that is as important as how the movie depicts its scares.

Viewing *The Evil Dead* is never a passive or intellectual experience. By understanding film grammar and then rewriting it, Raimi has directed a film that works powerfully on the gut. Since fear is a sort of irrational, hard-to-categorize feeling anyway, this approach works just fine. *The Evil Dead* is not only an "inspirational testament to a group of college students who put together a pretty decent horror film without studio support"[32] as one enthusiastic horror fan wrote, it is an intense, bravura bit of artistry that, like *Night of the Living Dead* and *The Texas Chain Saw Massacre* before it, rejuvenated the horror film. Most of all, *The Evil Dead* demonstrates how immediate and affecting a good example of the genre can really be.

CRIMEWAVE (1985)

NO BRIGHT SIDE

CAST AND CREW

EMBASSY FILM ASSOCIATES PRESENTS
A PRESSMAN/RENAISSANCE PRODUCTION, *CRIMEWAVE*.

DIRECTOR: Sam Raimi
PRODUCER: Robert Tapert
CO-PRODUCER: Bruce Campbell
EXECUTIVE PRODUCERS: Edward R. Pressman, Irvin Shapiro
WRITERS: Ethan Coen, Joel Coen and Sam Raimi
DIRECTOR OF PHOTOGRAPHY: Robert Primes
SUPERVISING FILM EDITOR: Michael Kelly
MUSIC COMPOSER AND CONDUCTER: Arlon Ober
"RIALTO" MUSIC: Joe LoDuca
SPECIAL EFFECTS: Marty Bresin and MB Special Effects
CASTING: Barbara Claran, Inc.

STARRING

LOUISE LASSER: Helene Trend
PAUL SMITH: Faron Crush
BRION JAMES: Arthur Coddish
SHEREE J. WILSON: Nancy
EDWARD R. PRESSMAN: Ernest Trend
BRUCE CAMPBELL: Renaldo, "The Heel"
REED BIRNEY: Vic Ajax
RICHARD BRIGHT: Officer Brennan
ANTONIO FARGAS: Blind Man
HAMID DANA: Donald Odegard
FRANCES MCDORMAND: Nun
TED RAIMI: Waiter
PHIL GILLIS: Priest

FILMED IN DETROIT, MICHIGAN, AND HOLLYWOOD, CALIFORNIA.

A DARK AND STORMY NIGHT...

FACING EXECUTION IN THE ELECTRIC CHAIR at Hudsucker Penitentiary, convicted murderer Vic Ajax proclaims his innocence to uncaring guards. He claims it was actually his boss, Mr. Trend, who connived the murder of Mr. Odegard, Trend's partner in the Odegard/Trend Security Company, all because Odegard wanted to transform the business into a girlie revue. Ajax's only witness is Nancy, a woman nobody has been able to locate.

Vic recounts the night in question, a night when a gusty thunderstorm rolled into Center City. While Vic, a hopeless romantic and wimp, attempted to romance the beautiful and urbane Nancy away from a heel named Renaldo, two exterminators, the ratlike Arthur Coddish and the oversized Faron Crush, set out to kill Mr. Odegard at Mr. Trend's bidding. Events went horribly wrong when Mr. Trend's wife, Helene, witnessed the murder from the high window of the Watchtower apartment building, and the two nefarious assassins then murdered Mr. Trend, the very man who hired them. Before long, Vic and Nancy's disastrous first date intersected with the two killers and Helen Trend's efforts to evade Crush.

As Vic's time runs out and execution looms, Nancy, now a nun, races to the penitentiary to clear him. But will she arrive in time?

STRANGE BEDFELLOWS

Not many people remember the team-up today, at least not those outside the directors' respective fan communities, but in the 1980s, the now-celebrated directors of *Spider-Man* and *O Brother, Where Art Thou?* co-wrote a film together. In some circles, that film is called *The XYZ Murders*, its working title during principal photography. For a time, the movie was to be distributed in the U.S. under the more expressive moniker *Broken Hearts and Noses*. And, though the project actually began its life as something called *Relentless*, it was eventually dumped in theaters and then the video market as the generic-sounding *Crimewave*.

This is a movie that Sam Raimi has all but disowned and that the Coens' actively ignore on their curriculum vitae, their so-called lost film. Considering such talents, it's a wonder this film hasn't been exhumed by scholars, or at least repackaged to exploit its makers' success, but then *Crimewave* remains a strange bird and not a particularly commercial venture, no matter how you cut it.

Watching *Crimewave* today, one might term it a sophomore slump. After a well-reviewed first effort, many directors find themselves battling this syndrome, a second project that doesn't cut the mustard. Steven Soderbergh (*Kafka* [1991]), Kevin Smith (*Mallrats* [1995]) and Spike Lee (*School Daze* [1988]) are three examples of talented artists who fell victim to the condition in the last twenty years.

Of course, whether or not this phenomenon is a reflection of a film's quality or a result of critical fickleness, since reviewers like to build up filmmakers and then tear 'em down, is another question altogether. Regardless, *Crimewave* is a unique chapter in Raimi's career because it's two for the price of one; the sophomore slump of the Coen brothers and Sam Raimi.

Crimewave came out of noble intentions and a friendship that commenced during editing of *The Evil Dead* in New York City. Joel Coen (who also helped edit the 1981 horror flick, *Fear No Evil*) hoped to get financing for his first directorial venture with brother Ethan, the suspense-thriller *Blood Simple*. Raimi recommended that the Coens shoot a short film first, like *Within the Woods*, to impress potential investors and drum up financial support.

More than that, Raimi and Bruce Campbell helped shoot the protean Coen promotional effort. Then, much later, when the Coens and their starlet, young Frances McDormand, attempted to distribute the finished feature, which cost 1.5 million dollars, they crashed at Raimi's apartment in Silver Lake along with actress Holly Hunter.

In 1981, Raimi and the Coens collaborated on a script entitled *The Hudsucker Proxy*, a comedic period film paying homage to the work of Preston Sturges. It was produced in the early 1990s, starring Paul Newman, Tim Robbins, Jennifer Jason Leigh and Bruce Campbell. In the same period, the team also wrote *The XYZ Murders*, a thorough change of pace. *Blood Simple* was a postmodern film noir, a grisly, bloody tale of murder, deception and infidelity. A gonzo horror film, *The Evil Dead* was gory to the max. *The XYZ Murders* was neither — an outrageous comedy that had more in common with Laurel and Hardy or the Three Stooges than such blood-soaked material. Raimi considered it a "send-up of film noir with a touch of comic book bedlam,"[1] but in point of fact, *Crimewave* fit in with Raimi's super 8mm canon because it blended genres, including comedy, melodrama, horror and slapstick, all for the sake of outrageous laughs.

A story "set in the present" yet boasting an atmosphere that is all "late forties,"[2] according to Raimi, *Crimewave* was a romp about a loser named Vic Ajax who discovered his own browbeaten manhood by protecting a damsel in distress named Nancy from two exterminators-cum-assassins, the ratlike Coddish and the oversized Crush. Avco-Embassy, which was riding high from its remarkable success with the John Carpenter films *The Fog* (1980) and *Escape from New York* (1981), financed the movie.

Originally known simply as Embassy in the 1940s when founded by Joseph E. Levine, the "Avco" in its name was added much later, in 1969. With the profitable Carpenter pictures, Avco-Embassy cornered the low-budget market left open by the disintegration of Samuel Z. Arkoff's American International Pictures during the late 1970s. One of the men in charge of green-lighting projects in those successful years, just before *Crimewave*, was executive Robert Rehme.

In 1982, *All in the Family* creator Norman Lear and Jerry Perenchhio purchased Avco-Embassy, and Rehme left Avco for a position at Universal Studios, where he had a banner year, working on *E.T.* and *Sophie's Choice*. But in 1998, he remembered his tenure at Avco-Embassy and that the organization "wanted out of the movies;" that "there was no budget for production."[3] According to an article on *POV Online*, a byzantine corporate structure prevented Embassy from borrowing money from brother Avco, which made budgets tight. By 1986, following *Crimewave*'s debut, Coca-Cola purchased Embassy, and the organization was consequently absorbed into Columbia Pictures[4] ... the same studio later responsible for Raimi's *Spider-Man*!

But for Raimi and Renaissance in the early eighties, Avco-Embassy offered a pot of gold to produce *Crimewave*: on the order of two to three million dollars, much more cash than the funds available on *The Evil Dead*! Tapert, Campbell, Shapiro and Edward R. Pressman (*Wall Street* [1987], *Reversal of Fortune* [1990], *The Crow* [1994], *Judge Dredd* [1995]) produced the film, to be filmed entirely on location in Detroit, the city that best approximated the old-fashioned feel Raimi sought.

One location was the famous Tuller Hotel, an old Detroit landmark known as "The Grand Dame of Grand Circus Park."[5] A massive structure built in 1906, the Tuller offered some eight hundred guest rooms and was a jewel of old Detroit, but had fallen into disrepair and ruin in the urban blight of the 1970s. Eventually torn down in the early 1990s, the building proved an expensive "get" for the *Crimewave* production team, a story recounted in Campbell's memoirs. Still, an important scene was set there. In particular, the Tuller doubled as the Rialto, a swinging night club where Vic and Nancy had their first date, washing dishes in the kitchen when they were unable to afford the tab for dinner.

THE ABCs OF THE XYZ MURDERS

Robert Primes A.S.C., a decorated cinematographer who has shot TV dramas including *Felicity*, *The X-Files*, *Quantum Leap* and *thirtysomething* as well as films like *They Call Me Bruce?* (1982), the Mel Gibson/Goldie Hawn vehicle *Bird on a Wire* (1990), *The Hard Way* (1991) and *Aspen Extreme* (1993), remembers how he was tapped to lense *Crimewave* following second-unit work on *Rumble Fish* in 1983–'84: "If I remember the chronology, I was shooting a big commercial on the introduction of the new Camaro. It was a million dollar TV commercial. We had giant stages over at MGM and special effects, and Sam Raimi came to visit me. He's such a technological guy. He loves every aspect of the mechanics of moviemaking, as do I. He hired me to shoot the movie based on the fact that he came onto the set of this very expensive commercial which we lit gloriously, and it probably impressed him."

Primes still recollects Raimi's enthusiastic presentation of the *Crimewave* screenplay. "He [Sam] would read the script and go 'Arrrrh, aaah, neerrrh!' and was so animated. The big impression I got was a comic book," Primes recalls. "It [the screenplay] didn't deal with the subtleties of human consciousness. It didn't deal with indecision and gray tones. It was almost like, 'This was a bad guy and he's really, *really* bad.' It almost seemed like caricatures of two-dimensional people. Because of that, I said, 'Okay, what's the approach to something like this?'

"I think my approach then became to color it like a comic book," Primes describes. "It was very gimmicky in the sense of the emphasis that Sam, at a given line, would want to zoom right into the mouth and see a tongue and two teeth, and the actor would say a final line. That's punctuation."

For Primes, a film lover influenced by Swedish director Ingmar Bergman and drawn to discover the same human truths as those highlighted in Bergman's work, *Crimewave*'s exaggerated style was not an easy fit. "I couldn't understand; why would you do this?" Primes remembers. "Why would you zoom into somebody's mouth?

"I'm a little older now," Primes continues with perspective, "and I understand it's incredibly entertaining. It's an exaggeration. It's a different style. It doesn't have to allude to the classical tradition of filmmakers. It's his [Sam's] world view."

Another talent drawn into Raimi's world was actress Louise Lasser, who starred in several Woody Allen comedies including *Take the Money and Run* (1969), *Bananas* (1971) and *Everything You Always Wanted to Know About Sex* But Were Afraid to Ask* (1972). She would take on the role of the much-hassled Mrs. Helene Trend, a character who, after multiple perils, ended up in a packing crate bound for Uruguay. "The appeal was that it was so clear to me it was a director's picture," she noted of *Crimewave* and Raimi. "I was willing to put myself in his hands. I like to be around people like that."[6]

Also cast, as Crush and Coddish respectively, were the late Paul Smith, who played beastly Rabban in David Lynch's *Dune* (1984), and the late Brion James, who proved so memorable as the violent replicant Leon in Ridley Scott's *Blade Runner* (1982).

Campbell was Raimi's first selection to portray the film's beleaguered lead protagonist, Vic Ajax, but Avco-Embassy and producer Pressman reportedly had issues with that choice and instead forced Raimi to audition other prospective leading men for the role, including *Cocoon* star, Steve Guttenberg. Eventually, New York theater actor Reed Birney won the assignment, and Campbell played a supporting role, the "heel" named Renaldo — Ajax's personal nemesis.

In the leading role of the beautiful Nancy, *Crimewave*'s other damsel in distress, was Sheree J. Wilson, an actress just starting out in film but who had extensive experience in commercials. "I was cast with a couple of lines in *Tootsie*," reports the actress, who later played April Stevens for five seasons on TV's *Dallas*. "I worked two weeks on that film and got left on the editing room floor. I think I'm Party Girl Number Two, but I got to work with Sydney Pollack, Dustin Hoffman, Dabney Coleman, Jessica Lange and Terri Garr, and I thought I'd just won the lottery. Then I got this phone call after *Tootsie*."

It was her agent. "She said, 'You know, they're trying to cast a young Shelly Long–type character in this low-budget movie,'" Wilson remembers. The agent also had some news about the director, a fella by the name of

Raimi. "She said 'He's a young director and he's gotten all this acclaim for *Evil Dead*,' and I said, 'I haven't seen it.'"

Despite her unfamiliarity with Raimi's first theatrical venture, Wilson flew out to L.A. and taped an audition. A few days later, in the middle of a move from New York to California, she was summoned for a call back. When she got back to the coast, she was surprised to learn she was the only actress present.

"I was thinking, 'Okay, I'm not quite sure how all this goes, but I'm the only girl here, and they're testing me with six different guys.' I was so naïve, so fresh and new. This was my first lead in a feature film and I thought, 'If I'm not crazy, I think they want me, and they're just testing me to see who I belong with.'"

After a long day of Raimi directing her with a variety of male performers, Wilson flew back to Tucson — where she had left behind her car and belongings. She resumed her cross-country road trip a second time, only to promptly receive *another* call.

"They called me and said, 'You've got it. You've got to be in Detroit, Michigan, on Monday.'"

Shooting on the film then known as *The XYZ Murders* commenced on Halloween and didn't finish until January 18 and, by many accounts, was a difficult shoot. "The whole film takes place in one night, so we were living that vampire schedule where you go to work at five or six at night, start filming at seven and work until six a.m., have breakfast and go to bed," Wilson explains. "It was a very challenging schedule as far as your health goes."

"You'd work Monday, Tuesday, Wednesday, Thursday, Friday and Saturday nights," cinematographer Primes details. "You'd sleep all day Sunday, and Sunday night was your day off. On Sunday night in the middle of winter, there is absolutely nothing to do in Detroit. We didn't see the sun for months."

Unfortunately, Raimi's sophomore effort also suffered from extensive interference by studio executives, who fretted he would not meet his financial and scheduling obligations. "We always had pressure to do it simply and bring it in on budget," Primes recalls. "He [Raimi] had a vision and it was ambitious. He couldn't just make a film where people spoke their lines and you had and an adequate page count everyday, and let it go. That's what all the business people wanted him to do. But it wasn't in him; it's not the way he was built. It was not his values; it wasn't what he wanted to do in life. He didn't want to make a simple film like everybody else. He had his own vision and his own life force."

And that meant some hair-raising battles over camera equipment, among other items. "We had wanted a luma crane," Primes remembers, launching into a description of that device. "You can put a camera up in the top [of the crane] and ... pan and zoom by remote control, so instead of having two, two hundred pound people and a camera up there, you put a fifty pound camera [at the top of the crane]. And because it is one tenth of the weight ... it can go higher, you can get into places, you can do very sudden moves. It had just been invented, and of course, Sam very much wanted to do those types of moves.

"The studio said, 'No, no, no, you're going over budget! You're spending too much time! You're playing with gadgets too much! No, absolutely you *can't* have a luma crane!'

"Sam, who is extremely ingenious, had what he called a shaky cam that he used on *Evil Dead*," Primes explains. "This means that you have a camera and you bolt it on a two-by-four, and you have two strong people, a key grip and the first camera assistant, and each one holds an end of it, and they go running up and down with the camera, over the top of people and stuff like that. So with this shaky cam we went running down a whole block. We had someone [Wilson] get out of a car and then she started running.

"We ran after her, and there was nothing that quite looked like the motion of this thing. Then the bad guy [Smith] came, and we turned around and did a 180 degree move and looped around, then ran back in the other direction, and did something else.

"It was a very flashy piece of camera work," Primes considers. "It couldn't have been a dolly, it couldn't have been a conventional crane, and it obviously wasn't hand-held, so when the studio looked at the dailies, they were sure that Sam had somehow connived himself into a luma crane to get the shot," Primes reveals. "They were furious, and they were on the phone ripping him a new asshole. 'How dare you?! We told you that you couldn't have a luma crane!' He just said, 'It was a seventy-five-cent piece of two-by-four!'

"And," Primes says with satisfaction, "it worked beautifully."

In addition to Raimi's typically unconventional approach to camera work, *The XYZ Murders* featured a bevy of bizarre set pieces and stunts. Probably the most memorable of these involved the "Parade of Protection: The Safest Hallway in the World." In essence, the set consisted of a series of locked doors and door arches through which a terrorized Louise Lasser was chased by the king-sized Smith character, appropriately named Crush.

"This was a strange, strange movie," Primes acknowledges. "The special effects man had designed these things [doorways/arches] so that if you knocked one over, it was like dominoes. The idea was that this was a burglar alarm shop, and you could test each [door] out and see it. So there were chases through there and Paul Smith, this big bull of a guy, would just bang through the doors. It wasn't made of steel, but rather wood painted to look like steel. Someone [Lasser] would shut the door and throw the latch, and then Smith would break through the door.

"We would dolly through and follow. From a graphic point of view, it was just as ingenious as it could be. It took a lot of shots, but it was pretty goddamned clever," Primes explains. It was also, he points out, treacherous. "At one point, all the doors were supposed to come crashing down. The bad guy would just huff and puff and shove one wall into another wall into another wall, and the dominoes would all go down. The stuntman ran through them, trying to get away. We did that, and there was loose lumber *everywhere*.

"All of those doors could have easily crushed a person," Primes considers. "Theoretically, it was built so that if you got right in the middle and crouched down, you'd be in the doorway and the doors would stack up a certain way."

Even Primes and the camera were not immune. "I got caught in the middle of that with a piece of two-by-four falling on the dolly track and I banged my eye into the camera. It hurt like hell. I also remember a stuntman getting caught underneath there and shouting for his life and being pissed off."

Phil Gillis, *Evil Dead*'s investor general and a budding actor himself, appeared in several equally strange sequences in *Crimewave* including a scene in Detroit involving stunt work. "When it was still *The XYZ Murders*, they shot a scene on the street in Detroit. The city gave them permission to block off the street, and they put up a telephone pole in the middle of it. It was hinged and bolted to the street with eight-inch-long bolts, so that it wouldn't move, and when it fell on the hinge, they would know within a couple of inches where it was going to fall.

"So, Sam shot this scene where they had a stuntman, and the telephone pole came down on top of the car this guy had been driving. And it was a full-sized telephone pole, believe me! And I was amazed at those stuntmen, how close they let the damn telephone pole get to them. Anyway, they rolled out of the way at the last minute. I played the bystander coming out of a building, and they had electric wires that sparked because they came down with the telephone pole."

Sounds simple right? "Nobody told me the wires were going to spark!" Gillis remembers. "So I came out of the door and they started sparking, and they were no more than six or seven feet from me. I must have jumped ten feet in the air, and afterward Sam told me what a great job I did.

"To me, the funniest part was the bargaining," Gillis notes of that night's shooting. "They [Sam and Rob] didn't like the scene and they'd already smashed up the car. There were a bunch of people, maybe 150 to 200 people from the neighborhood, and Rob Tapert goes out and says, 'Anybody got a junker I can buy?' Somebody volunteered, and they haggled over price. I think Rob ended up giving him a hundred bucks, but the guy wanted a hundred and fifty, so then they settled on a hundred, if the owner could keep the car battery. I'll tell you, it was priceless watching Rob negotiate with a bystander. So they used this car the second time and smashed it, and I don't know which shot they used.

"The car stunts were very sophisticated," Primes acknowledges. In fact, the climactic sequence in *The XYZ Murders* is an intense, sustained car chase in which good guys and bad guys jump repeatedly onto the hoods of various vehicles (as many as three) and trade fisticuffs, all at high speeds.

To accomplish that set piece, the production actually shut down the Henry Cabot Lodge Freeway for a night. "I remember closing it off and having it on the radio and television that they'd closed off a major freeway," Primes reports.

"My little joke I used to make about that is that to Sam Raimi, when the script says, 'The car pulls off the road,' that actually means the car is in the right-hand lane of a busy freeway, when suddenly the driver jerks the wheel left, goes into traffic — causing cars to spin out and tractor trailers to jack-knife. The car then jumps the divider, turning into oncoming traffic, which swerves around, and *then* the car pulls off the road ... six lanes over on the other side. That's what 'The car pulls off the road' means to Sam Raimi."

One of the cars so dramatically pulling off the road was Sam's Delta 88, the same vehicle that transported Bruce Campbell to the cabin of the damned in *The Evil Dead*. "He absolutely loved it, and it kept on getting destroyed, and he would rebuild it," Primes notes of the Classic. "He had a very sentimental attachment to that car."

Sheree Wilson is even more effusive about her scenes with the Classic — which she piloted throughout much of the chase. "That was an honor. Are you kidding? That's his baby! I got lots of privileges [with the car] — hanging off, dangling off..."

Indeed, the car chase climaxed when the Classic dangled over a bridge and plunged into the Detroit River. "We were hanging off of the Belle Isle Bridge!" Wilson exclaims. "We did the craziest stunts, but all of us were in it together. It was snowing, and we were trying to figure out how to make it so you couldn't see the snow. We had ambulances down there for hypothermia."

"At the bridge where we plunged the car in, it was so cold that everybody's beards were frozen up," Primes remembers. "The Detroit natives were in their heavy clothes. I got up in the crane to do a shot twenty feet off the ground, and it was so cold that I didn't care about the shot. I just cared about getting down!"

Inevitably, the winter temperatures and the night shooting led to one thing: *illness*. "I remember working a few nights with the flu," Primes recalls.

"We all looked a little gray by the end of it," Wilson adds. "Everybody was getting sick. We all knew we had to make it to the end of the film. And the minute they said, 'That's a wrap," I think everybody came down with the flu."

But even after the long winter nights came to an end, the difficulties didn't cease for Raimi and *The XYZ Murders*. Unfortunately, studio executives got more involved than ever, as Gillis recalls. "The film was shot in Detroit, but somebody looked at it and didn't like the thing and said it should be told in flashbacks."

And that meant one thing: a trip to Hollywood to do reshoots and additional scenes, mainly those set at Hudsucker Penitentiary. Naturally, this was an expensive process, and studio executives were quick to remind the Renaissance fellows that they'd already gone over budget and schedule.

An interesting historical side note regarding the reshoots is that future Academy Award–winner Frances McDormand played one of the nuns in the car rushing along with Nancy to save Vic. "Joel and Frances were dating," Wilson remembers. "Sam and Joel would drink coffee, and they would smoke, and they would pace and talk, and Ethan would sit and write. I saw so many sessions where they were just at it for hours, all night long."

Even with reshoots complete, long after principal photography, Avco-Embassy hadn't finished tinkering with *Crimewave*. "I think that in post-production the studio got very, very involved," recalls composer Joe LoDuca. "I think perhaps, in retrospect, I had a conversation that shot myself in the foot in what I was trying to tell some executive. He was concerned that the movie be perceived as a comedy, and I said that one of the ways you do that is to play the music straight, and the music is the straight man over the comedy.

"We've done that in horror movies and it's attested to by things like *Airplane*, where that's the joke. You play the music straight. I don't think that the person I was talking to got that, and it immediately made him nervous. Another composer was hired to do the score."

Looking at the *Crimewave* scoreboard, it became obvious Raimi had lost ground. No Bruce Campbell in the lead, no Joe LoDuca composing the score ... could things get worse? In fact, they did. In addition to casting and scoring considerations, Raimi also had final editorial control yanked out of his hands, as he later reported:

> They lost a lot of my favorite scenes, including a beautiful sequence in the sewers. The end product was incomprehensible to me, the beginning and end were so different, even I can't understand what's going on in that movie.[7]

At least a silver lining emerged for LoDuca. "What happened at the very end is that Sam brought me back in. I'm not credited, but I did the last three reels of the film, which were a little more action-adventure. That was a last-minute adjustment, so at the end I did get to work a little more on the film."

Still, LoDuca remembers it was a very difficult time. "I understood that it was a disappointment for me, certainly torturous for him [Raimi]."

Sheree J. Wilson didn't much care for the situation either. "I just think that's what's typical in Hollywood. First of all, these guys are young, and you go over budget and you take too much time. I mean, *you* try to do principal photography all night — the whole film takes place at night! And *you* start on Halloween and end in January. You don't think you're going to have weather problems and delays?

"And there were a couple of other issues," Wilson acknowledges. "Brion at the time was a little ... *unpredictable*. 'Where is he? He was supposed to be on the set...!' So there was a lot that was not Sam's fault, and it was a real shame. And they came in as, you know, the big heavies, vultures, making him wrong and bad and taking his film away from him in the eleventh hour, taking credit for all the good. I just think it was completely wrong and unnecessary."

Despite the battle with Avco-Embassy, Sheree still feels positive about the experience. "Shooting with Sam, Rob Tapert and Bruce, I felt like I was making a movie with my friends. They are complete professionals and they totally knew what they were doing, especially for being so young. We were all contemporaries; I had my twenty-fifth birthday on the set. Sam I and were the same age. I fell in love with Sam on that movie. First film, first big movie, first director — he's just the best."

If only Avco-Embassy had demonstrated the same faith in *Crimewave*'s directors as its stars did, history may have been very different.

CRIMEWAVE SINKS

Although *Crimewave* garnered honors at the Madrid Film Festival, a special jury prize at the Houston Film Festival[8] and an upbeat showing at the Seattle Film Festival, it is probably fair to state it is nobody's favorite Raimi film. Shown sporadically throughout the country, including New York, it opened in Manhattan at the Thalia on June 6, 1986, the same day as Arnold Schwarzeneger's *Raw Deal*, the family-friendly *Space Camp* and Tobe Hooper's remake of *Invaders from Mars*. For a time, the film also played midnight shows at the Waverly Theater, hoping to attract a cult following like the immortal *Rocky Horror Picture Show*.

Considering much of the negativity about the film in the press regarding post-production control issues, *Crimewave*'s reviews do not appear overtly unkind. *Variety* reported that Raimi's sophomore venture gave the "impression of having been storyboarded rather than directed" and that the film looked "cheap," yet also reported "that laughs are abundant enough to make this a passably funny entertainment."[9]

The *New York Times*' Vincent Canby also sprinkled kind words amidst the bad:

> It's full of film knowledge and is amazingly elaborate for a low-budget movie. The only problem is that it's not funny. One smiles at the inspiration of the jokes, though not at their execution. The chase that ends the movie is something of a technical feat, but it remains as dimly humorless as a smart film student's essay on how to shoot a chase.[10]

Although *Newsday*'s Mike McGrady called *Crimewave* a "turkey,"[11] the *New York Post*'s Jami Bernard was practically effusive, noting Raimi's second directorial effort was "more accurately a cartoon than any movie that ever pursued a comic book hero, including *Popeye* and certainly *Superman*," and, on a personal note, that "Raimi knows his stuff."[12]

The *Village Voice* had praise for the picture's style too. "Happily, *Crimewave* has a dazzling momentum and some brash, tasteless yucks," wrote David Edelstein. "Imagine a Jerry Lewis extravaganza about serial killers, with a style out of comic books and Warner cartoons — all pop-out foregrounds, loopy sound effects, and seize-you-by-the-collar performances."[13]

Despite such promising notices, few patrons sought out *Crimewave* and Avco-Embassy dumped it to secondary venues such as HBO and the home video market. It is a film that Raimi rarely talks about, dismissing it as "Slimewave" in many print interviews. His feelings are understandable since he devoted time, passion and energy to the film and it went out in a form he had little approval over.

Cinematographer Primes has come to some perspective about the off-beat film. "To be perfectly honest, I can talk about it now with Sam's unique vision, and what he did and all that, but at the time it wasn't really my thing.

"I guess I was in my early forties and Sam was twenty-five. I wanted to do more serious filmmaking, but now that I'm sixty-three, I can appreciate the twenty-five-year-old Sam Raimi more than I could at forty-two, just because I think I have become more tolerant of different kinds of film-making. At forty, I was very much at the point of my career that I wanted to make serious films, and this was kind of a comic book. I liked Sam, I liked his imagination, I liked the incredible passion, but I don't know if I ever believed in *Crimewave*," Primes acknowledges. "It's a hell of a thing to admit."

"In hindsight," he continues, "it was brilliantly imaginative, much more so than I could appreciate at the time. Let me just add this personal note:

I wish I had this perspective then, because I think I would have been much more empathetic to Sam. I think I could have been much more supportive to him with the insight I have now about the kind of artist he was, but that's because if he was immature at twenty-five — and trust me, he was — I was immature at forty-two."

A unique if oddball collaboration with two important filmmakers of our day (the Coens), and an experiment in adapting cartoon style to live-action film, *Crimewave* fulfilled Raimi's "sophomore slump" despite the game efforts of all involved. Its poor showing at the box office assured a period of retrenchment for Raimi and the advent of a more commercial venture, a sequel inevitably titled *Evil Dead 2*.

RAIMI RAP

CLOSE YOUR EYES: When Sheree Wilson learned she was cast in *Crimewave*, her first instinct was to go out and see Raimi's freshman film, *The Evil Dead*. That was an action Raimi was not keen on. "Sam wouldn't let me see it once he cast me in the film, because I hate horror movies," Wilson reveals. "They really affect me. Listen, it's my business; I know how they do all that stuff, and it still scares me to death. I hate them. So when I told him how badly I hated horror films, he didn't want me to see it. He thought I would lose faith in him as a director."

AN OLD-FASHIONED ROMANTIC: "In *Crimewave*, there was a relationship between this guy, the hero [Vic], and the woman [Nancy], and I believe it reflected a little bit Sam's very idealistic notion, which you even see in *Spider-Man*," suggests Robert Primes. "The man puts the woman on such a pedestal that he would throw his coat down so she would not have to step into the mud getting into the carriage, that chivalrous kind of thing.

"That was reflected a little bit in the heroic nature of this very wimpy character in *Crimewave*. He was a wimp, but he needed to be strong for this woman and go and deal with the bad people, even though they're much bigger.

"I think perhaps that all of his [Raimi's] relations with the opposite sex were out of movies: damsels, heroines and heroes," Primes speculates, "and people acting out a script about how chivalry is supposed to be."

A NIGHT AT THE RIALTO: One of the important scenes in *Crimewave* occurs at the Tuller Hotel, doubling as the Rialto. Here, while extras danced, composer Joe LoDuca indulged in a tribute to the music of the big band era. "The big band cues were pre-recorded. And what was fun about that experience for me was that I got to hand-pick a big band of some of my favorite colleagues at the time," says LoDuca. "I remember the drummer wearing a microphone on his chest. It was all recorded live; it was done sort of old style with everyone sitting in a circle around one figure-eight mike. Not only was it a throwback visually, but a throwback in the recording session as well."

FLYING PLATES: So much of the action in *Crimewave* is expressed with wacky, off-the-wall camera angles. One of Raimi's signature shots involves the camera tracking a flying or, more accurately, a hurtling object.

In one scene, Mrs. Trend defends herself from Crush's attack by throwing a barrage of plates and other dishes, and this distinctive camera angle is utilized. Cinematographer Primes remembers how it was done. "When we'd throw an object, we'd follow that object with the camera. What we would do was very simple: we just put the object on a monofilament on a stick in front of the camera, and we would just follow it into things. That was all Sam's incomparable mechanical imagination. It was absolutely incredible."

FATHER INVESTOR: When Sam Raimi was forced to create "book ends" to tell the story of *Crimewave* in flashback, he called upon his friend and attorney, Phil Gillis to lend a hand. "I went out to Hollywood, and Sam told me he wanted me to play the part of a minister while a character was being electrocuted or something," Gillis reveals of the scene set at Hudsucker Penitentiary. "I said 'Sam, I'm a Catholic not a Protestant; why don't you make him a priest? I'll recite the 22nd Psalm in Latin.' He thought that was so great, so that's what I recited when I led the guy [Birney] to the electric chair.

"That's also when I started to learn about Hollywood stuff, that jail cells are made of wood. And the sound of clanging jail doors was added later in post-production."

YOUR BIGGEST FAN: Achieving believable special effects on a low budget is never easy and *Crimewave* was no exception. "We had a pretty miserable little crane," Primes remembers. "I was up in the crane and Sam had these tremendous fans going because he loved the idea of leaves blowing. Ordinary fans wouldn't do.

"From Florida, he got these three-hundred-horsepower boat motors — marine engines! And they would create this incredible wind force that could almost blow people over. And Sam loved this; the more spectacle the better. He is a very flamboyant filmmaker, so we had this fan out there and it shook the hell out of the crane, and the camera was shaking all over the place too."

Primes tried to get the complicated crane moves down, but found them difficult because of the fans. "We did thirty takes and kept on trying to do it," he remembers. "I remember pleading with Sam, 'Can't we move the fan over there?' and he says, 'No, no, no,' he needs it.

"I remember the completion bond guy was on me like crazy to get that shot. He was very frustrated because he'd seen thirty takes go by. He was there because his company had guaranteed they'd complete the film on time and budget and had put up money to do it. I guess he had the power to shut us down, and he was a very unhappy camper."

THE MORE THINGS CHANGE: "I saw Sam doing one of the behind-the-scenes pieces they did on him for *Spider-Man* and there he was," Sheree Wilson notes. "His hair looked the same and he had the same intense, sweet look on his face: where he's holding his hands up in his little L shape, both hands, and he's 'walking through.' [On *Crimewave*] he would walk up, and he had his little camera that he made with his hands and he would zoom up and look at your face. Talk about an artist and an innovative director, he's really very special."

THE CRAZIEST MOVIE IN THE WORLD

What can be written about a film taken from a director's hands and then consequently disowned by that director? Well, in fairness, one can state that *Crimewave* is a problematic movie, and doesn't quite work in the ways it was intended. On the other hand, it remains inventive, unusual, and unlike any other motion picture ever produced, simultaneously a living, breathing cartoon strip and a funny throwback to the noir era.

"Noir sometimes played with unrealistic characters and situations and exaggerated them. I think that's basically what we did with *Crimewave*," notes cinematographer Robert Primes. "A comic book is an exaggeration, and when you're dealing with a movie that's more stylized than real, to exaggerate the techniques, the shadows, the camera moves, the lightness and darkness, seems appropriate. We didn't consciously imitate noir, but I think we made our choices for the same reasons that the masters of noir did."

Interestingly, *Crimewave* represents a deliberate throwback to the 1940s cinema in other ways, particularly in language and props. The dialogue is nothing if not purposefully old fashioned. "Come on, Pip Squeak, we're saving a seat for you," or "Hiya, Cupcake," or "A thousand guys would give a thousand bucks to have dinner with a girl like that!" It's jarringly anachronistic.

This stilted movie-speak comes right out of a 1940s dialogue vault, less realistic and more flowery than today's more "naturalistic," if less artistic, dialogue. It's played for humor, literally so straight that it is funny. It is difficult to take seriously lines like Victor's forceful admonition to "Taste justice!" and the film's dialogue consequently elicits a knowing smile about Hollywood's yesteryear.

The film's props also accentuate the feeling of 1940s era film. Raimi's camera captures such period items as a manual typewriter, rotary telephones, an oversized camera with big, silver flash bulbs, and other affectations that had passed into history when the film was produced in the 1980s. Even wardrobe, particularly Sheree J. Wilson's costumes, and the music of LoDuca's classy Rialto contributions reinforce the notion of a past world existing in the present.

"The lighting and the colors, everything — that was all on purpose," Wilson affirms. "It was talked about and really researched."

Though all of these touches remain interesting, one wonders why the film wasn't actually set in the 1940s, rather than in contemporary Detroit, with the 1973 Oldsmobile Delta 88 and other modern grace notes ultimately diminishing the carefully constructed period texture. Indeed, the film may have succeeded as a period piece because there would have been less audience confusion. But could 1940s Detroit have been captured successfully on three million dollars? Probably not.

Instead, the technique adopted here, which doesn't satisfy most viewers, is merely to suggest a feel, an atmosphere that is 1940s, with modern cars, video security cameras and skyscrapers still in evidence. The amusing use of the 1960s song "Cherish" in the Rialto sequence is good for a laugh of recognition, but a non sequitur in the loopy pseudo-forties world of *Crimewave*. Neither modern-seeming nor immaculately period, the setting is a little off-putting.

Handled much more successfully is the Three Stooges brand of slapstick comedy and violence. Coddish and Crush are exterminators, which harkens back to several Three Stooges efforts including *Ants in the Pantry* (1936), *Termites of 1938* (1938) and *Studio Stoops* (1950). In the case of *Crimewave*, the exterminators work for Center City Exterminators (motto: "We kill all sizes!"), as opposed to Larry, Moe and Curly's businesses, the Acme Exterminating Company (motto: "If you got 'em, we'll get 'em.")[14] or in *Ants in the Pantry*, the Lightning Pest Control Company (motto: "Got ants in your plants? We'll kill 'em.")[15]

Beyond that similarity and a tendency toward verbal puns (Crush's electrical weapon is powered not by megahertz, but mega*hurts*), *Crimewave* adopts the tradition of dramatic — but innocuous — slapstick violence familiar to Stooge fans. In one scene, Campbell's nasty character Renaldo gets crushed by a falling fire escape ladder and is crumpled before our very eyes, as though we're watching a Tom and Jerry cartoon wherein a piano has dropped from a tall building and smashed one of the characters.

Coddish's last minute plea for forgiveness, set to sappy, melodramatic music, is another cartoonish moment. Armed with a baseball bat, Ajax thoughtfully hears his argument, and in the time-honored tradition of slapstick, brushes aside his doubts. He accepts Coddish's apology and shakes the villain's hand, only to be tricked and attacked one more time. Similarly, Shemp begged for his life in *Fright Night* (1947), but the gag was slightly different since the roles were reversed, and Shemp actually escaped. In *Spider-Man*'s finale, Green Goblin attempts to pull Coddish's ruse on Peter Parker, begging Parker to take his hand in forgiveness while actually plotting to skewer the hero with his hovering glider. Unlike the dim-witted Vic, Peter knows better.

Raimi also has wicked fun with scene transitions. After Vic and Nancy are unable to pay for the dinner, it is announced that a dance contest is being held and the winners will get thirty-six dollars — the precise amount required to square-up the bill. An instant later, the camera captures the duo on the dance floor, entered in the contest, with phony smiles plastered on their faces. Then Raimi takes the joke a step further. The next transition cuts to dippy Vic merrily dancing about in the restaurant's crowded kitchen, blissful and smiling, but having lost the contest. Notably, Nancy is not so happy to be rendered a dishwasher. These moments are played well by Birney and Wilson and very amusing.

"The Parade of Protection: The Safest Hallway in the World" remains a brilliantly orchestrated visual joke, as well as the film's most talked about moment. A life-sized dominoes set, this bizarre test for burglar-proof doors makes the ideal location for a ridiculous chase, and the sequence boasts a surreal, charming momentum. Smith, the perfect cartoon menace, all bluster and rage, is filled with so much anger that one expects steam to fly out of his ears at any moment.

Despite intentional homage to the Stooges and cartoons of another era, this sequence's humor as in the majority of *Crimewave*, arises not from the actual, wacky events unfolding on-screen; but rather from an intellectual reckoning that the film artists have transferred the ethos of cartoons — clichés and all — to live-action film. Then, by understanding this joke, one must acknowledge how the gimmicky, and admittedly inspired, camera angles foster this echo of that other medium. That's a complex thought process, and not immediately conducive of easy yuks.

"It's about filmmaking," Primes stresses of the film's unique brand of humor. "The medium *is* the message. There's nothing wrong with that." Or to put it another way, "to appreciate the lunatic camera movements, it is necessary to have thought some time about how and why a camera moves at all."[16] This is a valid approach, but how is it possible that this strategy could be commercially viable, since it requires (a) an understanding of film history and (b) an understanding of film technique?

In some senses, to use a Raimi-centric metaphor, *Crimewave* is to *Evil Dead* as *It's Murder!* is to *Happy Valley Kid*. It requires more active thinking than a horror film does. Though *Evil Dead* works like a master's thesis on the genre, a stunning synthesis of textbook mechanisms and gimmicks, its audience need not study camera angles, editing or ambitious special effects processes to get the movie's feel. *The Evil Dead* generates fear and suspense, pure and simple, and that is what remains important about it. Though *Crimewave* is no doubt ambitious, a thesis on the mechanisms of a different genre — the forgotten Stooge-style comedies — its audience must process and be cognizant of movie history to comprehend the silly jokes.

That established, the Coens revived *Crimewave*-style humor in their 1987 movie, *Raising Arizona*. The tale of a small-time robber named H.I. McDonagh (Nicolas Cage) and his kidnap of a baby, the film featured, like *Crimewave*, a jailed protagonist and the guy even had job at *Hudsucker* Industries! The material was vetted in an arch, deliberately exaggerated manner, and framed much like a cartoon. The performances intentionally lacked subtlety, and McDonagh exhibited a chivalry to rival Ajax's, reacting violently to the notion of wife swapping and other improprieties.

Though there are no evil assassins in *Raising Arizona*, two escaped convicts (one fat, one skinny) played similarly over-the-top roles. Coddish and Crush's murderous tendencies were adopted by the "Lone Biker of the Apocalypse," another unstoppable rogue.

Raising Arizona featured POV shaky-cam shots, a la Sam Raimi's *Evil Dead*, especially in the dynamically orchestrated scenes of babies tumbling from a crib and seeking escape from their upstairs bedroom. Replete with deliberately "stagey" shots, *Raising Arizona* also spotlighted kinetic camera work during a grocery store chase, as well as eyes-bugging-out/mouth-open-screaming-style acting. It was *Crimewave* redux, with a bigger budget and no studio interference. The Coens got the feel right the second time and adopted many of Raimi's stylistic flourishes in the process

In the 1980s, mainstream Hollywood films were becoming more and more realistic, and a film as expressionist and bizarre as *Crimewave* bucked audience and studio expectations. It can be lauded on those grounds and appreciated for its technique and self-reflexive knowledge, but it isn't an easy film to love. One wonders what Raimi's cut looked like. One suspects it was wackier, wilder, and more worthwhile than the film that emerged. This viewer, for one, would like to see the "sewer sequence" Raimi discussed.

Director's cut, anyone?

EVIL DEAD 2: DEAD BY DAWN (1987)

THAT'S RIGHT! WHO'S LAUGHING NOW!?

CAST AND CREW

RENAISSANCE PICTURES PRESENTS *EVIL DEAD 2*

DIRECTOR: Sam Raimi

PRODUCER: Robert Tapert

WRITERS: Sam Raimi and Scott Spiegel

EXECUTIVE PRODUCERS: Irvin Shapiro and Alex De Benedetti

CO-PRODUCER: Bruce Campbell

MUSIC: Joseph LoDuca

SPECIAL MAKEUP: Mark Shostrom

DIRECTOR OF PHOTOGRAPHY: Peter Deming

DIRECTOR, NIGHT PHOTOGRAPHY: Eugene Shlugliet

ART DIRECTORS: Phillip Duffin and Randy Bennett

FILM EDITOR: Kaye Davis

SECOND UNIT DIRECTOR OF PHOTOGRAPHY: Tim Philo

MAKEUP: KNB

MINIATURES: Acme Special Effects

DANCE BY: Doug Beswick Productions

TARRING

Bruce Campbell: Ash
Sarah Berry: Annie
Dan Hicks: Jake
Kassie Wesley: Bobbie Jo
Theodore Raimi: Possessed Henrietta
Denise Bixler: Linda
John Peakes: Professor Knowby
Lou Hancock: Henrietta

Filmed in Wadesboro, North Carolina and Detroit, Michigan.

DEAD BY DAWN...

ASH DRIVES HIS GIRLFRIEND LINDA TO THE WOODS for a romantic weekend getaway. At a remote cabin, Ash plays a tape recorded by Professor Raymond Knowby, who discovered the Necronomicon, the ancient Book of the Dead, in the ruins of Kandar, and then inadvertently summoned a terrible evil by reciting demon resurrection passages.

The woods come to life, possessing Linda, and Ash is forced to dismember her, an action that drives him to the edge of sanity. Later, a dark force possesses his left hand and he chops off the offending body part with a chainsaw.

Meanwhile, Professor Knowby's daughter Annie is en route to the cabin with an assistant, Ed, and two local guides, rednecks Dan and Bobbie Jo. The group arrives at the cabin and concludes that Ash has killed Annie's parents. Thrown into the fruit cellar, Ash confronts Henrietta, a demonic version of Knowby's wife.

During a night of terror, Ash and Annie struggle to keep the terrible evil from consuming them. They endure a spectral visit from the deceased professor and learn that salvation rests within the Necronomicon's pages, in a translation of passages about a medieval hero who fell from the sky to save the land from the terrors of the Deadites...

THE MOTHER OF ALL SEQUELS

A sequel to the popular *Evil Dead* had been on director Raimi's plate for some time, even before his second effort, *Crimewave*, failed to propel his career into high gear and producer Shapiro suggested it was time to return to that cabin in the woods. "Sam had talked about there being a sequel when we worked on the first one," cinematographer Tim Philo reveals. "He said, 'Oh, after *Evil Dead 1*, Bruce goes back to 1300 to fight Deadites.' That was going to be *Evil Dead 2*."

Raimi developed that particular script scenario, according to an interview with Alan Jones for *Starburst* magazine, but monetary restrictions prevented that draft from becoming a reality. The troubled Embassy Pictures kept Raimi hanging for some five months,[1] repeatedly promising him the cash to produce a sequel, but never delivering it, or even a start date. Disappointed and waiting in limbo, Raimi severed his association with Embassy when a better alternative presented itself.

That alternative came in the person of a movie mogul, legendary Dino De Laurentiis, a man sometimes dubbed "Dino De Horrendus"[2] by sarcastic critics. Like Shapiro, De Laurentiis lived and breathed the movie business for decades, since 1940. Though De Laurentiis has been "behind some of the most pungent shlock in movie history,"[3] including Roger Vadim's *Barbarella*, the *King Kong* remake (1976) and the unpopular adaptation of *Flash Gordon* (1980) starring Sam Jones, the Italian producer also vetted many remarkable and worthwhile films, including Sydney Lumet's *Three Days of the Condor* (1975), David Cronenberg's *The Dead Zone* (1983), Michael Mann's *Manhunter* (1986) and David Lynch's *Blue Velvet* (1986), not to mention works by luminaries like Ingmar Bergman and Federico Fellini (*La Strada*).

An Irving G. Thalberg Memorial Award winner in the year 2000 for contributions to five hundred films, De Laurentiis may be an unrepentant mogul, not to mention flamboyant, but he also seems to recognize that movies have an obligation to be commercial *and* artistic, a distinction worthy of commendation in the era of the Hollywood blockbuster.

In the early 1980s, De Laurentiis was on a roll. He built his own movie studio in Wilmington, North Carolina. The largest moviemaking house on the East Coast, this facility boasts eleven sound stages, editing and screening rooms, a prop shop and more. Today, Screen Gems owns the property, following De Laurentiis Entertainment Group's (DEG's) monetary collapse in 1988. But twenty years ago, De Laurentiis built the facility to shoot *Firestarter*, a thriller adapted from Stephen King's best-seller. Also planned was the King anthology *Cat's Eye*, and *Maximum Overdrive*, which served as King's directorial debut in 1985.

De Laurentiis had already contacted Raimi about the possibility of directing another King adaptation, *Thinner*, but learned from King himself that Raimi was experiencing difficulties getting financing for *Evil Dead 2*, and offered to help.

When Raimi learned De Laurentiis could furnish funds, quickly, approximately 3.5 million dollars, he grabbed the opportunity, even though there were concessions. According to Philo, the Italian mogul "wanted basically the same movie made" as the first *Evil Dead*. Instead of fighting knights and monsters in another time period, the stalwart Ash would face a second adventure in the isolated cabin, with only a brief, surprise ending occurring in the distant past. Other off-message subplots were deleted, including one about escaped convicts returning to the Knowby cabin to find money they buried there before their capture,[4] leaving the story a spare variation on the original's theme: the siege on a cabin by a force in the woods.

But something funny happened on the way to the shooting stage: Raimi and co-writer Scott Spiegel, longtime Three Stooges fans, decided that if forced to repeat themselves narratively (same cabin; same Deadites), they need not tread familiar ground tonally. They opted to make their sequel ... *funny*. Writing from Renaissance HQ in Ferndale, Michigan, they fashioned a script that drastically revised the *Evil Dead* universe.

Like *The Texas Chain Saw Massacre* and *Night of the Living Dead*, some moments in the original *Evil Dead* were so horrific, over-the-top and gory they actually elicited nervous laughter. This factor was not lost on the Renaissance folks. Instead of shepherding a straight remake, they went beyond their template, infusing surreal, satirical and absurd moments into the concept. The bigger budget afforded the director a much broader canvas on which to paint, meaning wilder and wackier special effects. And the attention on laughter was in keeping with Raimi's personal preference to entertain rather than scare.

Thus Ash's severed, "contaminated" hand became the sequel's recurring nemesis, baiting the hero with obscene gestures and causing him grave bodily harm. Such humor derived not just from the unusual form of this antagonist, but Campbell's well-played physical battles with it. Before separated from the rest of his body, Ash's hand inflicted major damage, battering him with plates and dishes (shades of *Crimewave*).

"My own theory is that while they didn't intend for *Evil Dead* to be funny, they saw when people responded to it the potential for so much humor, and they capitalized on that for the next ones," Ellen Sandweiss explains. "I think they were very smart."

Another change concerned Ash, the square-jawed franchise hero. "In the original *Evil Dead,* Ash isn't a smart ass at all," Sandweiss reminds us. "He's just a nerd. He's the way Bruce used to be. Bruce is gorgeous, but he is such a geek and didn't believe in his own handsomeness. He was just a goof, and that's how he played the first Ash character."

In the new script, Ash evolved into an impressive Deadite-bashing warrior. Armed with a sawed-off shotgun, a chainsaw where his severed hand used to be, and funny one-liners (such as the Eastwood-like pronouncement, "Groovy"), Ash became larger-than-life, "the hero who fell from the skies" to defeat the Deadites. No longer merely an unlucky college student, Ash grew into an icon with a mission, not unlike the figures fronting other horror franchises of the mid-to-late 1980s, including Freddy Krueger (*A Nightmare on Elm Street*), Jason (*Friday the 13th*), Pinhead (*Hellraiser*), Leatherface (*The Texas Chain Saw Massacre*) and Michael Myers (*Halloween*). The new Ash gave fans a central figure of fun to identify with, and the new characterization and concept gelled well with Campbell's buffed-up physique and ironic sense of humor.

THE OLD GANG RIDES AGAIN – SORT OF...

Mounting an *Evil Dead* sequel proved more complex than one might suspect. For one thing, Raimi and Renaissance were not legally permitted to include footage from the original because of foreign rights issues. In order to get *Evil Dead* seen in theaters across Europe, Shapiro sold distribution privileges to various small companies across the continent. To acquire each company's permission to use *Evil Dead* footage in the sequel would have been time consuming and near impossible. Essentially, this development meant that the very artists who created a work of art where prohibited from re-using it in their own follow-up. This necessitated a brief reshoot of the first film's primary events, so as to familiarize audiences with the back-story.

For matters of simplicity, reshoots retelling the story of Ash included only two characters: Ash and girlfriend Linda. "The relationship between Linda and Ash did evoke some sweetness and gentleness, and in making Ash the character that he becomes in *Evil Dead 2*, there needed to be that softness and sentimentality," notes Baker of her character's inclusion in the sequel while Cheryl, Scotty and Shelly were written out.

"I met with Sam and Bruce, and they asked me if I would portray Linda in the second movie, but that was in 1986 and I was actually married by then and expecting my first child. The timing was just not going to be conducive for me to shoot and be gone," Baker reveals. "They told me when we met that it would be for a couple of scenes and a dream sequence, but God only knows what that dream sequence could have been..."

Linda was recast and actress Denise Bixler accepted the part. The remaining characters were new creations. Bobbie Jo, a part originally written for Raimi's roommate Holly Hunter in Silver Lake, and her redneck beau Jake were demon fodder, portrayed by soap opera star Karrie DePaiva and Dan Hicks, respectively. Earnest Sarah Berry signed on as Ash's new romantic interest, the lovely — if confused — daughter of Professor Knowby, Annie. Rich Domeier played her ill-fated assistant, Ed.

Though Campbell had a new band of thespians to dismember before the cameras, many behind-the scenes *Evil Dead* talents returned, including makeup artist Tom Sullivan. "*Evil Dead 2* was to be a four-month shoot for me," he explains. "Sam had asked me back in Detroit if I wanted to do makeup effects or stop-motion on *Evil Dead 2*. The script was huge. Lots of big suits and creatures and very complex effects. I had no way of tackling that scale of suit building," he notes, explaining his choice. "Focusing on stop-motion was a great opportunity to live out my Ray Harryhausen fantasy."

As before, Sullivan contributed to the art design of the movie. "My responsibility was for a list of shots including the Book of the Dead creation sequence," an opening explanation accompanied with visuals of the book's creation, long history and vile nature, "and lots of inserts of the Flying Deadite at the finale."

Evil Dead 2 offered Sullivan the opportunity to refine his original designs. "I built the 'Beauty' copy, three stunt copies of the Book of the Dead, and five sets of the Lost Pages. I had to update the Book of the Dead and the Kandarian dagger. I had given Sam the original dagger after filming *Evil Dead,* and he brought it to the Wadesboro, North Carolina, studio, a vacant high school. Molds of the hilt were cast by prop maker Tony Ellwood. I designed a blade based on the bladelike tail of the Flying Deadite. In my own lore of the prop, the tip of the tail would be the proper implement for a sacrifice. The blade, sculpted by Mike Trcic and Brian Rae, was added to the hilt, and stunt copies and FX versions were built.

"Sam wanted a bigger book," Sullivan explains of the new Necronomicon edition. "I enlarged the pages from the original book, and water-colored in the beauty copy, as well as adding a bunch of new pages representing some of the new elements in *Evil Dead 2*."

As *Evil Dead 2* began shooting in Wadesboro, hours from Wilmington and the eyes of De Laurentiis, Raimi made another concession, one involving his choice of cinematographer. "They made their plans," Tim Philo remembers, "and Sam in the meantime had done *The XYZ Murders*, *Crimewave*, and since I hadn't shot a 35mm feature, De Laurentiis wasn't necessarily going to go for me doing it."

Instead, Raimi retained the services of Eugene D. Shlugleit, who filmed *Crimewave* reshoots in Los Angeles. "We talked a little bit about it," Philo remembers, and "[Sam] felt bad that I wasn't going to be able to do it."

In the final analysis, it was a decision that didn't turn out well. Once principal photography began in the Wadesboro heat, Shlugleit's crew did not meet expectations and was subsequently released. Shlugleit himself remains credited with the *Evil Dead 2*'s exterior night photography since nighttime exteriors were the first order of business during his tenure.

SECOND GO

After losing Shlugleit, Raimi again turned to Philo, this time two weeks into a shoot that commenced the second week of May in 1986. With nine weeks left on the project, Raimi sent Philo the script.

"The *Evil Dead 2* script is an amazing document," Philo declares. "As a story it's probably impossible to read, but the level of complexity that Sam had jumped to in terms of elements in each shot was astounding. It would be shot after shot of two, three, four elements of either green screen, physical effects, matte shots or something. I read it and said, 'This is amazing, but it can't be shot in the schedule you're telling me, and I'm afraid I'll be the fall guy if I come down there and say hey, we're not making the schedule.'"

With a concrete finish date in August 1986, Philo declined to shoot *Evil Dead 2*, and Raimi found another talented cinematographer in a gentleman named Peter Deming. Today, Deming is among the foremost talents in the industry, having shot three *Austin Powers* films, *Scream 2* (1997), *Scream 3* (2000), *From Hell* (2001) and David Lynch's atmospheric duo, *Lost Highway* (1997) and *Mulholland Drive* (2001). Back in 1986, however, Deming had just two films under his belt, the long-in-production *Hollywood Shuffle* and a film shot in Michigan called *The Carrier*.

"I was actually surprised, because I didn't have a relationship with them [Renaissance]," Deming notes. In fact, he had met Raimi only once, and briefly, in Michigan. But that didn't stop him from seizing the opportunity. The first thing he did to prep for the assignment was watch the original *Evil Dead*, "because, as most people know, the second film starts at the end of the first and you get to know the characters, the setting, what they did, and what you need to do to go to the next step."

After that, Deming made the journey to North Carolina and took over shooting. "I was there, I think, for the better part of four months, and it was summer, so of course it was hot and humid," he recalls.

"It was difficult because I just came in on the fly and didn't really have a chance to analyze the script. I barely had enough time to read it," Deming remembers with a laugh. "Every day was an adventure where you would sit and have breakfast, and Sam and I and the first assistant director would talk about what we were going to do, and there were a few things that they told me right off the bat. There's a shot of Bruce being hurled through the woods by the evil force, and that was a complicated rig on a crane, so we had to shoot some tests for that, as far as what frame rates we wanted to use. Other than that, it was things popping up every day that we wanted to do."

One element that surprised Deming was the tongue-in-cheek approach. "It took me a while after I was there to get where they were going, because I had just watched the first one, which was very straightforward, and I was starting to wonder what they were doing. No one clued me in, but after a couple of days I was like, 'Oh, okay, I get it now.'"

Deming also found he had an easy shorthand with Raimi because of the director's experience behind the camera. "Sam came up making his own movies, so he's very knowledgeable in cameras and frame rates and forward and reverse, so he pretty much nailed that every time. He had done those things on his own for years."

By the time Deming was on board, many of the exterior shots had already been filmed, though one famous shot remained. At the end of *The Evil Dead*, the Force blasts its way through front door of the cabin, into the screaming face of Ash. *Evil Dead 2* recreates that shot and then one-ups it with a dramatic punch line: Ash spun through the air for miles and dumped head first into a muddy puddle. "I think that was actually my first or second day on the movie," Deming remembers. "It was actually pretty simple. The shot was hand-held with a 10mm; starting in the woods and basically running as fast as you could, and then having people who had rigged the [cabin] doors, and you would scream out the cues so they would open the doors at the last second, and you'd burst through the front and run right up to Bruce."

The final portion of the shot, Ash's unhappy flight, involved the famous Sam-O-Cam, a modified crane extending a long mechanical arm to a giant cross of sorts. Campbell was strapped to the cross, which would spin as the crane rolled forward. With a little fast motion and blurring to hide the apparatus, you have the Force pushing poor Ash through the woods.

Nearly as complex was a chase through the cabin interior, in which that pesky Force was back on Ash's tail, and harder to shake off. "That was another shot Sam designed," Deming explains. "The exterior portion outside the cabin was actually shot by Eugene and there was a hidden cut inside, where the front door bursts open. They did that and then the pull-out from the cabin on location, and we did the rest on the sound stage. So our shot started with the door bursting open and we followed Bruce into the bathroom and behind the wall, and as you look down at the floor at the start of the pull-out, I think there's either a quick cut or dissolve, so it's actually three shots.

"There was barely enough room for one person," Deming remembers of the fast-moving chase through the house's infrastructure, "and you're holding a camera out in front of you, not even looking through it. You're just kind of hoping you get the action. We did it a bunch of times just to make sure — I couldn't tell you exactly how many, but probably four or five times.

One of the most famous shots engineered by Deming involves the flying eyeball ingested by the unsuspecting Bobbie Jo. "The tricky shot was the one Sam wanted of tracking the eyeball," he explains. "Obviously, these were the days before wire removals and digital fixes, so I had an idea to use depth-of-field in our favor. I think we shot it with an 85mm or 100mm wide open, and Vern Hyde, who was our mechanical effects guy, made a rig out of wire that went way out from the camera and then back. They mounted the eyeball on it. There's actually wire in the background holding it, but it is so out-of-focus that it diffuses into not being seen."

And what did Deming think about masterminding such unusual shots. "It's good fun, basically. It's something that they hadn't figured out, and they mentioned it to me early on and asked if I had any ideas. A lot of that stuff was shot in reverse, like the eyeball going into the mouth, which usually involved acting it forward, breaking it down, and trying to act in reverse. Bruce was the best at that."

Shooting continued in Wadesboro and near Cheraw, South Carolina, into the hot summer months as temperatures topped out at over a hundred degrees. Cabin interiors were created in the J.R. Faison Junior High School gymnasium, a locale offering the cast a respite from sun-drenched days. But for Campbell especially, it was no vacation.

A scene in the cabin's kitchen required the actor to flip over and assault himself with dinner plates and other crockery as part of the "evil hand" sequence. Unlike other tricky shots, Campbell's intense performance showcased no gimmicks — it was just his own physicality on display. "A lot of that is Bruce, because he's really good at that stuff," Deming explains. "I think we may have undercranked a bit. It was maybe twenty-one or twenty-two frames a second; we rarely shot twenty-four frames a second on this movie — so really much of it is him, the illusion of his hand dragging him along the floor. Unfortunately, we put Bruce through the paces many times [testing different crank rates]. I know he did the scene where he broke the plates over his head a few times."

For Campbell, the action was welcome, if painful, as he explained to *Fangoria*'s Will Murray:

> I think it's great, I really do. Because you never have to do all this stuff continuously. You just might have a hard day every so often, where you have to do five things over and over and over. To me, I'd much rather have that than sitting around waiting for one shot during the course of the day ... I'd almost rather be injured than idle.[5]

After a long shoot in Carolina, the crew returned to Detroit for additional shots and post-production work. Deming remembers that the shoot was well-organized and progressed in smooth fashion. "No one was paid very much; they were just into it," he considers. "They shot for two weeks and I think I was there for thirteen weeks, so that's a pretty long schedule for a low-budget film."

The film also ran *over* schedule, missing the August completion date. Consequently, Tim Philo was recruited for a quick assist at September's end. "On the last day of shooting in North Carolina, I came in and shot," he explains. Specifically, he worked on the shot of the evil Force pursuing Ash's car, which then hits a tree and ejects poor Ash. Incredibly, the Force then swoops in *through* the Delta 88's rear window, smashes through the windshield, and continues the assault.

"It was an amazing set-up," Philo relates. "They'd been through it once before and not had success with it. It was done with a narrow camera at the end of a rig on a Western dolly, going behind the car, running down a ramp toward the thing." In Raimi lingo, this device became known as the Ram-O-Cam.

From there, Philo oversaw a series of quick set-ups in Detroit. "We had a warehouse studio outside of Detroit; two cameras, three sets, and no waiting," he explains. On one set, the lighting crew toiled. On the next, the camera was ready for action. And on the third, the special effects camera was stationed. "They had really professional production people working on it, and the set people were very good. The assistant director and production manager were great guys out of New York who knew how to coordinate a set. We were amazingly productive during that time, doing all specialty shots. We shot the scene where Linda is attacking Bruce with a chainsaw, and shot that blood flood scene with the hole in the wall that suddenly douses Bruce."

Philo explains how that memorable and wet sequence was accomplished. "It was crazy. The whole set was built on its side. Naturally the camera was on its side too, so it looked like Bruce was standing upright. He had a board going up his back and had to act as though he was pointing his gun at this thing and listening. And then, basically, a fifty-gallon drum of water colored to be blood was released on him all at once."

"That wasn't the sort of thing you could run a test for," considers Philo. "Basically we said 'Roll camera,' and we didn't know what this was going to do to his spinal column, to have fifty gallons suddenly hit him like a ton of bricks, but Bruce is a tough guy."

Other shots completed in Detroit included the vine attack scene, as well as some "inside-to-outside night attack stuff going through windows and breaking windows," according to Philo. "We did night stuff outside, because beyond the warehouse was a little patch of woods. And we also did some driving shots near the opening of the film that were done in a park in downtown Detroit."

Meanwhile, Sullivan and a small effects crew forged the film's memorable visuals. "Larry [Larson], Brian [Rae] and I set up shop at a studio with a blue screen for our composite shots," Sullivan remembers. One of their efforts included a planned scene involving a battle between medieval man and demon. "Larry had done a great job lighting the Deadite for the blue screen, but the battle sequence with the knights on horseback had been cut."

This left Sullivan to design and create the opening visuals, the explanation of the Book of the Dead's history. "The first Book you see is a stop-motion Book of the Dead with wooden covers hinged with a ball-and-socket joint, and the pages were glued over aluminum wire to facilitate animation," he details.

"The shot of the book being created represents four hours going by as I stood in front of the blue screen Larry Larson expertly lit, and I drew the book pages one frame at a time. As the pages turned faster and faster, I pasted pre-colored pictures onto the pages to accelerate the magic," Sullivan says.

"As the book falls into a rigid position, it was replaced by another stop-motion book that was hollow in the back and filled with stop-motion armatures supporting sections of a skull face," reveals Sullivan. "The brows and jaws could be animated separately under a highly flexible Smooth-On skin cast from the Book of the Dead. The stop-motion undulation was a cool effect, and as the Book's mouth opens, the camera pushes into the vortex."

The time vortex which pulled Ash back to AD 1300 was a spinning painting some four feet in diameter. "I had painted two vortexes," Sullivan describes, "and Larry and I photographed them rotating at different rates to be superimposed later, but it didn't happen." Also in this scene, strange apparitions traveled the swirling gateway. "The ghosts were sculpted in Super Sculpey over aluminum wire and painted with acrylics. Larry animated the camera pushing past the ghosts into the black background. Superimposed in the lab later, the ghost appeared to rush at and past the viewer."

Back on set, Deming also worked on the climactic vortex sequence, which saw Ash yanked from the safety of the cabin into a whirlpool of light and energy. "Bruce being pulled through time was blue screen, which was the standard at that time. Green screen wasn't really around yet. We put Bruce in a harness and spun him around and blew stuff on him," Deming recalls. "And then we'd shoot the elements, you know — the stove and different props from the house — and it was a combination of moving them away from the camera, the camera moving backward, and zooming out to create the illusion of [the props] flying away into the distance."

DANCE OF THE DEAD

Many animators contributed to *Evil Dead 2*, including Tom Sullivan and Rick Catizone, who animated Bruce Campbell's rebellious hand in some sequences. Also on board was Doug Beswick, an artist who had lent his expertise to a variety of notable productions, from Art Clokey's religious TV drama *Davey and Goliath* to the original *Star Wars*, for which he created Greedo's mechanical ears/antennae and lips. Beswick had also completed an assignment on *The Empire Strikes Back* at Industrial Light & Magic (ILM), developing armatures for the Hoth-dwelling Tauntauns, and is famous for animating the Freddy skeleton battle with actor Craig Wasson in 1987's A *Nightmare on Elm Street 3: Dream Warriors*.

In 1986, Beswick was in Los Angeles when he got the call to assist on *Evil Dead 2*, including one scene involving the headless Linda's dance through the woods. After renting the original *Evil Dead* on VHS, Beswick began telephone discussions with Raimi and Tapert about the shape of the sequence. Beswick was sent storyboards that he recalls as being "stick-figured drawings of the dance that they wanted to do."

From that concept, Beswick hired a choreographer to design the dance. "I believe there was some reference footage they may have sent to show me some elements of the set and things like that. But the actual dance that was in the finished film was created by choreographer, Tam G. Warner. We sat down with the choreographer and a dancer named Snowy Winters, and they rehearsed. We came up with a dance that seemed pretty cool for this character, so we set aside a time to film this dance. We filmed it in 35mm film with a background of a grid pattern."

Jim Aupperle served as the director of photography on the dance, and

Beswick remembers that the sequence was photographed from various angles. "We shot it as a master and a medium, and as a close-up and an extreme close-up. We only had one camera, so we had to film the dance over and over again. We sent this footage to Sam Raimi and Rob Tapert, who were back East, and they cut a sequence together.

"The editor on the show was Kaye Davis. She was heavily involved in helping us with what we needed to get this dance sequence done, because we were out in California and they were in North Carolina, where they shot the house," Beswick explains. "They sent me a 35mm cut that had all the surrounding live-action with Bruce Campbell, so it was actually the whole sequence from the movie, less the animation."

With the dance choreographed and live-action components understood, Beswick and his team built a small "Linda" figure based on a full-sized piece Mark Shostrom had constructed featuring her upper torso, arms and head. Seeking to match the live-action piece, Beswick and Yancy Calzada designed an armature, and Steve Wang sculpted the character, a miniature representation of the Deadite Linda about twelve inches high—with a detachable head.

"It was a pretty simple, straight-forward armature, nothing fancy except for the toes," Beswick explains. "She had toe joints so she could get up on her toes for the dance moves." Also critical was matching the background miniature with live-action footage. "I hired Jim Belohobek to build a miniature set that matched the [live-action] cabin exterior. We built it in forced perspective because the house was really just a backdrop. She [Linda] didn't really dance up to the house—it was in the distance. We built miniature trees and it was a full tabletop miniature set. There was no rear projection, nothing fancy, just animating on a table."

The table measured eight feet square, and it was this background diorama which Beswick used for the close-up of Linda's buried hand as it popped unexpectedly out of the grave. The hand was actually full-sized, and a forced perspective was deployed to heighten the reality of the scene. Specifically, a larger scale foreground component, with items like coal and dirt, was blended in one shot with the miniature background diorama (featuring the cabin), to provide the audience the feeling of depth.

With the Linda model and cabin grounds ready in miniature, animation commenced, and it was a slow process that continued for more than a month.

"It went pretty slow," remembers Beswick. "I had a moviola next to me when I was animating, and I would use that as reference to the timing of the dance. When we did the dance, we actually did it to what we call a *click track*—it gave you the beat; so that when the composer wrote the score, at least it would have the same beat."

Despite the laborious nature of animation, the process took less time than it might have, because Beswick didn't need to coordinate the sequence with any background projection, as Ray Harryhausen might have been forced to do.

"I had reference footage, but the animation was still a bit looser and free form. I was pretty much just trying to hit key poses, rather than match frame-by-frame."

What isn't immediately obvious to a neophyte is how—in a labor-intensive process, and working in such a small scale—the models aren't accidentally nudged or maneuvered out of their intended positions.

"We used what we call surface gauges, a machinist's tool, as pointers," Beswick explains. "They are used as a gauge of where you are in space with your [miniature] character. The typical way of using them is to have one on top of a head, and maybe one or two somewhere else on the body, so when you're advancing your character forward, you can see how far you moved it. Without those, you'd get lost and you wouldn't know where you were, especially if you had to back-up. The awful thing that does happen sometimes to an animator is he'll bump into his own surface gauge, or it'll move or tip over, and then you're totally lost."

The stop-motion dance sequence's most inspired two-step involved a funny move: Linda rolled her own severed head down her arm like an old-fashioned movie star rolling his top hat down his sleeve. It was a touch noticed and appreciated by Roger Ebert during his review on the TV program *At the Movies*. "We were having a blast, we really were," Beswick notes. "We knew this was going to be a really fun film. The first one was very serious and this was sort of remaking the same film with a different spin. Just as a note: the actual idea of the Fred Astaire hat move, if I'm not mistaken, was the choreographer's. It was something she came up with while we were rehearsing, and I thought that was so cool."

Linda's dance was not the only special effects moment orchestrated by Beswick and his crew. "We did the big tree limb that comes through the door" like King Kong's hand, and also "the giant Applehead character that's in the doorway," Beswick notes, referring to the demon-made-flesh that grabs Ash in the finale, a character named after a Three Stooges insult frequently uttered by Moe, along with the synonym, "Applebrain." "They were both full-size mechanical creations. They were huge. We built this huge mechanical tree limb that was sixteen feet long.

"We had a separate crew working on those props. Tony Gardner was heading up the Applehead crew and he used face casts of the actors to get the heads that are grown into it and the one that pops out. The [Applehead] eye was a big casting that they put some gelatin and other materials behind. And the tree limb was actually a big mechanical hand, built aluminum framed, aluminum hinged, and cableized—built by Phil Notaro at our shop. It was fabricated by Teresa Burkett and Mark Wilson. The actual bark was no more than mattress foam, cut, sliced, glued and painted to look like a tree. I remember they went out one day and took reference photos of various types of tree surfaces to get the right look. They hired a van to ship all those back East and our make-up crew went with them to operate everything."

Beswick loved working on the film, though he didn't meet Raimi until the film was finished, "but we talked on the phone and got feedback as the shots came in," Beswick explains. "He was very easy to work for. He had great ideas and it was a great experience."

Regarding *Evil Dead 2*'s other notable effects, Tom Sullivan designed, built and animated the Flying Deadite seen in the climax, as well as Henrietta's "pop-up" head shot and Ash's hand suddenly turning bad.

"The white streaking of Ash's hair was mine, as was the wilting flower," Sullivan recalls. "I built the Flying Deadite dummy for the finale head explosion Sam shot. For some reason, he included the cord [used] for flapping the wings. I wince every time I see it. I was wrapped up in plastic manipulating the Deadite's arms, so I never saw his framing."

THE RETURN OF JOE LODUCA

After scoring *The Evil Dead*, portions of *Crimewave* and the Josh Becker action-horror movie *Thou Shall Not Kill... Except* in which Raimi portrayed a villain inspired by Charles Manson, Joe LoDuca returned to score *Evil Dead 2*. This time out, however, LoDuca found that he faced a different challenge. The new film was not cut-and-dry horror, but a melding of tones from the overtly emotional to the humorous, to adrenaline-inducing.

"Sam had asked me early on to be involved with it," LoDuca notes of the project, "and it was a pretty quick turnaround, three and a half weeks or something."

One of the most memorable moments in the score involved the piano piece played by Ash and repeated during his emotional breakdown over Linda. "I tended to go operatic with it," LoDuca explains. "It didn't have to be what it was, that Ash all of the sudden is a brilliant classical pianist, but in some ways it was, once again, that combination of opera, horror and the Three Stooges."

The choice of composition works nicely there, heightening Ash's humanity, a necessity since throughout the film he would battle not to lose it to a demonic host. "The music is grand opera at that point," LoDuca considers. "I've often felt that with a lot of the work I've done for Sam and Rob, there's no such thing as going over-the-top. The idea is that the emotions

OP: Sam Raimi (kneeling) gets
eady to shoot more carnage in
e Tennessee cabin for The Evil
Dead on December 18, 1979.
Photo courtesy and copyright,
Tom Sullivan.

BOTTOM: Breaking up is hard
do: Bruce Campbell takes aim
at Betsy Baker's Linda in The
Evil Dead. Photo courtesy and
copyright, Tom Sullivan.

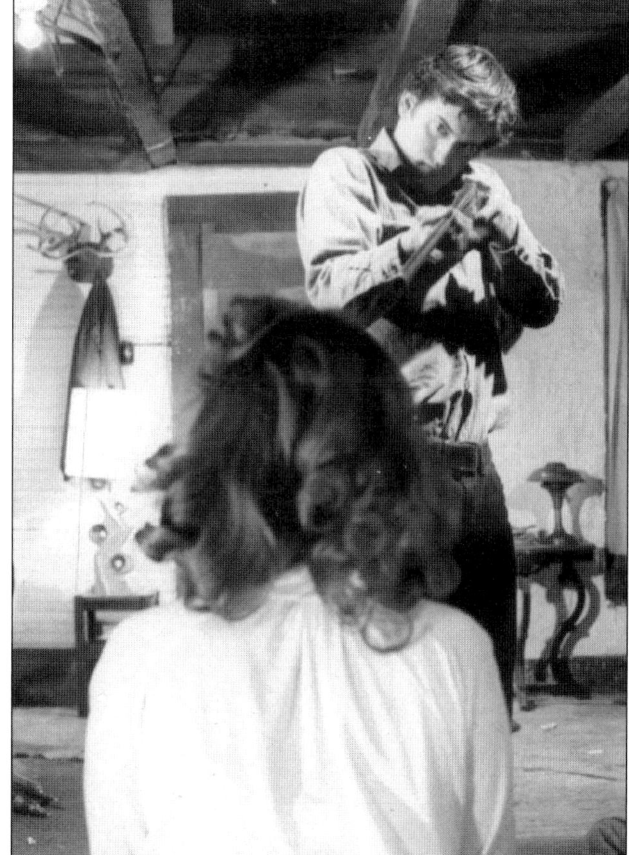

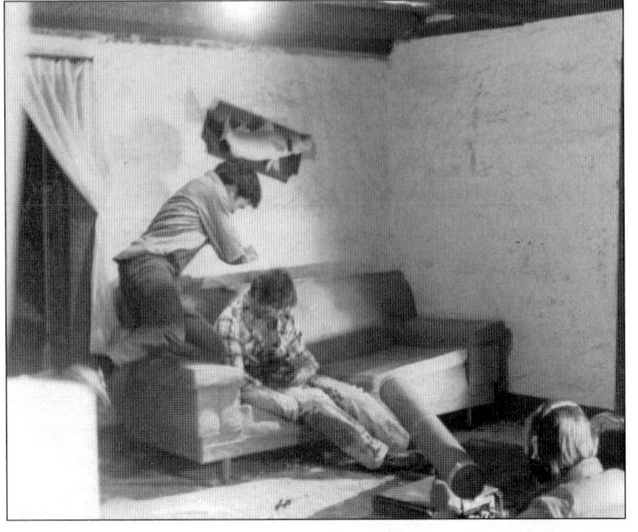

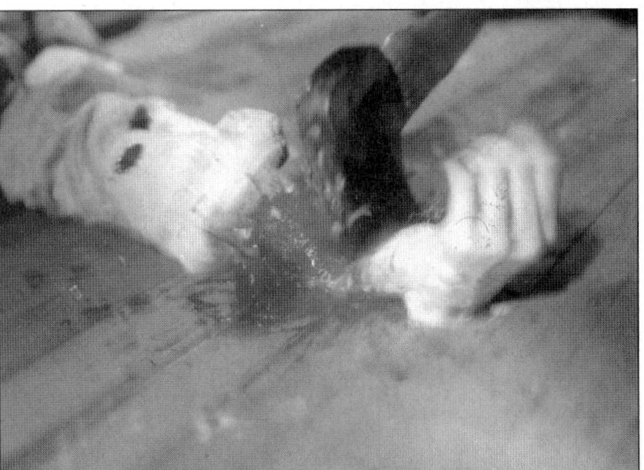

Top: Ash (Bruce Campbell) and Scotty (Hal Delrich), looking worse for wear, in the cabin of the damned for The Evil Dead. Photo courtesy and copyright, Tom Sullivan.

Middle: He's got an axe to grind. A close-up of an amazing special effects dismemberment for Evil Dead. Photo courtesy and copyright, Tom Sullivan.

Bottom: Director in the mist: That's Sam Raimi behind the wisps of smoke on the set of Evil Dead. Photo courtesy and copyright, Tom Sullivan.

Top: A view of Linda's burial site, crucifix and all from The Evil Dead. Photo courtesy and copyright, Tom Sullivan.

Middle: A view of Linda's burial ite by night, prepped and ready for shooting for The Evil Dead. Photo courtesy and copyright, Tom Sullivan.

Bottom: Tom Sullivan preps a severed head for an Evil Dead ffects shot. Photo courtesy and copyright, Tom Sullivan.

Top: Make-up artist Tom Sulliv surrounded by some terrifying props and figures for Evil Dea Photo courtesy and copyright, Tom Sullivan.

Bottom, left: Sullivan applie make-up scars and wounds to actress Betsy Baker for Evil De Photo courtesy and copyright, Tom Sullivan.

Bottom, right: Proud Papa: Tom Sullivan shows two speci effects creations for The Evil Dead, a decapitated head (left and Linda's ankle, replete with stabbing pencil! Photo courtes and copyright, Tom Sullivan.

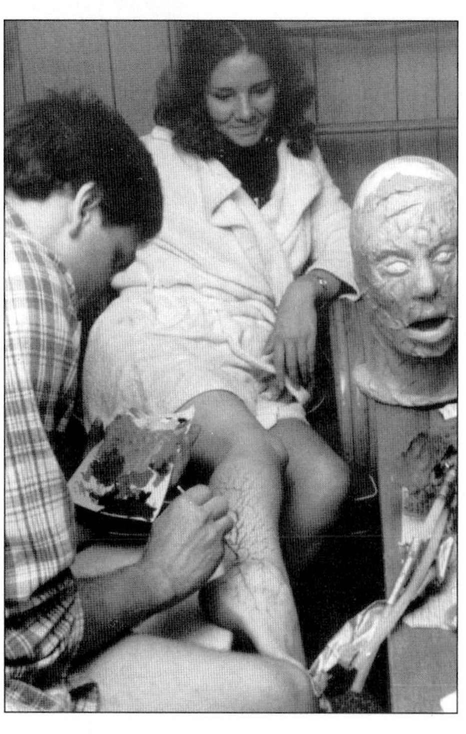

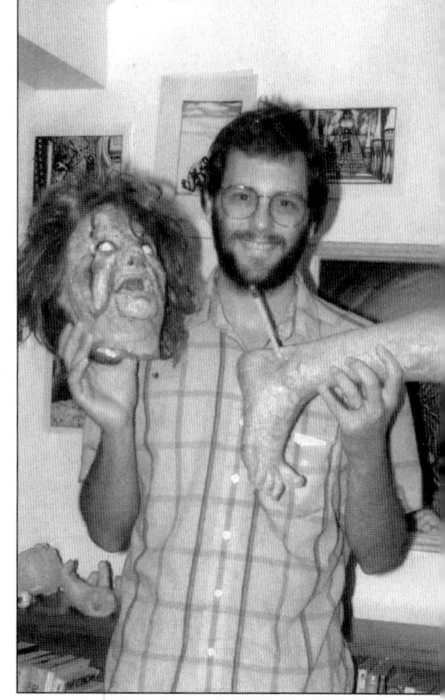

TOP: "Groovy..." A close-up of Campbell with shotgun at the ready from The Evil Dead. Photo courtesy and copyright, Tom Sullivan.

MIDDLE: Who's laughing now? Bruce Campbell's stunt double sits with the real McCoy inside e cabin interior in Evil Dead 2. Photo courtesy and copyright, Tom Sullivan.

BOTTOM: A view of the cabin interior reconstructed for Evil Dead 2. Photo courtesy and copyright, Tom Sullivan.

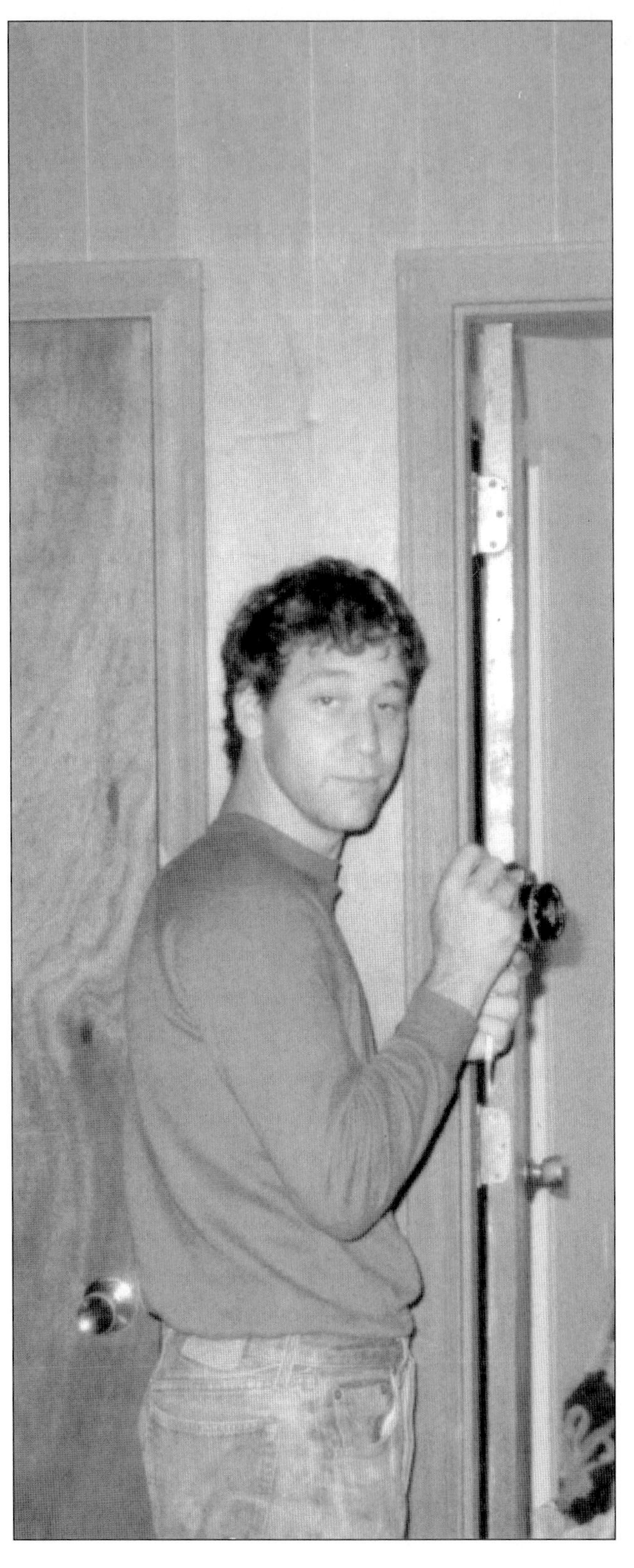

A candid shot of director Sam Raimi, circa 1986. Photo cour and copyright, Tom Sullivan.

TOP: Rob Tapert relaxes on the set of Evil Dead 2. Photo courtesy and copyright, Tom Sullivan.

MIDDLE: Inside the Faison School gym, Wadesboro, North Carolina, where the cabin interior was recreated. From Evil Dead 2. Photo courtesy and copyright, Tom Sullivan.

BOTTOM: A hero has fallen from the skies. Shooting the last scene of Evil Dead 2. Photo courtesy and copyright, Tom Sullivan.

Top: Sam Raimi, in old-age make-up, introd
Evil Dead 2: The Talent Show. Photo cou
and copyright, Tom Sull

Bottom: The villainous Applehead gets read
his close-up as the demon appears in the
for the first time during the finale of Evil De
Photo courtesy and copyright, Tom Sull

are so grand that they verge on opera. That's the point of view the music is taking, and everybody seems happy with it."

Another important riff, and one that quickens the blood pressure, arrives in the film's first third as Ash stands at the destroyed bridge only to realize that a demon is approaching. As Ash runs to the car, camera tracking at crazy speeds, the film borders on fast-motion insanity and the music heightens that effect. "I was trying to do something as urgent and dynamic as I could possibly come up, and the Delta 88 becomes the death coaster," LoDuca laughs. "The other levels in that score: there are some very creepy things in the mirror that take place. And there are those big bombastic action sequences, and finally in the last act, it turns operatic because you've opened the gates of hell."

LoDuca had written the ambitious score for *Evil Dead* and this time he didn't worry so much about technicalities. "At that point, the technical aspect was easily resolvable. By the time of my second film, *Thou Shall Not Kill ... Except*, there had been a little black box invented that enabled you to synchronize to a videotape, and give you a tempo match. At that point, it became a lot more organic in terms of how to write the picture."

COMING SOON – UNRATED – TO A THEATER NEAR YOU

Evil Dead 2 finished production slightly under budget. The real problem emerged when it came time for distribution. Though its tone was satirical, the film was fairly graphic in imagery. One scene saw Campbell cut his own hand off with a chainsaw, deep red blood splattering his face in close-up as he screamed. Other sequences were bloody, though the blood was green or black, so it was difficult to see why such moments would face objection from the MPAA.

Rather than get slapped with an X by the MPAA, DEG avoided the controversy altogether by not going to the ratings board at all. Like its predecessor, *Evil Dead 2* went out unrated.

But there were some interesting behind-the-scenes maneuvering too. Despite the fact that DEG footed the bill for the film's advertising and marketing, the film was technically released by Rosebud Releasing Corp. William Paul, author of *Laughing Screaming: Modern Hollywood Horror and Comedy*, explains what happened: Rather than "release *The Evil Dead Part II*, a certain X, DEG, the producing/releasing company, farmed it out to an independent releasing company to avoid having it rated at all."[6] Why bother? Well, DEG was a signatory of the MPAA, an agreement which meant it could not legally release an unrated movie. Thus the film was returned to the producers,[7] in this case, Alex De Benedetti, and released through Rosebud, which some insisted was not really independent at all, but actually just a shell corporation for DEG through which it could release this specific film and recoup its costs. After all, how could the unknown Rosebud company get a movie into more than three hundred American theaters without the muscle of De Laurentiis Entertainment Group?

When asked that very question, and about how much DEG would actually share in *Evil Dead 2*'s profits, Lawrence Gleason, president of marketing and distribution for DEG, and De Benedetti both appeared evasive. "That is a personal question. I am a private company and I don't have go into that kind of detail," De Benedetti told reporter Jack Mathews from his Beverly Hills office.[8]

In its unexpurgated form, *Evil Dead 2* launched its bid for box office supremacy on *Friday the 13th* of March 1987. It opened in the summer of Sylvester Stallone's *Cobra*, Richard Donner's *Lethal Weapon*, which also featured Three Stooges references, and New Line's *A Nightmare on Elm Street 3: Dream Warriors*. As was the case with the original, critics were mostly kind. In fact, many detected exactly what Raimi intended, a satirical sense of fun. Caryn James of the *New York Times* called the film "one of the goofiest, goriest movies this side of the grave."[9]

Newsday's Bill Kaufman noted that "independent filmmaker Sam Raimi knows the cliches of his genre well and he's incorporated virtually every one of them into this movie."[10] Writing for the *Time Out Film Guide*, Nigel Floyd noted that the film was "self parodic" and "delirious, demented and diabolically funny."[11] Writing for the *Chicago Sun Times*, Roger Ebert awarded the film three stars.

Despite accolades, *Evil Dead 2* fared poorly at the box office, proving more popular on the home video market and overseas such as in Italy and Japan. In the end, the film grossed less than six million dollars in theaters. However, this time Hollywood was finally ready to take notice of Raimi, Tapert and their inventive filmmaking style. As *Evil Dead 2* grew to become a legend on home video, Raimi tentatively took his first steps toward Hollywood's mainstream.

RAIMI RAP

FOR THE LOVE OF BRUCE: *Evil Dead 2* bears witness to the ascension of horror-action hero Ash and actor Bruce Campbell as a cult star. His performance reveals his versatility. "It's possible that [directors] thought he'd only be right for a horror film, but he's a very talented comedian,"[12] Raimi noted in *Entertainment Weekly*, an opinion supported by the people who worked on this sequel, including Tim Philo. "Bruce is in the line of great physical actors. The more physical the stuff is, the more he can go to town. I think of an American acting type — a physical actor; a guy who can do things with his body, subtle to broad things, like Tom Cruise. Bruce is like that. He does things on screen that are just great."

"It wouldn't have turned out as well without Bruce," Peter Deming adds. "They [Sam and Bruce] would refer to things — Three Stooges things; and he would just do it; he got it."

BROTHERLY LOVE: Raimi's brother Ted appears in *Evil Dead 2* as the possessed Henrietta, an oversized, lecherous demon. As Deming recalls, Sam Raimi didn't necessarily do his brother a favor giving him that part. It took four and a half hours to get into the suit and makeup, which included dentures and contact lenses. "When he was done, he'd take the suit off and they'd have to wring it out. He was so exhausted and dehydrated from sweating in that, and it was the kind of stuff that we did everyday for three months."

PANTS PROPHECY: There's an interesting discontinuity in *Evil Dead 2* regarding the prophecy of the hero who falls from the sky to rescue the past from the horrors of the dead. "The Lost Pages were all hand-drawn by me, including the Prophecy Page," Tom Sullivan explains. "I had asked Rob for a picture of Ash in costume and in the heroic pose Sam wanted. The polaroid had Bruce in tattered and torn *white* pants raising his chainsaw. Sam had me do a couple of versions. Later, of course, it turns out Ash has on *black* pants. Oh well. In my prophecy, the hero wears white."

THE FOG: One of Doug Beswick's greatest challenges in animating the headless Linda dance involved the atmosphere, literally. A mist had to accompany the miniature's moves — but how do you animate fog a frame at a time? "I hired another vendor to do some smoke that was match-moved into a scene," Beswick explains. "David Stipes Productions set up a motion-control system that they could program in by stop-motion moves. So you would take the footage, and by eye, match when my camera would pan as Linda did her little moves. Their stage camera would attempt to match that. It was tough, because some of my animation pans were very quick, so they had a bit of a problem with their motion control keeping up, but they managed to get some elements there which were later composited over the animation. That was really the only high-tech piece of those shots that the smoke, like a ground fog or some aerial haze, was motion tracked by a motion-control camera, and later composited in the shots."

CAMEOS: Tom Sullivan notes that many behind-the-scenes people and crew families actually made it on screen in *Evil Dead 2*. "Sam put Penny and I in a cameo in the airport scene. Penny is getting off the jet in her rust-colored turtleneck with a white strapped bag on her shoulder. I'm in about twelve frames in the background, loading luggage in the taxi. Rob Tapert, Dave Goodman, and I all wore the same shirt and cap to play our cameos as luggage handlers."

LEGACY: *Evil Dead 2* has joined its predecessor as a popular cult item, beloved by viewers and the movie industry, and even imitated in new films (such as 1999's *Idle Hands*). In Doug Beswick's house, the film remains a favorite. "I've seen it so many times. My kids loved it as they were growing up. They had it on laserdisc and they'd pop it in all the time. I just think it's so wild and unlike anything else that had been done at that time. It's a lot of fun to watch. Sam's direction and camera work — it was all breaking new ground."

"I was surprised," notes Peter Deming, "the first time I realized, which was probably in the early nineties, that they were using it in a cinema class at NYU. I thought that was pretty cool."

GROOVY...

Conventional movie wisdom advises that Francis Ford Coppola's *Godfather Part II* (1974) is Hollywood's finest sequel, a follow-up that equals the qualities of its predecessor and confidently stakes out its own identity narratively and visually. Yet movie buffs who get a kick out of severed limbs and blood baths may tout a different title for that honor, Raimi's *Evil Dead 2*, much because it works on those very terms. Sequence after ridiculous sequence goes for broke with visual and verbal puns, and there are a plethora of film history allusions and gags in the package too. The unpredictability factor Raimi's direction brought to the original, nightmarish *Evil Dead* is no less potent the second time around, but Raimi has tweaked the material, pacing the film not to frighten or repulse, but to generate laughs. In many situations, this simply means holding on a shot for an extra few seconds, yet it's a textbook case of how screams and laughter, responses existing on opposite poles of human emotions, can effectively be shepherded in a unified whole.

Noted film critic Roger Ebert described the film in this way:

> *Evil Dead 2: Dead by Dawn* is a comedy disguised as a blood-soaked shock-a-rama. It looks superficially like a routine horror movie, a vomitorium designed to separate callow teenagers from their lunch. But look a little closer and you'll realize that the movie is a fairly sophisticated satire. Level One viewers will say it's in bad taste. Level Two folks like myself will perceive that it is about bad taste.[13]

Peter Deming, Raimi's cinematographer, considers *Evil Dead 2* a "perfect representation of part of Sam's personality," in part because "it's a straight ahead horror film combined with the Three Stooges. Some of his early super 8s were total Three Stooges films — *The Nutty Nut* and things like that. And to be able, I think, to combine essentially two contrary genres is an amazing feat."

In *Evil Dead 2*, the blood flood behind the walls (and in Ash's face...) not only evokes memories of *Evil Dead*, where wall sockets and overhead pipes filled with blood, but represents a variation on *A Plumbing We Will Go* (1940), wherein Larry, Moe and Curly made a wet mess of a fancy home. It is not a flooded TV (dramatizing footage of a waterfall) that here redefines the idea of cinematic "wet work," but rather the torrent of fluids that eject from the wall and douse the hapless Ash.

Similarly, this sequel finds Ash waging constant war with his own hand, as if he is Larry, Moe and Curly all in one body, the physical abuse endured by all three shared among one man's mutinous body parts. This notion of Campbell doing Stooge schtick would re-assert itself more fully in the sequel, *Army of Darkness*, where Stooge-style sound effects play on the soundtrack and skeletal hands pop out of the ground and poke the actor's eyes and punch his nose. Still, *Evil Dead 2* reveals some pretty fine Stoogian form, which is funny because none of it seems out of place. When Ash's hand hides in a mouse hole and gets caught in a trap, the moment recalls 1941's Stooge entry, *Ants in the Pantry*, also involving pests like mice.

Beyond the Three Stooges riffs, movie allusions fly through *Evil Dead 2* fast and furious. There's a quick nod to Fred Astaire movies in the severed head roll during Linda's dance. There's evidence of old-fashioned horror pathos — the kind you'd find in a *Frankenstein* or *Wolfman* flick of the 1940s — in Ash's lost, dormant humanity once he is possessed. As he clutches Linda's necklace and cries heavenward, despairing the loss of his own humanity, he could be the Hunchback, the Frankenstein Monster, or any beast who has lost his beauty.

Some allusions are literally throwaways. When Ash's mutinous severed hand hides in a mouse hole, the audience instantly thinks of Tom and Jerry, but with Campbell as predator and the hand as all too clever prey. The trippy scenes of Ash alone in the cabin, surrounded by ambulatory lamps and furniture remind one of a demented *Pee Wee's Playhouse*, and Ash's debate about sanity with his mirrored reflection recalls Robert DeNiro's famous "Are you talking to me?" moment from Martin Scorsese's *Taxi Driver*. At one point, dialogue even references the Coen brothers when Jake comments about Ash having gone "blood simple."

Strange literary illusions also find their way into the movie. There's a touch of Twain's *A Connecticut Yankee in King Arthur's Court* and H.G. Wells' *The Time Machine* in Ash's arrival in another time period. He's a man from the future with gunpowder (like the former) and taking sides in a war between primitive man and monsters (like the latter). Far sillier is the off-the-wall reference to Ernest Hemingway. The author's *A Farewell to Arms* weighs down the garbage can imprisoning Ash's possessed hand, a totally irreverent, unnecessary, and brilliant joke stating the obvious; that Ash has said au revoir to a hand, if not actually his arms.

Unlike *Crimewave*, which required a knowledge of the source material, *Evil Dead 2* doesn't force its allusions down anybody's throat. One need know nothing of other productions to enjoy the flick as a horror ride, though a familiarity with film history makes any viewing of *Evil Dead 2* a full-blooded riot.

Campbell's bravura performance also makes the sequel enjoyable. Name another actor in Hollywood who could so successfully act unconscious at the same time as his hand drags him across the floor? Campbell's timing and overall physicality is remarkable, proving he's an adept stuntman as well as traditional film actor. Much of the enjoyment this time around arises from the fact that Campbell is on his own and is therefore center stage much of the time. He seems to be imbued with a new sense of confidence, but perhaps it is merely that the physical exertion of the role has freed him up to be himself. Maybe he didn't have the energy to overthink or nuance the part, and what comes out is pure instinct. Whatever the cause of his freedom and daring in this sequel, his performance glues the pieces together. He is ironically deadpan when the plot requires him to be dumb and forget the events of the original film (noting flatly, "So what is this place like?" as he sees the damned cabin for the first time). Oppositely, he verges gleefully on the edge of sanity in more intense scenes, such as his maniacal and self-destructive taunt to his own hand: "That's right! Who's laughing now!?"

If Campbell has flowered in the role of the dim-witted Ash, *Evil Dead 2* succeeds because Raimi matches him at every turn with humor embedded in the very camera work. Remember the brilliant final shot of *The Evil Dead*? The Force POV barreled down on hapless Ash and the film went black. When this sequel picks up that shot, it goes further. The camera zooms into Ash's face, lifts him off the ground, accelerates him through the air for miles, and spins him around. And how does the scene end? With a joke, naturally. Ash is dumped face first into a puddle, a horror movie pratfall. It's ridiculous, but timed to feel hilarious.

Later, the sun's rays save Ash after he has been possessed. He sits in the woods in silence, and slowly, calmly, Raimi's camera pans, looking for signs of evil in the woods. The pan continues and continues and continues, the audience fearful to see what it sees. But it's a joke — the camera eventually pans so far that it has gone in a circle and lands right back where it began, focusing on clueless Ash. Again, Raimi employs a certain shot, one meant to convey information, to generate a laugh. The audience expects the pan to be of a revelatory nature, but it reveals nothing to us, or to Ash, and that makes us laugh.

Another horror sequence becomes funny when Ash gives evil the slip. Ash runs inside the cabin, with the evil Force booming and chasing behind him. He flees from room to room and into the very infrastructure of the cabin, twisting and turning down long corridors, like Theseus escaping the Minotaur in the labyrinth. Then Ash hides and the stymied Force backs up out of the house as though those twisted corners never existed. Even evil forces, it seems, get confused and need directions. As with the long outdoor pan, the set-up is pure horror: a hand-held first-person subjective shot bearing down on a lone, terrified victim, but the end result is a joke. The force has lost track of its quarry. Who would have expected that?

The film's special effects also play up humor. Deadite victims fly through the air like Superman, screaming bloody murder and bonking their heads right into trees, light bulbs or walls. Another funny scene occurs following the humorous Astaire dance tribute, when Linda's decapitated head lands in Ash's lap. Just when it looks like the film might make a Lorena Bobbitt joke six years before that event occurred, it does something even funnier: dramatizing Linda's ambulatory noggin biting right down on Ash's palm. The bloody thing won't let go, which means Ash must bash the severed head into chairs, walls, doors, even the camera, to release its grip. This is made doubly ridiculous by the fact that this is his beloved's *skull* he is smashing into everything. Happy Valentine's Day, Honey!

The finest moment in *Evil Dead 2* involves the flying eyeball. Raimi's approach is again to foster surprise and shock. Ash stomps on Henrietta, her eyeball pops out and takes a flight across the room, where, naturally, it is swallowed by a screaming damsel! Utterly ridiculous, but revelatory of Raimi's willingness to crank up the horror imagery by using standard shots of the genre and then twisting them for comedic effect.

In a run-of-the-mill horror movie, an eyeball popping from its socket would be more than enough to please hardcore fans, but Raimi wants more than that, and who else could have imagined the eyeball landing in somebody's mouth? In including this over-the-top scene, *Evil Dead 2* effectively thumbs "its nose at the values of the country club that runs America, absolutely confident that its inventiveness and nonstop creativity will be appreciated by that target audience it *knows* is out there, and becomes so gory that it's funny,"[14] comments author J.P. Telotte.

But Ebert was right too. In the so-called moral majority, "family values" days of a conservative Reagan regime, *Evil Dead 2* champions bad taste and perhaps the ultimate American freedom: the right to be utterly silly for no other reason than you *can*. Fuck the MPAA.

From little touches, like the legend appearing in the cabin that reads "Home Sweet Home," to the grand fluorishes, like the scene in which Campbell wrestles himself to the ground, *Evil Dead 2* goes for broke. Its final twist, a reach for historical importance, is more than satisfactory. The final revelation that the Deadites exist in this time period because the hero from 1300 "didn't do a very good job" in killing them (Ash's words) works well in defining Ash as an ineffective boob and in granting the film a cyclical feel. Ash has fought the Deadites before and will fight them again, across the vast expanse of human history. For a horror movie about a few people stranded in a cabin in the woods, this is an epic finale, and one that sets up the sequel.

Fans tend to be divided about which *Evil Dead* film is best. The original was a terrifying example of its genre, an act of inspiration and an example of brilliance on a budget. Because of its humor and critic-pleasing reflexive approach, *Evil Dead 2* seems perhaps more indicative of Raimi the artist. His compulsion to entertain is on display in every gonzo sequence, pushing the film ever deeper into surrealism and laughs. It's a sequel that's an equal, in an off-the-wall sort of way.

DARKMAN (1990)

IF YOU'RE NOT GOING TO KILL ME, I HAVE THINGS TO DO.

THEY DESTROYED EVERYTHING HE HAD, EVERYTHING HE WAS.

NOW CRIME HAS A NEW ENEMY, AND JUSTICE HAS A NEW FACE.

CAST AND CREW

Universal Productions and Reinnaisance Pictures present *Darkman*

Director: Sam Raimi
Producer: Robert Tapert
Music Conducted and Composed by: Danny Elfman
Makeup Effects: Tony Gardner and Larry Hamlin
Costume Designer: Grania Prestin
Supervising Editors: Bud and Scott Smith
Production Designer: Randy Ser
Director of Photography: Bill Pope
Line Producer: Daryl Kass
Story: Sam Raimi
Screenplay: Chuck Pfarrer, Sam Raimi, Ivan Raimi, Daniel Goldin, Joshua Goldin
Film Editor: David Stiven
Special Effects: Peter Kuran
Special Visual Effects: Introvision Systems, International, William Mesa
Stunt Coordinator: Chris Doyle

STARRING

Liam Neeson: Peyton Westlake/Darkman
Frances McDormand: Julie Hastings
Colin Friels: Louis Strack Jr.
Larry Drake: Robert G. Durant
Nelson Mashita: Yakatito
Jessie Lawrence Ferguson: Eddie Black
Rafael H. Rablado: Rudy Guzman
Danny Hicks: Skip
Theodore Raimi: Rick
Dan Bell: Smiley
Nicholas Worth: Pauly
Aaron Lustig: Martin Katz
Arsenio "Sonny" Trinidad: Hung Fat
Said Faraj: Convenience Store Clerk
Nathan Jung: Chinese Warrior
Scott Spiegel: Dockworker #5
Bruce Campbell: Final Shemp

Filmed in Los Angeles, California.

A MAN WHO DESTROYS FOR REVENGE

SCIENTIST PEYTON WESTLAKE conducts experiments in creating synthetic flesh for burn victims, but meets with persistent failure, his artificial creations melting in the sunlight after only ninety-nine minutes. But Peyton soon faces bigger problems when his fiancée, attorney Julie Hastings, uncovers a secret memorandum incriminating millionaire construction magnate, Louis Strack Jr. Strack wants the evidence destroyed and sends crime boss Robert Durant and his vile gang to do the job.

Durant kills Westlake's assistant and blows up Westlake's lab, unaware that the scientist, horribly scarred and burned, survives the explosion. At a local hospital, a surgeon severs Westlake's nerve-controlling pain receptors, so he can survive with third-degree burns over 40 percent of his body. But without these nerve impulses, Westlake becomes prone to bouts of adrenaline-powered rage.

Hideously scarred and all alone, Westlake escapes from the hospital and sets out to kill those who stole his life. He reassembles his laboratory in an abandoned warehouse. Using his artificial skin, he mimics Durant and his lackeys, undercutting their crime operation. After a deadly confrontation between Westlake and Durant in the skies of L.A., Westlake sets his sights on Strack, who is now holding Julie hostage.

The final battle is waged on Strack's unfinished skyscraper and Westlake accepts his destiny as a hero called ... *Darkman*.

ORIGINS OF A HERO: A NEW "FACE" IN HOLLYWOOD

Although he'd made professional movies for nearly a decade, Sam Raimi's first bonafide studio production didn't come about until the end of the 1980s. After *Evil Dead 2*, a number of projects were discussed, including a sequel, but one effort gathered steam, in part because it was in synch with a trend that would dominate Hollywood for several years.

That project was *Darkman*, the tale of a grim avenger, a man who lost everything in his life and wanted to make his enemies pay. Originally entitled *The Darkman*, Raimi introduced the character in a short story and then a forty-page treatment.[1] He later described Westlake as a "throwback to the old Universal monsters, like the Wolfman" and a "poor sap who is cursed. His tormenters happen to be criminals, so that makes him a hero."[2]

For a long time prior to *Darkman*, Raimi sought an established superhero or comic book property he could adapt to the silver screen, and investigated acquiring the rights to the mind-clouding protagonist *The Shadow*, another hero with a pronounced dark side. When he failed to secure the rights to either *The Shadow* or *Batman*, Raimi forged ahead with his own creation, adding to his origin myth the singular notion of a man who could create synthetic flesh and mimic the faces of others, including enemies. In keeping with Raimi's knowledge of film history and desire to honor it, this element may have been a throwback to early cinematic antiheroes, notably one that appeared in a Warner Brothers movie called *Doctor X* (1932). That Michael Curtiz film starred Lionel Atwill and Fay Wray and featured an antihero with similar capabilities.[3]

Once Universal committed, developing the forty-page treatment into a workable script proved difficult. Raimi collaborated with brother Ivan, a doctor, to bring the film's medical aspects closer to reality. Then, thirty-three-year-old ex–Navy SEAL Chuck Pfarrer contributed a draft. Pfarrer, whose first produced screenplay was, appropriately, *Navy SEALS*, went on after *Darkman*[4] to work for executive producer Raimi on the screenplay for *Hard Target* in 1993, as well as other films including *Barb Wire* (1996), the remake of *The Jackal* (1997), and *Virus* (1999).

As Raimi and Tapert toiled with the script, awareness grew that they could be establishing the foundation of a superhero franchise. As Tapert reported to *Cinefantastique* on the set of the sequel, *Darkman II: The Return of Durant*: "In our case, Sam and I really want to see Darkman live on as a franchisable character and as an American superhero. In fifty years, Darkman should be on the damn tour at Universal with Frankenstein."[5] But for this to occur, the elements had to come together on the page, which meant another round of rewrites. To facilitate the improvement of the *Darkman* concept, writers Daniel and Joshua Goldin were retained.

"My brother and I had a written a script [*Welcome to Buzzsaw*] that was well-liked at Universal," Daniel Goldin explains, "and *Darkman* had been bouncing around Universal for a period of time before we came in. We'd met Sam Raimi just a few times casually and gotten along well, so everybody figured it would be a good mix."

And what did the *Darkman* script look like prior to their efforts? "It was a big, interesting heap of documents," Goldin explains. "There was a treatment that Sam had written, and then a draft that Chuck Pfarrer wrote. And we read another draft that was a combination of many drafts, that had Sam and Ivan's name on it. And there were lots of little story documents. There was just material everywhere; drafts that seemed to go in many directions."

As Goldin recalls, the brothers had a specific mission: "To turn this interesting mix of ideas into a coherent, emotional drama." Though Goldin stresses that they "did not attempt to take over this project and revamp it. It was just to make it work as well as possible and strengthen it.

"It was actually a very quick, tense process," Goldin says. "I think we did it over a month, a month of non-stop work. It was fun though. We were in a trailer on the back lot of Universal and had adjacent trailers with Sam and Robert Tapert. We had our own little world on the back lot."

Why the rush to polish the screenplay? "I think they wanted us to do another project at Universal, and I'm not sure if at the time *Darkman* was that high a priority. They wanted us to do a movie that we didn't really want to do, but they gave us a choice of two movies. We wanted to do *Darkman* and they wanted us to do *Problem Child*," Goldin reveals. "So we ended up making arrangements to do *Darkman* first, and they gave us a month to do it before we moved on to this not-as-exciting project.

"We spent a lot of time talking and pulling together a way of making the story work," Goldin describes. "I think that mostly we talked in terms of the nuts and bolts of the story, and it wasn't so much in big terms. Sam definitely had in mind a modern-day *Phantom of the Opera*, but mainly there was the notion of this existential hero bent on revenge — which was already there.

"One of the issues was trying to build a certain amount of suspense and interest in the story when it was pretty transparent that Strack was behind it all from the beginning," says Goldin. "At one point, we had Strack working for his father, and his father gets murdered while Strack witnesses it. He lets out a howl of pain and agony, and it isn't until the very end that we learn he actually set up the hit.

"There was also a subway scene that was cut out," Goldin remembers. "I think they didn't have the money to film it. It was a scene with Darkman, where Durant's minions chased him and suddenly they're in pitch darkness and one of them follows him into this tunnel, can't see anything, and then gets killed that way. It was a fairly early scene and was, I think, replaced in the film by the manhole scene."

The point of the Goldins' efforts, Daniel suggests, was to flesh out the *emotional* context of the film's hero. "He didn't just lose his life, the way he did in many other drafts, but was trying to regain the woman he loved, and it was hopeless in the end, and that's the story of how he became the man he is."

Equally important was making a brand new hero work for the big screen. "I remember that we talked about this a lot while we were writing this script. This was one of the first attempts that anyone had made to do a comic book movie without basing it on a comic book. That's quite a feat, because a lot of these projects depend on working with an icon that's already embedded in the public consciousness. We really had to make this a big, mythic story for it to work. It was a dangerous high-wire act in a way."

Of the process, Goldin has good memories. "It was really smooth sailing. I've worked with a bunch of directors and of all of them Sam is certainly the nicest. I have nothing but good things to say about him. The whole thing was interesting; it was Sam and Ivan and my brother and me ... just a bunch of brothers working on this thing."

DARK WORLD

With the work of the Goldins, Pfarrer and two Raimis combined (reportedly after twelve drafts), a budget of eleven million dollars was assigned, and it was time to design the film.[6] Peter Von Sholly storyboarded with Raimi, and Randy Ser was retained as the film's production designer.

For Ser, a graduate of Florida State University with a masters in fine arts, his involvement was a dream come true. "As I child, I was totally taken by the 1930s horror films from Universal," he notes. In his capacity as production designer, he would be reviving much of that world.

"You're creating the worlds and environments in which the characters live and the story takes place," Ser notes. "Anything that goes in front of the camera visually is part of something that a production designer deals with."

His thoughts on breathing life into *Darkman*? "Knowing Sam's work, and in particular after talking to him briefly, my take on it visually, which hooked up very well with what Sam was thinking, was that this would be a perfect homage to the 1930s Universal horror films. Without going into complete detail, if you look at Darkman's lab that he moves into, which is an old warehouse, what was on my mind was Dr. Frankenstein. There were a number of references visually to what we were thinking about in regards to those films."

Even with that idea, designing a film from the ground up isn't child's play, but Ser had his own process. "I come from theater, so I like to begin with the script. I come up with a back story for the character, and talk to the writer and director, if they are available, to see what it is they're thinking, where this character came from."

In developing a history for Darkman, Ser saw Peyton Westlake in a unique way. "He's definitely an urban dweller, but he's also living in the sunlight. He's living in a world filled with light and golden hues. If you look at his first lab, which is a combination laboratory, loft, and living space, the walls were painted a golden sun yellow, which were then lit to reflect the sunlight coming in. So even though he was ensconced in a world that kept him indoors to do his work, he was still surrounded and living in a world filled with sunlight and energy."

And as he moved into Darkman's world, that sunlight and lightness began to disappear, according to Ser, and his lair "becomes a place of darkness and more chaos; and the people he is dealing with are obviously traveling those worlds as well."

The Strack character also had a distinct feel. "As he says in the script, 'I built it all!'" remembers Ser. "He is always in control of the world, or at least the world in which he moves. What he had there [in his office] was something that was tasteful, with an undercurrent of, if not evil, then trouble. The man definitely had money and taste, and he would have a world people would be drawn to. That's what we were after with him."

Like many superhero films, *Darkman* spotlighted an array of amazing sets, gadgets and props, which needed to reflect the universe of the characters and the vision of the director. Darkman's second laboratory in the film, an abandoned warehouse, was one example.

"Sam, being Sam Raimi, moves the camera like nobody else can begin to imagine," Ser explains. "He wanted to do a number of shots that would require cranes moving through this set. Sam and I had a lot of fun and we spent a lot of time almost playing — just this creative energy — in his office, tossing ideas around, him [Raimi] telling me what it was he wanted to get to. When we got to the point where he understood the shots that he wanted and the kinds of cranes that would be required to do that, I built a scale miniature of the set, a full model, fully painted, and then got all the specs on the cranes he was going to use.

"And once he gave me the storyboards, we actually built little scaled miniatures of the cranes that swiveled and arced and did all the movements the cranes would. He and I took the cranes, with his storyboard and storyboard artist, and drove those cranes through the miniature set, and did the full camera moves to see how they would actually move, and what set pieces had to be hinged or moveable for specific shots. We very carefully planned this ballet of camera movements that Sam had envisioned in his mind."

To create this vast set, a real location was required. "We actually did not film it on a stage. We went to a warehouse, a very large one that used to be a refrigerated food warehouse in downtown L.A., which had never been shot in. We converted it into stages and the set was quite large. I can tell you that even when you looked up, that furnace, which we built, was two stories high."

Another creative challenge involved Westlake's strange skin-making machine, first seen in Peyton's high-tech lab and later recovered from the explosion and pressed into service in the warehouse. "I wanted to be able to give Sam the ability to shoot that machine so it would function all the way through the process without cutting, if we could," Ser explains. "We designed all these hand props and brought them to Sam and came up with the concept."

What resulted was a hybrid of a computer, photocopier, a hologram and skin mold — inside of which the audience could see the artificial skin mask pushing and bulging. The latter element was modeled on a real-life device.

"Sam had brought me the idea of the pin mold for the face," Ser notes. "Those were desk toys at that time, back in the 1970s and '80s. There were pin molds that you had on executives' desks around the country that you could push things into to calm yourself down."

Still, these elements had to be combined into one process that could go from start to finish without edits. "In order to facilitate giving Sam that option, I thought, 'Well, how can we achieve this?' I decided that we were dealing not with movie magic here, but magic. And I went to the people who built David Copperfield's magic acts and I told them I wanted to build an illusion.

"I told them, 'I want this illusion to operate all the way through.' The only place we had to cut was the moment when the face pushed out and you take out the new face Darkman was going to apply. We had to cut there, open the mold and put in the latex mask. The rest of that machine operated from A to Z. Then Sam could shoot it, multi-camera, and cut it the way he saw fit."

Another sequence in *Darkman* focused on the hospital where Peyton recovered from his burns after the lab explosion, only to learn that overeager doctors had tampered in God's domain and severed his nerve impulses controlling pain, making him a freak of nature.

"The thing we did in the hospital to make it creepy was the rotating burn platform that Darkman was strapped to," Ser explains. "We took a little license. We did a lot of research and went to the Sherman Oaks Burn Center, which is famous for Michael Jackson, and talked to them there.

"Even if you're going to dramatically interpret something, good filmmakers will go to the real world and do their due diligence," Ser considers, "and we did that." The production designer learned from his research that burn patients are often treated on moving platforms, to remove as much pressure as possible from the burns. But in real life, these treatment platforms rotate *horizontally*, so healthcare professionals can attend to bandages and replace sheets and otherwise interact effectively with the patient.

In this case, however, reality wasn't interesting enough. "We didn't feel, and Sam in particular didn't feel, that this was going to be visually arresting enough. We took that concept, and I came to Sam and said, 'How about if we take that concept and turn it into a two-fold Marquis De Sade [table], based on a knife-thrower's wheel?'

"So if you look at that design again, it's a Marquis De Sade X and it revolves in a way that is totally nauseating in that you are rotating 180 degrees upside down and over. This wasn't all my concept; these were things that Sam threw out that inspired me to come back to him with these ideas. We built that little set with a wall, which gave us the ability to blue screen the shot where the windows open, and of course, it's pouring rain and lightning outside."

Ser recalls the experience was not unique. The *Darkman* designer had the confidence of their leader, and the time to really go nuts. "I think we had somewhere between four and six months of preproduction, which was very luxurious, but that's why we were able to achieve what we did creatively, visually and financially. And I think I can proudly say for all of us, from Sam down, it came off without a hitch."

INTROVISION

From the earliest days of preproduction on *Darkman* it was apparent the project demanded a wide variety of effects, from miniatures and mattes to opticals. The man most responsible for this aspect is William Mesa, a talent who studied art, animation and storyboarding at the California

Institute of Arts. Having developed an interest in filmmaking at a young age, Mesa boasted a passion not just for the creative aspect of the art, but the technological side.

One of Mesa's earliest tasks involved visuals on the Sean Connery space-western *Outland* (1981), where he worked alongside noted effects man Roy Fields. In particular, Mesa supervised a process, then quite new, involving the film's finale, a battle between Connery and an assassin outside a mining station on one of Jupiter's moons. The effects involved live-action footage and miniature sets combined with a depth and reality not attained previously. The effects house was called Introvision, which also doubled as the name of the revolutionary process.

After *Outland*, Mesa supervised similar shots on many films, from Rob Reiner's *Stand by Me* to *Driving Miss Daisy* and *The Black Robe*. Recently, Mesa has headed Flash Film Works, a company producing visuals for hits such as *Holes* (2003), *The Italian Job* (2003), *Deep Blue Sea* (1999) and the TV series *24*.

Raimi first approached Mesa after completing *Evil Dead 2* with Dino De Laurentiis, while Mesa was still working on an early version of *Total Recall* in Australia for De Laurentiis and director Bruce Beresford. "They wanted us to get involved with *Darkman*, and Sam came in with Rob Tapert and basically took a tour of what we had as a facility," details Mesa. "At that time, which was before Digital Domain even existed, Introvision was probably the second or third largest visual effects company. We had three large stages and a complete model shop and machine shop. We did not have digital imagery, we had what was called a *dual process* and were the only ones in the world who had that. It would allow you to put people into picture imagery and project a picture on two screens at the same time."

Mesa details the process, which not long ago represented the vanguard of Hollywood technology, but now stands eclipsed by computer generated imagery. "It's one projector that projects onto two screens simultaneously and a matting system that allows you to matte out different portions of the imagery so an actor, when he's out on the stage, looks like he's behind objects in the picture. He is set back rather than just in front of the picture, which at the time was the technology of blue screen or projection photography.

"Sam saw that and started thinking, 'Wow, we can try things that we've never tried before!' That's what Sam loves to do at the beginning of each film," Mesa notes. "'What can I do or come up with that you haven't seen before? Can I now do something I visualized that wasn't possible to do before?' It's like having new toys to play with.

"So we sat down and started coming up with ideas, mainly working on that whole rooftop sequence," the film's climax. "The whole cluster of work is really in that scene at the end of the film, and we just tried to create at the time what was called *compound moves*, because anything you did with blue screen or projection photography usually didn't have complicated moves involved with it."

WHO IS ... DARKMAN?

Because *Darkman* was Raimi's first major studio picture, a whole new world of actors was available. Though he would have liked to see Bruce Campbell in the lead role, that wasn't a possibility given the scope of the project, where a more recognizable lead was deemed essential to commercial success. Though Campbell appeared as Darkman in the film's closing shot, billed as Shemp, the title role went to another performer.

"I knew at one point that Gary Oldman was going to play Darkman," Goldin recalls, "but for some reason it didn't work out." Instead, the part went to the imposing Liam Neeson, who, pre-*Schindler's List* (1993), was an up-and-comer with credits such as Leonard Nimoy's *The Good Mother* (1988), and *Next of Kin* (1989). Neeson, like Raimi, was attracted to the role because it evoked Frankenstein and the Hunchback of Notre Dame, "hideous, physically repulsive creatures who can still elicit sympathy in the audience."[7]

Casting Darkman's lady love, Julie Hastings, proved just as difficult. Julia Roberts was among the hopefuls, but ultimately it was Academy Award–nominee for *Mississippi Burning*, Frances McDormand, who accepted the part, having previously appeared in a Raimi film, *Crimewave*. "There was a lot of fighting about Frances McDormand," Goldin reveals. "I think at one point somebody wanted Demi Moore to play the character instead. All of these other possibilities just floated around at the time."

Larry Drake of *L.A. Law* took the role of Robert G. Durant, Darkman's most physically dangerous opponent. An actor of great size and stature, Drake appeared as a demonic Santa Claus in an early episode of HBO's *Tales from the Crypt* and played the title role in 1993's *Dr. Giggles*. Drake was joined by Colin Friels as the handsome brains of the criminal organization, the charming but perverse Strack. And Sam's little brother, Ted, appeared as a small-time crook who came to an untimely end when Darkman propped him up above a manhole on a busy street.

Raimi commenced principal photography with his largest cast, crew and budget yet. "The shoot, if I recall was fifty-four to sixty days," Randy Ser remembers. "You're talking about twelve weeks, five-day weeks, something like that. Three months." The carnival sequence in which Westlake succumbs to adrenaline-produced rage was shot on an empty lot in Los Angeles that is now the new wing of the convention center. Fellow director

John Landis appeared briefly in a scene set at another practical location, a local hospital, and there were stunt chases through Chinatown and dangerous drops from tall buildings.

The scene in which Durant pushed Pauly (Nicholas Worth) from a ninth story window was one such sequence. "That took the special effects department, the stunt department and the art department," Ser recalls. "We actually did that gig in a real hotel in downtown Los Angeles. The stuntmen actually did go out a ninth story window on a blind jump. He had to clear a parapit outside the window and then hit a bag nine stories below. We all had to work very carefully to make certain that it would visually work and that no one would get hurt while we were doing this."

Overseeing such impressive action was the film's stunt coordinator, Chris Doyle, who later worked on *Army of Darkness*, *A Simple Plan* and *For Love of the Game* for Raimi. Doyle, like Raimi, had a love for film history, a passion that brought him to the movies.

"I can remember when I was a kid watching Hopalong Cassidy and Zorro and stuff like that, and wanting to do it. I loved Errol Flynn and Burt Lancaster and Buster Keaton — though I'm not that old!" jokes Doyle. "I just enjoyed the physical things that those particular actors did.

"A first AD [assistant director] friend of mine knew the production manager/line producer of *Darkman*, which was Darryl Kass. This was Sam's first major film with a budget; they were interviewing people, and I prepped the script," Doyle remembers. "When I met Sam, we hit it off. I wanted to coordinate stunts and direct second unit because I wanted to be more involved in the creative part of filmmaking, rather than just falling on my face [as a stuntman]. He saw that in me, we hooked up, and it was great for those four pictures."

HANGING AROUND

Doyle's most unique challenge involved the action-packed finale of *Darkman*, a daring flight above Los Angeles. In the film, Darkman's lab has been destroyed and he attempts to ambush Durant aboard a chopper. Darkman then falls off the craft, hanging on by a long, dangling cable and hook. Making matters worse, the nefarious Durant is intent on losing his unwanted passenger by "shaking," and "dipping" him, even "blasting" him with a rifle. It was a complex sequence that could not be faked, but one that if handled well, would thrill audiences.

Before the scene was shot, however, Doyle had to know that the stunt was possible, and more importantly, *safe*. He went out to a small local airport with the helicopter pilot and the first double, Terry James. They discussed how the scene could be accomplished safely, and experimented with the cable the double would cling to during the airborne stunt. With the pilot, Doyle focused on the logistics of getting the stunt double up into the air and then safely back down to the ground.

"You have to do it a certain way because there's a lot of variables, including a cable that we cannot get in the tail rotor," Doyle considers. "And then, we just took it step-by-step and practiced to see what the problems were going to be. We worked out a lot of the bugs."

The flying sequence took two and a half weekends to complete, in part because the production could shoot only on Saturdays and Sundays. "It was a logistical nightmare, because of the permits you have to get to fly below five hundred feet, around people and buildings," Doyle explains. "So Terry was on two cables, and hooked up in three different spots, in case one failed. Then he had a back-up safety."

The scene was made even more complex by the fact that the stunt double could not communicate with the pilot, though the pilot was able to speak with him. The stunt double knew, "'Okay, we're going up,' or 'We're going down,' 'We're making another pass,'" according to Doyle. "Before the shot started, Terry could really hang on and save his strength, but then, when the shot started, he would dangle his leg and arm out and really flail.

"The first weekend we did that, and the second weekend we brought in Chuck Borden to double Liam, because we found out real fast that one person couldn't physically do it," says Doyle. "It was really exhausting. You're hooked on with the harnesses, but to make it look like a person, not just a dummy, with flailing legs and arms, it was very physically demanding."

The scene was accomplished with a minium of trickery and just a few tweaks of the camera to make it look faster paced. "Sam has a way of shooting stuff," Doyle notes. "He doesn't use those techniques so much anymore, but he would run the camera at twelve frames a second, seven frames a second, to get that jerky, erratic, panicked feeling, and it worked very well I thought."

Never content with simple thrills, Raimi wanted more. "Sam said, 'We'd like to have Larry Drake and his henchman up there using a flame thrower out of the helicopter,'" Doyle recalls. "Since I was a helicopter mechanic in the military and knew about helicopters, I said, 'That sounds interesting, but no, it's not going to work.' The way a flame thrower works, and with the prop wash on a helicopter, it would be a total disaster. It would just wrap the helicopter in flames. And if you had a malfunction with the flame thrower and it didn't ignite, it would spray out the oil-based fuel first. The helicopter would go up in a ball of fire.

"But I said, 'I have an idea. What about this 20mm round gun with explosive rounds?' That way, Durant could be shooting at Darkman," Doyle explains. "So I asked him to let me run it down, and I got together with him a few days later and told him my ideas. What's nice about Sam is that if you have an idea that works for the show, he doesn't have a problem incorporating it. He was the boss and he was the man, but film is a joint venture and he was smart enough to use a good idea when he heard one. Not that I inundated him with ideas. He's Mr. Idea Man himself."

The flight sequence had more to it even than that, as Ser remembers. Raimi wanted the helicopter to *drag* Darkman on a dangerous, impromptu tour of the city. "We actually shut down several blocks of downtown Los Angeles on consecutive weekends to do that," he reports.

"We did that over the Sixth Street Bridge," adds Doyle. "We were laying out this whole thing, and there was a bunch of stuff we didn't get to do, even though Sam liked it. There was a series of three or four breakaway billboards that were forty, fifty, sixty feet in the air along one of these stretches of road, and the bad guys were trying to run Darkman through these billboards. We didn't do that, but we did drag him on the concrete and bounce him up. That was a combination of a rig we made and a helicopter, so we could get in tight and have control over it. We actually hit the [Darkman] double, which was Terry, with a car; Sam's old 88."

This portion of the chase involved twenty-four cars. "And then we had to turn over a car and an ice cream truck," Doyle adds. "We also had the helicopter, and a helicopter ship photographing it. I was very familiar with working with helicopters, and we shot most of the action first unit with Sam."

One section not filmed outdoors involved the moment Durant's craft smacked Darkman into a skyscraper and smashed him through a window into a board meeting. "When Darkman swings through the window and lands on the conference table and is dragged back and says, 'Oh, excuse me,' that was a set," Randy Ser describes. "And what we had to do was figure out how to rig a cable that swung on the same arc a helicopter would swing. Then Liam came in and did that, not a stuntman. We swung him in the window and had to have the arc where he could land on the table, and then we'd yank him back out on this cable. It took quite a bit of geometry combined with matching angles to make that work so seamlessly."

The final destruction of Darkman's laboratory represented another combination of live-action locations, stunts and miniatures. "The warehouse is no longer there," Doyle sets the scene. "But it was the White King Soap Factory. For a few years before we used it, it was condemned, but the owners literally let us destroy the place because it was scheduled for demolition. We used air rams to blow Darkman over things."

If it sounds dangerous, know that Doyle is always a stickler for safety.

"There were explosions going on all around him [the stuntman], so we used this fire gel and also had the wardrobe treated with fire-retardant materials. We had safety people, and would do dry rehearsals until everyone was happy, and then shoot the thing."

Finally, the destruction of the warehouse was achieved via Introvision. "Bill Mesa came in and did that," Doyle explains. "They blew up a miniature and he superimposed that."

THE FINAL BATTLE

The last confrontation in *Darkman*, set atop a half-erected skyscraper, was one of the most difficult to arrange, a combination of unique approaches. The set-up read simply enough on paper. In order to rescue Julie, Darkman confronts Strack and his goons on the roof of an unfinished construction site. A conversation degenerates into battle, with Julie hanging on for her life by a metal pipe, and Darkman, the goons and Strack performing a dangerous high-rise hopscotch from beam-to-beam, level to level, as they fight. Props and stunts involved swinging hooks and a nasty rivet gun.

"This was the last problem we solved on the movie, because it was the most complex," Ser acknowledges. "It took months, numerous designs, models, approaches on how we could achieve this. And Sam gave me a lot of storyboards which clued me in to the shots and how I would have to design to facilitate our moving shots. The end result was the following: we designed a set that was an iron cross of steel so that you had a cross with four negative empty spaces in the corners. That was your key set.

"The set had to be three stories tall, and the easiest way to do that would have been to build it out of wood, glue it together and paint it to look like steel. But that was not going to work. Putting cameras, actors, stuntmen and quick motion on this set, we needed someplace large.

"We went out to Van Nuys Airport to the hanger that was built to house the *Spruce Goose*," Ser continues. "We rented that, and it had a concrete floor that was eleven feet deep. Then we went to an erector company, the companies that come in with steel and put up metal infrastructures for skyscrapers. We had it engineered, and the company came in with a crane and everything else. In half a day, all of the holes had been pre-dug for the well, and they put up this iron cross, which was sunk into the concrete floor. So now you basically had a real steel girder building."

"There was very little live-action set," Mesa confirms. "When I say that, I mean like a few beams. Almost all of that was projected work that we just shot and made plates of. We had a few beams and a couple of pieces to do close-up work on, and everything else was projected. All of the shots which showed a bigger vista, when we were on a particular story, were plates we shot to make it look like you were up several stories."

"We went to a company that shoots and makes TransLites, which are basically giant slides, photographs you light from behind and look real on camera," Ser describes. "Ten plates that appeared in individual shots were filmed from the top of the TransAmerica building, blown up and taped together into what ended being a 120-foot-long TransLite," which, Ser points out, was "at that time, the largest TransLite ever made in Hollywood, though we were beaten by *Ghostbusters II* (1989) shortly afterward."

"It hung 270 degrees around the set. Then we painted the stage floor black, and in the other 90 degrees we hung black curtains. We hung a black curtain as a ceiling over the top of the set, and that gave you your basic structure: negative iron cross with skyline."

Yet that was merely the live-action component. For the process to work, and to achieve the accurate scope, the set had to be doubled in miniature. "We were also shooting plates on the miniatures to facilitate things we couldn't do on that set, to project them in Introvision," Ser comments. The miniature Mesa built was highly detailed and eleven feet tall.

"We did a number of shots of what are called *after-composites*," Mesa explains. "Those are shots that we would shoot a tight plate element of on stage, and then project it back into a huge model shot," Mesa outlines. "We would shoot the model, and *inside* the model we would project the image. That way you could capture a super-wide shot of the characters with someone on a low story and someone else on a higher story."

Several elements were involved in the sequence: live actors on a carefully crafted, minimalist set, huge backdrops, and a highly detailed miniature into which action would be projected. But that wasn't enough to make the scene fly. There needed to be life in the background world too.

"Back then we did goofy stuff you'd never do today," Mesa explains. "We shot a miniature model with motion control so that we'd have a little helicopter on wires, and we'd pull it across — basically one frame at a time — and that would become our Vista Vision plate we could project, so you'd see a helicopter going across the background. It was like a one-fourth scale model that we put an electric motor in."

"We also pasted together imagery of some plates that I'd shot in Chicago from *Adventures in Babysitting*," Mesa notes. "I used some of those skyline pieces and pasted them together to make up our background plate.

"It took quite a few months," Mesa notes, "because it is much different today in visual effects than it was back then. This work had to be done either in principal photography or just post of principal photography, at the end of the shooting time. So all of your work is finished by the time you finish the movie. The only things that weren't done were some of those after-composites that we put into the miniature.

"We were working very early in the movie, starting right at the beginning, and having everything done by the last week of shooting," says Mesa. "We're talking about maybe six or eight months of working time overall. In today's movies, like *Spider-Man,* you're talking well over a year. So much is done in post, and you're virtually delivering shots two weeks before the movie is coming out."

The precise process of shooting the skyscraper finale was made easier, according to Mesa, by Raimi's organizational and personal skills. "He works from boards, so we can figure what's possible on the film, but as you're going along and you have the model in front of you, and you suggest that it would be cool to do something from a different angle or position, he gets on board with it and says, 'Yeah, that's really cool, let's do it.' As long as there isn't some terrible financial issue, he was always open to doing as much as we possibly could to add to the film."

DARKMAN LANDS IN THEATERS

In the summer of 1989, Tim Burton's *Batman* took America by storm. Far from the campy ethos of the 1960s TV series starring Adam West and Burt Ward, this big-budget film adopted the grim approach of Frank Miller's graphic novel, *The Dark Knight Returns* (1986), highlighting a far more serious and dangerous Caped Crusader. Burton's film was dark, violent, serious, and faithful to the idea of a nocturnal vigilante. More importantly, it was profitable. One of the most influential films of its generation, *Batman* launched a series of middling sequels, including *Batman Returns* (1992), *Batman Forever* (1995) and *Batman and Robin* (1997), but set off a new superhero boom in Hollywood.

Dark heroes like Alex Proyas' *The Crow*, Russell Mulcahy's *The Shadow* (1994), Todd McFarlane's *Spawn* (1997) and *Daredevil* (2003) seized on a revolutionary approach to filming superheroes and comic books. They lived by the maxim "the darker the better."

Released in late August of 1990, Sam Raimi's *Darkman* was among the first and best of this new sub-genre, a dazzling and heroic adventure that caught America by storm, and which many critics compared favorably to the "big" movie of that summer, Warren Beatty's *Dick Tracy*.

Ser remembers seeing *Darkman* for the first time. "I was blown away! My god, I'd gotten to live my childhood dreams! We saw the film at a screening room at Universal and everybody's heart and soul was in that movie. What can I say? Sam was tremendous to work with. He's a director that any designer would give his eyeteeth to work with." Daniel Goldin felt the same way. "I really thought Sam Raimi did a fantastic job. He's got an incredible visual sense; he's just an extremely inventive, ingenious director. I thought *Spider-Man* came out of *Darkman*, and frankly I like *Darkman* better!"

Critics found much to praise. Writing for the *Los Angeles Times*, Michael Wilmington commented that in "the recent flurry of comics-derived movies, *Darkman* may not be the most popular. But in some ways, it's the best: the only one that successfully captures the graphic look, rhythm and style of the superhero books."[8]

The *New York Post*'s David Edelstein called *Darkman* a "melancholy symphony for orchestra and whoopee cushion."[9] *Rolling Stone*'s Jim Farber noted that "Raimi's penchant for camp humor makes this malicious stuff fun."[10] *Newsday*'s Terry Kelleher reported that *Darkman* was "bursting with incredible action, horrible villainy, outsized emotion, overwrought music and exclamatory dialogue that belongs in balloons over the character's heads."[11]

But the *New Yorker*'s Terrence Rafferty best captured the film's spirit:

> Raimi works from inside the cheerfully violent adolescent-male sensibility of superhero comics, as if there were no higher style for a filmmaker to aspire to, and the absence of condescension is refreshing. The film's graphic style is all bright colors, high contrast, and skewed angles; its narrative is breathlessly speedy; its emotions are basic (mostly greed and revenge); and its dialogue is so crude and punchy that you can practically see the exclamation points.[12]

Less enthusiastic was *Time*'s Richard Corliss, who remarked that Raimi wasn't "effective with actors" though "his canny visual style" carried many a scene.[13] *People*'s Ralph Novak found something to complain about, calling *Darkman* a "loud, sadistic, stupidly written, wretchedly acted film" and "the most boring movie since Raimi's 1983 horror film *Evil Dead*, which persuaded some misguided souls to let him first do a sequel and then this relatively costly number."[14]

Mainstream America didn't concur with Novak's assessment, and viewing audiences made *Darkman* the number one film in the country the weekend of its release. The film was also a hit for Universal, making more than thirty million dollars on its investment. Thirty-or-so million may not sound like a cornucopia considering the big weekends of 2003, but this was 1990, before the "fifty million dollar opening weekend or die" principle hijacked Hollywood.

Two direct-to-video sequels followed *Darkman* in 1994 and 1996. Arnold

Vosloo replaced Liam Neeson as Westlake in both pictures, and Drake returned as Durant in the first of the follow-ups, *The Return of Durant*. The final sequel, *Die Darkman Die*, featured some interesting metaphors with the tale of Beauty and the Beast, and took the titular character into a new, would-be romantic relationship. Bradford May directed both pictures, which were produced by Renaissance Pictures.

RAIMI RAP

ROTTEN TOMATOES: "Sam used a lot of montages in that film," Randy Ser recalls about *Darkman*. "There is a little piece in there where Liam is seen as a puppet. If you can find that montage, in the script it said, 'Darkman is doing a jig wearing a funny hat.' I said, 'How about if we do this combining puppetry and *commedia dell'arte*?' So we built a little miniature puppet theater, which Liam has in his house, I think, to this day. It had these little tiny *commedia dell'arte* faces of Larry Drake as a jester laughing at him. And Liam put his head through a solid curtain and we put a little miniature hat on his head. He had an armature puppet below him in a kind of *commedia dell'arte* costume, which was then operated by the prop man watching the monitor below. We even made little tiny rotten tomatoes and threw them at Liam in that scene. That's a little sidelight that lasts about ten seconds on screen."

IF YOU'RE NOT GOING TO KILL ME, I HAVE THINGS TO DO: *Darkman*'s most famous dialogue, uttered by Frances McDormand, was quoted with admiration in reviews. "That was a line we came up with," Goldin acknowledges. "We had to figure out a way for the bad guys to follow Frances McDormand to Darkman's lair. She had already discovered the Bellisarius Memorandum, so why would Strack keep her there? Why would she leave? We had to figure out a clever, elegant way to get her out of that room. So we thought by adding just a little touch of ironic humor, it would work."

HIGH DIVE: One of the most memorable shots in *Darkman* involves the explosion of Peyton Westlake's loft/laboratory. In one amazing shot, the burning body of Westlake flies out of the explosion toward the camera. "They used a visual on that," Doyle explains, meaning animation. "But when he falls into the water, we were out at Long Beach off the docks and we used a stunt guy. We set him on fire on a crane about eighty feet above the water. To get the last part of that sequence when he hits the water, he did a fall. I had a couple of safety divers in the water in case he got knocked silly, but there were no accidents on the set and nobody got hurt."

CHINATOWN: Halfway through *Darkman*, Robert Durant meets Robert Durant (or Darkman pretending to be Durant) in a Chinatown revolving door. It looks like an easy shot to stage, but wasn't. Chris Doyle notes that he had a "pretty good double for Larry Drake size-wise, but they needed someone to fill the space and do some running and falling down. So I brought this guy in and we used him as a stunt double, but also as a *photo double* going around this revolving door."

"Again, we didn't have CGI in those days, which is what you do now in a film like *X2*," Randy Ser explains. "We had to do what was called motion control. So, in order to facilitate Sam's vision to make Larry Drake meet Larry Drake, there was a revolving door on the Chinese restaurant, which was a practical location in Chinatown. We built that door, the door unit, and a motor in that door unit that could be tied to a computer system that would make that door revolve *exactly* within one, one hundred-thousandth of a second. We shot him [Drake] going out of that door on location and then we took that film and went to a motion control stage and brought that door with us, matched the moves that were shot on location, and this was Sam doing his thing. My only involvement was to create something that could be motorized and hooked up to this rig to make sure you could do this seamlessly. We built that unit, brought it to the motion control stage, tied it to the camera so that the door and the camera all move past the computer within one, one hundred-thousandth of a second, and Larry Drake meets Larry Drake.

"There's a brilliance to CGI, but there's a unique creative brilliance that was non-computer facilitated in the old days," Ser reflects. "It shows you the difference in what you had to do to achieve those things in the old days. Let me put it this way, dreaming up the way to achieve that was a heck of a lot of fun and an amazing challenge. However, there were limitations to it. The effects were more physical than they are now."

CAMEOS: "There was this one big governor's ball scene," writer Goldin remembers, "and Sam invited everybody that helped out in the movie to appear in the film for the big party. We all wore tuxedoes and were extras in that scene. If you look at the exact microsecond, you can see me."

Raimi anoraks will also note that *Evil Dead* investor Phil Gillis appears in the cemetery as the priest assisting McDormand. This is Gillis' second appearance as a man of the cloth in a Raimi film. The first was in *Crimewave*.

WATCH YOUR STEP: There's a perfect visualization of the Raimi ethos during *Darkman*'s climax. Strack and Westlake face one another atop a skyscraper, and Strack reports that they stand 650 feet above the street. Then, packing a dynamic visual wallop, the camera pans down the *entire* skyscraper, visually validating Strack's claim. "We actually went down 650 feet on the model, what *would be* 650 feet," Mesa remembers. "But it wasn't enough, so we had to add about 50 percent more, and then we had the spikes sticking up at the bottom."

Raimi often uses "very distinct shots, like the shot going down 600 feet," Mesa considers. "Those are kind of comic book things that aren't necessarily normal filmmaking."

HANGING AROUND: The skyscraper finale gave stunt coordinator and second unit director Doyle a chance to get in front of the camera. "Chris is also an actor and he does second unit directing for Sam," Mesa says. "He's one of the bad guys in the closing sequence of *Darkman*. He's the one who pushes over Frances McDormand and gets hung upside down by a hook.

"I still have one of those hooks," Mesa notes. "They're actually made of soft rubber and they're very real looking even though they're light weight and rubbery."

NOT A BIMBO? "This is the first bimbo I've played,"[15] Frances McDormand told the genre press about her role in *Darkman*, which she later regretted not having a better time with. "I should have had more fun with it and embraced the damsel-in-distress thing. I was playing a character that has a masters in real estate law, but in the end, I was still handcuffed to a building waiting to be rescued. I really should have gotten into that."[16]

FAKE SHEMP: "When I saw *Darkman* and the very last frame of that picture, and there was Bruce when he turned around ... I was thrilled," says Verne Nobles. "They gave him the credit 'Shemp.' Only people who know these characters, that grew up with these two guys, would know what that credit meant. The Shemp thing became a very big deal. I felt like I was a bit of an insider at that time."

"Bruce wasn't in the picture," Nobles explains. "He was a fake. He was a Shemp."

WHAT IS IT ABOUT THE DARK?

Today, criteria for judging a film has mutated drastically from established academic standard, and one often wonders how, precisely, a critic decides if a production is praiseworthy or deserving of scorn. For instance, when writing a review, *Ain't It Cool*'s Harry Knowles takes into account where he's been the day he sees a movie, how he feels, and what his expectations are. Some may deride such a personal approach, but at least it is honest, enabling the reader to understand where the reviewer is coming from. And who can truthfully deny that a critic's mood probably plays a role in how much he enjoys a film? Anyway, the point is that such an approach is a contemporary, non-standard one, as is the boiling down of critical evaluation to a binary decision, like "thumbs up/thumbs down."

For this journalist, the equation to adjudge quality is different. The question I ask myself is simply this: Did the film accomplish the goals it set out to achieve? It makes little sense to deride an *Evil Dead* or a *Darkman* because it doesn't boast the thematic decorum or heft of a work by Shakespeare or Pinter. On its own selected terms and within its genre, does it work and, if so, how well? A way to answer that question is to apply the following test. Does the film's visualization match its theme; or more succinctly, does its form echo its content? Has the movie used film language, the grammar of moviemaking, to advance and enhance its story? Because in essence, that is what a good film *should* do. Discuss acting or dialogue as much as you'd like, but film is primarily a *visual* art form and its images are designed to make people respond a certain way.

Raimi's *Darkman* is a resounding success because it not only defines its parameters as a comic book movie that pays homage to Hollywood tradition, the Universal horrors of the 1930s and 1940s, but it then utilizes inspired techniques to visualizes its origin story in a way that registers emotionally with viewers.

An obvious example is the brief and artful scene transition early in the film, bridging the destruction of Peyton's lab to Julie's mourning over his death. Julie stands in the center of both shots, as one instant bleeds into the other, her shock morphing into grief. "That was strictly Sam," Randy Ser notes of this moment, which involves a switch of background plates (from lab to graveyard) and a quick-dissolve in wardrobe for McDormand, from smart business suit to black funeral garb. "I don't want to offend the writer, but I recall it was one of those things that Sam comes up with and astounds you when you see it."

Indeed, most films would probably include an artful fade out and fade in here; something to suggest the passage of time. But this is a *comic book* movie, and in comic books, the story jumps quite literally from frame to frame, across vast distances or ahead in time with no transitional device at all. There need not be an emotional winding down or a master shot introducing a new locale. Thus Raimi has accomplished a minor miracle here; unlocking the cinematic equivalent for a comic book frame transition, and thus reminding audiences of *Darkman*'s antecedents.

There are other examples, where Raimi discovers the movie shorthand for comic book language. "They do dynamic angles in comics and so did Sam in *Darkman*," William Mesa acknowledges, "as far as stilted angles or rotating stilted angles, meaning that in the shot you'll rotate the camera over just to get into the stilted angle. Those are things automatically done in comic books all the time, but in moviemaking you don't do that, and Sam wanted that in the film."

Raimi's mentor, Verne Nobles reminds us of another specific example. "When he had that blast in *Darkman*, and Darkman blasted out of the building and came right at the camera, they [movies] weren't doing that then. That was pure comic book. What he was able to do was take the obvious optical and make it into the 'Oh my god, look what he's done' moment. It was brilliant, absolutely brilliant."

The film's visuals reflects its content, comic book heroes and villains, in other scenes too, including the depiction of Friel's villainous Strack. "There's a scene in Strack's office where he shows Frances the model of the city," Ser explains, "and the model was transparent, reflecting the transparency of what was going on here [in the scene]. The water was not water, but *gold*, this hand-hammered, gold-hued reflective source. There's a beat where he looks down into it, and the way it was hammered, his face becomes completely distorted and broken up into a view that a fly's eye might see. That beat revealed the transparency of Strack's world," Ser considers. And thus the viewer was able to see *through* him. Strack's lust for money had deformed him, hence the fragmented view of his face, or as Ser notes, "his golden hues had become completely twisted."

Again, this is Raimi as the committed formalist, forging imagery which is not merely appealing to the eye, but noteworthy because it underlines the film's thematic aspects, making the viewer *feel* a certain way about the characters.

Since Darkman and his journey represent the heart of the film, it is appropriate that Raimi deploys crazy visuals to express the character's predicament. When Peyton escapes from the hospital, he ends up battered by a storm, rain pounding down upon him. Raimi's camera focuses on a whirlpool, a vortex spinning madly, and we see Darkman's eye superimposed at the center of it. The whirlpool is not there for plot reasons, merely a result of the watery thunderstorm, but a visual cue to Darkman's mental and emotional state. His life has been taken over by turmoil, flushed down the toilet so to speak, and this shot is a visual cue.

Later, Peyton comes to fear that he is a circus freak, a recurring motif in the film because of the surgery that removed his ability to feel pain. This fear comes to twisted life at the Carnival Round-Up. As Peyton's uncontrollable anger with a concession stand operator grows, a variety of techniques embody that anger.

A routine film would probably just depend on good acting. You know, let an actor dramatize his inner rage with a slow boil, that sort of thing. But Raimi expresses Peyton's anger via the camera angles and special effects.

The viewer is treated to strange views of demonic-looking mechanized clown-things that giggle, amusement rides spinning out of control in fast motion, and views of patrons through what seem to be distorted mirrors. When the concession stand operator insults Peyton, calling him a "weirdo," Raimi's camera adopts the POV subjective perspective, so the carnie is talking directly to the audience; so *we* feel Peyton's humiliation and rage. Then reality itself cracks (an optical effect) and splinters. The camera zooms into Peyton's eye where fire and orange light blazes... and then right back out again and finally Peyton reacts, breaking the carnie's fingers. It is an expressionist, formalist sequence in which we *feel* how Peyton's anger has built, the pressure around him and even the horror at his actions, as the camera pans around dizzily from the screaming victim to Julie to Peyton.

"It was scripted that there were unique things we were going to see," Ser describes. "And then there was Sam's vision of the script, and my interpretation of those things. I think we did a little homage to Dr. Caligari, the very German expressionist type of artwork, which was tied together with the skewed camera angles and the cuts, and the moves in on the laughing faces. It was somewhat Felliniesque in its approach."

By forging a visualization of anger, Raimi reveals something you might see depicted in a comic book, and fulfills the film's other purpose — homage, in this case to *The Cabinet of Dr. Caligari* (1920). Although purists get upset when the term "art" is applied to subject matter that is somehow considered common, as some consider comic books, *Darkman* is purely and simply artistic in its design and execution.

Whether it be unusual POV shots, like the perspective of a gun spraying out bullets, or a composition symbolizing social entrapment, as Darkman peers out through a vent grill at the society he can never rejoin, Raimi's choice of compositions augments the feeling of a comic book brought to life. Another notable comic-style sequence employs one of Raimi's favorite devices, which recurs in *The Quick and the Dead*, *For Love of the Game* and *Spider-Man*: the montage. Raimi again reveals time's passage without resorting to laborious shots that eat up precious screen time. Instead, he deploys the montage and superimposes handwritten equations, diagrams, and test tubes over views of Peyton as the scientist fruitlessly struggles to perfect his synthetic skin.

It is difficult to deny that *Darkman*'s helicopter battle and consequent chase through L.A.'s skies represents one of the finest comic book finales in film history. In 1999, *The Matrix* engineered a sequence of similar design and scope, with a helicopter, characters crashing into skyscraper walls, people dangling on cables, and lots of gunplay. Yet even with nine years of special effects advancements, that sequence cannot hold a candle to the kinetic, out-of-control and legitimately dangerous feeling of *Darkman*'s similar battle.

Why? Simply because Raimi utilizes his camera to express every aspect of the crazy fight, so the audience *feels* it is sharing the danger. This is not merely an opinion, it is a fact based on a dissection of the chase scene's components, the very anatomy of the sequence. Cataloguing the pertinent shots, there are POV shots from Peyton's perspective looking up the cable at a moving helicopter, POV shots from Durant's view, aiming down at Peyton below, and POV shots from a bullet, traveling the distance from one helicopter to another. In film grammar such compositions are the equivalent of the first-person voice, landing audiences smack dab inside the action.

There are also hand-held shots, wild pans heightening the motion and speed of the helicopter during the battle, and crazy zooms into extreme close-ups of Durant's shocked eyes as the helicopter crashes into a tunnel wall. Finally, lengthy and amazing long-distance aerial shots reveal that the chase is no fake. Real copters weave and dodge, dip and ascend, traversing narrow corridors between glass-lined business offices.

One shot at a time, the sequence represents a collection of brilliant notions. Edited together, it is an unsurpassed masterpiece of the action format because Raimi's desire to involve and entertain the audience is behind it. Certainly, *The Matrix* is a great film and its helicopter battle is involving, but some digital aspects take the wind out of its sails. It never feels as dangerous and off-kilter as the insanely paced *Darkman* finale.

Boasting a cameo from everybody's favorite hero, Bruce Campbell, *Darkman* comes replete with homages to everything from Hitchcock, in the form of a McGuffin (his term for a diversionary plot device) called the Bellisarius Memorandum, to Caligari. It also displays Raimi's impish sense of humor, notably the opening sequence involving an assassin whose gun is built into his prosthetic leg. Naturally, for anyone to actually *use* the weapon, the poor guy must hop around on one foot, not a good situation when bullets are flying.

Its form reflecting content, *Darkman* represents a high point in the superhero genre, a successful experiment in translating comic book ethos to film. As Ethan Alter wrote in *Film Journal International*, "Sam Raimi's *Darkman* remains the closest Hollywood has come to capturing the unique spirit of comic books on film ... every frame could easily have been drawn rather than filmed."[17]

ARMY OF DARKNESS (1993)

WELL HELLO, MR. FANCY PANTS!

TRAPPED IN TIME...

SURROUNDED BY EVIL...

LOW ON GAS.

CAST AND CREW

Universal Productions, Dino De Laurentiis Communications and Renaissance Pictures present *Army of Darkness*

Director: Sam Raimi
Producer: Robert Tapert
Co-producer: Bruce Campbell
Director of Photography: Bill Pope
Music Composed and Conducted by: Joseph Lo Duca
"March of the Dead" theme: Danny Elfman
Visual Effects: Introvision International and William Mesa, director of effects
Special Makeup: KNB
Ash and Sheila Makeup: Tony Gardner and Alterian Studios
Art Director: Aram Allan
Book of the Dead Animation and Design: Tom Sullivan
Stunt Coordinator and First Assistant Director: Chris Doyle

STARRING

Bruce Campbell: Ash
Embeth Davidtz: Sheila
Marcus Gilbert: Arthur
Ian Abercrombie: Wiseman
Richard Grove: Duke Henry
Michael Earl Reid: Gold Tooth
Bridget Fonda: Linda
Patricia Tallman: Possessed Witch
Theodore Raimi: Cowardly Warrior

Filmed in Acton, California, and Hollywood, California.

CRY HAVOC AND LET SLIP THE DOGS OF WAR

TRANSPORTED TO THE YEAR 1300 by the powers of the Book of the Dead, twentieth century S-Mart employee Ash is promptly captured by the knights of King Arthur. Arthur's wise man believes the displaced Ash may be the "Chosen One," a legendary figure who will protect his people from the evil of the Deadites. But Arthur is not convinced, and Ash is thrown into a demon-infested pit. Ash escapes and sets loose Arthur's nemesis, Duke Henry.

Hoping to return to his time, Ash sets out to recover the Necronomicon, which possesses the knowledge to transport him there. But on his quest, Ash confronts the Deadite evil, which creates an exact — but malevolent — doppelganger. Worse, Ash bungles the words that make the book safe to remove from its demonic altar and thereby spurs the formation of a Deadite army ... an army of darkness.

Ash converts his car, the Delta 88 into a rolling arsenal called a "death coaster" and with his knowledge of gunpowder and twentieth century fighting techniques, defends the realm. He rallies the troops and is aided by Duke Henry, but if Evil Ash should possess the Necronomicon, all hope is lost, and the Good Ash will never return to Housewares.

UNCLE SAM WANTS YOU, FOR THE ARMY OF DARKNESS!

Before *Darkman* came together, plans were afoot for a third installment in the *Evil Dead* series. The second film's overseas grosses were good, and Dino De Laurentiis offered to provide financing for a sequel that would pick-up where the second left off — with a confused Ash trapped in the year 1300. Sam and brother Ivan partnered on a script throughout preproduction and production of *Darkman*.

When *Darkman* proved a success, Universal opted to share the risk on the new project, putting up half the film's twelve million dollar budget alongside the Italian mogul. For Raimi, Tapert and Campbell, the third film — to be titled *Army of Darkness* rather than *Evil Dead 3* — offered the opportunity to leave behind the famous cabin in the woods and film a grand period adventure.

There was less studio oversight on *Army of Darkness* than *Darkman*, but the movie's vast scope necessitated cost-cutting measures. For one thing, the production was a non-union job. For another, many talents, including Raimi, Campbell, and Tapert, took pay cuts. This was all done in an effort to shepherd money to the most crucial place: the screen.

Richard Grove, an actor who studied at the Yale School of Drama with classmates Angela Bassett and John Turturro, was cast in *Army of Darkness* as Duke Henry and recalls being impressed with the film's preparation. In particular, Raimi "had done a complete visualization of every single shot," says Grove. "Every shot was mapped. Everything was storyboarded very dynamically ... the whole movie! It was just fantastic because the way he had the shots set up was so neat. It was almost done in that old *Vault of Horror* style, which I thought was just magnificent."

William Mesa, the effects genius who accomplished miracles on a budget with *Darkman*, returned to collaborate on *Army of Darkness* with Raimi. "Sam was very happy with what we did on *Darkman* because we came up with a lot of crazy, wacky stuff, which he loves," he remembers.

"So when *Army of Darkness* was being written, he wanted to know what he could do to make it go beyond what you've seen in other movies. He uses all the stuff that Harryhausen did, not just in *Jason and the Argonauts* (1963) but in *The Seventh Voyage of Sinbad* (1958) and other productions. But because we had this army of rotten people, we wanted to make sure that we didn't just have people in skeleton suits, but actual skeletons."

And that meant a twist on stop-motion animation utilizing the

Introvision process to blend components. "Stop-motion was something that Ray Harryhausen did, but the way stop-motion animation is traditionally done is that you shoot the live-action scene and *then* you project it and add the stop-motion character in front of it," Mesa informs us.

"The other thing about the way Ray Harryhausen did stop-motion animation: it was basically projected 35mm, or rear projected Vista Vision. It was always rear projected and the character was put in front of it and you could never get the picture quality that way. We didn't want to do that. We wanted to front project Vista Vision elements with Bruce. That way the quality would be beyond anything that had been seen before. That was the approach we took."

Once again, Raimi stood at the effects vanguard, working with sixty-foot-tall Scotchlite front-projection screens, miniatures, and background plates shot on an Eastman S248. He told *American Cinematographer* that the advantage of Introvision was "the incredible amount of interaction between the background, which doesn't exist, and the foreground, which is usually your character. Because you can see what's happening through the camera, you can really play with the back and forth."[1]

Beyond a new take on effects, *Army of Darkness*'s battle sequences between man and monster also came out of lucky happenstance and film history. "I happened to have, from a long-time friend, some storyboards that were given to him by the director of *Joan of Arc*," Mesa explains, referring to the 1948 film starring Ingrid Bergman and directed by Victor Fleming.

"I brought those in and Sam just flipped out over them because there were huge battle scenes of soldiers lifting up ladders and going up the top of the wall and being pushed off. There were all these great angles that you don't see in films today, and he'd say, 'We've got to do this shot!' and he picked out some twenty-five shots from the storyboards.

"The storyboard artist worked really closely with Sam in coming up with those angles, blending in all of these shots from *Joan of Arc* into the battle scenes," Mesa explains. "And these shots which we did in *Army* have been copied again in *The Mummy* and *The Two Towers*. Same layout, same angles, and it is so close that it's almost a tribute to Sam Raimi because they did so much that seemed pulled right out of *Army of Darkness*."

RECRUITING AN ARMY OF DARKNESS

From the beginning, one thing was certain about *Army of Darkness*. Only one man could play the lead role, the inimitable Bruce Campbell. *Army of Darkness*'s script represented a different approach to the character, making him a figure of fun. Campbell himself expressed satisfaction with a role in which he could do more than dismember other cast members. "I don't just say a few words and blow the guy away," he noted. "I get to talk myself out of situations."[2]

Army of Darkness also offered Campbell the chance to work with a more diverse group of actors than the previous *Evil Dead* adventures. The accomplished veteran Ian Abercrombie, *Seinfeld*'s 'Mr. Pitt,' joined up as Campbell's foil and straight man, the humorless Wiseman. Before *Army of Darkness*, Abercrombie had played Merlin four times already, so was well-prepared to counsel Ash and the film's King Arthur, British actor Marcus Gilbert.

To get into the role's spirit, Abercrombie viewed the first two films in the franchise. "I rushed out and rented them both," he says. "I didn't know what to think in the beginning, but I saw this clever side of Sam and realized they were very funny. I saw what he was doing — the tongue in cheek. And seeing Bruce, I really got into it and realized it was going to be a great deal of fun."

Of course, as straight man, Abercrombie couldn't *look* like he was having fun. "I had to play it straight. I was Merlin; the Merlin who is the protector of his people and knows the danger of the Deadites. My purpose, I felt, was to be keeper of my people and this young man, though I had great doubts about him. But I still had to play it straight," cautions Abercrombie. "I couldn't be fooled by him, even his jokes. I tried to bring a heaviness, a presence, like everything was at stake for us. We would have been totally lost without the Necronomicon."

Cast as Arthur's rival, Duke Henry, Grove came to the production with an affection for the genre and the series' previous installments. "I've always been a big fan of horror films and *Evil Dead*, and when I was living in New York, I always had big Halloween parties," Grove explains. "I always picked one or two films that would be shown in a separate room and always had *Evil Dead* on. I was a huge fan, I'd seen it maybe a dozen times." Grove also understood the crew biographies. "I'd read about the background of Sam, coming out with Bruce and Rob Tapert, and how they put it [*Evil Dead*] together, so I knew all about it."

A young actress from South Africa, Embeth Davidtz also appeared in *Army of Darkness*, her first film in America. Later, she starred in *Schindler's List*, *Murder in the First* (1995), *Bridget Jones's Diary* (2001) and *The Emperor's Club* (2002). Grove recalls being impressed with her from her first scene. "She was focused," he notes. "She was passionate. There's a scene when Ash first comes in, and she's spitting and yelling at him. I was there for that shot, and she was great. It was 100 percent real for her. She wasn't kidding the material at all, she wasn't playing with it."

Another notable cast member was Bridget Fonda, who appeared in the film's opening, which recapped the events of *Evil Dead* for the second time. Fonda became the third actress in three films to play Ash's Linda, following Betsy Baker and Denise Bixler.

TO THE BATTLEMENTS!

Principal photography on *Army of Darkness* occurred over a period of fifty-five days. Stage work stretched across thirty-seven days, while twenty-seven days were spent on location at a massive castle set and other outdoor locales. "We were out near Acton, where they built the castle," Abercrombie notes. "It was such a drive. We drove every day until we did the night shooting, and then we stayed in a hotel out in Lancaster."

The castle itself was an impressive set. "This was a mountain that had the entire front of the castle. It was incredible to look at from a distance," Grove considers. "We were right near Tippi Hedren's lion preserve and occasionally you'd hear a lion roar."

But it was mid-summer as shooting progressed, which meant difficult weather conditions. "You have to remember that out there, in this in-between woods/in-between valley, the days are extremely hot and the nights are extremely cold," Grove explains. "So the contrast in temperature is dramatic. As soon as the sun goes down, it's freezing, and as soon as the sun comes up, it's boiling. Most of us were wearing some variations of wool or heavy clothing, so it was uncomfortable for everybody during the day."

Much more fun than braving temperature swings was the opportunity to see Raimi direct on a spectacular, medieval-style set. "The comparison I always use when people ask me about working with Sam Raimi is that he's like a big kid with a camera," says Grove. "He had enormous amounts of energy and enthusiasm for what he was doing. He was constantly excited. If somebody did a really good scene, or a stunt came off really well, he would just be absolutely thrilled by it. That enthusiasm was infectious.

"I felt that he was a sensitive person," Grove adds. "I think that the kind of defense mechanisms you develop when you're supposed to be a leader or director ... I don't think Sam had those. I've worked with lots of other directors on big shows. Some directors are bossy and pushy and want to control everything. That's not Sam. Sam was just like a kid with a camera. He was so excited to be making movies. You could obviously tell he just loved it, so when problems came up, he just didn't like them. He was uncomfortable with them, which is why I think Tapert is so important to him. Robert Tapert is Sam's bad cop. When you work on a big film, it's just controlling these levels of chaos. There's so many things going on — and everything has to stop, everything has to focus, and shots have to be set up."

"From my limited knowledge of working with him on the film, I'd say he's a truly dedicated film man," adds Abercrombie. "He knows film backward and forward. He's like Martin Scorsese that way. He doesn't play around too much, even in the down time, and he's got his eye on everything."

Abercrombie recalls that on the *Army of Darkness* set, Raimi's parents visited him and watched him shoot. "He keeps grounded in his roots," Abercrombie considers. "That's why he's surrounded by his friends. That's why he has Bruce. A part of Sam's success is that he's very grounded and that he works extremely hard. He delegates authority, but when it comes to the bottom line, he is at the helm. You *listen* when he's talking to you. He has little patience for slackers, for which I don't blame him, because this is his dream. He's got that cherubic face, like a choirboy gone wrong. That's my reference to him. I always say he reminds me of a choirboy who's done something naughty."

As for Raimi, he enjoyed a little more freedom on the set. "This is back to kind of hands-on filmmaking that we grew up with,"[3] he told Steve Biodrowski in *Cinefantastique*.

BATTLE ROYALE

Though the released version of *Army of Darkness* runs a scant eighty-seven minutes, the last third involves an attack on Arthur's castle by the Deadites, led by Ash's evil double. Finding the hero within, Ash defends humanity by using twentieth century ingenuity. In his car trunk are two items no time-tripping protagonist can do without, a chemistry textbook and an issue of *Fangoria* magazine! Ash's twentieth century know-how references not only a literary model, Mark Twain's *A Connecticut Yankee in King Arthur's Court*, but also naturally, the Three Stooges. In *Fuelin' Around* (1949), the Stooges developed a powerful fuel based on their reading of a text called *Elementary Chemistry.* The Stooges also fiddled in matters medieval in *Restless Knights* (1935) and *Squareheads of the Round Table* (1948).

Behind the camera and capturing much of the ridiculous action was William Mesa. "My involvement with the movie would be a lot more than visual effects supervisor, because I worked so closely with Sam," Mesa explains. At the time, cinematographer Bill Pope could not be paid his standard fee because of money problems, and the production agreed he would shoot only certain hours Monday through Friday. This left Mesa to shoot many of the action sequences on the weekend, including the moment with Campbell on a dolly, walking and delivering an inspiring speech to the troops.

A complex sequence in concept and execution, Mesa recalls that his charge on the battle scenes was the same one Raimi established on early projects. "We wanted to come up with stuff that was wacky and different," he describes.

More often than not, this meant choreographing Campbell to deliver live-action jabs and punches to figures that weren't really there, stop-motion skeletons that had already been filmed and would be combined with the live-action footage using the Introvision process.

These shots depended on crackerjack timing and precision but came out beautifully on screen. "You totally believed he walked up to a skeleton and knocked this thing—and it went spinning around," Mesa recalls. "It was a timing thing. 'At number six, you have to hit the skeleton...'"

But even though it looked good, it was no cakewalk. "Bruce was cussing and swearing some of the time because you had to work on the number system," says Mesa. "Sam would tell us to make it as complicated and hard for Bruce as possible. 'Make him go through torture!' So we'd come up with these shots that were really, really difficult, and sometimes they would take thirty-seven takes.

"Some of the scenes were really complicated, because there would be multiple skeletons in one frame, where they would jump over a wall and Bruce would swing around and kick one's head off, then chop one's arm off. We would rehearse for basically maybe half an hour or so before doing it, because Sam wanted the timing perfect, and didn't want to cut up the shots. He wanted them all to work in one take."

One joy of *Army of Darkness* is this adroit mix of special effects, prosthetics and stunts, often within the same shots. Tony Gardner, who created the makeup for *Darkman*, returned to create many of the glorious ghouls for *Army of Darkness*. Like Raimi, Gardner grew up making home movies with family and friends, and as an artist counts a few films from his childhood as career inspirations, notably *Planet of the Apes*.[4]

For Mesa, the chance to integrate so many effects approaches was a challenge he appreciated. "Some takes, we would trick the audience and do a stop-motion animation mixed with live skeletons that were mechanically rigged. The time Evil Ash was walking along in the graveyard, and the skeletons were pulling another skeleton out of the ground, it was stop-motion. But Evil Ash would grab *another* skeleton and pull its arms off, and that one was *mechanical*. All of the elements were blended together, and as a supervisor I loved the idea of blending prosthetics, mechanics and visual effects into one thing. I still do that today. It's a great avenue to really make shots work and blend together."

Stunt coordinator Chris Doyle also contributed to that process, staging the spectacular battle royale's live-action component. "We layered the whole thing with actors and stunt people. We had lots of action in the background with stunt guys getting blown up and flying, using these air rams. We had a couple of different sizes; one will send you about forty feet and thirty feet high," he remembers.

One element Doyle worked on was the Classic, Raimi's Delta 88, converted into a "the death coaster." "He [Campbell] drives this thing, and it's got blades in front, so it is chopping up skeletons as it goes. In that sequence, as he's driving it in the castle, I had three guys on air ratchets," Doyle explains. "They wear a vest underneath their costumes, and they're hooked up high on their backs. And they would literally run five or six feet and the cable would come to a stop, and that triggered the solenoid, which would jerk them up and out of the shot. And we timed that as the death coaster was coming toward them. With the camera angle, it looked like the blades actually hit them and knocked them into the air.

"We discussed this sequence, and Sam drilled me on how all of this would work, and I worked with him on the storyboards," Doyle lays out. "Sam likes to have the storyboards and keep everything straight. When you have a busy action show with lots of elements, they really come in handy to keep you oriented to where you are and what goes where. It really helps you keep things together when you have drawings of the puzzle. We got that all on the storyboard, and we tested everything that night and we shot it.

"Bruce drove the death coaster in some sequences," Doyle reveals. "For the wider shots, there was a double driving it. Some of the stunt people would jump on it as it was going by, and he'd knock them down.

"One of the things I really enjoyed was the sword play," Doyle considers. "When Sam and I first talked about this picture, it was like, 'Oh man, this is great!' I get fire, high work, I get to jump a car into a castle and turn the car over ... just a lot of different stuff. And the medieval material was great anyway. Some of the sword stuff we could put together early in the day before we would shoot, but a lot of the major stuff were things we worked on for weeks in advance."

This meant that Doyle and Campbell spent a lot of time together, a span Doyle enjoyed. "Bruce is very professional. One of the things about Bruce is that when he gets on the set as an actor, he knows his lines. There's none of this blowing line crap you get with some actors. He's so professional, and has respect for the crew's time and the effort they're putting out. He just feels like that's his job. He's prepared and there's no waiting. Bruce is ready to go when he walks on the set.

"Bruce is very physical," adds Doyle. "I can talk to him like a grown-up. When we first started the show, I gave him a bag with knee and elbow pads. 'Here's your pads, you're going to be needing these things, and when I tell you to put 'em on, I want you to put 'em on. I know you're physical, but you have to get through this with the least amount of bruises as possible.' And he was great about that kind of stuff."

THE END?

As conceived by the brothers Raimi, *Army of Darkness*'s climax would have set up a sequel. Instead of returning to his time, Ash "overslept" and awakened in futuristic London, a postapocalyptic world where he would again face Deadites. This climax fit with the idea proffered in *Evil Dead 2* that it was Ash's destiny to serve as perpetual opponent of the Deadites throughout time. However, Universal hated the concept, feeling it was "negative." "They made us change it because of some political issues," Doyle explains.

Instead, a more upbeat ending was deemed necessary. "He [Sam] had to get Bruce back to S-Mart at the end, instead of leaving it on this dark note where he ends up in downtown London after a nuclear holocaust," Doyle relates. "We shot that end sequence [S-Mart] probably a month after we did the picture. We came back to do that and shot at Malibu in some lumber store. If I'm not mistaken, we shot three or four nights there."

The new climax involved Ash returning to Housewares, but bringing the Deadite scourge along. "Sam told me what he wanted to do, and I said, 'Sure, we can do that.' He wanted to have these guys [the Deadites] flipping through the air, so we used an apparatus called a Russian swing. It's a funny-looking thing. It's an A-frame with a flatbed swing on it. When it's standing still, the A-frame fulcrum at the top is ten feet up, so we have a nine foot swing that's really sturdy. The platform at the bottom is flat, and they use it in the circus for flying people up into chairs."

The stunt double for the Deadite Witch was Jack Verbois, who performed a double flip with a twist, utilizing the swing. "We also put squibs on him, so this was really challenging," Doyle notes. "He pulled it off really well."

Campbell performed much of his own stunts, including the moment when Ash jumps atop a moving cart and blasts Deadites with a rifle. "We put him on a cart and pulled him, with people next to him so he wouldn't fall off," Doyle notes. "We pulled the cart through the shot as he was firing up at the roof. That was a fun, challenging sequence to do."

And not the film's last, either. Two months after the film was deemed finish, a round of reshoots began in Santa Monica. These were interior sequences involving Ash's stay in a windmill. Other reshoots occurred in the hills north of Glendale, depicting Ash's tumble into a puddle, as well as scenes with Bridget Fonda.

"We did several reshoots," Grove explains. "The level of money spent on the reshoots was minuscule, which must have meant some problem with money. The first reshoot I did was in Bronson Caves, a very famous place. I knew it because of *Batman* — it was the Batcave — and endless amounts of *Outer Limits* episodes were shot there. So Sam was shooting simple reshoots of the early moments in the film when Henry was captured; I think they had a crew of five to eight people there, it was all on the fly.

"But I remember telling Sam about Bronson Caves. I pointed to one cave and said, 'Don't you recognize that entrance?' 'It's the Batcave!" He saw it, his eyes lit up, and he said, 'You're kidding!' As soon he he knew what it was, he was so excited to be in a place that was so historic.

"Bridget Fonda shot her scenes very quickly," Grove continues. "Finally they ran out of time, it was getting dark, and they realized they had to do some pick-up shots of me on the horse, swinging that thing [a mace]." This particular shot was an insert to be used in the battle, at the moment Henry's cavalry rides over the hill to aid King Arthur and Ash.

"We pulled off the side of the road at a very large rest area and they brought out a little dolly, a little platform with wheels," Grove explains. "They put on a rocking horse with a rug on it and Sam set this thing up in micro-seconds. And they had some guy rocking the horse, and I was bouncing as well, and I thought this was the most ludicrous thing I had ever done as an actor. The helmet was too large, and if you look closely, it falls down in my face at the last minute, and I can't actually see what I'm hitting." Though Grove was not enamored of the shot, he notes that it turned out fine as it appears on film, briefly glimpsed. Of Raimi he notes, "He's a very bright guy and he knows how to match shots."

When reshoots were complete, Joe LoDuca, *The Evil Dead* maestro, returned to write the score, and found he was composing in a different style. "In terms of score, it does have more fun with the movie," he notes. "There are times when we absolutely go along with the humor. There's an Irish jig, and that's where we sort of get into animation music, but done in such a way that there's a little bit more needling, mischievous quality to it."

For Ash's battle in the pit with a Deadite monster, LoDuca also found himself working on a grander scale. "That's more an Indiana Jones moment. I think that once again, it seemed to me that where we were, and everybody's reaction to Ash, was really what the score should focus on. We talked about treating Ash in a certain modernistic way and giving him some kind of Spaghetti Western moments in terms of music. I think that ultimately, it just didn't fit. I think the fish out of water played better; playing it straight and letting the music be the straight man. So that when Ash has his little moral collapse and looks like he's going to be a coward, there's this solemn Gregorian chant. Or when they create the death coaster, there are moments of a mystical, magical female choir, and it's much more the convention of a fantasy or adventure score than anything to do with Ash."

Fans of the earlier *Evil Dead* films will also note that *Army of Darkness* has a nostalgia factor, reviving bits of *Dead by Dawn*'s score. "In the prologue, I reprised *Evil Dead 2* when they repeat the vortex sequence. The difference is that now we've added a choir for a couple of reasons. One is that we had a budget. But it also seemed appropriate, given that you have this sort of epic tale."

Having scored the entire trilogy, LoDuca considers *Army of Darkness* his favorite contribution. "I feel close to it because I think that's the one that Sam and I worked most closely on. We were in a period of time there when I could actually play orchestral mock-ups of the cues before we went to the stage with them. There was a way to keep informed and get feedback.

"And," LoDuca considers, "the fact that we had resources by the time we did the third one."

THE CUTTING ROOM FLOOR

Though De Laurentiis afforded the *Army of Darkness* team great freedom while shooting, Raimi discovered in the editing room that he would have to deal squarely with Universal. The studio was unhappy with several edits of the film, the ending and other elements. The original opening, which would have dramatized more of Ash's "real" life, was jettisoned because it slowed down the action. Subsequent cuts, some by Raimi and some by film editors outside of Renaissance, came in variously at 96 minutes, a scant 81 minutes, and the theatrical version that lasted approximately 87 minutes. Basically, everything not related to the central plot, including a romantic scene with Campbell and Davidtz, was trimmed.

"I watched the uncut version of it, because the true ending is when Ash comes into the future, and it is a science fiction future," Richard Grove explains. "I thought that was brilliant, and was expecting all of that. And when I saw it, it was this cut version. I heard that Universal had chopped it to shit, and I was very upset. Not just because of my scenes, but because I felt it didn't make sense."

In particular, Grove felt that the removal of the scene in which Ash goes to Henry seeking help, weakened the movie's narrative. He sets up that missing scene as it was conceived and shot: "It was a short scene, a transitional scene, to check in with Henry the Red to establish the fact that he could possibly be the cavalry coming at sunrise.

"Bruce was riding on the road, and I believe he stopped because there was something unusual he heard or saw. He either got off his horse or was thrown off, and a net was thrown around him. All of Henry's cronies rushed in around him, and Henry showed up with a sword in his hand and had that line that Ash said to him at the beginning of the film. I said, 'Well hello, Mr.

Fancy Pants' or 'Well, well, if it isn't Mr. Fancy Pants.'" At that point, Henry's men would have released Ash, letting him explain what was happening and that Arthur needed help.

The scene consisted of close-ups of Campbell, and Grove was to "give no indication of whether I would or wouldn't help, to keep it suspenseful," says the actor. Without that scene, Grove feels the film lost something. "Suddenly Henry the Red shows up with all of his guys. Why? You never saw the scene with Ash in order to connect them! I don't think Sam would have let that go if it had been left to him."

When asked about other deleted scenes, Grove recalls at least one. "There was also Arthur's funeral scene that was cut. I don't remember much about it because I wasn't there when they shot it, and I didn't go through the script very carefully. But what I recall is that there was a fairly elaborate funeral scene after Arthur was killed in some way. It was very much like the scene in *Lord of the Rings* where Boramir is killed and they put him in a boat and float him off. It was apparently an ancient Norse, Viking ritual to put the dead in boats with the weapons of the enemies they conquered at their feet. I believe that's how it was set up. It was very beautifully rendered in the storyboards. As I recall when I spoke with Marcus, he said it went really well."

ASH VS. HANNIBAL LECTER

If the cuts in *Army of Darkness* weren't troubling enough, the film soon became a pawn in a power struggle between Universal and De Laurentiis over serial killer Hannibal Lecter. *The Silence of the Lambs* was 1991's most celebrated motion picture, generating a huge profit and earning Academy Awards for Best Picture, Best Director (Jonathan Demme), Best Actor (Anthony Hopkins) Best Actress (Jodie Foster), and Best Screenplay based on material from another medium (Ted Tally). Universal wanted to continue the franchise, but De Laurentiis owned the rights to the Lecter character, having once produced the Michael Mann thriller *Manhunter*, a prequel Lecter story by novelist Thomas Harris titled, in book form, *Red Dragon*.

When Raimi needed three million dollars to complete *Army of Darkness*, Universal stonewalled and held up the picture's release.[5] Raimi explained the situation to interviewer Bill Warren in a *Fangoria* exclusive: "The only thing [Universal and De Laurentiis] had in common was *Army of Darkness*, so until they finally settled on the *Lambs* sequel, which they did, they were using *Army of Darkness* as something between a hostage and a bargaining chip."[6]

The matter was finally resolved, paving the way for 2000's Lecter adaptation *Hannibal*, co-produced by Universal and DeLaurentiis. As for *Army of Darkness*, it was released in February of 1993, though it would have made for a perfect summer movie. Adding to audience confusion over the film was its title. Hardcore fans wanted *Evil Dead III*, or the long-rumored title, *Medieval Dead*, or even *Evil Dead 1300 AD*. Adding insult to injury, the film also went through a grueling ratings battle with the MPAA, and emerged in defanged terms, rated a light R. For fans of the unrated predecessors, this represented a shift in the content of *The Evil Dead* series from horror, to horror laced with comedy, to comedy laced with thrills. "A lot of people who were squeamish and who hadn't even seen the others thought that was fun. But the real hardcore people were like, 'You sold out,'" Campbell told the *San Francisco Examiner*.[7]

Army of Darkness divided critics. On the plus side, John Anderson wrote in *Newsday* that Raimi "packs *Army of Darkness* with so many whacked-out movie references that it's like a hysterical *Finnegan's Wake* for horror/action/postapocalyptic/ninja/sci-fi buffs."[8] "When he's really cooking," wrote Peter Rainer for the *Los Angeles Times*, "[Raimi] knows how to make the techniques of fantasy-horror seem funny all by themselves." He also noted that "Raimi builds our awareness of movie technique into our response, he makes us laugh at our own connoisseurship because, after all, it's really a connoisseurship of shlock."[9]

Jami Bernard noted that "Raimi is one of those directors like Joe Dante who have absorbed the history of pop culture through their skin and right into their bloodstreams;"[10] and Jonathan Romney reported in the *New Statesman and Society* that the movie "is like Tom and Jerry with broadswords and bad jokes."[11]

On the downside, *Entertainment Weekly*'s Owen Gleiberman suggested it was "time to let these dead rest in peace;[12] and Ralph Novak, while admiring the film's sense of homage, noted that *Army of Darkness* "seems to last three hours."[13]

RAIMI RAP

SKULLS AND STOOGES: "Sam wanted each of the skeletons to have its own character," William Mesa reports. "'Let's not make 'em like Harryhausen did,'" Raimi would say. "'This skeleton is going to be Moe; this skeleton is going to be Curly. Each is going to have his own stupidity.'" And just to help get the Stooge connection across, "Sam used his voice a lot on the skeletons."

Three Stooges fans will also recognize the influence of the famous comedians in the scene following Ash's theft of the Necronomicon. "In

Army when Bruce is leaving the grave site and gets tripped up by the skeletons, that's a tribute to the Three Stooges, but then Sam has to take it much further," says Mesa. "Doing the Three Stooges just isn't enough. He's got to go as far as he can go with it, like the hand in the mouth and everything else. He took the thing as far as it could go."

THE GOOD BOOK: Tom Sullivan was recruited briefly for duty on *Army of Darkness*. His mission: to re-create the Book of the Dead over a single weekend. He built a new book, re-inked it, and water-colored in the pages. But the book wasn't the right size! The book "had to be larger to allow Ash to get sucked into it during the Klaatu, Verata, Nikto scene," Sullivan explains. "A Ten Commandments size book was built, and four pages from my copy were pieced together to make one big page."

THE MONSTER IN THE PIT: "When the Deadite comes out of the well and Ash blasts him with the gun and he does a back flip and falls back in, that was performed by a stuntman named Rick Blackwell," Chris Doyle explains. "He was dressed up as the creature in the pit. That was interesting because he had to do this one-and-a-half back flip and he was half-blind in that makeup and costume, but some of these guys just amazed me with what they could pull off."

"We had a pad down there [in the pit] and spotters on the side. He fell down about eight feet into the pit. It was more than eight feet, it was probably twelve or fifteen feet deep, but we padded it up to eight feet," Doyle continues. "It really helps to see because you need to spot yourself. When you do this stuff for so long, you get this air-sense. He did it half-blind and pulled it off perfectly. We did it twice, I believe, and he did it perfectly both times. Sam was just beside himself."

KLAATU VERATA NIKTO: Wiseman John instructs Ash very carefully to speak three important words that will release the Necronomicon from its demonic altar and make it safe to carry. Those words are significant in Hollywood history. They are the instructions actress Patricia Neal (as Helen Benson) gave to Michael Rennie's powerful robot Gort in the finale of the 1951 Robert Wise classic, *The Day The Earth Stood Still*. This dialogue immediately rung a bell for actor Ian Abercrombie, but it took him some time to figure out why. "When I read it, I said, 'Why do these words sound familiar? This is stolen from some place!' I mentioned it to my agent and he said, 'You idiot, it's from *The Day the Earth Stood Still* starring Michael Rennie!'"

MIRROR IMAGE: "I doubled a bunch of times as Evil Ash," Chris Doyle reports.

"They shot over my shoulder sometimes and I'd double as Ash. We [Bruce and I] had something going there. At one point, we did have somebody else doubling Ash, and it was working okay, but it seemed to work better if I jumped in there and did it. When I do stunts, when I'm doubling somebody, I really take on their mannerisms and the character as much as possible. Not all stunt people who double do that. Especially this kind of campy thing ... I love that stuff. It's really easy for me to get into a character like that. It was so much fun."

HORSE SENSE: Abercrombie recalls that Raimi's incredible technical knowledge of filmmaking sometimes caused miscues with actors. "I was on a horse when we had just arrived back after finding Richard and Bruce, and they were in the shackles," he explains. "We arrived back at the fort and they fell down and I was on the horse and came into the shot, and Sam was behind the monitor setting up another shot and said, 'Ian, can you move your horse a quarter of an inch?' And I said, 'I beg your pardon?' And he said, 'Can you move him a quarter of an inch to the left?' And I said, 'Well, how do you move a horse a quarter of an inch?' And then he looked up from the monitor, and I realized that to him that quarter of an inch was *in the monitor*. I could move the horse forwards and backwards, but I couldn't move it sideways."

GIVING ASH THE FINGER: In the deleted scene involving Henry the Red and Ash, Grove recalls that a small physical deformity came in handy. "I remember Sam collaborated on that scene. On my left hand, I'm missing a little bit of my forefinger, and it's an ugly looking finger. So I said to Sam, 'What if as Bruce is riding off, you get some sense of people out here? And this hand comes up in the frame with this ugly nail, and the palm is open and it closes like a signal?' And Sam loved that idea and we did two or three shots of my hand making this signal for the guys to jump Ash and throw the net over him."

DOCUMENTARY: One thing that makes Raimi's films special is his humor. That humor extended behind the scenes too, as William Mesa recalls. "Sometimes I would take a videotape to look at the layout of the set because we were remaking it in miniature, and Sam would go around interviewing different people who were working on the set and kind of force them to say they were having a great time, even though they'd been working for twenty hours or something and were totally burned out. He'd get them at the worst times and make them say how wonderful this all is.

"It's wonderful working with Sam, and his philosophy is that you get the most out of people when they can have fun making the movie," muses Mesa. "That really holds true of any of the films I've worked on with Sam.

If you create an environment where you are going to have fun, then you're going to put your effort into making this movie the most. Sam does that. He wants the experience to be a good experience."

EVIL DEAD 4: A fourth film in the *Evil Dead* series has long been rumored. "They all make money, but over a long period of time," Campbell noted of the franchise. "The last, *Army of Darkness*, didn't do the slam dunk at the box office."[14] Still, Mesa reports a sequel has been a topic of conversation. "I went to a book signing of Bruce's book, and Bruce happened to be there with Rob [Tapert] and Lucy [Lawless] and they were talking about trying to put together another *Evil Dead*."

THE PROMISED ONE RETURNS

Published in 1889, Mark Twain's novel *A Connecticut Yankee in King Arthur's Court* spotlighted the adventures of a Yankee industrialist named Hank Morgan who is inexplicably catapulted back in time from his mechanical plant in Hartford to the Middle Ages. Trapped in the year 528, Morgan is captured and rushed to King Arthur's court, where he escapes execution only by his (accurate) prediction that an eclipse will soon occur.

Granted a reprieve, Hank becomes Merlin's right-hand man and introduces telephones, bicycles, guns and explosives to the unenlightened denizens of the sixth century. Much of the novel's humor emanates from the medieval response to this technology. The novel's point, according to scholar William Dean, was to dramatize "a New Deal for the downtrodden common people — transforming Arthur's England into a technically efficient state in which gunpowder and mechanical skills triumph over superstition, injustice and oppression."[15]

Devised a hundred years later by Sam and Ivan Raimi, *Army of Darkness* is an irreverent yet not unfaithful rendering of a similar story, at least thematically. In the film, an average twentieth century fellow named Ash is catapulted back in time to the year 1300, where he meets a King named Arthur, and introduces a brave new world of technology including gunpowder and a modern vehicle — not a bicycle, but a death coaster. A Merlin-like character, in the film called "Wiseman," is the individual in both works with the ability to return the hero to the correct epoch.

Why adopt the template of *A Connecticut Yankee*? As Raimi has explained in the past, he wanted to make a film that took the concept of "technology versus the supernatural" further than ever before.[16] Twain's novel offered a near-perfect prototype to accomplish that mission, and though Raimi may dramatize very different villains, demonic Deadites rather than a socially unjust and superstitious Catholic Church, the tools by which to defeat these villains — human ingenuity and technology — are identical, making comparisons between the Twain novel and *Army of Darkness* not quite as far fetched as it seems at first blush.

Certainly, the source of humor in both cases is identical: our "contemporary" thoughts on the backward denizens of the past, and their bewildered responses to a man from the future. On the latter front, Wiseman's ill-advised experimentation with gunpowder — waving it over an open flame — spurs a disapproving response from Ash. The merging of these time periods in *Army of Darkness* not only results in a story about technology defeating the supernatural but, in theatrical terms, resulted in an intentional blending of acting styles, which baffled some on the set and had to be carefully monitored by Raimi.

Grove explains. "Sam delighted in watching Bruce's performance, and the more Bruce would kid the material, the bigger Bruce would get, the more excited Sam got. Now I thought that was curious, because everybody else in the movie was taking it, for the most part, 100 percent seriously. I always felt there was a divergence of style in the film. Bruce's style of acting in the film didn't match the style of others. However, his style of acting matched all of the effects; matched all of the monster characters perfectly. The movie works."

Abercrombie agrees and remembers an incident when Raimi directed him to maintain that distance between approaches. "I think at one point I did laugh at something in one of the takes, and Sam said '*No*, that's not funny to you.'" In other words, the *Connecticut Yankee* template, fish-out-of-water humor and all, could not succeed unless each contingent of the film's actors (Bruce vs. the Arthurians) played as *opposites*.

Also, one must never forget that Raimi is master of the homage, from both literature and film sources. So it is not just *A Connecticut Yankee in King Arthur's Court* acknowledged and ribbed in *Army of Darkness*, or merely Arthurian lore, it is Jonathan Swift's *Gulliver's Travels*, another satire. The *Army of Darkness* windmill sequence, wherein a dozen "tiny" versions of Ash tie the prone hero up, echoes the first part of *Gulliver*, "A Voyage to Lilliput," in which the normal-sized protagonist is bound and restrained by the forces of little people. This film is a tour of fantasy classics, but with Larry, Moe and Curly as guides.

Regarding film history, references to adventures past are equally rich. "He's not afraid to use things from the past," Mesa acknowledges. "That's what *Army* is, a tribute to *Sinbad* and *Jason of the Argonauts*, *The Day the Earth Stood Still* and the Three Stooges — all in this comic book way." Indeed the references are numerous. *The Day the Earth Stood Still* riff comes about when Ash mis-speaks the magic words to free the Necronomicon ("neck tie, nektar, nickle..."). The Three Stooges come into play as Ash steals the book and skeletal hands poke his eyes, smash his cheeks and otherwise pummel him. Also, Ash's battle with a flying Book of the Dead reflects Larry's similar predicament with strafing birds in *Back to the Woods* (1937).

The skeleton attack on Arthur's castle references the 1948's *Joan of Arc* in visual terms and *Jason and the Argonauts'* similar battle, the most discussed scene in that film, according to creator Ray Harryhausen. "When one pauses to think that there were seven skeletons fighting three men with each skeleton having five appendages to move each frame of film, and keeping them all in synchronization with the three actors' movements, one can readily see why it took four and a half months to record,"[17] Harryhausen once noted. *Army of Darkness* is not just a reference to this incredible sequence, but a multiplication and advancement, featuring more fighters and new techniques, but always a deeply felt love for what Harryhausen established.

Ash's weapon of choice, a chainsaw, represents the sword of Excalibur, heightening the Arthurian connection to the material. Ash's sword battle on the castle staircase recalls a duel in Michael Curtiz's *The Adventures of Robin Hood* (1938); and when one of the Deadites yells, "Cry havoc and let slip the dogs of war!" even Shakespeare (*Julius Caesar*) is referenced. The title card of *Army of Darkness* actually reads "Bruce Campbell vs. The Army of Darkness" and thus revives a defunct Hollywood tradition of putting actors' names in titles. Kind of like *The Bowery Boys Meet the Monsters* (1954) or *Bela Lugosi Meets a Brooklyn Gorilla* (1952).

However, there is another more subtle homage that makes *Army of Darkness* enjoyable. It involves Campbell. In many ways, Ash in this movie seems a needling variation on the Charlton Heston image highlighted in films such as *Planet of the Apes* (1968), *The Omega Man* (1971) and *Soylent Green* (1973). Read the following description by the late Pauline Kael, and imagine she is writing about the character of Ash in *Army of Darkness*:

> Physically, Heston with his perfect, lean hipped, powerful body, is a god-like hero built for strength; he's an archetype of what makes Americans win. He doesn't play nice guy; he's harsh and hostile, self-centered and hot-tempered. Yet we don't hate him, because he's so magnetically strong; he represents American power — the physical attraction and admiration one feels toward the beauty of strength as well as the moral revulsion one feels toward the ugliness of violence ... He is the perfect American Adam to work off some American guilt feelings or self hatred on.[18]

Like Taylor, Heston's character in *Apes*, Campbell's Ash is a "man out of time" in *Army of Darkness*. Both characters romance the most beautiful women of their new time period (Nova and Sheila), find themselves captured and abused by the dominant cultures of the "alien" world, and then launch themselves into wars to preserve mankind from an outside evil (Apes or Deadites). More to the point, both characters are given to invectives like "Damn you!" and curse-laden monologues ("Where in the hell...?") Also, they verbally condescend to the establishment culture. Ash calls his captors "primitive screwheads," and Taylor calls his new world "upside down," likening it to "a madhouse."

Ash and Taylor share another commonality: they both return "home" with surprising results. For Taylor, the discovery of the Statue of Liberty makes him aware that his race is doomed, and that he is indeed on Earth. For Ash, he awakens in his own time only to find that the Deadites are still with him.

The original ending, in which Ash lands in a ruined, postapocalyptic downtown London probably would have been a closer approximation to the *Planet of the Apes* scenario, but the theatrical ending is close enough to draw out the parallel.

Where these characters are really different is in how their directors view them. To director Franklin Schaeffer, Taylor is mankind's savior and defender, even if he has some arrogance to overcome. Ash, by director Raimi, could be mankind's savior, but he's also a boob. Both heroes are fish out of water, but stranger-in-a-strange-land Ash is the more overtly funny of these arrogant snipes, sounding Stooge-like in his empty threats ("Oh, you...," he waffles, trying to sound dangerous). Much humor is derived from the fact that Ash is so much bluster, and that his primary foil, Abercrombie's Wiseman, is a model of long-suffering dignity.

"I've found this in some of the things that I've done," Abercrombie notes of his performance as the straight man. "When I'm listening to people, there's a slight quizzical feeling like I can't quite believe what they're saying, but I don't register any emotion until they've finished. I'm weighing what they're saying, and I think you can see my brain working. And I have a little disdain for what people are telling me."

In conjunction with Campbell's blustering and thoroughly enjoyable performance, Abercrombie's restraint brings out the film's humor in an effective way. In some ways, he is the most interesting character Ash ever appears beside because he does not become a villain (which would necessitate killing), does not beat up Ash (which would necessitate killing), but instead *needs* Ash and vice versa. It's a fun twist, especially in a film rife with Campbell's sarcastic one liners.

From a visual standpoint, Raimi engenders humor by taking accepted camera techniques and extending them to absurd length. An early scene in

Arthur's courtyard involves a pan across a crowd. The extras in the scene pivot as the camera cruises by them, gazing at something off screen. This shot soon encompasses a line of a dozen or so, until the camera at last pinpoints Ash, who is to be cast into the monster pit. Again, a pan is mostly used to convey something *nearby* in space, but not so here.

In line with that shot, *Army of Darkness* seems timed for laughter. Trapped in a windmill, Ash screams as the Deadite force pounds on the door, but then the sound effects and scary music suddenly silence themselves and Campbell is left screaming all alone, sounding like an idiot.

Homage, humor and Campbell's performance open up the world of *The Evil Dead* to epic proportions. *Army of Darkness* isn't scary, but it is involving, and rarely have effects and skeletons been more ... fun. "When you have an *Evil Dead* film marathon beginning with *Within the Woods*, you will see the tone of each movie change by about twenty degrees," Tom Sullivan says, "from the dark, grim and jarringly frightening, to the more humorous, to Three Stooges slapstick." As Raimi develops as a director, his films became more and more a reflection of his personality and desire to entertain rather than merely frighten.

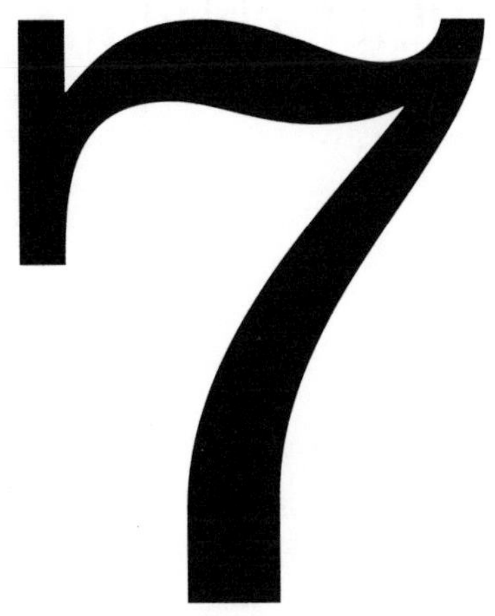

THE QUICK AND THE DEAD (1995)

IS IT POSSIBLE TO IMPROVE ON PERFECTION?

THINK YOU'RE QUICK ENOUGH?

CAST AND CREW

TRI-STAR PICTURES PRESENTS, IN ASSOCIATION WITH JAPAN SATELLITE PRODUCTIONS, AN INDIE PRODUCTION, *THE QUICK AND THE DEAD.*

DIRECTOR: Sam Raimi
CASTING: Francine Maisler
MUSIC: Alan Silvestri
COSTUMES: Judianna Makovsky
FILM EDITOR: Pietro Scalia
PRODUCTION DESIGNER: Patrizia Von Brandenstein
DIRECTOR OF PHOTOGRAPHY: Dante Spinotti
CO-PRODUCERS: Chuck Binder and Sharon Stone
EXECUTIVE PRODUCERS: Toby Jaffe, Robert Tapert
WRITER: Simon Moore
PRODUCER: Joshua Donen, Allen Shapiro and Patrick Markey.
ART DIRECTOR: Steve Saklad
GUN COACH AND ARMORER: Thell Reed
SPECIAL MAKEUP EFFECTS: KNB

STARRING

Sharon Stone: Ellen
Gene Hackman: John Herod
Russell Crowe: Cort
Leonardo DiCaprio: Kid
Tobin Bell: Dog Kelly
Roberts Blossom: Doc Wallace
Kevin Conway: Eugene Dred
Keith David: Sgt. Cantrell
Lance Henriksen: Ace Hanlon
Pat Hingle: Horace the Bartender
Gary Sinise: Marshal
Mark Boone Junior: Scars
Olivia Burnette: Katie
Fay Masterson: Mattie Silk
Raynor Scheine: Ratsy
Woody Strode: Charles Moonlight
Jerry Swindall: Blind Boy
Scott Spiegel: Gold Teeth Man
Sven-Ole Thorsen: Swede
Bruce Campbell: Wedding Shemp

Filmed at Old Tucson Studios.

THE GUNFIGHT IS IN THE HEAD, NOT THE HANDS

IN THE TOWN OF REDEMPTION in the late 1870s, the yea rly gunfighter's quick draw contest kicks into high gear. Among the contestants vying for $123,000 in prize money are Ace Hanlon, a flamboyant gunman and wanted criminal, Spotted Horse, an Indian who claims he cannot be killed by bullets, the mysterious Sgt. Cantrell, and the town's despotic tyrant, John Herod, who views the gunfight as a crucible through which he can confront and destroy his many enemies out in the open.

This year, however, the contest is different. Herod's son, Kid, has entered the contest and is gunning for his Pa; and Herod has abducted an old friend turned preacher, Cort, and is forcing him to participate.

Into this hotbed of confrontation and deceit, a female gunslinger, Ellen (a.k.a., Lady), arrives in town, harboring her own terrible secret from childhood. With the help of the Kid and Cort, Ellen tests her mettle and targets Herod, for whom she has a burning hatred.

THE NEW OLD WEST

In the early nineties, the Western was alive and kicking for the first time in years. *Pale Rider*, *Silverado* and *Young Guns* had set the stage in the late eighties for a full-blooded genre comeback, and Clint Eastwood's Academy Award–winning Best Picture, *Unforgiven* (1992), spurred the trend of new, and in some instances, revisionist Western flicks. *Tombstone* starring Kurt Russell and Val Kilmer became a surprise hit in 1993, despite a troubled production, but then the tide turned once more. Westerns concerning women (*Bad Girls*) and African American gunfighters (*Posse*) came and went with little notice and Kevin Costner's epic three-hour biography, *Wyatt Earp*, landed in theaters with a thud in 1994.

One of the most unique and stylish Westerns of the modern revival came at the end of the revival cycle, in February 1995: *The Quick and the Dead* starring Sharon Stone and directed by Sam Raimi. Unlike other films directed by Raimi up to that point, *The Quick and the Dead* was born from the imagination of another writer, making the film Raimi's first experience in Hollywood as a "hired gun." Instead, the knowledgeable screenplay came from an unusual source — Englishman Simon Moore.

Independent filmmaker Moore, writer and director of the crime-thriller *Under Suspicion* (1992) starring Liam Neeson, remains one of Hollywood's finest fantasy writers, having adapted *Gulliver's Travels* to television in 1996 for stars Ted Danson and Mary Steenburgen. His other credits include the popular miniseries *The Tenth Kingdom* (2000) and *The Snow Queen* starring Bridget Fonda in 2002. Despite this success, it was not always so for the young writer. In the early nineties, he wrote a script, a Western, and nobody seemed interested.

"At the end of 1992, I just started working on an idea to do a Spaghetti Western," Moore explains. "I had this idea about a knock-out, quick-draw contest.

"I had seen lots of movies that were about how the West wasn't really how it had been portrayed in film, and it was *really* much more ethnic, or much more about money, or more civilized, or whatever. And I thought, no one has done a Western for a while which is a really fast paced 'Who is going to survive the quick draw?' kind of thing. I wanted to go back to the fundamental image of what I believed the Western was, which is two people at either end of a street, and only one of them is going to make it.

"What I was trying to access was really much more the Italian Westerns of Sergio Leone and the Spanish–Italian Spaghetti Westerns rather than the more classical American Westerns." Moore explains. "People often think that writing is primarily about writing dialogue, and what I love about these Westerns is that they're beautifully constructed; beautifully written, almost scored like a piece of music. And yet the characters remain very mysterious. They don't say who they are in conventional terms through dialogue and back story. It's a very different kind of writing."

But Moore also wanted to tweak the Western. "The one thing I'm not interested in doing is remaking something that works, or remaking something that I'm aware exists," he reveals. "In pretty much everything I've ever done, there's a mixture between a conventional idea, if you like, and something that comes out of left field. That's what gives me the energy. I love action films, but I'm not very interested in the door bursting open and some super strong male hero coming in, killing everybody."

So Moore decided his hero should be female. "When you introduce women into that kind of world, something very interesting happens and you have an interesting dynamic straight away," he considers. "And so I wondered if you could have 'The Woman with No Name.' That was the central idea for me. I wondered if you could have someone occupy that role, and then something that was very familiar, that macho gunplay, is recycled through the eyes of someone who shouldn't be there. Someone who should be a school marm or something."

Then Moore provided his main character, Ellen (or "Lady"), with a back story, a childhood trauma that she unwittingly played a role in and had yet to fully recover from. "That's all stolen, or as writers say, *homaged* from the Spaghetti Western, where there's not only a back story, but a back story that involves guilt of some kind," acknowledges Moore. "Something that I particularly took from a lot of these stories is the idea that you see something as a child and you're helpless, but you're somehow implicated in it and it drives the whole of your life. And again, the Spaghetti Western is a form where there isn't a lot of room for talking and explaining conventional psychology, but you'd see why this woman would devote her life to being able to shoot fast."

After developing his major character, Moore infused the concept with literary allusions that would augment the tale's archetypal feel. "I knew I wanted the town to have Biblical connotations, which is why I called the lead villain Herod and the town Redemption. It felt to me that there needed to be an Old Testament feel to it. I wanted to say to the reader — and to the audience — this is a movie where you're either quick or you're dead."

The only problem was getting the script produced. "I was going to direct it myself and just shoot it as a low-budget Western in Spain or something," Moore remembers. "I sent it to a number of studios, and indeed Sony and Columbia both passed on the picture. At that point, we were really offering it as a three or four million dollar movie."

Nothing happened with *The Quick and the Dead*, even as Hollywood rediscovered its love of the Western, until one day in May 1993. "At that point I was really broke and I had just come back from a restaurant with my friends; there was another film I had in development, and they wanted to take out an option for another year, and it was money, but I didn't think they were going to make the movie, so I was saying, 'I've got to turn it down.'"

When he returned home, the writer found a message on his answering machine from his American agent, who told him that "somebody wants to buy your script and they're really serious, and they want to buy it now, and they want to pay a lot of money for it," Moore recalls. "It's the call you dream of having. It was one of those Frank Capra moments when you're trudging back thinking, 'I'll always be poor.' I got this message and thought, 'Which script is he talking about?' I had several scripts out, and none of them were thriving."

But his agent informed Moore that the deal was going to happen and furthermore, that it was going to happen over that very weekend. "It was one of those bizarre things where one minute nobody wants do anything, and then on Monday you're on the plane and the deal is closed. The studio was convinced that on Monday, as soon as business opened, the other studios would be bidding on this project, so they made me an offer I couldn't refuse."

Despite their enthusiasm, the studio (Columbia/Sony) played its cards close to the vest. "They wouldn't tell me who the star was, or who the director was, so when they actually said Sam Raimi is going to direct it, I was thrilled," relates Moore. "The thought that some independent filmmaker was going to be part of this was very exciting to me. I was steeling myself for some crap, middle-of-the-road, sixty-five-year-old director saying, 'Simon, we've got to change it all.' So it was great to get a young hip director who said, 'Simon, we've got to change it all.' I was really excited Sam was doing it. It all happened very quickly in May, and in a couple of weeks, I was starting the first of many rewrites."

HEART OF STONE

On the other side of the Atlantic, Moore's screenplay intersected with an up-and-coming power in Hollywood: actress Sharon Stone. After years in the business and appearances in films such as *Action Jackson* (1988) and *Total Recall* (1990), Stone had become an overnight sensation with the release of Paul Verhoeven's sexy thriller, *Basic Instinct* (1992). Stone's follow-up, *Sliver* (1993), though plagued by controversy, was also a huge hit. After filming *Intersection* with Martin Landau and Richard Gere, Stone found Moore's script and felt the Western would be a perfect vehicle. Columbia agreed and purchased Moore's script.

When searching for a director, Stone made it known that she would only work with one talent: Sam Raimi. "He was the only person on my list, and if Sam hadn't made this movie, I don't think I would have made it," she revealed in the *Los Angeles Times*. "It's the kind of picture I don't think just anyone could have made, even any great directors, because of the kind of material it is."[1] What qualities, precisely, did she admire? She told author Bill Warren that she was a particular fan of *Army of Darkness* and was impressed by Raimi's growth as a director.[2]

For Raimi, *The Quick and the Dead* represented an opportunity to visit a very different genre and escape the so-called ghetto of low-budget, exploitation horror movies. He described the project in the press as "a fun, entertaining Western for a nineties crowd,"[3] but what wasn't acknowledged in that remark was that as a director he was taking a grand leap into Hollywood's mainstream. He was working with big actors like Stone and Gene Hackman, who was cast as the villainous John Herod, and had to meet with their approval if he was to direct the feature. Because he was directing a studio film, Raimi also had to compromise. For example, his visual effects supervisor from *Darkman* and *Army of Darkness*, William Mesa, was Raimi's first selection to supervise that component on *The Quick and Dead*, but because the project was a Sony movie, Sony Image Works received the contract to create the film's visual effects.

Sharon Stone had more clout. During casting, she insisted that a little-known Australian actor named Russell Crowe play the key role of Cort, the repentant preacher. "The studio went berserk, but people don't threaten me a lot," Stone said of her battle to get Crowe. "I don't take a bluff."[4] Consequently, principal photography on *The Quick and the Dead* was delayed for Crowe, in Australia at the time.

"We had a conference call, and I was sitting with Sam in this hotel in Tucson," Moore recalls and "Russell Crowe began by saying, 'I read the script, and it's obvious that everyone but me has a character.' That was his opening gambit. And I thought, 'Fuck! Where are we going to go with this?'" On working with Raimi, Crowe later described the director as sort of like "the fourth Stooge."[5]

Another casting choice proved equally controversial. Sharon Stone wanted — and got — Leonardo DiCaprio, fresh off the success of *This Boy's Life* (1993) and *What's Eating Gilbert Grape* (1993), to play the crucial role of Kid. Again, the powers-that-be weren't confident about that decision, and Stone reportedly softened them by paying DiCaprio's salary.

Working with a big-name, Hollywood cast, at least for Moore, was an eye-opener. "I'm afraid people like Sharon Stone just treated me as though I was the guy who brought her latte or something," he recalls. "The first meeting I had with her, she sat down and told me who this character was and what this character would do. She never once asked a single question."

And Hackman? "Gene Hackman is probably my favorite film actor of all time," Moore establishes. "And I can't tell you how excited I was that he was doing the film. We had a read-through in a hotel in Los Angeles and during the reading he just stopped every five minutes or so and said, 'That's a terrible line,' 'God, that line stinks,' or 'We've got to change that.' You imagine that there will be a moment in your life where you sit in a room and all these people are doing the thing you've written, and it is going to be the best day of your life, but in reality, it is close to the worst day of your life because there's no acknowledgment that you're sort of instrumental in this film happening. You go from being the center of the universe to being an entirely marginal figure who is quite literally asked to stand outside the door when the meetings are going on. It's a tough road."

One joy of *The Quick and the Dead* remains the marvelous and colorful supporting cast that brought to life the denizens of Redemption. Pat Hingle played Horace, the gentle bartender, Roberts Blossom was Doc, Ellen's only friend, Sven-Ole Thorsen played the bombastic Swede, and Keith David portrayed the arrogant Sgt. Cantrell. Gary Sinise was also cast in a critical role, as was Lance Henriksen, the star of the much-mourned Chris Carter series *Millennium* (1996–1999) and film efforts such as *The Terminator* (1984), *Aliens* (1986), *Pumpkinhead* (1989) and *Scream 3*.

"That was a really interesting period for me," Lance Henriksen remembers of the period leading up to 1994 and his casting as the flamboyant Scourge of the Sagebrush, Ace Hanlon. "I did three Westerns in a row. One was *The Gunfighter's Moon* and the other was *Dead Man* with Johnny Depp, which Jim Jarmusch directed. Then they asked me to do the role [of Ace] and I read it and thought it was a wonderful little cameo in this movie. I started building a character, and Sam hired this incredible wardrobe lady to design the wardrobe, and she put me all in leather, and it had this embroidery on it and was beautifully done.

"Normally when I work, I pick my hat, boots and guns. If I'm doing a Western, I want my own hat. So I went to a guy in Tucson that is one of the great makers of real authentic Western hats and I had one made," notes Henriksen, an actor who loves getting into a character. "When I went to Tucson to do a reading with Gene Hackman and everybody, and we were all around the table to read this thing, I'd already started. I had dyed my hair black, put extensions on it, and grown a moustache and had this whole thing going, and Sam kept looking at me wondering what the hell I was doing. I saw the guy as very flamboyant."

Another veteran actor who co-starred in *The Quick and the Dead* was Kevin Conway, a performer who has given acclaimed performances in films including Tobe Hooper's frightfest *The Funhouse*, *Thirteen Days* (2000) and the Civil War epic *Gods and Generals* (2003). He was shooting a film in Germany and France when Raimi sent him the screenplay. "I'd never met Sam," Conway explains, "but I guess he saw some of the pictures I did and wanted me to play this guy."

Of his character, Eugene Dred, the town pimp, Conway laughs. "I loved Eugene. First of all, he was a guy with minimal talent. He wasn't very good with women, so that's why he was a sort of child molester. He wasn't very good with a gun, which is why he didn't want to enter the contest, but Leo DiCaprio['s character] kind of forced him into it by insulting him. I thought this guy was a real slob, a pimp and a back shooter, but I loved doing Westerns, so I said, 'Yeah, I'd love to do it.'"

THE QUICK AND THE REWRITTEN

As the big-name cast assembled for Raimi's sixth feature film, writer Moore found that studio executives were increasingly concerned about the screenplay. "As I understand it, one of the rules of Hollywood is that the nearer you get to production, the more anxious everybody becomes. There's really only one thing you can keep changing, and that's the script."

With so many producers involved in *The Quick and the Dead*, including Rob Tapert, Sharon Stone, Joshua Donen, Toby Jaffe, Allen Shapiro, Patrick Markey and Chuck Binder, there were many folks to please. "In every stage of script development, more and more people were coming in, and they all just wanted to change it," says Moore.

Firstly, they wanted to keep Stone happy. Secondly, they had a fairly new writer and director to contend with. Thirdly, Moore's proposed four million dollar film had ballooned into a big-budget extravaganza, costing at least thirty-five million dollars.

"All that stuff comes together and you've got studio heads and people whose comments, as they come to you filtered through various levels of management, are often completely crass and stupid," Moore considers. "And Sam, who is far more experienced than I was in that sort of meeting, would do meetings with people and whenever they'd raise an issue, he'd say, 'Yeah, that's great. Sure, we'll take that on board. Simon will fix that.' We'd go from interest group to interest group throughout the day and he'd be promising we'd fix all these things."

"Sam is a nice guy and I like him very much, but Sam is really a player," considers Moore of Raimi's approach in dealing with the contradictory and asinine Hollywood upper echelons. "I think he's someone who believes that the base of operations always has to be fluid. In other words, you always have to deal with who you are in the room with at the time."

And what was the concern about the script? "There was pressure from the studio all the time to keep opening the film up, and make it a more conventional American Western, in the sense of more talking scenes. And I kept saying, 'That's not the way this works. This needs to be very lean and visual;' pretty much how the movie ended up," Moore explains.

"So what we were doing a lot of the time was not fundamentally changing the film as much as pulling it in one direction. All the stars felt their parts were underwritten and wanted more dialogue, and more scenes where they talked about their pain, so we went through all that. But there came a point when I said to Josh Donen, 'Look, I'll rewrite this script until I'm blue in the face, but if you or the studio get someone else to rewrite it, then I'm off the picture and I'm not coming back.'"

As Moore toiled to rewrite the script — over and over — a personal crisis arose. His girlfriend underwent major surgery, and he needed to stay close by, in England. On the surface, studio executives were supportive of his decision, which involved a few days off the film. "'Don't even think about coming out; that's fine. You need to be with her,'" they told Moore. He took them at their word and stayed home to care for his girlfriend rather than continuing rewrites. He received a surprise call after one weekend.

"Monday evening they called up and said, 'You've been fired from the picture,'" Moore reveals. "Just when you think you've reached rock bottom in terms of the moral universe of Hollywood, you think, no, there are subterranean depths."

At that point, Hollywood script doctor and independent filmmaker John Sayles rewrote the film to grant it a more authentic sense of the Old West. "So they did that, and a script that was a conventional length suddenly became a two-and-a-half hour movie," Moore describes. "Then, about three weeks from shooting, they phoned me back up and said, 'Look, would you consider coming back on the picture?' And despite what I had said to Josh Donen, I said, 'Sure, yeah, of course I will.'

"So I went back over and had this insane meeting where the same studio executives who fired me and wanted to change the script said, 'We like the new script, but it feels kind of fat and bloated and padded now. Could you have a look at it?' I had a look at it and pretty much cut out all the stuff he'd [Sayles] put in. Not all of it, but pretty much all of it. So we got to a week before shooting and they said, 'Yeah, it's good now.' It was a completely fucking pointless exercise."

GUNFIGHTERS

Bringing the Old West to life was an important element of the filmmaking process for Raimi and the cast and crew of *The Quick and the Dead*. To achieve that goal, Raimi embarked on a great deal of research on the era of the film, circa 1878. He also hired Thell Reed, the world-renowned Fastest Gun Alive to train his cast in the art of gun fighting. Reed is one of Hollywood's true gentlemen, and as a teen in 1958 was introduced to the business by the legendary Gene Autry. Over the years, Reed worked on *Gunsmoke* and *The Rebel* and, because of his vast knowledge of American history, remains the industry's go-to-guy for accurate Westerns.

Reed served as the film's armorer, and reports on his work process. "I break down the script per character, for what gun I think they would be using and how they would be carrying a gun. And then we have what is called a show-and-tell, where you have a whole big table full of guns with different holsters," he explains. On *The Quick and the Dead*, Raimi requested a variety of fancy rigs. "He was very detailed," Reed stresses. "He knew it all, believe me. He just wanted to make sure I did!"

In particular, Raimi wanted the film's guns to be accurate. "Sam wanted the authenticity of the rigs for 1878, so I had to make sure all the guns and gun rigs were correct. There's a lot of open-top, cap-and-ball-type guns in there," Reed reports. These conversions were popular between the time of the Civil War and the release of the first successful cartridge revolvers, like the Smith and Wesson in 1869 and Colt in 1873, and are not often seen in Westerns. "Sam wanted those guns in there, which was great, because they were carried by guys who couldn't afford new guns, so that's what they had."

"It was Sam's vision," Reed stresses. "He allowed me to get guns from the era."[6] Reed found those weapons by searching private collections and accessing his own collection. Among the weapons used was a tiny gun called a Knuckleduster, a fairly expensive little piece at some $3,000 dollars, that Stone's character used in her attempted assassination of Herod. "That's a hide-out gun for gamblers that you could drop in a vest pocket," Reed explains. "You could hide it in the palm of your hand or turn it around, and put your middle fingers through that big hole in the grip, and it becomes a brass knuckle."

After consulting with Raimi about weaponry selection, Reed had approximately three to four months to train the actors in their use, a process the armorer thoroughly enjoyed. He describes DiCaprio as "a top professional who would buckle down and train with those guns." He also has words of praise for other cast members, many of whom he has worked with since.

Reed enjoyed his time with Stone, who learned how to perform a complex quick draw for the saloon shoot-out with Eugene. "Sharon trained hard for that," he remembers. "She had to cock those guns all the way back when they fire. If you pull any of those old, single-action guns for that era and just pull the trigger, nothing happens. You have to throw the hammer all the way back for each shot, every time it's fired." Reed recalls that Stone's guns rode high, due to the old-time rigs she wore. This meant the actress had to cock the hammers while pulling the guns out of leather, all while keeping her elbows close at her side, much like a pool player. Then, as the muzzles lifted up, she had to pivot and fire. "It's quite a process to do ... it's not an easy thing," Reed considers.

But Reed found Stone in top form. "She was excellent. She had a good sense of humor, she used to tease a lot, and she took her guns very seriously. She was safe with them, and told me how she grew up on a farm, hunted with guns and knew gun safety."

"I trained with Thell a lot," adds Henriksen. "He's a genius with a gun, and a world champion. He and I used to shoot every day. Real shooting. And we all got very, very good with guns."

"I had Sam's permission to let the actors take the guns to their hotel rooms to practice, which is not a common thing," Reed explains. "Usually, they don't want the guns to leave the set, but I discussed this with Sam. No ammunition of course, just empty guns, and we were all staying in the same hotel, so I could go by their rooms and check on their training. And they just practiced religiously with them, and that's how they got good."

"We trained all the way through the film, everyday," Conway confirms. "You couldn't let a week go by and then pick 'em up. I took the guns back to the hotel and used to practice at night. My hands were bloody, because those guns were real and you had to cock them to fire. You couldn't just pull them out and squeeze the trigger. They had double hammers, so as you're pulling them out of the holster, you had to be pulling back on the hammer to cock it. It's like walking and chewing gum at the same time. If you're not ambidextrous, you have to will your left hand to cock the gun as your right hand is firing, to keep up the rapidity. In the old days, you could shoot your foot off. You'd snag the gun in the holster and you'd shoot down and end up missing a toe."

Part of Reed's gift was matching weapons with characters. "I'm not very tall," Conway explains. "Because it was a fast-draw contest, everybody else was picking these short barrel guns that you could whip out of your holster real fast. It makes it easier. But I have short arms and I'm not meant to be a gunfighter, so I said to Thell, 'Give me the long barreled guns, two of them, because when I pull them out it's going to look funny.' I wanted that little humor."

Henriksen also had special guns to enhance his speed while firing, as Ace Hanlon was described as one of the finest gunfighters in the land.

"They put double springs in my guns, so I would have to work really hard to pull the hammers back. Then, when we finally did the movie, they put a lighter spring in, and I was like lightning."

"My favorite thing about my character is that I wore my guns the way they were really worn in those days. They wore them very high and I practiced a hip draw that was Thell's idea. I felt like I *was* that guy, Ace, and my wife used to walk on the set and say, 'My heart be still!' The crew even signed a petition saying, 'Don't Kill Ace Hanlon.'"

The actors fell in love not just with Reed, but with the notion of playing gunfighter. "Even prop guns can be dangerous, but I guess they all thought we could be adults," says Conway. "They were wrong! Lance, Keith, David, Russell and me — every time we passed each other — we'd say, 'How are you?' and then go for our guns to see who could outdraw the other one. Every time you went to the set, it was like a huge game. You could stay in costume, you had your guns, and you just walked around this town and could stay in character if you wanted. It was a really wonderful experience."

Unless, of course, you happened to be on the mean end of the barrel. "Everybody on the set was panicked because, 'God, you're going to hurt yourself!'" Henriksen laughs. "You have that silly aspect of making films where the politically correct thing to do is not what your character would do, so you end up offending somebody. You're standing by the craft services table, and you pull your gun on somebody and that's not really politically correct. We didn't actually do that, but we were always working toward that."

SHOOTING THE SHOOTISTS

The Quick and the Dead was filmed in Mescal, Arizona, some forty miles southeast of Tucson.[7] The production company recruited extras from the ranks of the local unemployed, seeking colorful characters like "corn woman" and "posole lady," all of whom bore the brunt of a "million miles on their faces."[8]

The film lensed from October 1993 through the winter of 1994 and endured notable weather problems. At one point, it snowed in Mescal, causing delays since a snowy Redemption would not match footage already in the can. The devastating earthquake of 1994 rocked Los Angeles and the production shut down for a day so crew members could return home to check on their families. All the while, the tabloid press stalked Sharon Stone, trying to dig up dirt on the popular star, while the actress herself proved a good Samaritan by working Christmas day of 1993 to feed the 1,000 homeless and unemployed people at the annual Salvation Army Christmas Dinner.[9]

Shooting in the desert of Arizona, in a full-fledged old Western town, not only augmented the actors' performances and sense of reality, it reflected the film's content. The town of Redemption was created by Academy Award–winning production designer Patrizia Von Brandenstein (*Amadeus* [1984]) to mirror the twisted ethos of its despotic "benefactor," John Herod: "Nothing lives in the town. Even the cactus is dead, like the spirit of the people. Graves and abandoned safes are landscape hallmarks," she described. "The grand town clock serves only to define gunfights. The civic monument is Herod's house, dominating the town just as its occupant does. I wanted it to reflect a bloated predator."[10]

Of principal photography and the cast, Henriksen has only fond memories. "Leonardo was just a kid in that, but boy was he thrilled to be playing that Kid," he explains. "The whole thing was like that. We were all excited about it."

In fact, Henriksen practiced some new moves to enhance the character of Ace Hanlon. "I had a buddy whose name is Rex Rossi, who worked with Tom Mix when he was twelve-years-old and worked on Wild West shows. He was my mentor, and he's the one who taught me how to ride horses to begin with. So a month before the movie started, I said to him, 'I've got to shoot a card out of this kid's hand, and I think there has to be more to it than that.' So we worked on the horse trick where I flip off the horse backward. We worked on that for a month before we even got to Tucson.

"I got there and said, 'Sam, I want to show you something.' I asked the stunt guy to bring a horse over, and he brought a big white horse. I said, 'This is how I'd like to shoot the thing out of her hand,' and I jumped on, and then flipped over the horse, and shot under the belly. Sam got really excited and said, 'That's in the movie!'

"One of the things that Sam was really about was *ideas*," Henriksen stresses. "He is such an enthusiast about shots he wants to do, but if you come up with ideas, he gets very excited if it's a good one. He's got the same enthusiasm about film as I do. I will never reach the stage where I'm just walking through something."

In fact, Henriksen's gung-ho attitude resulted in a funny moment with co-star Gene Hackman. "When Gene Hackman and I did our first scene together, Sam put the camera on the ground and said to Gene, 'You step in front of the lens like this, with your legs spread,'" Henriksen relates. "Through his legs, you see Ace Hanlon standing there, taking a bow for what he just did.

"And Hackman said, 'What is that? What's that mean? That's just a camera shot, right?' So then he says, 'I'm going to walk over to him.' And I said, 'Gene, wait a minute.' I'd never worked with Hackman before and had waited twenty years to work with him. I said, 'Gene, don't walk to me, let *me* walk to you. It makes you stronger. If you walk to me, you're weaker, so let me walk to you.' And then I did that little turn where I said, 'I'm the best you'll ever see.'

"But I remember after that day was over, I thought, 'What the *fuck* did I just do? You don't tell Gene Hackman where to walk!' But he held his ground. It was that kind of environment where I was so much 'the guy' [Ace] that there was no ego involved. If he'd told me to fuck off, it would have been all right."

The only portion of the film that Henriksen didn't enjoy was his character's humiliating demise at the hands of John Herod. "I had to do it, but going down that way wasn't the way I saw Ace Hanlon getting done in," Henriksen explains, "putting bullets through both hands and turning me into a dancing idiot. But you know, there are a lot of things you do as an actor. Who wants to get killed? I didn't want it to be over. Ever. I really didn't."

Conway's character, Eugene, also came to an unpleasant end in the film, shot in the genitals by Stone's protagonist during a ferocious rain storm. Conway remembers shooting that sequence. "We had to create a lot of rain for the film and that scene was probably the most difficult I'd ever done in my life. It took a couple of days to shoot that scene with Sharon; about two and a half days. What a lot of people don't realize about rain towers is that when the rain falls from the sky, it hurts. But with the rain towers being closer to the ground, when it hits you, it *really* smarts. You can get a headache just from getting pelted on the hat.

"Because I had to fall back in the mud and say my lines up toward Sharon, I was getting hit in the eyes and it was really hard to concentrate. We were freezing too, by the way, because it was in the desert and it wasn't warm. Every time we'd finish a take, we'd have to run into the saloon and stand by the heaters. It's a bonding experience working in the rain like that. Gene got to stand there with an umbrella and say his lines, but Sharon and I were soaked. Basically two and a half days of being soaking wet."

And did the actor have any apprehension about his character's castration by bullet? "I remember questioning very carefully the guys that rigged that squib. In fact, it disappointed me a little because I think they underloaded it. I think it would have been great if the shot had blown the whole crotch out."

Though the last day of filming the movie was frantic, because the cast stayed up all night to shoot one final sequence in the saloon gallery, Conway agrees with Henriksen that it was a great time and place to be a working actor. "I remember a great sense of satisfaction when it was over because I knew it was a great movie. I felt a great sense of camaraderie."

"I just came off a movie called *Tombstone*, which was very grueling," Thell Reed considers of his tenure on a Raimi set. "When I came on this show, Sam was such a pleasant, nice gentlemen to talk to. He treated everybody equally, whether the guy was a grip or an armorer or whatever. He said, 'We're all part of making the movie, and we're all important,' and he's like a commanding general that you can actually talk to. Just a wonderful experience working with him."

TRICK SHOTS

With principal photography on *The Quick and the Dead* completed, Simon Moore kept abreast of the film's developments from London. "I saw the rushes every week and so from a distance, I could give my views on it. When I saw the rushes, I just thought, 'This is really kind of sensual and terrifically achieved.'"

Raimi's visceral epic, however, might have been even more sensual had things been a tad different. A sex scene involving stars Stone and Crowe was deleted from the final cut in America prior to the film's release in February 1995, because Stone felt the scene did not fit in with the picture's established reality. American fans felt quite disappointed by the scene's removal, though many have been able to see it via downloads on the Internet.

Finally, after more than two years since Moore first imagined his new brand of Spaghetti Western, *The Quick and the Dead* was released and the critics had their say. Reviews were mixed. Roger Ebert noted that the film displayed Raimi's "zest for stylistic invention"[11] and *Newsweek* praised Stone's "nice, brooding performance" and the fact that Raimi kept the "humor and arty shots coming."[12]

While not giving the film a perfect score, the *New York Times*' Janet Maslin noted that Raimi's taste for "visual and crazy, ill-advised homage" made for "sly, sporadic fun."[13]

Peter Travers opined in *Rolling Stone* that viewers would leave the film "dazed instead of dazzled, as if an expert marksman had drawn his gun only to shoot himself in the foot."[14] Writing for the *Christian Science Monitor*, David Sterritt was more enthusiastic:

> Sam Raimi has juiced up the action with the energetic style he developed in the sardonic horror movies that launched his career. To my eye, Raimi shockers like *Darkman* and *The Evil Dead* are more tricky than scary, using an onslaught of gimmicks to mask an absence of thought and feeling. His new Western also has plenty of self-conscious devices, from super-swift editing to the year's weirdest camera angles. But what makes them more than ostentatious inside jokes is the respect he shows for the conventions he affectionately parodies.[15]

Despite nice, if reserved, praise, *The Quick and the Dead*, did not pack the box office punch its makers had hoped for. Moore recalls that he was in America with Raimi after the opening weekend, at a restaurant, when the bad news came. "Someone arrived from the studio and said to us, 'It looks like we're only going to do seven million dollars on the first weekend.'" At a final budget of thirty-five million, that wasn't a satisfactory number.

"If you'd told me [when I was writing that screenplay] that I'd be sitting by the ocean in a restaurant in Santa Monica with someone saying my film is going to do seven million dollars in its first weekend, I'd have been absolutely thrilled," Moore considers. "But I realized at that moment, in terms of investment, it was like the kiss of death. They were mourning it. We all had one glass of wine and went home."

Still, the clouds over Redemption had a silver lining. "I came back to find that the film was number one in Paris and opened really well across Europe," Moore remembers. "But I think for the studio it was a flop. End of story. They spent too much money on it. And it came at the end of the Western cycle. Still, as time goes by, more and more people have said, 'I really like that movie.' That's not unique in the history of cinema."

The Quick and the Dead grossed eighteen million dollars; more than *Army of Darkness,* but less than *Darkman*, and for Raimi its failure was a difficult thing. What followed in his career was a period of reflection and self-examination. He didn't direct another feature until 1998's *A Simple Plan*, instead spending time with wife Gillian and his children. He toiled within the world of television, overseeing production on such ventures as Shaun Cassidy's genre soap opera, *American Gothic* (1995–1996) starring Gary Cole.

Later, Raimi blamed himself and his well-honed visual style, likening it to a drug addiction, for *The Quick and the Dead*'s failure. "I was very confused after I made that movie. For a number of years I thought, I'm like a dinosaur. I couldn't change with the material."[16]

As for Simon Moore, he feels that Raimi's period of self-reflection had nothing but a positive outcome on the artist's film style and directing process. "It's quite interesting what's happened to Sam. I believe something fantastic has happened to Sam, which is that he's become much more interested in actors. I think that the sort of middle period, where he went out of his way to work more with actors and make his work less constantly visual has been enormously helpful for him, and that's part of his maturing as a really excellent director. But I think at that time he was still very anxious that thirty seconds would go by without there being a wham-o-cam or something."

RAIMI RAP

ENGLISH COWBOY: Simon Moore's screenplay pleased studio executives, but they had no idea it came from this unlikely source, from across the pond. "It was quite funny, because when the script was finally picked up by the studio, they wanted me to come out immediately. I think they probably had in their mind that it was written by some leathery old Midwesterner," notes Moore. "So when they saw this fresh-faced London boy, they had a few qualms. When I got all the inevitable notes coming out of the studio, at one point someone said, 'This is a great script and we really like it, but somehow it doesn't seem to have the authentic *smell* of the Old West.' I knew they were on to me then."

MOST WANTED: Lance Henriksen had so much fun on the set of *The Quick and the Dead* that Raimi gave him a souvenir after the shoot: Ace Hanlon's "Most Wanted" poster. "I have my reward poster on a wall," reports Henriksen. "I put it up, I had to."

And the text? "Reward of $10,000 for Leslie 'Ace' Hanlon. Wanted dead or alive," Henriksen reads. "On the night of May 26, near Campbell, Santa Clara County, Leslie 'Ace' Hanlon brutally murdered John B. Shaw and then robbed the victim and his widow of all their money and possessions. About forty years of age; 5'11"; weight: 165–70; has sharp features; black hair; blue eyes; medium complexion. When last seen wore a black suit, black shirt, black hat, number 9 shoes. He used ace of spades as a trademark. Walks very erect. He carries two Colt peacemakers with pearl handles."

KISS KISS, BANG BANG: Kevin Conway's Eugene is an unsavory character and one brief scene brought that to life. When Lady confronts him about his attempts to deflower Horace's daughter, a creepy close-up of Eugene reveals strange "pow pow" sounds emanating from his gold-toothed mouth. "That wasn't in the original scene," Conway remembers. "I guess my mouth moved. When I went out to loop it a month later in California, Sam said, 'This bothers me here because it looks like you're saying something, but you didn't say anything.' I didn't want him to cut my close-up, so I said, 'Well, what if he just makes a little sound? What if he just looks at her and goes '*pssht, pssht, pssht*' like he's imagining blowing her away?' And Sam loved it."

GUN DETAILS: The detail on the weaponry in *The Quick and the Dead* is extraordinary. The Kid's gun features an inlay of an American eagle, Herod's a snake, and Ace's pistol, of course, bore the ace of spades. To age Cort's 1851 Navy Colt, which was originally a cap-and-ball percussion gun, armorer Thell Reed took drastic measures with the guns used. "I took them out by my swimming pool and dipped them in chlorine water to let them rust. They looked rusty and old, but were brand new guns."

Such detail, including the nickel plating and ivory handles on Ellen's Colt Peacemakers, was accurate to the period. "It cost about $2.50 extra to get nickel plating and $5.00 extra for ivory grips in those days. Remember, a cowboy made about $30.00 a month, so that was all relative.

"In those days, a lot of gunfighters had pretty guns," Reed muses. "If their guns were getting a little beat up, they got new ones. That was their tool of the trade so when you see a guy he might have rough-looking clothes on, but he'll have a beautiful, well-cared-for weapon because that is his life. When you see a guy in 1878, he couldn't tell you about his summer home; what you saw is what you got. His saddle, guns, hat and boots. That's how he established himself."

DANCES WITH WOLVES: In the early scenes of *The Quick and the Dead*, there's a subtle feeling of tension between Ace Hanlon and John Herod, who eventually end up fighting on the street, only one of them surviving the encounter. "We were in the bar and I'd talk to Sam," Henriksen remembers. "I'd say, 'Sam, you know what? When wolves are in the same proximity, they never make very long eye contact because that means aggression; that's battle.' So when Hackman comes in for the first time, I said, 'I'd like to do it like a wolf in the sense that I'll make eye contact, but just long enough ... otherwise I'll shoot him.' There was always that kind of subtext going on."

NO SEX: One scene missing from *The Quick and the Dead* in the American theatrical version is a love scene, an interior sequence at the bordello (The Pigeon's Nest) between Cort and Lady. Though it appears in the European and Japanese versions, fans have wondered about this scene, which begins with bondage (Cort in shackles) and culminates with the not-too-subtle suggestion of oral sex. "We shot a sex scene, but it didn't really play," Stone reported of the wet sequence (it was raining inside, for some reason...). "Why would she stop gun slinging and all of a sudden have sex? So I removed it. Even though Tri-Star had a heart attack."[17] Another scene shot but missing from the final cut: Sharon Stone nude in an old bathtub.

THE BROTHERS HANLON: "I used to say we should do a sequel to this movie where Ace Hanlon is killed and his three brothers, Hearts, Diamonds and Clubs, come looking for him," says Lance Henriksen. "And Hearts wears white leather with red hearts on it. He's a little gay, but he's the deadliest of them all. It would have been great, and I would have played all the roles."

IS YOUR HEART BEATING FASTER? IS YOUR BLOOD PUMPING?

The Quick and the Dead is a lean, mean, cinematic machine in which all of the genre's fat has been burned away, leaving the film a simple crucible: *the gunfight*. As a result, much of the film's running time dwells inside a single, important moment, that critical instant when two gunfighters stare into each other's eyes, draw their weapons, and learn for the ages who is best.

All counted, there are eleven gunfights in the film, each circling ever closer to a final round of confrontations and the audience's almost accidental realization that some of the protagonists will, by necessity of the game, be forced to fight each other to survive. And that means some characters the audience likes and is invested in will, inevitably, be killed. Not only is this a brilliant method by which to foster sympathy for a character, and indeed the Kid's death is pretty heartbreaking, but a unique and singular structure that separates *The Quick and the Dead* from virtually all other Westerns.

Moore recalls that the repetitive gunfight structure was a concern for some. "'Isn't it going to be the most boring film in the world? How can you do that? How can you keep one step ahead of the audience?'" he was asked. "The appeal for me of something like *The Quick and the Dead* is that you have more than one hero. If it's just Ellen, then everybody else is expendable, but if you start to care about Herod's son, and you start to care about Cort, then you realize it gets worse and worse. The fewer the numbers get, the more you think, 'Soon two people are going to face each other, and I don't want either of them to get killed.'"

"Sam immediately embraced that idea visually and said, 'I'm going to make every gunfight look different,'" Moore reveals. "That was a smart choice, because I think it comes naturally for him to look for a different visual style to express everything. The people who don't like the movie? That's what they don't like about it. You know, 'Well, it's just one gunfight after another.' And the people who love the movie say that 'It's so clever that you can live in such a contained world.'"

Another unique facet of *The Quick and the Dead* involves the moments surrounding the gunfights. Stated simply, these scenes function as foreplay, conveying the thrill of the duels and leading back to that penultimate moment, the orgasm of the gunfight. I describe it in sexual terms, because I believe that this is, in fact, the language of the film, both within Moore's dialogue and in light of Raimi's visuals. "It looks like you're having a pretty good time playing with yourself," Ellen tells cocky Ace Hanlon when he tries to challenge her, seducing her as it were, into a gunfight.

"Is your heart beating faster? Is your blood pumping?" asks Herod, after Ellen has survived her first duel, aware she feels more alive than before. What, one may ask, is he really describing? *Afterglow*? Before his first contest (against the Swede), Kid asks Herod, "What if someone gets excited and starts shooting early?" Is he talking about a gunfight or premature ejaculation?

In addition to sexual innuendoes, there are dozens of loving close-ups of guns, and guns slipping — with a leathery snap — smoothly into tight-fitting holsters. Even the virtuous Cort is seduced by the allure of guns. He is a Man of God, abstaining from violence (and presumably sex?) but Herod brings him to the NRA equivalent of a bordello, a gun shop, and Cort immediately feels uneasy there.

As Kid describes the weapons for sale, Raimi's camera captures Cort pacing in the background, anxious, a glint of silver from an exposed gun glittering on his eye, as if winking at him. Then Raimi's camera zooms in on the customized Remington pistol as Kid removes it from a fabric sleeve, undressing it in loving, nearly ritualistic fashion. There's another close-up of Cort, more unnerved than before, and then an insert shot of his twitching, impatient hands. When the Kid subsequently spins the gun's chamber, the camera moves in even tighter on Cort's face, capturing the burning desire in his eyes.

Finally, after Cort's first gunfight, Herod wants to know if it felt "natural" and "nice and smooth," more coded language for sex. The point is not hard to discern, really. These characters live and die by the gun. Yet we also know what guns often represent in film, going as far back as Warren Beatty in *Bonnie and Clyde* (1967), if not further: they're phallic symbols.

Even the Cort and Herod relationship seems to have a sexual component. "I always wanted to fight you Cort," Herod proclaims nervously. "Since the first time I met you, it was just this itch I had to scratch." Again, a burning desire is coupled with the moment of the kill, the emission of violence each duel symbolizes.

"It wasn't entirely conscious, but I think there is something there," Moore commented to this author with some amusement. "So much is done in the American cinema, particularly, with guns. There are obvious points to make about guns and what they might represent, and I guess if you have two guys saying, 'My gun is bigger than your gun' or 'My gun is faster than you're gun,' then at some level you're into other territory as well. I wasn't consciously trying to create a homoerotic Western, but I'm quite happy if people read it that way."

Notably, each of the dramatis personae uses the gunfight just as a person might use sex. Herod is the most accomplished and experienced gunfighter, a skill he uses to dominate others, to control people, as an abusive husband might dominate his wife or a rapist might threaten someone. Kid employs the gunfight as a way to earn his father's respect, to prove he is really a man like Dad, no longer a virgin, as it were. Ace Hanlon is all show, but no delivery, effectively impotent, a fact belied by that inglorious and humiliating death that Henriksen didn't like.

Into this sexually charged environment strides a woman in leather, and it is she who sees the gunfight in the most unique manner of all because, unlike her competitors, she is female. Ultimately, Ellen uses the gunfight not as a perverse thrill or a bullying tactic (like Herod), a test of manhood (like Kid), or an aphrodisiac (like the unwitting Cort). For Ellen, the gunfight is a constructive instrument, a tool by which to achieve justice. According to the authors of *Reel Knock-Outs: Violent Women in the Movies*, the character of Ellen is a "celebration of the anti-sexist female avenger," one that "centers upon her nameless heroine's violent yet principled retribution."[18]

With pistol in hand, Ellen undoes sexual injustice, freeing a young girl from Eugene's advances. With her careful aim, she takes down Herod, freeing a community from a despot that exploits it. Where men use the gunfight (i.e., "sex") for selfish gain, Ellen, though clearly bent on revenge, seems able to manipulate the crucible of the gunfight in a more nurturing, distinctly female manner — to help others, to achieve a *positive*. The gun may be a male symbol, but Ellen has been forced to master it. Her early failure with the gun, resulting in the death of her father, has endowed her with a sense of the gun's power, and the responsibility that comes with it.

The Quick and the Dead works so beautifully because Raimi, as the hyperformalist that he is at heart, understands where the emotional core of the story rests. The gunfight is a thrill, but since the audience isn't standing there on the street, facing down an opponent, how does a director make the viewer feel that thrill? One way is to follow the essence of the screenplay and focus on the gunfight. But another way is by filling the edges of the tale with all of these sexual innuendoes and undercurrents. We aren't living in Redemption, so we can't feel the heat of battle, but the characters are constantly telling the audience, often in coded, sexualized terminology, how it makes them feel to fight. On that level, as sexual beings, we understand the fight even if we can't participate in it.

On a visual level, Raimi keeps interest in the gunfights alive by filming, essentially, the same sequence (two competitors fighting) differently some eleven times. In Kid's battle with Swede, as the moments tick down on the clock and the fight begins, Raimi deploys a sudden tilt of about 30 degrees and then a zoom, then a tilt and then another zoom, then another tilt and a faster zoom, until the shots are a kind of frenzy of movement and acceleration, a perfect build-up to the shoot out.

When Flat Nose Foy faces Cort, Raimi utilizes slow motion photography and exaggerated sound effects to punctuate the contest. The audience does not even see the two men draw. There is the jarring sound of a beer glass shattering on the ground, then a gun blast, then a close-up of Foy's shocked eyes as he is struck, and the point is established visually: Cort is so fast the camera could not even capture his quick draw.

Oppositely, when Herod and Ace face off, the camera observes Hanlon's draw. A super-fast pull-back propels us backward during that action. The point here is the opposite of the one established in Cort's fight. Ace is so fast, the camera had to literally step back to catch his quick draw, and yet Ace *still* isn't fast enough. Herod is faster. This gunfight visually reveals that the man in whom the audience had the most confidence, Ace, is actually a slow poke next to the real challenge, the evil Herod.

On a much broader note, one might view *The Quick and the Dead* as the most accessible of modern Westerns and also the most fun, simply because it gazes so squarely at this unique moment of confrontation, the gunfight, and those who participate, depicting them as the ultimate, extreme competitors. These gunfighters are like today's bungee-jumping daredevils, adrenaline junkies getting a high off the thrill of danger; or as Herod notes succinctly, "You passed a test, you feel alive." Just like skydivers or snow boarders, there seems to be a fetishistic obsession among the duelists with their equipment (guns, bullets, holsters) as well as the rules of the sport. So efficient at capturing detail, Raimi places these items in prominent compositions and in close-ups throughout the film to augment this sense of boys with toys and the woman who bests them all.

As students of Raimi, we have seen his homage to the films he grew up with, including the 1930s Universal monster movies (*Darkman*) and the stop-motion adventures of Ray Harryhausen (*Army of Darkness*). *The Quick and the Dead* continues this tradition by honoring Moore's inspiration, the Spaghetti Westerns of Sergio Leone.

Accordingly, Raimi applies tried and true Leone techniques, including a concentration on close-ups, often of just the eyes. Perhaps more importantly, he also recreates the Leone universe, a place of "blighted, surreal" landscapes and "grotesque characters with awful teeth."[19] All those elements are in place, and yet the true Raimi genius has always been his ability to adopt the style of his favorite films out of tribute, tweak them, and finally, go one step beyond.

As Clint Eastwood once noted of Leone, the director had his "own vision of what a Western should be" and that "some of his ideas were truly crazy."[20] The same comment could be applied to Raimi. Here, he stages a shot audacious enough to equal the flying eyeball in *Evil Dead 2*. Following a nasty gunfight between Cantrell and Herod, Raimi's camera gazes through a hole in one gunfighter's skull, coincidentally revealing a view of the dead man's opponent through the gaping wound.

Another inspired shot reveals a bullet wound to an injured combatant when light from the sun shines indelicately through the impact site. These are *not* compositions one is likely to find in a conventional American Western or in Leone's cinema, but a step beyond such traditions.

Raimi's early mentor, Verne Nobles, who has directed Westerns himself, remembers his shock upon seeing *The Quick and the Dead*. "What he did with the camera was incredible. And then, that damn bullet going through the guy's head ... I fell on the floor! That is so Sam, that is what he *is*. He has the ability in a normal picture to take you to the other side."

Some reviewers don't care for that other side. Ray Greene noted in *Hollywood Migraine* that in *The Quick and the Dead*:

> There's a deconstructive impulse about announcing one's influences that borders on hysteria. The film blends Sergio Leone's Spaghetti Western cartoonishness with the genuine cartoonishness of the Road Runner... using such devices as a bullet hole blown through a character which lets through light, but not blood. It's a pseudo-hip mishmash ... in a way that seems almost defensive. Raimi seems to be operating under the assumption that ... the audience has seen all this Western stuff before.[21]

Greene is correct about Raimi's gleeful cheer in announcing his influences, an essential element of any homage, and part and parcel of the movie-brat ethos, but he may be off the mark regarding Raimi's confidence in the material.

As cinematographer Tim Philo noted so insightfully in this text's introduction, Raimi the artist is a man always concerned with his audience and how they are enjoying/responding to the moviegoing experience. In designing and executing these radical and inventive camera angles and shots, Raimi grants the thematic material a new veneer, one that energizes the audience rather than fostering ennui. The Western is an old genre at this point, and *The Quick and the Dead* diffuses that problem by incorporating many twists on convention. That the gunfighter is a woman is just one twist in Moore's clever script. That the story removes all extraneous material and focuses on the crucible of the gunfight is another.

Though Raimi has seemingly come to believe that his formalist, inventive visuals are wrong for this material, this author would counter that claim. These visual grace notes, from the gunfighting montage, to the slow-motion photography, to the wild angles, succeed in making the material a fresh experience. These touches energize an audience that might rather go see an effects-heavy modern action-thriller rather than an old fashioned Western. The very shots reveal not Raimi's intrinsic boredom with the material, but his incredible joy with it, hence the tribute and his attempt to make it new all over again. The sun-through-the-bullet-hole moment is no mistake, but a victory wherein, according to reviewer Owen Gleiberman, "you can taste the comic book impudence of Raimi's imagination."[22]

Lance Henriksen notes that "Sam made the film accessible by putting his style into it," and this author believes this is a correct assertion. *The Quick and the Dead* isn't your father's Western, thanks to the creative efforts of all involved, and that is why it is a popular cult item today, probably the most talked about Western of the last decade, especially now, given Raimi's high profile. It is an endlessly entertaining movie, made more so by Raimi's insistence on shooting it with the visual flair that only he could bring to it.

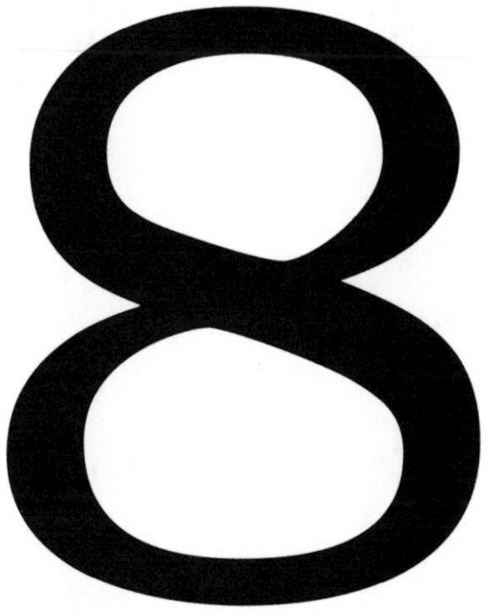

A SIMPLE PLAN (1998)

NOBODY WOULD EVER BELIEVE THAT YOU'D BE CAPABLE OF DOING WHAT YOU'VE DONE.

SOMETIMES GOOD PEOPLE DO EVIL THINGS.

CAST AND CREW

Paramount and Mutual Film Company present, in association with Savoy Pictures, *A Simple Plan*

Director: Sam Raimi
Casting: Ilene Starger
Music Composed and Conducted by: Danny Elfman
Costume Designer: Julie Weiss
Film Editors: Arthur Coburn and Eric L. Beason
Production Design: Patrizia von Brandenstein
Director of Photography: Alan Kavilo
Based on the novel by: Scott B. Smith
Co-producer: Michael Polaire
Executive Producers: Gary Levinsohn, Mark Gordon
Producers: James Jacks and Adam Schroeder
Stunt Coordinator: Chris Doyle
Screenplay: Scott B. Smith

STARRING

Bill Paxton: Hank Mitchell
Billy Bob Thornton: Jacob Mitchell
Bridget Fonda: Sarah
Gary Cole: Baxter
Brent Briscoe: Lou Chambers
Becky Ann Baker: Nancy
Chelcie Ross: Carl
Jack Walsh: Tom Butler
Peter Syvertsen: Freeman
Tom Carey: Dwight

Filmed in Ashland, Wisconsin, and St. Paul, Minnesota.

IF IT'S BROKEN, FIX IT.
IF YOU HAVE AN ITCH, SCRATCH IT.

IN FROZEN NORTHERN OHIO, Hank Mitchell lives a happy but modest life with his expecting wife Sarah, toiling at a low-paying job at the local grain store. One wintry day, Hank makes a discovery in the woods with his dim-witted but good-hearted brother Jacob and the loud-mouth redneck Lou Chambers: a crashed plane with a satchel containing four million dollars.

The three men resolve to keep the money and divide it three ways after a suitable amount of time has elapsed and Hank can be certain the money isn't marked or counterfeit. But Hank finds that he and Sarah are increasingly obsessed with the money, and impatient with Jacob's plans to re-establish the family farm. Soon the plan to keep the money spirals out of control, leading to distrust, paranoia, and ultimately murder.

When a man claiming to be an FBI agent arrives in search of the missing plane, Hank and Sarah wonder if the mysterious Agent Baxter is really who he claims to be, or the criminal who lost his ill-gotten ransom and now hopes to reclaim it.

The startling answers are revealed on a bleak, snowy landscape as Hank makes decisions affecting the rest of his life.

A SIMPLE BREAKTHROUGH

In 1993, twenty-eight-year-old Scott B. Smith was paid the princely sum of a million dollars for his first novel, an intense thriller about human nature called *A Simple Plan*. A psychologically adroit drama about good, corn-fed Midwesterners corrupted by their accidental acquisition of four million dollars, the book was, in the words of Smith, a former psychology student at Dartmouth, "dark and unheroic."[1]

More than that, the novel was an involving morality play, asking the question, "What would *you* do to keep four million dollars?" The answers, played against a bleak snowy landscape, were grim and involving. "I think there's something very seductive about the first-person voice," Smith told the *New York Times* about his decision to write the book in that tense. "You sort of fall into it, no matter what horrible things the character does, and I wanted to keep that up until the very end, at which point the reader would have to sort of pull back."[2]

Published by St. Martins Press, *A Simple Plan* generated extraordinary buzz and was praised by Stephen King, not unlike *The Evil Dead* back in 1982, as the finest thriller of the year. the *New York Times* accurately described the novel as an "absorbing story of choices made, both well and badly, and consequences stalled, evaded, suffered and escaped."[3]

The notion of adapting Smith's thriller to film was a no-brainer, and it wasn't long before that process began. For a time, John Cusack considered playing Hank. Brad Pitt and Nicolas Cage both reportedly showed interest, and Tom Cruise turned the role down. Among those talents planning to direct the film were Mike Nichols, John Boorman and Ben Stiller. Way down that list of dream directors, some fifteen names down, was a fellow by the name of Raimi.[4] He was a guy who hadn't shot a feature film since 1994, and had settled comfortably into the world of television, a venue allowing him to be home for dinner every night with wife Gillian and young children.

Actor Gary Cole starred in the 1995–1996 CBS TV series *American Gothic*, produced by Renaissance talents Tapert and Raimi and creator Shaun Cassidy. He remembers Raimi's role during that span. "Sam's part in that at the time was more of putting all the elements together, and then finishing it in post, in his style, which always has its own originality to it."

A SIMPLE SHOOT

Scott B. Smith adapted his own novel when penning the screenplay for *A*

Simple Plan, excising the ending of his literary work, which some reviewers complained seemed over-the-top. In the movie as it was released in 1998, Hank's brother Jacob survives almost until the climax, whereas in the original novel, Hank murders Jacob in the same sequence wherein Lou is killed, about half the way through the story. Then the novel culminates in very graphic terms when Sarah, believing she is in the clear after Baxter's death, spends a suspect bill, possibly marked, and precipitates Hank's final killing spree in a convenience store. He is armed with a machete, of all things.

This ending rubbed reviewers the wrong way, including columnist Michiko Kakutani, who noted that Smith's narrative devolved into a "grotesque compendium of *Grand Guignol* violence and senseless sensationalism" and that if the book began as a sort of film noir, it ended as an "inane parody of *Friday the 13th*."[5]

"I was kind of surprised how violent the book was compared to the film," remarks actor Chelcie Ross, who has appeared in numerous films, including Mike Nichols' *Primary Colors* (1998), and co-starred in *A Simple Plan* as Carl, the town Sheriff. "The film is violent, but I think Sam made a very serious effort to weed out some of the mayhem.

"There's a point, I believe, at which audiences become numb, inured to violence," the actor considers. "I think it is more effective when used sparingly and in exactly the right places, and I think Sam made a real effort to do that. My memory may be faulty about the book, but I think Hank loses control a good deal earlier. He's so over the line that, I don't know, he's irredeemable.

"My point — and I can't get inside Sam's head — is that he knew for the tension to build, for the violence to have the effect that it should have, he had to keep the pressure cooker on Hank from all sides. From his buddies, from his wife, from Carl; so he becomes this unpredictable animal, because you don't know which way he might go."

Starring in the rewritten *A Simple Plan* was Bill Paxton, who Raimi had acted with in the 1993 Mike Binder film, *Indian Summer*. Paxton was a veteran of many popular films including *Aliens*, the horror movie *Near Dark* (1987) and Carl Franklin's *One False Move* (1992), a movie Raimi had turned down the opportunity to direct. Paxton had become a bankable leading man in the late nineties thanks to roles in blockbusters such as *Twister* (1996) and *Titanic* (1997), the latter of which was in release as *A Simple Plan* filmed. Paxton proved perfect as the Everyman Hank, in part because he had a clear understanding of the hero's dilemma. "Unless you've been in a situation like that, you don't really know what you'll do," he told *Entertainment Tonight*, "and it depends on how desperate you are for the money."[6]

Already cast when Raimi came aboard was Billy Bob Thornton, who would be playing the simple-minded Jacob. The casting of Thornton, then riding high from the success of *Sling Blade* (1996), also represented a shift away from Smith's novel. In the book, Jacob was an obese bald man and a dullard, but not the humorous simpleton created by Thornton.

Bridget Fonda, who appeared briefly in Raimi's *Army of Darkness* as Linda, was cast as Sarah, a role she inhabited to chilly perfection. Gary Cole, the evil sheriff of *American Gothic*, was hired in the critical role of the enigmatic Baxter. "That was all due to Sam," Cole notes. "He was looking for somebody — not for a large part, but a pivotal part. It's my favorite movie, in terms of movies I've been in, even though I'm not in it a lot,. It's a great script, and Sam shot it great, and the whole thing works."

A powerful and robust actor named Brent Briscoe (*The Green Mile* [1999], *The Majestic* [2001]), lobbied for the part of Lou, a role for which Meat Loaf (*Fight Club* [1999]) was considered. "Billy [Bob Thornton] and I got close, and I ended up doing *Sling Blade*," Briscoe explains. "When he was going into *A Simple Plan*, Billy called me and said, 'Look, this is the perfect role for you.' I grew up in a small town in Missouri and I knew that guy. The moment I read the script, I knew that guy."

Briscoe tested with Thornton, and won the role in part because Raimi's wife saw his audition on tape. "To this day, I thank his wife, Gillian. I thank her for a career. Sam told me straight out. He said, 'Gillian saw the tapes and said, 'That's the guy!'"

Ross was one of the last actors cast, but proved crucial to the film's suspenseful equation, playing the representative of law and order, the sheriff. "I think Carl is most important as a window for the audience through which they can see how this town saw these four people," Ross considers. "I have to include Bridget's character in that. I think that otherwise you have three northern rednecks. You've got one fellow who seems to be mentally and emotionally, and every other way challenged. And then you've got the henpecked husband and Lady MacBeth, and the town drunk. And there's no reason to pay a whole lot of attention or have much empathy for these people unless someone validates them. I think that Carl gives that."

EXECUTING THE PLAN IN THE FROZEN NORTH

The plan was simple: to shoot Raimi's seventh movie in and around Minneapolis. Unfortunately, the weather had a different agenda. "We were supposed to shoot in Minneapolis, like a thirty-mile radius around it, the whole time," Briscoe explains. "but when we flew up there, and there was no snow because of El Niño. We were stuck."

With no snow on the ground, *A Simple Plan*'s production team had to find a new home, which meant a trek north. "I immediately got rerouted to

Superior, Wisconsin," Briscoe continues. "It was freezing. You couldn't go outside without snow getting in your eyes."

The movie crew found a new location in Ashland, Wisconsin, a small hamlet founded in 1854 and known as "Lake Superior's Hometown." The base of operations was a Victorian-style, grand hotel with sixty-five rooms, the Hotel Chequamegon on Lake Shore Drive. "Ashland was where the hotel was," Ross describes. "You find Ashland by going straight north from Minneapolis until you hit Lake Superior, and then drive east and north around the Lake, headed toward the Upper Peninsula. Ashland is on the lake, about as far north as you can get in Wisconsin."

"The main street had, like three lights," *A Simple Plan*'s stunt coordinator, Chris Doyle, says of the quiet, charming town. "Normally they would have snowdrifts fifteen- to twenty-feet high on the roads, but they only had them between four- and six-feet high, and it was really, really cold. It was a beautiful little town and the people were so happy to have us there. A bunch of us went to this forty-year-old theater to see *Titanic*. Billy Bob Thornton and Bill Paxton made friends with some of the locals, and I think both of them went ice fishing with some of them."

"These other places, the locations, were a good driving distance from there [Ashland]," Chelcie Ross continues the tour. "The trip out to the plane crash location was probably a thirty-five- to forty-minute drive north from Ashland."

And a perilous drive it was. "We drove out there, and a couple of times I drove out in a blizzard and couldn't see ten feet in front me," Doyle remembers. "Everybody had to be careful that they had warm clothes with them because people would break down on the side of the road in this type of climate and freeze to death. The locals would say, 'This is mild, this is nothing.' And we'd say, 'You're kidding me; it's freezing here!" Of course, we were from California."

"Long days," Ross recalls of the fifty-five-day shoot. "That kind of weather makes days longer because all of the simple tasks are more difficult. The cast has it easier than the crew, always, but in those kinds of conditions, it is especially true. They would set up little warming tents and get heaters for us. During set-ups, actors would be inside the tents, but the crew members didn't have that luxury."

"Bill [Paxton] to this day swears that his mouth was frozen," Briscoe remembers of the day that Paxton and Thornton shot the scene at the dilapidated Mitchell farm. "It was fifty-six below with wind chill. Literally *fifty-six below*. Billy Bob said one day, which I thought was so funny, 'Okay I've decided what my next movie is.' And we all stood back and listened. And he said, 'It's going to be Billy Bob on a porch in Hawaii drinking iced tea.'"

"The worst day for me was the scene where we all roll up, get out of the pick-ups, and are going to search for the plane," Gary Cole describes. "That day was about ten degrees, and with wind chill, about ten below.

"During some of that stuff on the road, there was just no place to go, no place to be warm," Cole explains. "But the trade-off is worth it. There's something about snow in movies. It looks so good, and cold causes things to happen to actors and their faces, and it's just an element of reality you can't deny."

"There's a whole lot of the acting job eliminated because of those conditions," Ross agrees. "You don't have to act cold. You wake up and you're in it. You don't have to pretend you're in Minnesota or Wisconsin."

In particular, Ross remembers his baptism by ice, his first day on the film. "The first day that I shot was actually a night. I drove to the base camp and got wardrobe and makeup, and it must have been at least one in the morning by the time they drove me out to the site where they were shooting. This is one of those scenes that I will never forget. Driving out across the snow-covered farmlands for miles on these country roads, and in the sky was this enormous orange globe hanging on the horizon that looked like something out of *Dune*, or some sci-fi production. The Red Planet or something.

"What they had done is hung what they call an *artificial moon*," Ross explains. "It's a helium-filled globe that is lit from inside and tethered with three or four lines that run down to the ground. They lifted it up, so they could put a general illumination over a large area — in order to shoot outside at night without having to put lighting instruments everywhere. Then, of course, you have to light close-ups, but for general illumination it gives a wonderful look to a snowfield. So for miles driving across the snow, we could see this huge moon hanging on the horizon, getting closer and closer.

"The temperature at that hour of the morning was at least ten below," says Ross. "All they wanted me to do was drive up and do that little scene where they [Hank and Jacob] come over and talk at the window of Carl's truck. I drove it the first time for rehearsal, and noticed there was no outside rearview mirror. They'd taken it off to get it out of the shot. There was an inside rearview mirror, and the road was icy. So I drove up and did the rehearsal and Sam said, 'Okay, let's shoot it. Back it up to the marks.'"

Ross attempted to comply, but the truck's back window was frozen over, and he had no exterior mirror to check his bearings. "So I'm hanging out the truck window, at ten below, trying to back it down the road, and I slid the truck off into a ditch!

"Once I started sliding, there was just no stopping it," Ross explains. "I had my foot on the brake and was pumping the brake, but it was just like a toboggan or a luge. The ditch was deep enough that I was sitting there looking straight up at the windshield with the rear end down in the ditch.

"Sam is back down the road maybe twenty-five yards, and he yelled to the grip 'How long to get it out?' The grip says, 'Twenty minutes or half an hour;' and Sam says, 'That's a wrap!' That was my first day's work on *A Simple Plan*. It was one of those times when you get out of makeup for a forty-minute drive home thinking, 'I'm fired. That's the end of that!' But it's a good indication of how Sam reacts under pressure. He didn't throw a tantrum or say nasty things."

The cold climate played havoc with *A Simple Plan*'s cast in other locations too, including the Victorian-style house where Hank murders Nancy, Lou's wife. "I think Bob Dylan played out there one time, because he is still painted on the garage. It's not in the movie of course, but his big head was painted on the garage up there. It's just a vacant house," Briscoe describes, "and it was one of the coldest places I've ever been in my life."

Lou's death scene took two days to shoot. "We shot that scene in the first day [involving Hank and Jacob's illicit tape-recording of Lou's mock confession] and on the second day I had to come back and lay in that Karo syrup and be dead, and there was no heat," remembers Briscoe.

This sequence of *A Simple Plan* proves one of the most harrowing to watch, in no small part because it degenerates quickly into terrible, unexpected violence. At one point, Hank is forced to shoot Nancy, and the poor woman is literally lifted into the air and blown backward into a kitchen wall by the blast. It's terribly disturbing, and that is precisely the way stunt coordinator Chris Doyle wanted it.

"The story is very dark. The nature of these guys finding the money and slowly turning on each other ... it gets so ugly," he considers. "I had to sell that. When Lou's wife gets shot and flies up against the cabinet, I had to sell it to Sam. He was afraid it would look like *Army of Darkness*, too comic bookish, and I said, 'Not the way we're going to do it, Sam. If you don't like it, you can always cut away from it, but I think you're going to like it.'"

Doyle remembers how he came to plan and choreograph the scene. "The sequence reminded me of a black-and-white television show I saw as a kid. It was about the Civil War and these young people, teenagers, fighting. I remember a scene that really struck me was of this kid inside a house, soldiers break in, and this kid is trying to get away. They find him and shoot him, and it affected me. It was so ugly. That sequence in the script, when I read it, brought to mind this whole thing. That was the feeling I got when I saw that scene.

"As the story progressed and these men end up fighting each other, it turns tragic. And how tragic is it that he [Hank] shoots this woman because she won't put the gun down, because there's panic going on. He's scared for his life, but for her not just to get shot and fall down, but to get *blasted three feet and hit the cabinet*, to me, just made it so ugly. That's what I explained to Sam.

"What's fun about this business is when you do something that comes across exactly as you wanted it to," Doyle muses. "That was one sequence that I remember in particular, after the screening. I heard people say, 'When that woman got shot it was ugly; it was terrible.' That's the feeling I wanted. Everything has beats, like music building. In this instance, it builds up to this, and that shot is the drum beat and you say, 'Oh my God!'"

SUSPICION AND SUSPENSE

As *A Simple Plan* nears its conclusion, suspense grows exponentially under Raimi's direction. One particular scene is a real gut-buster. In Carl's office, Hank prepares to show Agent Baxter the location where he and Jacob heard the plane crash. Carl is there, blissfully ignorant of everything. Hank is there with a secret — the stolen money — and his uncertainty about Baxter's real identity. And Baxter is revealing absolutely nothing, but watching Hank very closely.

"He [Raimi] didn't want that part to be a throwaway," Cole considers his role. "He told me, 'I know this is not a big part, but I want this done delicately. When this guy shows up, I don't want the audience to know what is going to go down.' And I agreed with that, and he tweaked me however he needed to tweak me, and basically I didn't really have to do anything but pull back.

"There was no need to show anything," Cole continues. "That's more threatening. Sam and I had a discussion about this. Either way, this guy is trouble. If he's from the FBI, he's trouble because they could get caught. If he's one of the guys that lost the money, they're also in trouble. So better to hold off and not show things. It was written that way, not to reveal anything, because it leads to the moment where Baxter shoots the sheriff. You don't know until that moment what his deal is. But you certainly know that Bill Paxton is not thrilled he is in town."

For Ross, the scene was a difficult one, not emotionally, but physically. "First of all, it was prop hell for me. I had donuts and guns and bullets and paper weights and keys and all kinds of crap. And, as Sam noted, I'm probably the most right-handed person in the world. I don't do anything with my left hand. So all these things became right-hand props to figure out the choreography with." Ross also had the pleasure of eating deep-fried donuts, purportedly cooked by Carl's wife in the film. "They had somebody make some deep-fried donuts in odd shapes, just clumping the dough into the foil. They were ugly, nasty-looking things."

Cole continues to describe the scene. "Bill is on the phone with Bridget Fonda, she's telling him not to go, and he's just kind of faking the other half of the conversation. I thought Bill did that great. He's saying so much with his face about not knowing and really delivering the tension of what's about to happen. There's a lot going on in that scene, and the script is full of stuff like that. Sam got the best out of him."

Ross offers praise not only for Paxton and Cole, but Fonda. "All she had to do [for that scene] was record that phone call. I have done a lot of films where there's a phone call and you need to answer a specific question, and they'll have the script coordinator on the other end of the line or just talking to you across the set, and you answer on the phone. Bridget was there. *Insisted* on being there. Did that phone call live, all day long. And she could have had the day off."

This suspenseful scene of competing motives and secrets led up to the film's finale: a series of confrontations at the plane crash site where the whole thing had started with the discovery of the money. Because it was an exterior sequence, and because of its import, the scene was another difficult one.

"You can see the inclination, the hill that Bill runs down to go to the plane crash," Ross describes the setting. "In fact, Gary is coming down from the opposite direction. Because we were going to shoot in that snow-filled valley with the plane down in the bottom of it, we were going to be there for a long time. We had to have one path that was ingress and another that was egress, because otherwise you mess up all the snow and you can't shoot it. You get a big crew going up and down all day long, and you just ruin the entire location. So there was one path up and one path down, which quickly became ice. So the grips tied ropes from tree to tree so we could pull ourselves up, and also because otherwise you would be skating down on your butt. The crew could do that, but the cast couldn't because of the costumes.

"The last scene is critical you know," Ross weighs. "Nobody was ever quite convinced that we had it, so it became a project of rewriting, sometimes between takes; of Billy improvising within the take. We kept sneaking up on it, kept reworking that scene, improvising and improving it until we were comfortable with it."

Ross pauses to consider Thornton, and his remarkable ability to make even the most difficult scenes work. "Billy Bob Thornton, man, what can you say? Billy Bob and I have done *Primary Colors, Waking Up in Reno* and *A Simple Plan*, and of course, he wrote *The Gift.* We've been around each other quite a lot; I'm really still in awe of the guy, even after all this time, and I consider him a buddy. When I was in the Air Force, I worked for a four star general who was from Oklahoma. He was 6'5" and seemed like an old redneck, but he had this computer for a brain. You could mention something to him that was very technical and full of statistics, and three weeks later he would quote it to you. Billy Bob is like that. He does that Good Ol' Boy, and that's who he is, but he does it so convincingly you think he's a little slow. But man, he's way ahead of all of us. He's also a great mimic, like a sponge. Anything he sees and hears, he takes it all in." For the heart-wrenching role of Jacob, Thornton was nominated for an Oscar for Best Supporting Actor.

As for Raimi, he was a new man on *A Simple Plan*, taking lessons learned from *The Quick and the Dead* and other projects, and shooting his thriller in a different style. "The movies I make are usually screaming to entertain loudly with great insecurity, the camera racing around as much as possible," he told the press. "But I had so much confidence in the script that I felt the only choice for me was to put the camera not in the most exciting or dramatic places, but in the proper place, and really allow the actors to tell the story."[7]

WINTER WONDERLAND

A Simple Plan opened on December 11, 1998 against *Star Trek: Insurrection*, *Shakespeare in Love* and the comedy *Rushmore*. It was a crowded season at the movies, but critics singled out Raimi's feature, making it the intellectual's must-see film of the season. *Rolling Stone*'s Peter Travers termed it "sharp, subtle work"[8] and *Entertainment Weekly* raved it was "lean, elegant, and emotionally complex — a marvel of backwoods classicism."[9] Writing for the *Christian Science Monitor*, David Sterritt acknowledged the change in Raimi's directing MO: "Raimi makes his first steps into grown-up moviemaking, and an impressive step it is."[10]

A Simple Plan awarded Raimi the best notices of his career. "Raimi turns the screws of the relentless plot with quiet precision, aiming for queasily escalating suspense,"[11] David Ansen reported for *Newsweek*. And John Powers, critic for *Vogue*, went further. "Most neo-noirs are simply an excuse for hip wisecracks and stylish violence, but Raimi recaptures the human dimension of theft and murder. In this film, crime has an emotional weight that crumples some characters, brings out self-protective violence in others and reveals the wide vein of sadness that runs through daily life."[12]

A low-budget production, *A Simple Plan* earned back its budget but little more, grossing $10,069,000. More rewarding than box office reception, the film racked up nominations and awards. Thornton's performance was nominated for an Academy Award, a Golden Globe, a Golden Satellite and a Saturn Award. His portrait of Jacob also garnered him a Boston Society of Film Critics Award and a Chicago Film Critics Association Award. Co-star Fonda was nominated for a Blockbuster Entertainment Award and her future husband, composer Danny Elfman, was nominated by the Chicago Film Critics Association. Smith was also recognized, nominated for a Best Writing Academy Award (material from another medium), a Broadcast Film Critics Award, and a Writer's Guild Award. He took home the prize for best screenplay from the National Board of Review. It was a bonanza of praise and recognition that Raimi had selected the right path directing this thriller.

RAIMI RAP

AUTHOR ACCOLADES: "I got a hardback copy of the book and I have it right here in front of me. I have it displayed," reports Briscoe with a sense of pride. "I'm going to say what Scott Smith wrote me, which is really nice. 'To Brent: who made Lou come alive on the screen; a better Lou in many ways than the one I wrote. More complex, more poignant, more human. Your pal, Scott.'

"To me that was one of the nicest compliments you can ever get," Briscoe considers. "From a screenwriter — an Academy Award–nominated screenwriter. And personally, I think he should have won!"

THE APPRENTICE OF SUSPENSE: "Sam has a nature...," Cole considers, "where you think about Hitchcock. He's a real artist like that. He wears the suit and tie, and maybe he's even wearing it under that parka ... I don't know. He's got a very 'old Hollywood' kind of feeling. 'Lights, camera, action!' — that kind of animation comes out of him."

SECRET GARDEN: "What I think Sam would love to talk about is the fact that he's a gardener," Briscoe says. "He's planted all these trees in his yard. It's a big deal for him. He thinks that's what his life really is."

PSYCHOANALYSIS: "Sam and I talked about the character [Carl] on almost a daily basis," says Ross. "A lot of actors fly by the seat of their pants and think that they instinctively will do what is right for the character. I always want to talk to the director. And Sam is like a good psychiatrist or analyst. He always turns it around and says, 'What do you think about it?' You end up with a dialogue instead of him just saying, 'This is what I want you to do.' A neat thing about Sam is that even if it is something he wants to impart to you, if you hit upon it, if you say it, it's your idea, and he never says that's what he wanted to tell you. It's always, 'You're right.' He encourages the fact that you have made the right discovery about who your character is. He leads very gently where he wants you to go."

READY FOR YOUR CLOSE-UP: "He's so funny," laughs Briscoe. "One thing I would say about him that I love is when he was blocking a scene he'd say, 'Brent, here's what I want you to do. I want you to bring your miserable face and look right over here and stand and say the line.' Then, 'Billy, you and your miserable face...'

"It's hysterical. He's being degrading, but he's not. He's screwing with you. It's one of the funniest things on earth. 'I've got a close up of you — oh, that's going to be *disgusting* — but anyway...'"

NOSEY: "It was crazy," Doyle notes of the weather on location near Lake Superior. "They set up tents for the cast and crew with heaters inside and also for the camera equipment. Our still photographer got her nose stuck. Her nose touched a metal case and she actually got it stuck on the thing. She pulled it off and had this little red, round thing on her nose the whole time we were there. That's how cold it was."

OBSERVE AND LEARN, MY FRIEND...

There's a new, more mature Raimi at work in the harrowing *A Simple Plan*. Some people who worked with the artist over the years term the film the beginning of his "middle period," the time in his career when the camera angles stopped being of paramount importance and performances were elevated to a threshold equal to visual composition. It's an interesting shift for such a dynamic filmmaker, yet one should not assume that Raimi no longer has "the gift" so far as mise en scène. He still knows precisely where to position the camera and how to stage sequences to wring out maximum emotional impact. It's just that in *A Simple Plan*, *For Love of the Game*, *The Gift* and *Spider-Man* the angles are a little less over-the-top. Raimi remains the formalist we know and love, bound and determined to forge entertainment of the highest order; it's just that he has struck a balance between the acting component and the camera work.

In *A Simple Plan*, Raimi found a perfect template to usher in this new phase. There are only a few characters in the compelling novel, and their degradation from happiness to paranoia and misery is one well-charted by writer Smith. Raimi need not push to impact the audience; he has but to allow these characters to tell their tale. And the core of that story is not just that money is the root of all evil, but that, according to Hank's narration in the novel, the money "by giving us the chance to dream, had also allowed us to begin despising our present lives."[13]

The money is like a cancer in the book and film, overcoming the characters' souls a piece at a time until unacceptable choices somehow become acceptable. Choices like murder. Like fratricide. The story remains universal, and therefore affecting, because everybody has wondered what it would be like to be rich. To win the lottery, or find stolen money. How would we react? What would we do? What would we give up? In allowing these questions to rise to the forefront, Raimi has engineered all the special effects he requires.

As in all Raimi's films, strong visuals reinforce the screenplay, and many are symbolic. For instance, when Hank, Lou and Jacob first wander into the nature preserve in search of the fox, the camera is perched far above the trees, watching from a high angle. Traditionally, the high angle represents entrapment or doom in film and it does so here, but the imagery is more powerful even than that. Three crows squawk in the foreground, close to the camera, resting on branches that intersect the frame, cutting it up into jags and conveying the impression of disorder.

The crows watch the men traverse the snowy landscape and Jacob remarks that the black birds are "waiting for something to die," as if they are already cognizant that death will come to these interlopers. Crows are not only scavengers, as Jacob correctly points out, they are mythological harbingers of death, and a gathering of crows is called a "murder." Furthermore, myths reveal that crows indeed gather at a time and place when it is expected someone will soon die. So the presence of these intruding crows in the frame (and there are three; mirroring the three conspirators) signifies doom and also foreshadows murder, a desperate measure Hank and his brother will soon resort to. The birds are not there by accident, but as a symbol of foreboding.

A Simple Plan communicates adroitly in the language of legend and literature. There are visual symbols that tie each character to well-known, and often corrupt, figures in literature. Hank eventually kills Jacob, his own brother; and early on at the plane, Hank injures his head, staining himself with a mark of Cain, the mark of the first human to commit fratricide on earth by killing his brother, Abel.

Hank's wife Sarah represents another famous character in literary history, Shakespeare's Lady MacBeth. Both women push their husbands into ambitious, murderous action. "You have to go back and return some of the money," Sarah obsessively plots in bed by dead of night, as when Lady MacBeth anticipated the death of Duncan. "You'll have to go in the morning, so when it storms later, it'll cover your tracks..."

Later, Sarah allows baby Amanda to suckle from her breast, while explaining, in excruciating detail, how Hank and Jacob should trick Lou into confessing while recording his words on a miniature tape recorder. This behavior recalls MacBeth's wife, a woman who feels she must take charge of her husband's career ambitions (and therefore a murder conspiracy) because she fears his weak nature, that it is 'too full o' th' milk of human kindness to catch the nearest way."[14] In other words, Sarah does not trust Hank to be as brutal as he must be to accomplish the job, so she plots and plans for him, even as an innocent baby nourishes from her "milk of human kindness."

Though Sarah does not explicitly curse her womanhood, as does Lady MacBeth in act one, scene five ("Come to my woman's breast and take my breast for gall."), she dramatizes a total coldness of character. Just as Sarah plots betrayal, a baby suckling at her breast, Lady MacBeth so describes in act one, scene seven a horrible image. She would take a smiling baby, pluck it from her nipples and "dash" its brain out rather than fail at the enterprise of murder. In our culture, women are known as nurturing souls, and their ability to nourish the young with breast milk symbolizes this nature. Sarah and Lady MacBeth represent the *opposite* of female nature, and therefore have much in common.

Lady MacBeth is a character that cajoles her husband by insulting his manhood and courage, and near the end of *A Simple Plan*, Sarah adopts the same tactic, dressing Hank down and painting a picture of a most unhappy future should his courage and fortitude not return. At least Lady MacBeth boasted a semblance of conscience about her actions, a fact that eventually led to suicide. In *A Simple Plan,* the manipulative Sarah never expresses remorse or conscience, still grasping for the money even when it is learned the bills are marked and therefore worthless.

Jacob seems primarily evocative of another figure in literature, a much less corrupt one than either Cain or Lady MacBeth: Lennie Small from John Steinbeck's novel *Of Mice and Men*. Both men share the dream of one day owning a farm, and both are simple minded. Like Lennie, Jacob is always paired with another man, one who seems to be much smarter than he. It is tempting to view the film and note that one brother is stupid, the other smart, but it is Hank who seems the emotional idiot. Jacob may not possess traditional "book smarts," and indeed he is bitter that Hank went away to college at great expense, but Jacob is emotionally open and intelligent. He knows that their father committed suicide, whereas Hank doesn't put the facts together. Jacob also feels guilt over the death of Lou, asking Hank if he ever feels evil. He is the moral compass of the film, despite his lack of traditional "intelligence." If Sarah is Hank's id, pressing forever onward to take the money no matter the cost, Jacob is his ego, his moral sense of restraint and decency.

As Raimi watchers recall, his films often feature homage to literature and the cinema. *A Simple Plan* follows this pattern with allusions to characters from scripture and literature, but there is another source of tribute too, Raimi's favorite film: *The Treasure of the Sierra Madre*.

John Huston's brilliant black-and-white film explored the story of down-on-their-luck prospectors in search of gold, but instead finding themselves bedeviled by jealousy, paranoia and greed. Like *A Simple Plan*, *The Treasure of Sierre Madre* was adapted from another format, a novel by B. Traven. It likewise featured three important characters, Dobbs (Humphrey Bogart), Howard (Walter Huston) and Tim Holt (Bob Curtin). Like the Hank–Lou–Jacob triangle of *A Simple Plan*, these men needed each other, even though they didn't like or trust one another. They were all in on a conspiracy, aware of a gold vein's location on a mountain, and in the unenviable position of splitting up their booty three ways.

Dobbs in that film is very much like Hank. Early in *The Treasure of the Sierre Madre*, the audience roots for him. He seems a decent, if down-on-his-luck fella, and the audience sides with him when an unscrupulous employer cheats Dobbs out of his hard-earned wages. When Dobbs strikes back to get his money, it is not the act of a bad man, but a desperate man who has been cheated. It is only later that the audience detects that Dobbs is the weakest link, suspicious to the point of insanity, and willing to kill to protect his share. He shoots Holt and abandons his partners so he will have the treasure for himself.

The story of *A Simple Plan* takes Hank on a similar trajectory. The audience sees that he is a likeable family man, just trying to make a living, and is with him even as he discovers the satchel of cash. The audience wants to see him succeed, and worries that Lou will mess everything up for everybody. Yet it is Hank that kills Dwight. Yet it is Hank (with Sarah's prodding) who pushes to frame Lou. Yet it is Hank who kills Nancy, an innocent. Yet it is Hank, finally, who murders his own flesh-and-blood just so he can keep "the story straight." Like Dobbs in Huston's film, Hank is not the man the audience believed him to be and so closely identified with. He is weak emotionally and morally.

If anything, Smith's novel makes this more apparent: by the end of the story he has also killed Lou's neighbor (to frame as Nancy's lover), shot Mary Beth, Jacob's dog, and Sarah worries that he might turn his murderous attention to her.

There are other similarities between Raimi's film and Huston's. In both, the landscape plays a crucial role — proving harsh and unforgiving, and shaping the environment in which terrible actions occur. In *Sierre Madre*, the heat of the desert brings about a sort of murderous fever in Dobbs. In *A Simple Plan* it is almost the opposite equation, the cold of Wright county permitting Hank and Sarah to icily plan and execute murder.

The conclusions of both films are thematically close. The treasure — the thing for which Dobbs and Hank lose their souls — is an empty victory, metaphorical fool's gold. In *The Treasure of Sierre Madre*, Dobbs steals the money, goes off by himself and is promptly killed by bandits. They ransack his belongings, not realizing the gold is there, and it is cast to the four winds ... literally blown away like dust. In *A Simple Plan*, Hank learns that FBI agents randomly marked bills, making the stash worthless. He has killed his brother, lost his innocence, and gained nothing.

"He's a brilliant master of film and he's my favorite director, the absolute number one," Raimi has said about Huston. "There's been a focus on the visual over the past twenty-five years ... but that will pass, and Huston will come back into vogue. It's the human story that is powerful, meaningful, and lasting."[15]

By understanding what made John Huston and *The Treasure of The Sierra Madre* so special, Raimi was able to direct his film in similar, though not derivative fashion, highlighting the human story, making the audience feel Hank's "breach morally and epistemologically, as a sucking wound in the soul and the way Everyman sees the world."[16]

Huston's films have been described by writer Stuart Kaminsky as a "moving canvas" on which the director explores his thesis, "the effects of the individual ego on the group and the possibilities of the group's survival."[17] *A Simple Plan* argues the same thesis, examining how Hank's world collapses when he attempts to dominate the group for his own selfish gain. Had he not tried to force Jacob to take sides, Lou would not have been killed. Had he not (unwittingly) made Jacob a murderer, Jacob would not have felt so much guilt that he could no longer live. By trying to impose order, Hank has wrought only chaos, much like Dobbs, who wanted it all and lost everything.

This author has written repeatedly in these pages about form expressing content. Raimi students may watch this film and feel the director reigned himself in on that front. Yet Raimi's compositions in *A Simple Plan* are every bit as successful in vetting the story as in other films he has directed, just tweaked to augment the human story, the one Raimi views as lasting and meaningful. Note for instance, how the film is bookended by similarly lensed scenes at the Delano Mill and Grain Store. At the beginning of the film, Hank goes about his business and in voiceover describes his father's "simple" definition of happiness (the respect of neighbors, love of a good wife, etc.) A very similar scene closes the film: Hank back at work, but this time miserable, having been expelled from paradise by his own hunger for something better. The physical similarities in the two scenes reveal how much things have changed from film's opening to denouement. What once seemed innocent now seems corrupted.

A Simple Plan is a chilling tale of manipulation and murder. To echo that cold feeling as well as the barren, almost hopeless nature of life in Wright county, Raimi stages a number of dramatic exterior long shots, where characters appear little more than tiny, moving figures on a vast, wintry landscape, their movements captured by a stationary camera. The message of these shots might very well be that the land doesn't change, evolve, or forgive. It is bigger than the characters, literally, and plays a part in their decisions. What would *you* do to escape the loneliness of this cold frontier, not precisely the Mexico of *The Treasure of the Sierra Madre*, but not too different, either. Would you kill?

Raimi also designs effective compositions expressing the characters' plights. Near film's end, Hank gets a haircut and he is seen in the foreground. Behind him, Carl enters the shop and asks questions. This scene might have been filmed with traditional two-shots, over-the-shoulder views, or any array of less effective choices. Instead, Raimi's camera captures Hank's worried face up-close, trying to maintain composure, as Carl probes deeper. By making Hank the primary figure within the frame, Raimi focuses on the human intrigue, the universal fear of being caught. Within one shot we get questioner and questionee, and in Paxton's expressive eyes, fear and anxiety. Importantly, the inquisitor behind him does not see these things, and so the shot reveals not only Paxton's guilt, but Carl's total inability to see it. It is a simple shot, not a flashy one, but one that reveals the nature of the characters in spades.

Another composition reveals everything the audience need know about Sarah, and the stolen money's impact on the Mitchell marriage. Hank has just come home with the ill-gotten cash. Raimi's camera is positioned on the kitchen table, and Sarah is the only person in the frame, her back to the audience as she prepares dinner. She hears a noise and turns around. In the foreground, falling piles of cash crash down on the table, eclipsing our view of Sarah. The rack focus shifts from Sarah in the background to the money in the foreground, and the shot expresses the notion that the money will be a factor in their lives "bigger" than both of them. The cash buries Sarah in the frame, just as it does so morally, and she becomes determined to keep it.

A Simple Plan is a cinematic perfect storm, an ideal marriage of a literate, involving and human story with the visuals of a confident director who knows exactly how to present it. The film received so much praise not because Raimi had “reigned himself in,” but because he took a page from Huston’s book in his cleverest homage yet, and put the people first. That is a stylistic decision as much as is the use of the shaky cam, or a Ram-O-Cam. In quietly trusting his actors and his own story sense, Raimi achieves a new confidence, proof that sometimes subtlety can entertain better than fireworks.

FOR LOVE OF THE GAME (1999)

CLEAR THE MECHANISM

CAST AND CREW

UNIVERSAL PRODUCTIONS PRESENTS A BEACON PICTURES, TIG PRODUCTION, MIRAGE ENTERPRISES PICTURE, *FOR LOVE OF THE GAME*.

DIRECTOR: Sam Raimi
CASTING: Lynn Kressell
MUSIC COMPOSED AND CONDUCTED BY: Basil Poledouris
MUSIC SUPERVISOR: G. Marg Roswell
COSTUME DESIGNER: Judianna Makovsky
FILM EDITORS: Eric L. Beason and Arthur Coburn
PRODUCTION DESIGNER: Neil Spisak
DIRECTOR OF PHOTOGRAPHY: John Bailey
EXECUTIVE PRODUCERS: Ron Bozman and Marc Abraham
BASED ON THE NOVEL BY: Michael Shaara
PRODUCERS: Armyan Bernstein and Amy Robinson
SCREENPLAY: Dana Stevens
VISUAL EFFECTS SUPERVISOR: Peter Donen
VISUAL EFFECTS: Cinesite, Hammerhead Productions

STARRING

Kevin Costner: Billy Chapel
Kelly Preston: Jane Aubrey
John C. Reilly: Gus Sinski
Jena Malone: Heather
Brian Cox: Mr. Wheeler
J.K. Simmons: Frank Perry
Vin Scully: himself
Steve Lyons: himself
Carime D. Giovnazzo: Ken Strout
Bill Rogers: Davis Birch
Hugh Ross: Mike Udall
Greer Barnes: Mickey Hart
Scott Brean: Brian Writt
Michael Papajohn: Sam Tuttle
John Darjean Jr.: Warble
Ricky Ledee: Ruiz
Rick Reed: Home Plate Umpire
Tracy Middendorf: Blond Player's Wife
Ted Raimi: Gallery Doorman

Filmed in New York City, New York, Aspen, Colorado, Universal City, California, and Hollywood, California.

SUMMER WINDS...

BASEBALL LEGEND BILLY CHAPEL HAS SEEN HAPPIER DAYS. After eighteen years in the game, the pitcher has been traded from the Detroit Tigers by the team's new, corporate-minded owners. And worse, Billy's girlfriend, Jane, stands him up for a romantic dinner date right before the season's last game.

As the day of the game approaches, Chapel makes important decisions about his personal and professional life. Should he and Jane marry? Should he allow himself to be traded, even though he has always identified himself proudly as a Tiger? Or is now the right time to bow out gracefully?

Feeling alone and unsure, even with the counsel of his good friend and catcher, Gus Sinski, the idealistic Chapel pitches his final game at Yankee Stadium. The contest begins as a tense one, with a battle of wills between batter Sammy Tuttle and Chapel.

As Chapel inches nearer to pitching the perfect game, he reflects on his past, his first meeting with Jane, and memories of the game.

YOU COUNT EVERYTHING IN BASEBALL

After *A Simple Plan* finished post-production, director Sam Raimi began his biggest-budgeted film yet, a fifty-million-dollar baseball/romance flick starring Kevin Costner. But before Raimi ever came aboard the project, it was a long road to get the film made.

For Love of the Game almost never was. Written by Michael Shaara, the Pulitzer Prize–winning author of the Civil War epic *The Killer Angels*, the short novel gathered dust in a drawer until 1988, following the author's untimely passing. Shaara's son, Jeff, author of *Gods and Generals* and *The Last Full Measure*, discovered the manuscript and introduced the world to a hero named Billy Chapel, a baseball player whose "time is nearly over" because "the harsh reality of the modern game is surrounding him, and so he begins to see beyond, to what might lie ahead..."[1] But as he looked forward, Billy also made peace with the past and pitched a perfect game. Written in spare, efficient style, Shaara's novel was heart wrenching, inspiring and romantic all at once. It reads like a Hemingway novel, lean in prose, but macho and tough in its portrayal of the lonely man on the mound.

One day in the mid-1990s, the novel found its way into the hands of one of Hollywood's premier producers, Amy Robinson, whose movies include *Running on Empty* (1988), *White Palace* (1990) and *From Hell*. "I'm a big baseball fan and I happened to read a little blurb about a book that sounded intriguing to me, so I went over to the bookstore and bought it, and that was *For Love of the Game*," Robinson says. "It's a slim little volume written by a man named Michael Shaara, and I just fell in love with the book.

"At the time, I had a deal with Universal and I wanted to get them to option it, but I was having trouble convincing them, even though it would not have been very expensive," the producer relates. "I mentioned it and then gave it to Sydney Pollack, with whom my ex-partner and I had produced *White Palace*.

"Sidney and I are friends, so I gave him the book and he sat out in his garden and read it, and cried at the end," Robinson continues. "Coincidentally, someone on his development staff also read it, so he got it from me and also heard about it from her. We went back to Universal and all of the sudden they were quite interested, naturally. So we optioned it together and developed it."

A first draft was written by one of the screenplay authors of Robert Redford's paean to classical baseball, *The Natural*, but Robinson and Pollack agreed it wasn't the right take. "It was not a bad script," Robinson elaborates, "just in a sense a little too reverential of the book."

In particular, the novel was set in the 1970s, replete with references to Neil Diamond, *Charlie's Angels* (which plays on a hotel TV) and other pop culture touchstones of that era. There was agreement among the producers that *For Love of the Game* might be more compelling as a comment on the state of contemporary baseball, with all its ups and downs, rather than a look at a simpler era. But could Robinson find the right writer to tackle the material?

Fortunately, writer Dana Stevens stepped up to the plate, fresh off the Madeleine Stowe hit thriller, *Blink*, and evidenced enthusiasm for the subject matter. "Basically, after *Blink*, I took a job with Amy Robinson," Stevens sets the scene. "I wrote a script for her at Universal which was a thriller [*The Lion Sleeps*] based on a Joyce Carol Oates novel. After I finished that, it was well received, but all I was getting offered were thrillers with tough women characters. Amy and I had become pretty good friends through the course of working together and we went to lunch and she said, 'Well, what do you really want to write?' And I said, 'The truth is that I want to write *The Way We Were* (1973). That's my favorite movie of all time.' She looked at me and said, 'Do you like baseball?' And it so happens that I love baseball — I've been a huge baseball fan all my life! So I said, 'I love baseball' and she said she had this project with Sydney Pollack, who had directed *The Way We Were*. He was the original director on *For Love of the Game*, and she had this book and this project, and the script wasn't right."

Stevens came aboard and promptly read the Shaara novel, assessing its cinematic qualities. "It's a novella. It wasn't really finished. It was found in a drawer after Michael Shaara died, and then they published it. It's kind of dated, so they needed to completely reinvent the love story part. The baseball part was pretty good.

"I felt like the structure in the book was so brilliant, and it gave me an opportunity to do something half-and-half," Stevens considers. "The baseball, the relationship, and of course the metaphor of the game. You play a game, and you play games with each other in a relationship. And it also had something in it that I loved. A lot of times when you do a baseball movie, it doesn't feel universal because how many people are professional baseball players? I felt this story had a universality because Billy Chapel being a baseball player was just a metaphor. He's the ultimate guy, and he's like *every* guy. He's not sure he wants to grow up. He's not sure he wants to commit. Any guy can identify with that, whether he's a professional baseball player or not."

When the movie was released, some critics complained it was neither fish nor fowl, too much romance or too much baseball. This is actually a common complaint regarding Raimi's films, including *Army of Darkness* and *Evil Dead 2*. His movies tend to mix moods, often funny and scary, blurring the lines between comedic moments and serious ones, so *For Love of the Game*'s tale of romance and baseball is hardly out of the norm. "I really wanted it to be half-and-half," Stevens notes of the film's structure. "I wasn't really worried about the love story. I knew that would turn out pretty good. I wanted to make people love baseball as much as I do, and see the game and what a wonderful game it is, and see the gamesmanship between the pitcher and the batter; and the drama of a pitcher pitching a no-hitter, a perfect game."

One thing that Stevens did change, in keeping with the times, was Chapel's lover. In the book, she was Carol Grey, and in the movie she became the less drab-sounding Jane Aubrey. Essentially, the Chapel/Carol–cum–Jane relationship remained the same from book to film, focusing on how much Chapel really needed a woman when his true love was baseball, though Stevens updated the specifics. "I read the novella quite carefully, but I completely invented the character of the woman and the love story aspect of it, that she has a daughter and how they meet. The original adapter had stuck really close to the book, so it had this really old-fashioned quality, and I very much modernized it and brought it into modern baseball."

LINE-UP SHAKE-UP

While Stevens forged a script, the rules of the game changed abruptly. "It's a very convoluted story," producer Amy Robinson notes with a sigh. Before long, Sydney Pollack was not planning to direct the film, though he remained involved, and a new talent came in, *The Big Chill* (1983) director Lawrence Kasdan. Stevens met with Kasdan to discuss the script.

"Everybody was telling me that I had no chance of getting this job because it was so high profile at the time. Those are pretty big directors," Steven remembers. "But I did get the job. I wrote the script, and it really changed my career completely. My original script is somewhat different from the final product."

At that point, Kasdan brought in his pal from *Silverado* (1985), star Kevin Costner, who had already made a splash with baseball movies in the past, including the classic *Bull Durham* (1988) and *Field of Dreams* (1989). Although Costner struck gold in the sports world with 1996's successful *Tin Cup*, critics had ripped to shreds his 1997 epic *The Postman*.

"It was always sort of designed to be Kevin's third baseball movie," Robinson acknowledges. "It was the perfect capper, and that made sense to everybody, obviously including Kevin." Costner brought in his own producer, Armyan Bernstein, who also felt instinctively that Costner could play the part like no other. "Kevin *is* Billy Chapel,"[2] he opined in one interview. Costner accepted the role, noting it was "probably the role" he'd been headed for his whole life because it "was so much about things" he knew about, "a perfect game set against an imperfect life."[3]

Things went swimmingly until Kasdan told Stevens he didn't like her script. "The only person that didn't love it was Larry," she acknowledges. "It kind of laid there and I took the job doing *City of Angels* and became very involved in that process."

While Stevens was away, things became even more unsettled. "There was this whole big drama in the middle of this where Larry Kasdan's son — Jake Kasdan, who was twenty-one at the time — did his own version of the movie, and then Larry and Kevin hooked up, and basically tried to take the project away from Amy and Sydney. So it became this big drama for a long time, and that's why I had so much time to write *City of Angels*, because Universal was kind of stuck. You know, 'We love Sydney and we love Kevin and Larry, so what do we do?'" Stevens details. "Then, basically, the final hurdle was that Kevin decided I should be the writer, so Larry ended up dropping off the project because his son wasn't going to be the writer.

"And then it became Kevin and this producer, Armyan Bernstein, who was sort of his guy, and Amy and me trying to get the project in order to get a director," says Stevens. "But it was hilarious, because it was just like the movie: the women thought one thing and the men thought another thing."

At this point, Raimi entered the picture most unexpectedly. *A Simple Plan* had not yet been released, and Raimi was still seeking a spot in Hollywood that suited him. Never really a fan of horror films, though he enjoyed their artistic qualities, he wanted to direct other types of films. "For a long time, I was content making entertaining horror romps," he revealed. "Then after I was married and had some kids, I looked around and said, 'What do I want to do now?' My tastes had changed. I'd gotten older....Now I think I'd like to make a movie that I'd like to see."[4] Raimi's approach to win the director's perch on *For Love of the Game* might accurately be termed a stealth attack. He used an upcoming horror picture, an Arnold Schwarzenneger millennial film entitled *End of Days*, as his way of getting to the baseball picture.

"This is, of course, just a story. I wasn't there," Stevens relates. "But Sam went ahead to meet with Armyan under the pretense of discussing *End of Days*. He sat there with Armyan, and Armyan gave him this whole spiel about *End of Days*, and I don't even know how Sam got the script for *For Love of the Game*, but Sam says to Armyan, 'I'm here under false pretenses, because I don't want to direct *End of Days*. I want to direct this baseball movie you have.'"

"It was a surprise," producer Robinson acknowledges, "and he was just finishing up *A Simple Plan*. He showed us a rough cut of that, and it was such a different kind of movie from his other movies; I love it when directors stretch themselves. In some cases, I just go by instinct, and I could see that he really liked the material and really understood it. I could see that baseball meant a lot to him. It was an exciting and interesting way to go."

Stevens was thrilled. "I happened to know Sam a little bit, so I was happy to hear Sam wanted to do it. I always thought he was a cool guy and that his films were really innovative, and I thought he was the right guy to work with Kevin because he was young and hip, and also, Sam is a guy that crews love. I felt he wasn't going to be pushed around by Kevin, and that was very important to me because I was being pushed around by Kevin a lot. I knew that Sam loved my script and was going to stick up for it as much as he could."

But there was just one question. Would Costner, an Academy Award–winning director in his own right — and one wielding veto power on this film — agree Raimi was right for the job? Raimi was sent on a pilgrimage to seek an audience with Costner and solicit his approval.

"Kevin was shooting *Message in a Bottle*; he was on some island off the coast of Maine or something, and Sam had to go meet him and talk to him about doing *For Love of the Game*," Stevens relates. "So he got there and was flown on this little puddle jumper over to the island, and there are these people there from the movie, and they told Sam there were a lot of mosquitoes on the island and gave him some stuff to put on, and he put it on his face. Well, his face became completely swollen, so when he met Kevin Costner for the first time, he was completely miserable and couldn't really, in Sam's mind, do as good a job as he wanted."

"I was sure Kevin never heard of me," Raimi told *Entertainment Weekly*. "After we met, I honestly didn't think he was interested in me, but I guess he must have liked the other directors he met even less."[5] Soon Raimi was attending meetings and was slated to direct his biggest movie yet.

BATTER UP!

With Raimi aboard, preparations began for the shoot, and sooner rather than later, the director found himself playing umpire to various factions. "Gradually, as things progressed, I clued Sam into the whole history of the project," Robinson explains "Sam is just a very singular, interesting, smart, courtly and politically astute person in my opinion. He was able to navigate all the waters very, very well and he had a real love of the material. The studio responded to the idea of Sam doing it, so it was a great situation."

"There were so many little behind-the-scenes battles about what I wanted and what Kevin wanted, and really Sam came in and was almost editorial," notes Stevens. "I don't remember that he came in with new ideas

Top: "Why you little!" Bruce Campbell gets a mouthful in a Stooge-like sequence from Army of Darkness (1993).

Middle: Cry Havoc and Let Slip the (stop-motion...) Dogs of War. The Deadite Army makes preparations for war in Army of Darkness.

ttom: Sam Raimi (left) directs e Campbell (far right) while a rimitive Screwhead" watches the set of Army of Darkness.

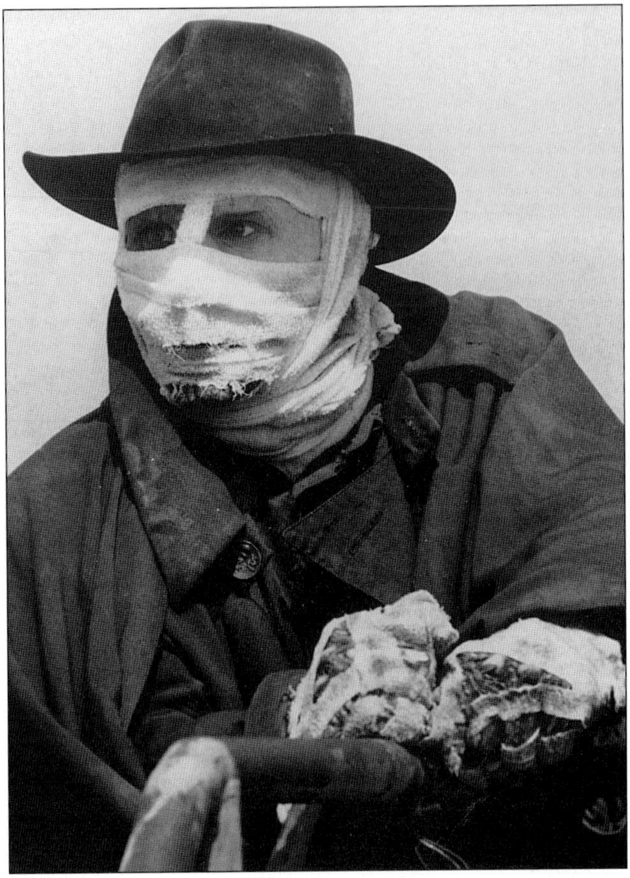

Top: Vengeance has a new fa
It's Liam Neeson as Darkman

Bottom: On the run: Darkma
flees from Durant's helicopte
assault during the climatic
showdown of Darkman (199

"Some people deserve to die." Lady (Sharon
e) challenges John Herod (Gene Hackman) to a
ght in The Quick and the Dead (1995).

OM: Duel in the Sun: Cort (Russell Crowe)
nt and center with nemesis John Herod
e Hackman) to his immediate left, during
se moment in The Quick and the Dead.

Master of the quick draw (and shaky cam): Sam Raimi directs the action in his postmodern Western, Simon Moore's The Quick and the Dead.

Top: From left to right: Lou
nt Briscoe), Hank (Bill Paxton)
nd Jacob (Billy Bob Thornton)
ake a discovery in the woods.
From A Simple Plan.

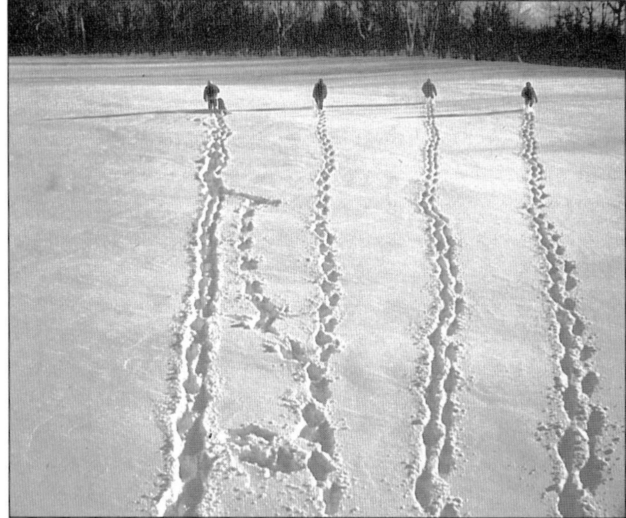

Middle: Cold blooded: The
arch for a downed airplane in
frozen north is about to turn
tragic in A Simple Plan.

Bottom: From left to right:
l Paxton, Sam Raimi and Billy
Bob Thornton brave sub-zero
nperatures on location during
hoot of A Simple Plan (1998).

Top: Clearing the Mechanism: Billy Chapel (Kevin Costner) pitches a perfect game in Yankee Stadium in For Love of the Game (1999).

Bottom: Teammates: John C. Reilly (left) as Gus and Kevin Costner (right) as Billy share a light moment during production of For Love of the Game.

Top: He doesn't like witches. onnie (Keanu Reeves) accosts nnie (Cate Blanchett) during a tense showdown in The Gift.

Bottom: Annie Wilson (Cate anchett) studies her cards and the hand fate has dealt her, during The Gift (2000).

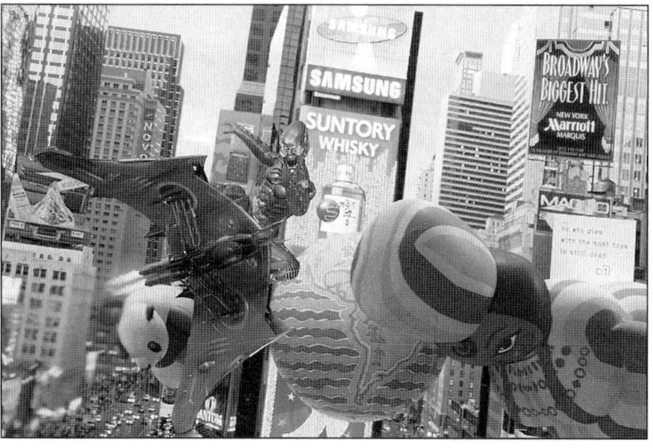

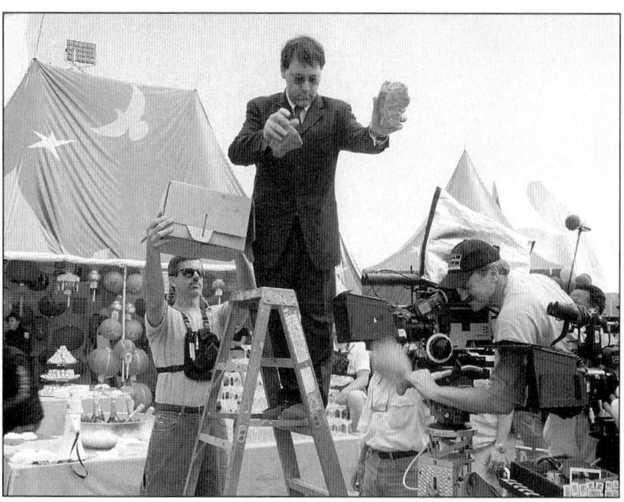

TOP: Action is his reward: Pete
Parker (Tobey Maguire), in Spi
Man regalia, clings to a ceiling
Sam Raimi's Spider-Man (200

MIDDLE: Action Goblin! The ev
Green Goblin, in full costume,
attacks the World Unity Fair in
Manhattan from atop his glide
perch. From Spider-Man.

BOTTOM: Rocks and ladders:
Raimi gets hands-on for a spe
shot on the set of Spider-Man.

to add to the script, so much as weigh in on some of the arguments that were going on."

Such as? "About the how the two characters meet," Stevens specifies. "I wrote many different scenes of how they meet, and it was hard. The version in the movie is not my favorite version, though it's fine. It was a bit of a thicket he was walking into, and I do think he was good to work with."

Casting represented another battle. Eventually filled by charming Kelly Preston, the Jane Aubrey role was turned down by Helen Hunt and Natasha Richardson.[6] John C. Reilly, the Oscar-nominated star of *Boogie Nights* (1997), *Magnolia* (1999) and *Chicago* (2002), was cast as Gus Sinski (Orsinski, in the book) and was loved by everyone, even though there was controversy over his selection too.

"I was supposed to do for *For Love of the Game*. I was supposed to be the catcher," Brent Briscoe, Lou from *A Simple Plan*, reveals. "I went out with people who were training me because Sam said, 'I need you; I want you to do this part.' I said, 'Okay, I will go out and become the best catcher on earth.' I got the catcher's mitt, I went out with the trainer, I had balls thrown at me. When I was right out of high school, I had three college scholarships to play baseball; I knew how to play baseball."

But, as Briscoe discovered, Raimi didn't have final say on casting. It was Costner's decision. "Sam went to him three different times and said, 'This is the guy I want to play the pitcher,' and I would have gotten to catch the perfect game in Yankee Stadium, which would have been a dream for me," Brisoe relates. "I'm an insane baseball fan."

Unfortunately Briscoe was vetoed.

Navigating equally difficult waters, Robinson decided the film needed to reflect the authenticity she felt the script deserved, and there was only one place in the world to film it. "I kept insisting that it had to be Yankee Stadium. I'm a New Yorker and Yankee Stadium is the temple of baseball. Everybody was very worried about it, so one day I just picked up the phone and called George Steinbrenner, and literally ten minutes later he called me back. It was so strange. I was so terrified.

"'Well, hello, Mr. Steinbrenner,'" Robinson recreates the call. "'My name is Amy Robinson. I'm producing this movie and we want to shoot in Yankee Stadium and it stars Kevin Costner.' Well, those were the magic words! 'Kevin Costner?'" Robinson leaps into a dead-on imitation of the Yankees' owner. "'He's a wonderful young man. I watch his movie *Dances with Wolves* all the time! I just love Kevin Costner! Anything that young man wants to do must be very good!'

"Well, cut to four months later after negotiation, and this and that for his people," Robinson says. "In the end, his people and the guys who run the stadium are wonderful, and it was logistically a very big deal shooting there. It was very expensive, but it was truly great to have the run of Yankee Stadium and be able to go on the field and into the locker room. It was like being in some kind of fabulous church. It was unbelievable, and we were there for almost a month."

"It was a dream for all of us," Stevens adds. "That was probably one of the happiest times of the shoot."

THE PERFECT GAME

The cast and crew of *For Love of the Game* spent the better part of a month in Yankee Stadium, shooting long days. Costner performed a large percentage of his own pitching, sometimes for nine hours a day in an effort to achieve the authenticity the production sought. Sometimes doubled by Dave Eiland, Costner was a real trooper, throwing eighty-mile-an-hour balls, sometimes with excruciating pain in his arms and shoulders.

"Kevin was very insistent on that," Robinson remembers. "He worked very hard at that, and had a very sore arm. We used the Yankees' real trainer to work with him. He was so excited about standing on the mound at Yankee Stadium. His parents came and watched him."

For Reilly, who was trained by San Francisco Giants catcher Brent Mayne, playing a catcher was intense. "There's this guy on the mound, and he's coming at you with animal energy ... You squat into position and brace your arm and you think you're ready. Then this guy hurls this missile at you, and every last ounce of composure, all of that training, just goes flying out of your head."[7]

Unlike *A Simple Plan*, where the crew dealt with frigid weather, New York enjoyed mild weather during shooting in October 1998. "They had a very short World Series, so it wasn't too cold, and we had gorgeous weather," Robinson reminisces. "It never rained the whole time, so we were just blessed. It was a little chilly at night; we had to shoot day-into-night since the game went on and on. There were all kinds of logistics, and Sam worked on his shot list."

Stevens was amazed by Raimi's preparation for the film. "He had volumes of storyboards," she reveals. "He storyboarded the whole damn screenplay! You know, most people don't storyboard love stories, but he just had it all in his head." Accordingly, Raimi the entertainer had a goal in synch with his stars, producers and writers. He wanted to share the joys of baseball, and that meant accuracy was priority number one. "With *For Love of the Game* what I was really trying to do was make the baseball seem as real as possible," he told *Cinescape*.[8]

Despite the novelty of shooting in Yankee Stadium, the time spent in

New York had an impact on the director. "Coming to New York was not conducive to raising a family, and I have a wife and three kids," he said in one interview, indicating that he felt homesick.[9]

PACKING THE STANDS

Like all Raimi movies, *For Love of the Game* features state-of-the-art effects work. Unlike most Raimi films, these effects exist within a reality-based context (no Deadites, superheroes or bulletholes in skulls).

"It's very interesting seeing Sam use the techniques that he uses in other kinds of films in this movie," producer Robinson reflects. "I think for students of Sam, it's an interesting way to look at this movie, as opposed to just saying, 'Well, gee, I wonder why he did a movie like this. It's not anything like his other movies!' And in some ways it isn't, and that's completely wonderful, but in other ways, he utilizes a lot of things that he is extremely talented at in the movie.

"We had a lot of CGI [computer-generated imagery] in *For Love of the Game*," Robinson reveals. "We had to fill the stadium with people and various things. We had two thousand extras, and what we called these 'dimensionally challenged' people, which were cardboard people, but even with the dimensionally challenged and our real people, Yankee Stadium seats fifty or sixty thousand people."

Making certain those seats were filled was a special effects company called Cinesite. "Getting the opportunity to work on a Sam Raimi film doesn't come around every day, so the whole crew was very excited about being a part of it," reports Thomas J. Smith, a talent with a BFA and MFA from San Francisco's Art Insitute. Before moving to Cinesite, Smith worked on the revolutionary special effects for *Who Framed Roger Rabbit?* (1988) at ILM. He labored with thirty artists for two months to complete some seventy shots on *For Love of the Game*.

"Peter Donen was a former client of mine at Cinesite and he was the overall supervisor of production," Smith details. "He presented a plan to Sam and executed the plate shoots at Yankee Stadium. We would take all the element shots, sections of the stands filled with people, and composite them together and film them out," Smith explains. "Blocks of crowds were shot and manipulated to film whatever the camera angle was. Any character that crossed over empty seats [that we filled in] would have to be rotoscoped, a process by which you cut out that character and then composite him back over the new filled-up sections.

"In one scene," Smith remembers, "there was a 180-degree panning shot around Billy Chapel. We tracked and composited CGI characters into the seats. Because the background was out-of-focus, we used some rudimentary toy models that had simple movements built in, and it worked just fine.

"What really sold those shots was the fact that on each of our elements, Peter had people moving around, walking up and down the aisles, just as you would have at a real game," Smith reveals. "The seams where we rotoscoped the edges to match were overlapped in a way that you couldn't detect any problems. In the case where we were using sections over and over, there was a problem with repetition, like someone's shirt color showing up too often. As a solution, we selected those individuals and changed their shirt colors from red to blue so the pattern would disappear."

Another critically important effect was establishing the right light for the time of day the game occurred. "There was a big establishing shot of Yankee Stadium from a building nearby," Smith explains, "and we did extensive work on that. There was a complete sky replacement to match the time of day in the film, early twilight. Because the shot was a zoom, there was a lot of tracking and finesse work that went into making it look real."

These effects shots work beautifully, primarily because they don't stand out as effects, but appear absolutely real. "There's a saying in our business: if the work goes unnoticed than you've done something right," Smith comments. "The best compliment is someone saying, 'Oh, I didn't know there were any visual effects in *For Love of the Game*. Photo-real visual effects are the toughest to pull off, and it's always satisfying when you accomplish it."

SHADOW AND SUNLIGHT

A solid script faithfully adapted from an honored literary work, a high degree of authenticity in the photography and action in Yankee Stadium, and brilliant effects selling the illusion of a perfect game were elements of *For Love of the Game* that, if edited well, could forge a new pinnacle for sports movies.

But problems arose in editing that very soon became a public brawl. "Basically, Kevin, as you can see from all of his films, is not concerned with a film being too long, and they are too long," Dana Stevens stresses. "Basically, what it came down to was Sam had a version that was shorter, and Kevin had a version that was longer. They were still working together. It wasn't like Sam and Kevin had a falling out, they were trying to work it out. But then Universal says, 'Let's test the two versions.'

"Up until this point, Kevin Costner would come up to me and Sam and everybody and say that this was the best film he's ever been in, and it is his favorite film he ever made," Stevens describes. "Everybody had a great time doing it. Sam handled it great, Kevin handled himself great. He let Sam make his movie, let Sam be the director. He was just as smitten with Sam as Alfred Hitchcock as the rest of us — Sam has a take-charge quality. So Kevin was willing to go ahead and be the actor and let Sam be the director once we got the script problems ironed out.

"There were two tests," Stevens relates. "There was the Sam cut and the Kevin cut, and the Sam cut tested huge. And the Kevin cut also tested pretty well, but not as big as Sam's. And that was because Sam's was shorter. It was as simple as that. Then there came the wrangling where every single thing got fought over in terms of the length in each little scene."

Costner felt unhappy with the cuts, though Stevens notes they were minor. "Basically, I'm telling you, the differences are about three scenes. They're tiny little scenes that don't matter. There's a nudity scene in the shower. There's a scene that has a bunch of ad-libbed jokes that I didn't write, where everybody says 'fuck' a thousand times. And there was maybe a couple of other really minuscule scenes that ended up coming out of the film that saved it from an R rating, and made it a little shorter. But the final movie you're seeing is not Sam's cut, and it is not Kevin's cut. It's a compromise."

In fact, compromise is the name of the game in Hollywood, especially with so many egos and interests involved. "The star and director have to compromise with each other, and the studio had a deal that Sam had to deliver a PG-13," Stevens explains. "There were compromises made. That happens on every film. Maybe not on *A Simple Plan*, and that's why it is so good. It's independent; it cost less money; it's a movie that didn't have the scrutiny our movie did."

Just days shy of the movie's release, the issue exploded in the press, with Costner complaining that Universal had damaged the film with its insistence on cutting the scenes he preferred. "[For Universal] this movie has always been about the length and the rating. It's never been about the content," he said in *Newsweek*. "And you feel a studio would want to release the best version of the movie, not the one they think appeals to the biggest common denominator."[10] In *Variety*, Costner noted that "[films are] all worth defending if you work a year on them. They are for me."[11]

The star's point is a noble one, that creators should be granted the freedom to express their vision regardless of arbitrary restrictions on ratings and running time. Ye this is the rub: his comments also might be construed to mean that the "best version of the movie" was *not* the one playing in theaters come opening day ... not exactly the type of remark that stimulates people to see a movie. Also, this sort of bloody battle in the press all but guarantees a critical feeding frenzy. Again, not the way one wishes to open a fifty million dollar film. Of Costner's press offensive, Robert Bucksbaum, a film analyst with Reel Source Inc., expressed this view: "It reminds me of a baseball player making ten million. He should take some time to sign autographs once in a while."[12]

Given the atmosphere, *For Love of the Game* became a target for abuse when released in mid-September 1999. The *New York Times*' Lawrence Van Gelder termed the movie "routine entertainment, because the love story doesn't strike sparks or really tug the heartstrings."[13] Writing for the *New York Post*, Rod Dreher termed *For Love of the Game* "*The Postman* on a pitcher's mound" and warned audiences that "if you want an Ingmar Bergman–style yuppie baseball movie, look no further."[14] Stanley Kauffmann, writing in the *New Republic* wrote that "Costner is so credible that, even more than usual, the story is an irritating interruption of the game that he is pitching. The woman is Kelly Preston, who tries bravely along with Costner and the director, Sam Raimi, to brighten up the basically stale romantic scenes."[15]

Critics singled out Raimi, who had done the unthinkable — escaped the genre prison the media had placed him in back in 1982. "A talented genre filmmaker ... [Raimi] directs down to this movie, as if to say that if you've paid to watch this stuff, you must be a chump," noted Stuart Klawans in the *Nation*.[16] "It's surprising to find so much schmaltz in a picture by Sam Raimi," the *Christian Science Monitor* opined.[17] Richard Corliss in *Time* magazine wrote that the "nattering violins, orgasmic from the first moment, alerts you that director Sam Raimi has either no control of the production or no belief in the material."[18] In July 2000, *Sight and Sound* critic Andy Richards joked that the Evil Dead were presumably turning in their grave.

It was pretty devastating stuff, but not nearly as devastating as the film's box office plummet. During its opening week, *For Love of the Game* struck out while Martin Lawrence's comedy *Blue Streak* hit a homer. The baseball pic earned only $14 million to *Streak*'s $19.2 million. Ultimately, the film grossed in the neighborhood of $35 million, well short of its $50 million budget.

Reviews were ugly to Costner, too. There are folks in the industry who have been gunning for him ever since he won the Best Director Oscar in 1990. *Waterworld* (1995) and *The Postman* were two opportunities to give him a kick, just as reviewers have recently taken to abusing Ben Affleck (witness the not merely negative but blistering reviews of *Daredevil* and *Gigli*).

"There's no doubt they went after Kevin," Amy Robinson considers. "They just did it in a cheap way, and I think part of it was brought on because there was some publicity surrounding the release of the movie. It was all a terrible shame because while we were making the movie, Kevin

Costner was very happy making the movie, and he really liked it. There is so much in his performance, and it is absolutely one of his best performances. I love Kevin's work. The scene where he sits on the bed and cries is quite a scene. I do think they went after him personally, and for whatever reason there was a lot of animosity in the air that the picture caught."

"Here's my two feelings about it," Stevens weighs in. "If Sam's version had been released, it could have been a bigger hit, but perhaps if Kevin's movie had been released without his negativity about the movie, it could have been a bigger hit.

"I would really just want people to know that up until the eleventh hour, Sam Raimi and Kevin Costner were working well together and making this movie together on the same team, so to speak. It was very unusual at this point in Kevin's career that he was willing to let Sam go ahead and make his film. They got along great. And all the cliches you hear about Kevin were not apparent in this film until the last minute, and I think that is due to Sam's personality and his skill as a director."

"I do think it's overlooked," Robinson notes of the film, in many senses a victim of bad publicity and poor timing (it opened just months after another Costner film, *Message in a Bottle*). "They never mention it when sports movies are mentioned. I think that Sam did a really wonderful job on the movie. I think there's a lot in that movie that will hold up as years go by. Unfortunate things happened at the end, only when it came out."

RAIMI RAP

CASTING: IMPOSSIBLE: "There was a time when Tom Cruise was begging Sydney Pollack to do the movie with him," Dana Stevens reveals. "Sydney didn't want to do it with Tom because of the autumnal nature of the thing. This wasn't about somebody who *wasn't* at the end of their career. If it had been Tom, we would have had to rewrite it to say he had an injury or something. That was something we wanted to hang onto, and that's why Kevin was perfect for it."

ON THE MOUND: "I remember when I first saw Kevin at Yankee Stadium, we were like big kids," Stevens reflects. "We were so thrilled to be there. George Steinbrenner would come and see us, and wanted to hob knob with Kevin, and I remember two things about him. First, he was shocked that a woman had written this, and I also remember the moment he realized Sam was the director, because he thought Sam was some kid on the set, a runner or something. I was standing there when Steinbrenner realized it and was like, 'You're the director?! You're just a kid!'"

MOST VALUABLE PLAYER: "He is very polite and likes to call everybody 'sir.' 'Yes sir,' 'Yes ma'am,'" Robinson describes the feeling of a Raimi set. "It sort of trickles down. Not militarily, but politely. People really worked hard and are really, really dedicated to Sam and what Sam is trying to do. It's a very good atmosphere on his set. He also has a terrific sense of humor; he's sly, complicated and smart, and has real vision. He's the kind of director people like to work for because there's a lot going on there."

CLEAR THE MECHANISM: The film's famous phrase is "actually Kevin's ad-lib," according to writer Stevens, "and it became a big touchstone for him. I didn't write that. He had to bring in his own mantra as an athlete, and I really liked that."

SOUVENIR: "My cherished memento is a baseball signed by Sam that said we made it possible for 56,000 people to see Billy Chapel pitch a no-hitter," says special effects guru Thomas Smith. "It doesn't get any better than that."

YOU CAN SMELL THE FALL ... AUTUMN IS JUST AROUND THE CORNER...

Because *For Love of the Game* is an expensive Hollywood movie headlined by a major star and featuring a romantic angle instead of drooling zombies, Raimi aficionados are tempted to view it as an anomaly in his film oeuvre. But that may not necessarily be an accurate reading. Though the film represents a compromise in some important ways, accommodating competing viewpoints and ideas, there's more than enough of interest on screen to render it a worthy addition to the Raimi canon, if only one looks closely. For one thing, Raimi remains adroit with his imagery and choices of compositions, again deploying state-of-the-art special effects to vet a narrative. Watching *For Love of the Game* unfold, one immediately senses a mastery of technique, a wedding of pure entertainment with visual style. There is nobody in the business better than Raimi at marshaling effects to make a movie feel "real," but perhaps more to the point, Raimi deploys his compositions to tell a story that fits in well with his genre efforts.

At first, Billy Chapel may seem to have little in common with Peyton Westlake, Ash, or *The Quick and the Dead*'s Ellen, but in fact, he is a similar character. The venue is different, the world of professional sports, but this guy is every bit as much a grand hero as these protagonists. Like, *Darkman*'s Peyton, Billy Chapel no longer fits in with his world, an outsider because of the increasingly corporate nature of professional baseball. And, like Ellen, Chapel constantly finds himself competing in a very personal crucible. Here, it is not the Old West arena of the gunfight, but the contemporary and personal confrontation between pitcher and batter.

Throughout the film, as Chapel sizes up each new challenge at the plate, one is reminded of the dusty streets of Redemption. There is more in common than one might imagine: two contestants meet some distance apart, glare at each other, and wait to see who "brings the heat." Like the gunfight, only one of these men can be victorious. In framing baseball in this fashion, Raimi reminds the audience that baseball is a battle, and that for every such conflict there is a hero, a guy to root for.

"It's a hero's journey," writer Stevens affirms, "which in a way is archetypal ... which is what Sam does so well. It's mythical in a way; that's what Sam is drawn to, and what he's so great at. That's why it's not so weird when you think that Sam would do this film."

Indeed, Raimi's choice of composition buttresses the notion of modern day heroes among us. After a nostalgic series of old film clips which actually feature Costner as a youth, learning to play baseball, the audience sees adult Billy Chapel striding through an airport concourse, his teammates alongside and behind him in a pack. This sequence is rendered with slow-motion photography, extending the audience's view of the Detroit Tigers, and fostering the almost subconscious feeling that these guys are akin to astronauts walking to their launch. They clearly have "the right stuff," and their heroic parade, captured in this lingering fashion, along with the nostalgic home-movie clips and iconic Sinatra tune on the soundtrack, sets up the notion of modern day heroes. This depiction of Chapel lands *For Love of the Game* squarely in context of Raimi's earlier career selection, defining battles between good and evil and not limiting itself to such things as romance or a love affair.

Costner noted that the role of Chapel was "fairly close to the bone,"[19] and that description calls up another aspect that makes the film worthwhile. This is not just any hero, this is a veteran on the last day of the job, giving up the thing he loves most in his life, baseball. And yet, the game has isolated him from others, including the woman he wants to be with. "That's the moment in *For Love of the Game* when Billy pitches the perfect game and comes back to the hotel room and there's no one there," Costner reflected in an interview with the authors of *Reel Baseball*. "To me, that's a very real moment for American cinema and the world of baseball. That the athlete just wept..."[20]

Costner is perfect in this role, not because he is "intrinsically convincing as a star athlete,"[21] but because he is very much in the same place, careerwise, as the protagonist he portrays. He too has had difficulties in personal relationships over the years; he too is no longer the crowd pleaser he once was, around the time of *The Untouchables* (1987), *No Way Out* (1987), *Dances with Wolves* (1990) and *The Bodyguard* (1992). And he too is often a voice for individuality in a corporate environment.

Costner films often evidence a simple and wholesome world view. *The Postman* was widely ridiculed in 1997, and yet it spoke plainly about patriotism, American values and what democracy represents. People thought it was corny, but it really just seemed painfully earnest, and therefore not in tune with the more cynical, slick entertainment of this era. Chapel, who has "always been a Tiger" is confronted with the same issue. He is a little bit older than other players and his world is no longer about "the love of the game," but about money instead. "Everything's changed, Billy," Mr. Wheeler tells him, "the players, the fans, the TV rights, the arbitration. The game stinks.'"

Chapel replies that it isn't the game that stinks, and coming out of Costner's mouth, that line has a certain resonance. This could be a metaphor for the movie business, couldn't it? In which everything is dependent on an instant home run, the big opening weekend. It was not always so, and Costner knows that, and carries that baggage on his face. We are witnessing the end of an era both for Billy and, perhaps, for this actor.

In many ways, *For Love of the Game* is about this feeling of melancholy, of endings, of *autumn*. "It's something in the book, but something I embellished," Stevens notes. "It's the end of the season. It's the end of Billy's career. And baseball has this poetic feeling. If you're a fan of the game as I am, and as Sam is, and as Michael Shaara obviously was, you are struck by that feeling. In the summer, you're a boy, and then it's autumn and the game is over and you have to go back to your life. It's part of baseball lore; it just so happens that this is the last game of the season and it is autumn, and the love story is envisioned as being between people who are a little older, which adds to that autumnal feeling.

"It's autumnal because athletes have a short life span," Amy Robinson adds. "That makes them moving creatures. There was a big full-page ad in the *New York Times* when Michael Jordan retired again, and he kept saying, 'I did it for the love of the game, and what basketball gave me.' And when I saw that, I was thinking of Billy Chapel."

Again, this author's criterion for judging a good movie is simple. Do the film's visuals reflect and augment the film's story? Does form mirror content and make that content more relevant or affecting? In this case, the answer is affirmative. Taking into account the melancholy, autumnal nature of Chapel's story, Raimi has effectively filled his film with "sunlight and shadow," compositions and moments that buttress this notion of time passing.

That opening montage of the Chapel/Costner home movies is the perfect example: acknowledging Costner's (Chapel's) mortality and history even as it trumpets his accomplishments as a player. Since it is actually a very young Costner in those shots, the audience sees the hero as a young man in an era long gone. When the viewer then sees a mature Costner, there is a sense of connection to his past, and then, finally, to the end of that history as Chapel plays his last game.

The screenplay also acknowledges time passing and the nostalgia that many feel for baseball. *Remember when athletes were heroes?* The movie does, noting often "the old boys" who nobody had to "show the door" when the time came to retire. When the Fox TV announcers note in the film that "you can smell the fall, and autumn is just around the corner," Raimi's choice of shots reflect not only Shaara's novel and Stevens' well-pitched script, but the very nature of the main character. As he pitches the perfect game, Chapel's last baseball game stretches into orange twilight, a metaphor for the sun setting on his career.

"You look old...," Chapel says to one character, "are we that old?" Again, there is an obsession with age and endings, changing seasons. Raimi addresses this theme in a way that is rather touching, augmented by the script and one of Costner's most insightful and overlooked performances.

For Love of the Game arrived in theaters with a nearly impossible charge. It was part chick flick, and part sports movie, and those two genres boast totally disparate fans. The film may please one section of the crowd and alienate the other. It is this structure of half-and-half, mirrored quite accurately from the novel, that is the film's greatest hurdle. People interested in seeing Costner pitch a perfect game may not care about his meet-cute with Jane, a frequently rewritten scene. Stevens' screenplay accurately adapts and augments the emotional issue of the book — that Chapel doesn't really *need* Jane. Baseball is his first love. That is an interesting dynamic, but the movie's length plays against the realization. At a running time of over two and a half hours, the film is Raimi's longest, and the relationship is not compelling enough to stay the course. The fact of the matter, it seems, is that as long as Billy has baseball, he really *doesn't* need Jane.

Oppositely, the baseball scenes are enormously effective and realistic, perhaps the best and most authentic ever captured on film. There has never been a film that better captures the mindset of a pitcher. Raimi's visual sense comes into play as Yankee fans heckle Chapel on the mound. There is a spinning camera on Costner, representing his discomfort. Then he "clears the mechanism" and tunes out the noise of the stadium. The screaming is silenced, and then, the background is blurred, visually silencing the hecklers. By blurring out the people in the stands, Raimi makes viewers understand the focus required to pitch a game in front of millions.

For Love of the Game would benefit from a shorter running time, and a lead actress more Costner's equal in age and stature (Stevens saw the character as Michelle Pfeiffer), but it had a nearly impossible charge too. It had to impress both those who loved the game and those who wanted to see the latest Meg Ryan flick, a latter day *You've Got Mail*, set in a ballpark. The film has found a new audience on video/DVD because it has many fine qualities, not the least of which is a sincere, emotional heart — which made critics despise it. The film is about baseball, youth, endings, growing up, leaving things behind, and these themes come across very effectively. It is good, mainstream entertainment made less satisfying by an audience's expectation that movies be either fish or fowl, a comedy or a romance, a horror film or a comedy, a sports picture or the latest Meg Ryan movie. By remaining faithful to the structure of Shaara's novel, *For Love of the Game* flouts expectations, probably to its own ultimate detriment.

It remains an interesting historical footnote that so-called horror directors Wes Craven and Sam Raimi both took big steps outside of the genre in 1999, with *Music of the Heart* and *For Love of the Game*, respectively, and that both productions were savaged by critics. One must wonder, was this critical drubbing due to the actual quality of these fine films, or the fact that these artists had challenged accepted notions about them?

10

THE GIFT (2000)

ALWAYS USE YOUR INSTINCTS

THE ONLY WITNESS TO THE CRIME WAS NOT EVEN THERE.

CAST AND CREW

LAKESHORE ENTERTAINMENT AND PARAMOUNT CLASSICS PRESENT A LAKESHORE ENTERTAINMENT/ALPHAVILLE PRODUCTION, *THE GIFT*.

DIRECTOR: Sam Raimi

CASTING: Deborah Aquila

CO-PRODUCER: Richard S. Wright

MUSIC COMPOSED AND CONDUCTED BY: Christopher Young

COSTUME DESIGNER: Julie Weiss

FILM EDITORS: Arthur Coburn and Bob Murawski

PRODUCTION DESIGNER: Neil Spisak

DIRECTOR OF PHOTOGRAPHY: Jamie Anderson

EXECUTIVE PRODUCERS: Sean Daniel, Ted Tannebaum, Gregory Goodman and Rob Tapert

PRODUCER: James Jacks

VISUAL EFFECTS SUPERVISOR: Peter Donen

RRING

Cate Blanchett: Annie Wilson
Giovanni Ribisi: Buddy Cole
Keanu Reeves: Donnie Barksdale
Katie Holmes: Jessica King
Greg Kinnear: Wayne Collins
Michael Jeter: Gerald Weems
Hilary Swank: Valerie Barksdale
Kim Dickens: Linda
Gary Cole: David Duncan
Rosemary Harris: Annie's Granny
J.K. Simmons: Sheriff Pearl Johnson
Chelcie Ross: Kenneth King
John Beasley: Albert Hawkins
Hunter McGilvray: Miller Wilson
Nathan Lewis: Cornelius
Benjamin Peacock: Tommy
Danny Elfman: Tommy Lee Ballard

Filmed in Savannah, Thunderbolt and Springfield, Georgia.

THE SOUL OF THIS TOWN

STILL IN MOURNING OVER THE ACCIDENTAL DEATH of her husband a year earlier, psychic Annie Wilson labors on, caring for her three young boys and earning a living by reading the fortunes of the locals in Brixton, Georgia.

One of Annie's clients is Valerie Barksdale, a woman being beaten by her brutal husband Donnie, an "insecure redneck" that feels threatened by Annie's involvement with his wife. Annie's simple-minded but loyal client, Buddy Cole defends Annie's family from the violent Barksdale, even as he deals with a dark secret from his upbringing.

When sexy young socialite Jessica King disappears without a trace, Annie is recruited by Brixton police and Jessica's father, Kenneth King, to discover what happened to her. Annie experiences a vision of Jessica's murder, but is unable to determine the perpetrator. When the police discover Jessica's corpse in the Barksdales' pond, the crime seems to be solved, but Annie is not so certain. Donnie is sent away to prison after a sensationalistic trial, but Annie's visions of the dead girl persist.

As she develops affection for Jessica's fiancé, town principal Wayne Collins, Annie utilizes her unique psychic abilities to solve the terrible crime.

MAMA-THON

In the year 2000, after the box office failure of *For Love of the Game*, Sam Raimi came home to horror. But he carried the tools of the trade he had learned on *A Simple Plan* and his 1999 baseball epic, casting charismatic, top-of-the-line actors in what would prove to be an emotionally wrenching story about a woman isolated from her family. The woman was psychic, yes, but the supernatural overtones were less important than the emotional ones, and the personal story was one that resonated.

The Gift originated in the mind of co-writers Billy Bob Thornton and Tom Epperson. Friends since the third grade, Epperson and Thornton grew up in rural, poverty-stricken Arkansas.[1] *The Gift* was their third collaboration after *One False Move* and *A Family Thing* (1996), but it was, perhaps, the most personal film of Thornton's career.

The story of Annie Wilson was very much the story of the actor's own mother, a woman who used to speak at medical conventions on parapsychology and even had her abilities tested at Duke University, and yet was married to a hot-headed high school basketball coach.[2] Mrs. Thornton's accuracy in seeing the future was apparently pretty good: she once predicted that her son would work with Burt Reynolds,[3] and indeed, Billy Bob and Reynolds ended up on *Evening Shade* together.

"Personally, I knew that Billy was telling — with a little bit of underscoring and poetic license — about growing up with this woman who was considered the crazy lady of the town, because she was psychic," reports actor Chelcie Ross, Thornton's friend, who appeared in *The Gift* as Kenneth King. In fact, many characters were based on the clientele Thornton had observed as a youngster.

"The one at the beginning of the film, whom she's talking to about the fact that he's bleeding and needs to go the doctor, Billy said that was a real character," Ross explains. "That guy really came in to see his mom all the time and had women all over the county. Billy said he was this short, homely, horny little guy who knew where every woman was who wasn't getting any attention. So these were real memories for him."

The screenplay, which had once been designed as a Jodie Foster vehicle (think *Nell* meets *The Sixth Sense*),[4] landed on Raimi's desk by coincidence, having nothing to do with the fact that Raimi and Thornton collaborated on *A Simple Plan*. In fact, it was Raimi's wife, Gillian, who suggested he consider directing the film.[5]

When Raimi read the script a second time, after initially dismissing it as too dark, he found it to his liking. "Billy Bob and Tom Epperson ... created some very real characters," he enthused. "It seemed like they knew this small town in the South, and there was such attention to detail that I felt I was reading a great piece of American gothic literature, like a Faulkner piece. Only it happened to have the supernatural."[6]

A small film budgeted at a scant $9.5 million,[7] less than one-fifth the cost of *For Love of the Game*, *The Gift* was to be distributed by Paramount Classics, the "indie" arm of mega-giant Paramount Pictures in anticipation of the reality that it might not generate wide appeal. "Their studio system is geared to put 2,000 prints or more over a national market where they can come up properly with an advertisement and sell it as Rite Guard or Kool-Aid, or something that people understand and can buy tickets to," Raimi noted in an interview with *IndieWire*'s Anthony Kaufman. "So I don't think that the studio ever would have made this film ... It would appeal to a small group of people and therefore [was] not right for them."[8]

But something funny happened. Big name actors in Hollywood like Keanu Reeves, Greg Kinnear and twenty-four-year-old powerhouse Giovanni Ribisi signed on. Not merely because they liked the script, but because they were admirers of the newly cast leading lady, *Elizabeth* (1998) star Cate Blanchett, who learned of the screenplay from Thornton while shooting *Pushing Tin* with him. "Actors hold Cate in high regard," Raimi noted of his lynchpin. "So I ended up with a high-caliber cast I never thought I'd get."[9]

Oppositely, his new lead actress insisted it was the opportunity to work with Raimi that cemented the participation of so many Hollywood players. "We had almost no budget. Everyone was there to work with Sam,"[10] she reported.

"I remember him [Raimi] asking me my opinion of Cate as an actress when I was in his office," Ross explains. "The only thing I'd seen her do was *Elizabeth*, and on the basis of that, I said 'I think she's a wonderful actress,' and boy, was I shooting way below the target there.

"He also told me that Keanu was being considered for Donnie. Right after that, I went to shoot *Waking up in Reno* and talked to Billy about it, and Billy was pretty upset about the prospect of Keanu playing that role. He didn't like that idea at all. He said, 'I could name about a hundred guys that I think would be right for this role, and Keanu wouldn't be on the list,'" Ross continues. "I've worked with Keanu a number of times. We did *Bill and Ted's Bogus Journey* and *Chain Reaction* together, and I like Keanu a lot. He gets busted a lot, but I don't think anybody works harder than Keanu does. Where Billy came from with this whole thing was that it [the script] was roughly based on his life growing up. Somehow Keanu wasn't fitting into his memory of childhood in Arkansas."

Another actor in consideration for the role of the abusive Barksdale was *A Simple Plan* veteran Gary Cole. "I went in and actually read for two parts," the actor says. "In the same audition, I read for Duncan and also for Donnie, the character that Keanu played. I think I did the lawyer first and peeled off the suit and put on the wife-beater T-shirt and read for Donnie."

Cole was cast as Duncan, the corrupt prosecutor engaged in a secret sexual liaison with the murdered girl, Jessica. Like his character in *A Simple Plan*, Cole found that his role in *The Gift* had a very specific purpose. "He's a red herring," Cole explains. "Part of that movie is that you don't want to know where to go. We don't want the audience to finger anybody. We want everybody guessing. You kill two birds with one stone, because the movie obviously required a court scene, a big plot point, and it underlines the small town. So you have the lawyer, but he's also involved in this triangle and possibly murder. That was basically the reason he was there."

This was Cole's third opportunity to work with Raimi counting the series *American Gothic*, and the third time he played a corrupt establishment figure, a law-enforcer. "Sam is a director who feels confident with people he is familiar with," Cole reports. "He knows what to expect, possibly what he's going to get. I think certainly Sam spent a lot of time watching me in *American Gothic* because he did all of the post-production, so he had a sense of the personality that I put across, and you know, if he thought it would be useful in a story, that's where it fit. Obviously [Sheriff] Lucas Buck [in *American Gothic*] was that. He was an authority figure that was also corrupt, so Sam was familiar with me in that way."

SONG OF THE SOUTH

Cate Blanchett was cast as Annie in *The Gift* in 1999, and began to research her role as a fortuneteller. "I met quite a few psychics here in L.A., which was interesting," she noted. "And then I met several in Savannah ... I did a lot of different things. I didn't just have my palm read; I had my feet read, I had tea leaves, I had Turkish grounds, I had someone touch my head and my crystals done and my aura read and my angels explored, I had the whole lot."[11]

She developed her Southern accent by hanging around a Wal-Mart in Georgia, and also interviewed several psychics to glean a sense of the work. "I met one woman who had done quite a lot of work with the FBI in Savannah, and she was really extraordinary. She said that when she was younger she placed herself unwittingly in really dangerous situations ... she would have angry husbands coming around at three o'clock in the morning with shotguns saying, 'Don't talk to my wife any more about the affairs you think I'm having.'"[12]

Blanchett wasn't the only researcher. Reeves reported early to location in Savannah, rented a pick-up truck, bought some tight-fitting jeans and began hanging out at bars to get the mood of the place.[13]

Also joining the cast in Savannah for the forty-four-day shoot were Kim Dickens, future Best Actress Oscar–winner Hilary Swank (as Valerie Barksdale) in her first role after *Boys Don't Cry*, J.K. Simmons, who appeared in *For Love of the Game*, and Katie Holmes of *Dawson's Creek* fame, as the murder victim. The film shot in Thunderbolt, Georgia, approximately five miles southeast of Savannah, overlooking the Wilmington River, for the scenes involving the Wilson home. Some shooting was also completed in Springfield, Georgia, a good 150 miles northeast of Savannah in Effingham County. Greg Kinnear described the colorful locations as being like "the eighth character in the movie. There's a haunted vibe and unusual spirit to the town that we tried to use in the movie."[14]

"I like the South," Ross, a Texan, considers, "and I think the value of shooting there is right in front of you on film. You can't fake that. I had been to the South quite a lot, and there's something about settling down in Savannah for a while that just changes things, being around the people and the history, and then physically the trees and the moss. If we'd shot it somewhere in L.A. and faked it, it would have required some more suspension of disbelief from the cast and the audience.

"We had a dialect coach helping us with the sounds, which are confusing, because in Georgia there are about three different dialects that are very distinct. But what you get being on location is to hear the differences, and converse with people on a daily basis who have accents, and that helped us all."

Raimi, who had once shot a different sort of supernatural movie in a different Southern state, also felt that the setting contributed to *The Gift*, one of his most atmospheric efforts:

> We had very little money ... and we had to establish we were in the Deep South quickly, so we chose the town because it had such outrageous trees — they were fantastic creatures with gnarled arms and weird faces. It looked like something out of *The Wizard of Oz* and one of the premises of the movie is that the world of the supernatural exists. We wanted to make it real for the audience ...[15]

But if the Southern locale was a powerful boon to production, Blanchett was even more appreciated. "I love Cate. Oh god, I want to work with her again," Chelcie Ross comments. "She is so honest, just *so* honest, every take. When she was doing her testimony on the stand in the courthouse, even when they were doing the close-ups, I sat in my place in the court house, off-camera, because I didn't want to miss it, for one thing. Every take, I was there because I was learning. I was taking an acting lesson. I don't know how she got there, but you're never gonna catch that lady acting. She's what we all aspire to, and such a sweet lady too, so nice."

"Simply put, Cate Blanchett is a force of nature," Raimi told the press. "She not only is a great technician ... but something happens when the camera hits that face. With a lot of actresses you move in close with the camera just to get a bigger face on the screen. With Cate, when you move in, you get something else. You get warmth and goodness and intelligence."[16]

The shooting of *The Gift* went smoothly, with the performers embodying their characters in a deep and meaningful way. But if Raimi was enjoying himself on set, watching intense interpersonal scenes play out, the news he received from Hollywood during the shoot must have pleased him even more. He had been selected to direct the long-awaited big screen adaptation of a popular superhero, Spider-Man, beating out other Hollywood big names, including wunderkind David Fincher, in the process.

FOREVER YOUNG

As *The Gift* went into post-production and Raimi found himself embroiled on preproduction for *Spider-Man*, a project certain to be a logistical challenge, composer Christopher Young entered the picture. Danny Elfman, who appeared in a cameo in *The Gift* as a fiddler and scored such Raimi efforts as *Darkman* and *A Simple Plan*, was unavailable to write the score, and Young, a horror movie fan from childhood, wanted the job. "It so happened that we had the same agent, Danny and I," Young explains. "I said to my agent, 'I have to get the opportunity to at least interview with him [Raimi]. Can you set that up?' And he said, 'Here's the good news, Danny is a tremendous fan of your music, and I don't think it would be any problem for Danny to recommend you in his absence.' And I said, 'God bless Danny!' So Danny made the call and paved the way for me to meet Sam.

"Ever since seeing *Evil Dead*, I always fantasized about finally connecting with Sam," Young continues, "and felt instinctively after seeing that movie that, my god, our lives have to cross! I thought his work had precisely the same kind of nightmarish demons that had been responsible for a lot of the stuff I worked toward with music.

"I remember going to see Sam at Sony," Young recalls. "I was surprised. Here he was doing post-production on *The Gift* and the majority of his time was being spent on preproduction for *Spider-Man*. Under normal circumstances, you would have thought that anyone in that position would have been pulling their hair out of their head and been slightly neurotic and on edge to the degree where they would probably snap at everyone around them at one time or another, but he was Mr. Cool, Calm and Collected."

After introductions and coffee, Young and Raimi got down to spotting *The Gift*. Young recorded the session on cassette so he could play back the dialogue later. "Sam said something to me that was surprising," Young remembers: "'Chris, to me the single most important thing that I want you to bring out in the score is the emotional journey that Cate Blanchett takes throughout the course of this movie. Yes, she has second-sight power, and through her visions we as an audience witness some pretty horrific things, and this is a murder mystery. But more important to me, the film is about a woman at the onset who is incapable of connecting with her children because of the fact that she has not resolved emotionally the unexpected death of her husband.' He said that everything that happens in the course of the film and her participation in the solving of the mystery, from his point of view, was really just a means for her to learn how to resolve this issue, so that she could finally embrace her children and be a part of their lives in a way that she hadn't been able to."

And, Young remembers, Raimi was incredibly encouraging about accomplishing that mission. "He said, 'I know you can do all the spooky stuff. I'm sure that is going to turn out wonderfully well, but what I'm really interested in hearing you do is something that is *thematic*, that acknowledges the location of the picture and allows the audience to feel for Annie and act as a window into her heart.'"

Young accepted his charge and from his studio in Seattle crafted a haunting score, one recorded in two marathon days — thirteen-hour sessions each, with fifty-one musicians participating. His score featured instruments he felt captured the gothic feel and Southern locale. "I wrote out a list of instruments that that would indicate location," he describes. "It seemed to me that the solo fiddle ultimately was the most successful, because it's a very expressive instrument, number one. Number two is that in terms of its range and capacity, it made available lots of notes. I didn't think there was any other instrument that would represent the location and allow for as great a range of notes as a fiddle."

In addition, Young utilized a variety of really bizarre instruments, including a psaltery for the sequence involving Annie's dream sequence at the swamp. He also used a berimbau (a long bent stick with one metal string going from top to bottom, and a hollow gord strapped to the top, acting as a resonator). "You whack this thing with a stick and then you bend it so it reverberates," Young explains. "There were a couple of those whacks in some of the dream sequences, and Sam heard it and said, 'You have to put this in my score!'"

Also drummed into service: a devil chaser (a bamboo stick cut in a manner that when struck, it buzzes), nature chimes, and a gord pipe from Burma, which creates a sound Young likens to a "sick bag pipe or sick harmonica.

"The core of the score is a string orchestra and some French horns and some normal, traditional orchestra percussion instruments and keyboards, pianos." Young stresses, "The odd things are embedded in something that is traditional."

Because Raimi was involved prepping *Spider-Man*, he sent editor Bob Murawski to work with Young at the recording session, but Young nonetheless felt empowered by the director. "He said, 'You're going in the right direction; I trust you, just do your best.'"

A CHRISTMAS GIFT

Raimi's ninth feature debuted for a week in December 2000 in order to qualify for Academy Award selections, and went into general release on January 12, 2001. Like *A Simple Plan*, *The Gift* garnered excellent reviews, impressing critics with its emotional tenor and performances. "Putting his faith in a sturdy script and a fine cast led by the ever-remarkable Cate Blanchett, director Sam Raimi eschews trendy over-emphatic effects in favor of a straightforward approach that makes for a solid tale well told,"[17] wrote *Variety*'s Todd McCarthy. *Rolling Stone*'s Peter Travers noted that the film delivered "the lurid goods as a scary, sexy, twist-a-minute whodunit."[18] Ebert and Roeper gave the film "thumbs up" and Ebert noted in the *Chicago Sun Times* that the film was "ingenious in plotting, colorful in its characters, taut in its direction, and fortunate in possessing Cate Blanchett."[19]

The Gift did not fare much better than *A Simple Plan* in terms of box office, grossing $10.5 million in general release. Blanchett, Ribisi, Swank and the screenplay by Epperson and Thornton garnered Saturn Award nominations. Ribisi was also nominated for an Independent Spirit Award for Best Supporting Actor. Raimi's next movie, coming a year and a half later in May 2002, would gross more than ten times as much as *The Gift* and nearly more than all of Raimi's previous films combined ... in its opening weekend!

RAIMI RAP

RED HERRING: "I like to have as much back story as possible, even though there are people who think you don't ever see that on the screen," Ross notes of his creative process forging a performance. And how did he see *The Gift*'s Kenneth King? "He was a red herring. We stuck that in there with Kenneth King, but Sam didn't follow through quite as far as we played with the idea. At the dance, for instance, we shot some stuff of King and his daughter dancing in a way that was a little bit strange for a father and daughter to be dancing. And I think they decided in post that it went a little far and they couldn't quite take it there, but we wanted to plant the idea that it was a possibility, that King could be the culprit."

SAM SCREAMS: If you listen to the score for *The Gift*, you'll detect more than evocative, compelling music, you'll hear the director's vocal contribution. "He [Raimi] came over here to my studio maybe three times so I could play him things either on the piano or synth mock-ups of things," Christopher Young remembers. When the director visited, the composer was in the process of recording some high-pitched screams, having a vocalist performing what he terms "banshee cries." "They appear in a number of cues in the film. I don't know whose idea it was, but I said, 'Sam, why don't you try some?' So we put him in the hall and put on a microphone and he ended up screaming, and some of his screams are in a couple of cues."

911: "I had a police paramedic tell me about heart attacks," Ross remembers of his preparation for King's big scene, a cardiac arrest at the crime scene where Jessica's corpse is recovered. "He had been a paramedic for about twenty-some odd years and told me about various kinds of heart attacks. I made a decision that the stress of the moment, the condition of my arteries, and the cold of the water were going to make this a pretty intense heart attack, and Sam had talked to me early on about it. And I had been talking to Willy [the paramedic], and sometimes it's just kind of a tingling in the arm, but he said that it could also be a sharper pain that hits the left arm and the chest.

"We went for it, and Sam had one camera set up in the water, one from above, and I think he was shooting a third camera up on the dock with Cate, Keanu and all those people," Ross describes. "So there was a whole lot of stuff going on. It was cold that day and the water was cold and we underdressed with wetsuits, J.K. and I. And the poor stunt girl that was in the water was just frozen. It was a tough scene for everybody, because there are so many things going on in that scene, up on the dock, in the water, the two of us going into the water," but as Ross recalls, it came off very well on screen.

THE UNIFORM: On *The Gift*, Raimi donned his usual uniform: suit and tie (and often sunglasses). "That's respect for his craft, respect for the people he works with," Ross considers. "He understands that he should show the profession the respect that a doctor shows his profession."

"The thing that distinguishes him is a kind of gentleness. Sam is not only a gentleman, but a gentle man, because he brings that kind of gentleness to every person and every situation on the set, and you don't see him shouting, raising his voice. Things can go completely ass backward and Sam has this gentle control which makes him more powerful than if he were screaming and shouting and threatening people. I think that as a general rule, the tone of a set goes from the top down. The director sets the tone for the entire set, so when you have a man who has a smile on his face, has his crazy little imp-like sense of humor, wears a tie, and is gentle and listens to people, everybody else follows suit. 'Well, this is the way this runs;' 'This is the way we act on the set.'"

THERE'S A STORM COMING...

Following on the heels of *The Sixth Sense* (1999) and *Stir of Echoes* (1999), *The Gift* is a supernatural thriller that delves into parapsychology and extra-sensory perception. More dramatically, it explores the heart and soul of a lonely widower who has buried herself in work. By doing so, Blanchett's Annie has denied her personal life and the emotional needs of her sons. Annie's job as a fortuneteller may be an unconventional one, yet it serves its purpose; distracting her from the painful matters closest to her heart. Raimi's triumph in *The Gift* involves characterization, and Annie's slow-building recognition that she has used her gift of sight only to blind herself to the emotional needs of those closest to her.

Because *The Gift* is primarily an emotional journey, the genre elements play a part, but do not overtake the movie. Raimi renders the supernatural world in wholly believable fashion here, so much so that identification with Annie is heightened rather than diminished, often a concern in fantastic horror scenarios that require suspension of disbelief. As a character, Annie seems sympathetic and touching, not a crackpot who believes in psychic powers, and that broadens the movie's appeal. Annie might well be a therapist, a hairdresser, a forensic scientist, or any person who stumbles upon a mystery. Therefore, her second sight is not the film's central obsession, but simply the instrument, like Sherlock Holmes' powers of deduction, by which she solves a terrible crime.

How does Raimi make the world of parapsychology feel utterly believable, besides treating Annie's choice of career as a work-a-day job, replete with a home office? In most cases, by coupling images of the "other" or supernatural world with those of the natural world. Make note, for instance, how many times *water* serves as the focal point of Annie's psychic visions. A pencil rolls off Wayne's desk in his school office and lands, surprisingly, in a puddle — *and wham!* — the audience is inside Annie's vision, gazing at a corpse's dirty feet beside the soaked pencil. Two worlds have suddenly overlapped.

The visual key to this overlapping or adjacency of worlds may just be an early shot in the opening credits, in which the image of a local swamp is crosscut directly with straight-on, large-scale close-ups of Annie's symbolic cards. The melding of the cards and the swamp in contiguous compositions symbolizes the co-existence of different worlds, at least in terms of film grammar.

Throughout the movie, water and second sight are connected visually. Annie walks outside her home, looks up in a tree, and sees a sky composed of water, and a corpse floating above her. Likewise, it is the sound of dripping water that leads to another frightening vision: an unquiet corpse sulking in Annie's bathtub. These instances reinforce the notion that water and the world of supernatural, exemplified by Annie's visions, go hand-in-hand.

This conceit to couple images of water, an element of the *natural* world, with second-sight, an element of the *supernatural* world, succeeds on two levels. Firstly, the water represents an overt clue to Jessica's final disposition. Her corpse was thrown into the Barksdales' pond, so water is one clue from beyond the grave. But more thematically, water is a unique medium. It is a carrier. It ebbs and flows. It crests, builds, and floods. It crashes into — and can occupy — almost any space, even places it doesn't belong. Similarly, the supernatural world follows the same set of precepts, flooding in on Annie, soaking her in its reality, then leaving suddenly, as if a wave has broken and receded.

Raimi selected locations for *The Gift* based in part on the unique and unearthly trees he discovered there. He attempted to forge an interesting equation, that the natural world (symbolized by trees) can be wholly strange and unfamiliar. By similarly utilizing water imagery to signify the supernatural, Raimi continues this motif, the blending of two worlds. He reveals that the supernatural world is not so far-fetched or different than a 500-year-old tree, or the water of a nearby swamp, things we might look at every day but not really see or consider.

On a different thematic level, *The Gift* seems obsessed with secrets, and hurtful ones at that. Wayne bears a murderous secret, and fears Annie will learn it. Valerie attempts to hide the secret that she is abused by her husband, but bruises betray her, despite the sunglasses. Buddy's secret, sexual exploitation by his father, has driven him to sanity's edge. Duncan and Barksdale hide their illicit affairs, in hopes of preserving reputations. *The Gift*'s main thematic strand, suggested nicely by the screenplay, is that for Annie to face her own secret (the denial of her husband's death), she must navigate this path of abuse and secrecy.

Michael Betzold wrote in *Magill's Cinema Annual* that for being "the product of male writers, the script is unusually perceptive — and so is Raimi — in delineating the many nefarious ways in which violence and threats can permeate the lives of women."[20] He is correct, but it isn't just women who are threatened in *The Gift* — it is the Wilson children and men like Buddy. The town of Brixton is a hotbed of secrets and danger, and that's why it is the perfect story to tell in the South, a region replete with many layers, beliefs and secret histories. It is reputedly the most "haunted" region of our country, and other kinds of ghosts, cultural boogeyman including slavery and inequality, dwell side-by-side with conventional normality, just as, Raimi suggests, the world of the supernatural does.

The South, or a Hollywood perception of the South anyway, works as a metaphor in *The Gift* for virtually all the characters. It is civilized and normal on the surface, but just underneath there are secrets to unearth. Annie discovers abuse, both physical and sexual, desires wanton and perverse, and other ghosts among the so-called respectable people of Brixton. It is in facing and vanquishing these demons that Annie realizes that she too has a secret to conquer. She has never accepted the death of her husband, and what brings her to this recognition of her own denial is not just the act of righting a wrong, solving a murder, but the tangible evidence of her "gift" of the other world. Buddy returns from the other side and protects Annie from harm. This suggests hope; hope that another world exists, perhaps where Annie's husband somehow "survives." In sharing this hope with Annie, Buddy is not merely protecting a friend, he is serving as a sort of psychic Boo Radley, the enigmatic character depicted in Harper Lee's Pulitzer Prize–winning novel, *To Kill a Mockingbird*.

Actually, *The Gift* has much in common with that classic novel, spotlighting Raimi's continuing predilection to pay tribute to past literary and film works. Consider that book and film both occur in the contemporary South and concern themselves with a widowed parent raising children alone, in the book Atticus Finch; in the movie, Annie Wilson. Both works involve a homicide and an ensuing, sensationalistic court case. And, at the last minute, the real murderer is stopped from committing another crime by the unexpected intervention of a kindly but mysterious person, Boo Radley in the book; Buddy Cole in the film. Even the core social issues are not far apart. *To Kill a Mockingbird* concerned racism and the untoward underside of Southern society. *The Gift* also addresses that underside, here presented in the form of domestic abuse.

This author's film instructor always insisted that if a reviewer resorted to discussing performances in a review, the reviewer had failed miserably in his task, since many critics consider acting just a minor piece in the overall scheme of a film. Yet this is a study of Raimi's films *and* his development as a director, so it would seem remiss not to mention that he makes the most of this cast. His collaboration with Blanchett results in an affecting film that transcends any particular genre or stereotype.

Playing against type, Keanu Reeves makes fine use of his physicality, creating a threatening individual who is terrifying precisely because of his physical dominance. Others in the cast are equally good, but the point is really that Raimi as a director has pulled back, found the best way to tell his story, and then let the actors tell it. He showcases their talent in cogent, effective shots, and brings on the Raimi whammies when necessary (including a few *Darkman*esque zooms during the Jessica-in-the-tree vision), but otherwise lets the work speak for itself.

Only a director with confidence in his ability to entertain can forge a genre film of such restraint and razor-sharp suspense. And that's a terrific thing, even if one misses the inspired craziness of *The Quick and the Dead* or *Evil Dead 2*. This is Raimi's so-called middle period, and the director succeeds by playing against expectations. Critics and students of his work expect Raimi to be big, operatic, even overbearing, and instead he pulls a switcheroo and is subtle, focused and controlled, so that the eventual letting loose is all the more terrifying.

11

SPIDER-MAN (2002)

COLORFUL CHARACTERS A MUST!

GET READY FOR THE ULTIMATE SPIN.

CAST AND CREW

COLUMBIA PICTURES PRESENTS
A MARVEL ENTERTAINMENT/LAURA ZISKIN PRODUCTION OF *SPIDER-MAN*

DIRECTOR: Sam Raimi
WRITER: David Koepp
BASED ON: the Marvel Comic by Stan Lee and Steve Ditko
CASTING: Francine Maisler, Lynn Kressler
CO-PRODUCER: Grant Curtis
MUSIC: Danny Elfman
COSTUME DESIGNER: James Acheson
VISUAL EFFECTS DESIGNER: John Dykstra
FILM EDITOR: Bob Murawski and Arthur Coburn
PRODUCTION DESIGNER: Neil Spisak
DIRECTOR OF PHOTOGRAPHY: Don Burgess
EXECUTIVE PRODUCERS: Avi Arad and Stan Lee
PRODUCER: Laura Ziskin and Ian Bryce

STARRING

Tobey Maguire: Peter Parker/Spider-Man
Willem Dafoe: Norman Osborn/Green Goblin
Kirsten Dunst: Mary Jane Watson
James Franco: Harry Osborn
Cliff Robertson: Uncle Ben Parker
Rosemary Harris: Aunt May Parker
J.K. Simmons: J. Jonah Jameson
Joe Manganiello: Flash Thompson
Gerry Becker: Maximillian
Bill Nun: Joseph Robertson
Jack Betts: Henry
Stanley Anderson: General Slocum
Michael Papajohn: Carjacker
Bruce Campbell: Ring Announcer

Filmed in New York City, New York, and Los Angeles, California.

SPIDER-MAN, WHERE ARE YOU COMING FROM?

DIFFIDENT TEENAGER PETER PARKER lives a simple life with his kindly Uncle Ben and Aunt May, often missing the school bus and secretly longing for the love of his life, next-door neighbor Mary Jane Watson. However, Peter's life changes on a school field trip when a bite from a genetically engineered spider imbues him with super powers, including the ability to scale walls, shoot webs from his wrists and sense danger with tingling spider senses.

When Ben is killed in a car-jacking that Peter could have prevented, Parker comes to understand the magnitude of his powers and sets out to help people as a costumed hero, Spider-Man. But the hero gig doesn't pay the bills, and Peter takes a job at the *Daily Bugle* as a freelance photographer. His first assignment: snap a photograph of the mysterious Spider-Man for curmudgeonly editor-in-chief, J. Jonah Jameson.

Meanwhile, Norman Osborn, father to Peter's best friend, Harry, and head of his own corporation, learns that the U.S. government plans to pull the plug on his project to develop super soldiers and advanced military hardware. Norman experiments on himself, but the performance-enhancing formula transforms him into a maniac. Equipped with a green armor suit, a terrifying helmet, and a powerful new glider, Osborn terrorizes Manhattan as the Green Goblin.

When Peter rejects the villain's offer to team up, matters become personal. Osborn learns the hero's identity and threatens Aunt May and Mary Jane, spurring a final confrontation and Peter's subsequent realization that with great power comes great responsibility.

ALONG CAME A SPIDER

Way back in 1962, Marvel Comics' writer Stan Lee envisioned a new brand of superhero, one who was neither a father figure like DC's Batman and Superman, nor a wholesome teenage sidekick like Robin. Instead, this fellow was an awkward teenager named Peter Parker who had been granted superpowers by accident, courtesy of a bite from a radioactive spider, and who faced the same day-to-day problems we all do. "Suppose a teenager really got superpowers," Lee asked himself. "Wouldn't he still have the normal problems of any teenagers? Girls, family, acne, dandruff, ingrown toenails, allergy attacks, anything?"[1] With that concept in mind, artists Steve Ditko and Jack Kirby fashioned the new hero's gear, including a blue and red, tight-fitting costume, a black spider emblem on the hero's torso, and a weblike network across the outfit.

Lee's editor didn't like the concept, and *Spider-Man* first appeared sans fanfare in the final issue of a magazine called *Amazing Fantasy* (number fifteen). Today, that comic is worth $95,000 dollars in mint condition,[2] because Lee's concept exploded. Within a year, Spider-Man became a sensation and headlined his own comic book title. The character has become so popular that he is now a universal trademark for Marvel Comics and poses a real challenge to Superman and Batman for the title of most popular superhero of all time. This is not merely because of his nifty wall-climbing superpowers, but because Lee overturned many precepts of superhero comic books when creating him.

Spider-Man is not the beloved, universally accepted hero that Superman is in Metropolis. Peter quickly discovers that his own version of Superman's Perry White, *Daily Bugle* editor J. Jonah Jameson, is a cranky, ill-tempered lout that hates Spider-Man. More to the point, Parker does not face a static universe where good always triumphs. His Lois Lane, girlfriend Gwen Stacy, is killed by Spidey's nemesis, Green Goblin, a character introduced in 1964 in the comic's fourteenth issue. Later, one of Peter's friends, Harry Osborn, goes bad and becomes a villain. Despite his unreal powers, Parker lives in the real world.

Lee wrote nearly a hundred issues of *Spider-Man* and very quickly saw his creation jump to other media, including television. In 1967, an animated series (with Lee serving as story and art consultant) appeared courtesy of Grantray Lawrence Animation under the title *The Amazing Spider-Man*. The series pitted Peter and girlfriend Betty Brand against comic book villains including Mysterio, Dr. Octopus, Sandman, Elektro and Green Goblin.

In the early 1970s, Spider-Man appeared in live-action form on the educational program *The Electric Company*, this time in a series of brief sketches entitled *The Adventures of Spider-Man*. The hero was never dramatized out of uniform and was mute, his thoughts displayed as comic-style balloons. Among Spidey's opponents on PBS was Count Dracula played by Morgan Freeman.

In 1979, CBS aired a more adult version of the myth on a short-lived, primetime series, *The Amazing Spider-Man*. Nicholas Hammond was Parker, Robert F. Simon played Jameson and Irene Tedrow was Aunt May. The series eschewed the more outrageous aspects of the comic, particularly costumed villains, and focused on Spidey's conflicts with nuclear terrorists, evil scientists and kidnappers. The series limped along for two seasons before disappearing from the airwaves.

And so it went. *Spider-Man* appeared on television again, notably in a 1982 cartoon called *Spider-Man and His Amazing Friends*, in which Parker roomed with superheroes, Firestar and Iceman. But unlike Batman and Superman, Spider-Man never really had the kind of success on the tube he deserved. And even as the Man of Steel and Dark Knight fronted major movie franchises in the early and late eighties respectively, Spider-Man found only dead ends on the road to the silver screen.

In the 1980s, the Cannon Group, home of movie moguls Manahem Golan and Yoram Globus, the "world's leading purveyor[s] of B movies,"[3] acquired the license to Spider-Man from Marvel for $250,000 dollars.[4] Many fans of your friendly neighborhood Spider-Man did not consider this good news, because Cannon's other superhero films, *Superman IV: The Quest for Peace* (1987) and Albert Pyun's *Captain America* (1991), the latter based on another Marvel icon, were not successful. At one point, *Texas Chain Saw Massacre* auteur Tobe Hooper, who had directed *Lifeforce* (1985), *Invaders from Mars* (1986) and *The Texas Chainsaw Massacre Part II* (1986) for Cannon, was slated to direct.

In the 1990s, the rights to produce a Spider-Man film bounced around again, from Cannon to MGM to Viacom. In 1991, after *Terminator 2* blew away all comers at the box office, director James Cameron adopted *Spider-Man* as his pet project and developed a lengthy, nearly one hundred–page treatment. Like the Hooper production, Cameron's didn't get off the ground, though his treatment featured an important and controversial plot point. In his version, Spidey had organic web slingers, a concept different from the one established in the comic book, wherein Parker designed a mechanical shooter.

Finally, in spring of 1999, the Spider-Man license landed at Columbia/ Sony Pictures. Fortunately, Sony acquired Spider-Man at exactly the right moment. Although the *Batman* film franchise had been tarnished by Joel Schumacher's *Batman and Robin*, a gaudy exercise in excess, film's digital technology was rapidly improving, to the point that the superheroic actions of Spider-Man could be achieved realistically. In the summer of 1999, George Lucas' *The Phantom Menace* and *The Matrix* ushered in a new era of CGI movies, films boasting breathtaking effects in action scenes. Better yet, superheroes were trending hot. Wesley Snipe's actioner *Blade*, a film based on a vampire hunter featured in the early 1970s comic *Tomb of Dracula*, grossed $112 million in 1998, and in the summer of 2000, Bryan Singer's adaptation of Marvel's *The X-Men* raked in an impressive $294.3 million.[5] Hollywood executives felt their box office senses tingling, and *Spider-Man*'s development hit warp speed.

ALONG CAME A RAIMI

The pieces for a Spider-Man movie came together at the turn of the new millennium. David Koepp, author of *Carlito's Way* (1993) and *Mission: Impossible* (1996), as well as director of *The Trigger Effect* (1996) and *Stir of Echoes*, penned a script detailing Spider-Man's origin. Eventually given a polish by Alvin Sargeant, the script went through many drafts. Cameron's treatment established the film's villains as Elektro and Sandman, but they were eventually replaced by two others, Green Goblin and Dr. Octopus.[6] Very late in the process, Dr. Octopus was removed and shunted off to the prospective sequel, leaving Norman Osborn, the Green Goblin, as the primary antagonist.

Finding the right director for *Spider-Man* proved a tougher task than writing an acceptable story. *Apollo 13*'s Ron Howard was slated to direct at one point,[7] and other names in the mix included *Batman* helmer Tim Burton and *Home Alone* director Christopher Columbus. Young David Fincher, auteur of the stylish *Seven* (1995) and the bold *Fight Club*, was also a top contender until the last minute — though he was apparently keen on using the tragic Gwen Stacy storyline rather than the preferred origin tale. Fincher's fortunes looked good because *Spider-Man*'s producer, Laura Ziskin, had already worked with him on *Fight Club*.

Raimi wanted the opportunity to direct *Spider-Man*, but considered himself a long shot. He had pursued comic book franchises before, attempting to launch films based on *The Shadow* and *Batman*. And according to Stan Lee on the *Spider-Man* DVD, Raimi attempted to adapt *The Mighty Thor*, another Marvel property. None of those efforts bore fruit, which is why Raimi created his own superhero, *Darkman* in 1989. But even if Raimi did get the job, he understood it would be an incredible challenge.

"I was tantalized and at the same time terrified," he admitted to James Mottram of the BBC, "because I didn't know how anyone would make a good Spider-Man picture ... It's one thing to use technology to create fantastic sights that we're unfamiliar with ... But we look at people 90 percent of our waking day, it's most difficult to trick the audience with what they know so well, the human form, and how it moves and reacts, and how gravity affects it."[8]

Despite misgivings, Raimi interviewed for the job, and unbeknownst to him, the studio higher-ups were impressed with his knowledgeable, insightful and heartfelt presentation. As it turns out, Raimi had "everything we were looking for," according to Columbia Studios executive Amy Pascal. "He was incredibly stylish, he had tons of heart, and he's a total *Spider-Man* geek."[9] Indeed, Raimi had been a fan of Spider-Man since childhood, with that mural emblazoned on his bedroom wall, so his expression of love for the character was genuine. Still, when he learned of his good fortune on the set of *The Gift*, Raimi — ever modest — was surprised he had been entrusted with the important assignment.[10]

NOT AN ITSY BITSY SPIDER

Shepherding *Spider-Man* to theaters in the twenty-first century was not easy. At first, Raimi and producers eyed a 2001 release, sometime in the fall, but as it turned out, that was overly ambitious, and real world events would make that a difficult time for a grieving nation, following September 11.

With shooting scheduled to commence in January 2001, so much had yet to be decided, including designing and casting. On the former count, *Spider-Man* retained the services of three-time Oscar-winner James Acheson. Though Acheson was known primarily for designing period pieces, having picked up gold statuettes for *The Last Emperor* (1987), *Dangerous Liaisons* (1988), and 1995's *Restoration*, Acheson proved the perfect selection by skillfully updating the famous Spider-Man gear.

As Raimi noted to *Cinescape* editor Steve Hockensmith, Acheson added "some dimensionality to it, to take a slightly more subtle approach to the coloration of the outfit, to increase flexibility."[11] Eventually some twenty-three suits were created for the production at a staggering cost of $100,000 each. Acheson's costumes were not only well-received, they assured him future superheroic assignments, and after *Spider-Man*, the designer outfitted Ben Affleck's *Daredevil*.

Another critical talent was visual effects expert John Dykstra, the mastermind behind the impressive special effects for *Star Wars* in 1977. Since *Star Wars*, Dykstra had created the visuals for *Star Trek: The Motion Picture* (1979), *Lifeforce* and the last two *Batman* films. It was his job to make possible Raimi's unique vision of *Spider-Man*. "Sam's idea... included a lot of daytime stuff," Dykstra reported to the *Inquirer News Service*. "Daytime visual effects shots require more detail and are generally harder illusions."[12]

To Raimi's surprise, Dykstra suggested that the whole Spider-Man character could be created with "full CGI."[13] In other words, a fully digital superhero! For Dykstra and his team this approach meant not just creating "the look of the character," but the "soul of the character," which Dykstra admitted was "the toughest part."[14]

Back in the non-digital world, casting of the movie's titular character became Hollywood's hottest guessing game. Heath Ledger, Leonardo DiCaprio, Freddie Prinze Jr., Jude Law, Chris O'Donnell, Wes Bentley and Raimi buddy, Bruce Campbell[15] were among the names bandied about, and many in the industry were surprised when the announcement came that Tobey Maguire had landed the role.

Well-respected for dramatic roles in Woody Allen's *Deconstructing Harry* (1997), Ang Lee's *The Ice Storm* (1997), *Cider House Rules* (1999) and *Wonder Boys* (2000), the California-grown young man began devoting himself to acting at age sixteen and was known widely for his friendship with *Titanic* star DiCaprio.[16] Raimi and wife Gillian were impressed with Maguire based on his beguiling, innocent performance in *Cider House Rules*. Also, there may have been a sense of identification. "Tobey looks a bit like Sam did when he was younger," Raimi's mentor, Verne Nobles, suggests. "He and Sam clicked. They're both shy in their own way."

"Tobey's an Everyman," said producer Ziskin. "He's adorable, but not a classic hunk. He's not a model. He looks like an ordinary kid."[17] Those very qualities made the actor the perfect choice to play unassuming Parker, but there were concerns. No one at Columbia Studios believed that the role of ungainly Peter Parker was beyond the acting abilities of the studious, accomplished Maguire, but could the small-framed vegetarian pull off the dramatic action scenes?

Maguire knew he could, and furthermore, identified with the Everyman aspects of Spider-Man's character. "It's almost like you can put yourself in Spider-Man's shoes," he mused, "whereas Bruce Wayne is a billionaire and Clark Kent is an alien."[18]

Fortunately, Maguire had an ally. Raimi believed in his ability to carry the film and shot an elaborate, *Dirty Harry*–like screen test of a topless Maguire violently dispatching a gang of thugs in a makeshift alley. Replete with props, a damsel in distress and pulse-pounding action-movie music, the sequence revealed a muscular, taciturn, highly focused Maguire, and was enough to land the actor the plum assignment.

Maguire then embarked on a herculean training regimen to bulk-up, exercising four hours a day, six days a week on a regimen that included martial arts, cycling, gymnastics and yoga.[19] Because he was a vegetarian, it wasn't easy to create muscle mass, but Maguire kept at it, having his blood consistency checked on a daily basis.[20] For his efforts, the twenty-six-year-old actor was paid four million dollars, with the guarantee of twelve million for the sequel.[21]

With Maguire set, speculation turned to the man that would challenge him onscreen as Green Goblin. Any actor cast would face the specter of superhero villains past, including Jack Nicholson's Joker, Gene Hackman's Luthor, and Ian McKellen's Magneto. A big name was definitely required if the ranks of that select group were to be filled. Nicolas Cage was mentioned, and John Malkovich was also considered,[22] but it was the wiry and intense Willem Dafoe who was finally cast. Like the other great actors playing villains, Dafoe brought a vast and varied body of work with his name. He had won Oscar nominations for roles in *Shadow of the Vampire* (2000) and *Platoon* (1986) and played Jesus Christ in Martin Scorsese's remarkable *The Last Temptation of Christ* (1988). The Independent Spirit and Saturn Awards had honored his performance in *Shadow of the Vampire*, and the actor has also been nominated for Golden Globes and Screen Actors honors. A man dedicated to his craft, Dafoe promised to become the perfect comic book villain.

A friend of Joel Coen and Frances McDormand, Dafoe recalls that he used to hear Sam Raimi stories often, and so the director was always on his mind. "And when I heard he was going to direct *Spider-Man*, I thought that was an inspired choice," he says.

Raimi contacted the actor while Dafoe was out of the country, and then ran up a considerable long-distance phone bill. "Sam started talking and two hours later he was still talking," Dafoe revealed in *TV Guide*. "He told the story in such precise and psychological detail: 'Ultimately, the Green Goblin goes after Spider-Man because he feels rejected. He'd wanted Spider-Man to join him like a father wants his son in the family business.' I thought, 'This guy is nuts. But he just might make a fantastic movie.'"[23]

When asked about the Jekyll-Hyde nature of his character, Dafoe indicates the comparison is apt. "Clearly that's what comes to mind. It's a classic kind of evil alter-ego that is born. That's really all in the writing, so it's not so much my interpretation as addressing myself to the story. Having said that, although he didn't direct me to look at any films, Sam did give me a copy of the novel *Dr. Jekyll and Mr. Hyde*. It's the one thing he gave me on the movie."

Taking her second shot as a superhero love interest (after 2000's *The*

Crow: Salvation), was young actress Kirsten Dunst, a performer who generated buzz over her sexy performance in *Bring It On* (2000) and haunting role in Sofia Coppola's *The Virgin Suicides* (1999). She was overseas filming a movie called *The Cat's Meow* for Peter Bogdonovich when she tested with Maguire.[24] They had instant chemistry, and Parker found his Mary Jane.

Another big gun was Academy Award–winner Cliff Robertson, a decorated and highly respected figure in movie history. Having won an Emmy in 1963 and an Oscar for Best Actor for 1969's touching science-fiction tale *Charly* (based on the short story *Flowers for Algernon*), Robertson was *Spider-Man*'s touch of class and elegance, a reminder of Hollywood history.

"They [Sam and Laura] approached me and in effect said, 'Look Cliff, Marlon Brando did his gig in *Superman* and Alec Guinness did his in *Star Wars* and we've got a similar little situation with Spider-Man's avuncular Uncle Ben. We would like you to entertain the thought," Robertson says. "And I said, 'Okay.' They came to New York and I met them; we seemed to get along, and I was particularly impressed with Sam."

In preparing for the role, Robertson went back to the comic book to learn about his character. "I did talk to Stan Lee, based on what we were trying to do. He had a certain allegiance and fidelity to the original, having been the creator. He emphasized the need for a very loving and respectful relationship between the two characters."

Forging that relationship was much easier because Peter Parker was played by Maguire, an actor Robertson found delightful. "He was very kind and nice and spoke almost reverentially about my work. He treated me with great respect, probably undeserved," Robertson says modestly. "But he was very kind and nice to work with."

Robertson also enjoyed working with Rosemary Harris, who was cast in the film as Aunt May; she had appeared in *The Gift* as Annie's granny. "She's a charming, delightful, beautiful lady and I've been a fan for many years. We knew each other socially and were looking forward to working together."

Though Robertson had once played the cowboy villain named Shame in episodes of the 1960s Adam West series *Batman*, it had been some time since he dwelled in the superhero universe. He discussed with this author how his approach to Uncle Ben differed from that which he adopted to play the villainous president in John Carpenter's *Escape from L.A.* (1996) and the protagonist of *Charly*, genre roles of vastly different stripe: "When you're doing a character like that in the Carpenter picture, you're playing a character that is a little bit exaggerated, obviously. It's almost like a cartoon. So his character is a little overblown, and you instinctively put the dial in your inner mentality to about a seven on the overblown scale. It's an instinctive thing; not study. When you're doing [a character in] *Charly* — a sci-fi thing that hasn't became a reality yet — because it's a very human story, very warm and delicate, you do not go that over the top at all, you stay within the boundaries of credibility. *Spider-Man* was strictly human. In terms of the relationship with Tobey, with whom I work in the sequel, it's very avuncular. The uncle who is really the father who loves the son."

Raimi also provided the veteran with insight into his character's purpose. "Sam kept saying, 'Cliff, this character is the moral spine of the picture.'"

THE TANGLED WEB OF FANDOM

Boasting a stunt crew of over 150, the big-budgeted *Spider-Man* shot throughout the winter and spring of 2001. Some exteriors were lensed in New York, while interiors were recreated in Los Angeles. The lab where Peter Parker was bitten by a spider (a steatoda) was created at the Natural History Museum near U.S.C. Spider wrangler Steve "Bugs Are My Business" Kutcher trained the spiders used in the sequence. Many stages at Sony doubled for New York locations. Stage 27 was decorated as Times Square for the World Unity Fair action set piece, built to collapse on cue a piece at a time to simulate the Green Goblin's aerial bombardment. Stage 30 recreated the pilings of the Queensboro Bridge, a set required for the climactic battle.

As Raimi filmed, news of the screenplay's details leaked out and a few dyed-in-the-wool Spider-Man fans were not happy. For one thing, the script changed Spider-Man's origin. In the comic, he was bitten by a radioactive spider, and in the movie it was a genetically engineered spider.

Spider-Man's nemesis, Green Goblin, also had a face-lift for his big close-up. "The development of the costume was extraordinary," Dafoe recalls. "They did much trial and error about not only the design, but how you could build it. It [the costume] was quite tight and had all of these formed pieces, so I had very, very long fittings for it, where they would actually take the little pieces and adjust them like pieces of a puzzle on my body. At one point, the Goblin had all this circuitry on his skin. At one point, he had a big backpack. There was a long period of research and development, let's say, and it was quite involved."

"Initially they tried a mask, even before my involvement," Dafoe continues, "but they found it too silly and not scary enough. It's difficult, because in the comics there is something comical about the Goblin. He's kind of a silly figure. I think they felt he had to have a technological base and hardness and evilness that the Goblin doesn't have in the comics."

More importantly than these cosmetic changes, at least to some fans, the Koepp screenplay retained the idea first introduced in Cameron's decade-old treatment, that Spider-Man would have organic webshooters not mechanical creations. Many fans found this change unacceptable, believing it made Peter less intelligent. "We want to make sure that this isn't screwed up," said Jo O'Malley, a fellow who worked on a Web site dedicated to changing this notion, No-Organic-WebShooters.com.[25]

"I've seen the Down with Organic Webshooters Web site," Raimi later acknowledged. "I'm putting out a petition myself, Down with Down with Organic Webshooters Web site."[26]

Jokes aside, Raimi felt there was just cause to tweak Spidey's powers. "There's a very good reason for going with the organic webshooters," he explained. "First, Peter is supposed to be one of us. He is supposed to be an average, middle-class kid, and he would have to be a genius and a chemical engineer to devise a webshooter that was powerful enough to produce a web that would stick to buildings and allow him to fly around the city."[27] Raimi's point was valid. Why would Aunt May and Peter worry about money if he could invent something with so much profit potential? Ever the storyteller, Raimi pinpointed a logistical weakness in the tale, probably something that bothered him as a child, and then improved the reality of it.

Still, Raimi and his unfinished film were under a spotlight, and that was discomforting. "It preys upon my insecurities when so many people don't like a casting choice, or don't like some creative decisions," Raimi wrote in *Entertainment Weekly*. "I finally told myself that the best way to please the fans is [to] not necessarily listen to them, but follow in my heart what I love about the comic book and bring that to the screen."[28]

On one hand, it is easy to understand fan trepidations about comic book-to-movie adaptations. Hollywood had bungled the job before, with *Superman III* (1983), *Captain America*, *The Fantastic Four* (1994), *Batman and Robin* and *The League of Extraordinary Gentlemen* (2003) jumping immediately to mind. Fans *care* about their favorite characters, but what they had no way of realizing is that the film's director felt the same way. All Raimi could really do to protect himself from more unkind remarks on the Internet was wait for the film's release. As in so many situations, the proof of the pudding would be in the eating...

ACTION GOBLIN

"The days tended to be quite long and I was on the film maybe on and off for four or five months," Willem Dafoe remembers when asked about *Spider-Man*'s principal photography. "For that kind of movie, that's pretty standard."

What wasn't so standard however, were the Goblin's accouterments, including a helmet that obscured Dafoe's face. "It may or may not have been a good idea to have something that covered so much of my face," the actor considers. "In theory then, what you try to do is find different modes of expression. And that is a certain physical language. But that was a little difficult to find too, because you didn't want it go get too baroque, or too refined, and you don't want to steal Spider-Man's thunder. He's the dancer. He's the agile one. So what we are left with is the Goblin's toys and the Goblin's sheer weight, his heaviness, his strength."

In developing how he would move, we did all kinds of things," Dafoe continues, "all kinds of martial arts. It all looked vaguely *Crouching Tiger*, and we didn't want it to go in that direction, so the Goblin ended up being pretty much a puncher. I think, looking back on it, whenever there was a scene with much dialogue and with the mask, it was difficult to play the scenes well, because you couldn't see the eyes. That was a challenge, but I think the design worked well emblematically. It's a very strong visual."

The part was also very physical, a fact the theater actor appreciated. "I like doing that stuff," Dafoe comments. "I think that's part of the experience of the character. If you have someone else do all your action stuff, there's a huge hole in your story. It may not be felt by the audience, but it will be felt by me, and then I won't have the authority to pretend. I won't be able to claim the role as mine. Whenever you work on something, you want to create this history with it, this contact with it, find a way to be committed to it, and for me that is usually through the body. Sometimes, I think I'm more of a dancer than an actor, and I feel most comfortable doing the physical stuff. As the Goblin, when I could, and even Norman Osborn, I would approach it from a place of physicality and a task-oriented approach to the scenes."

That approach included wire work and high jumps, particularly in the scene following Green Goblin's birth in the lab. "That was my first day of flying, being up on a ratchet and being sent through the air," Dafoe explains. "It was thrilling to do, and it was very difficult because I had to do a long leap, quite high, and then stick the landing right in front of the camera. The truth is it was hard to get, and we finally got one that was beautiful, but it didn't bring the scene to the next level."

Eventually, the shot was cut. "We loved it and were proud of it as a great event, but it didn't really work in the storytelling," Dafoe says. "And of course, Sam is disciplined enough not to fall in love with the process and hang onto it just because he feels sentimental about it."

SWING TIME

Two hundred technicians labored to create the visual effects of *Spider-Man*, more than five hundred CGI shots in all. It was a cutting-edge, high-wire act, and the conceived final shot was a show-stopper, a thirty-second jaunt through the sky that would carry the audience alongside the airborne Spider-Man. No rain (a la *Godzilla* [1998]) and no black night (a la *Batman and Robin* or *Daredevil*) would cloak the flaws. After all, Spider-Man didn't dwell in a dingy, pitch-black Gotham, but a vibrant, colorful, daytime world, and Raimi sought to honor that vision. But how to make Spider-Man fly, or rather, swing?

"We tried all sorts of different combinations to see if we could fake Spider-Man swinging, including using a human in front of a green screen," Raimi revealed to *American Cinematographer*'s Ron Magid. "Spider-Man is the graceful dancer of the skies, and those attempts just weren't fluid or free enough."[29]

And that led Raimi back to Dykstra's bold initiative to achieve everything with the computer. But that meant that Raimi had to understand the new world of digital effects, even as he shot the film. "He had to figure all that out in his head, because a lot of that is done optically," Verne Nobles says with awe. "In *Spider-Man* there was a lot of CG work that was being done, but Sam had to understand the process to make it look like it wasn't CG, number one. And number two, the camera was always in places where you wondered how the hell he got it there.

"I am almost sure, knowing him, that Sam must have gone back and looked at some of the early films, like the silent *Napoleon*," Nobles speculates. "It was one of the first times, that I know of anyway, where they actually put the camera on some kind of rope or camera and swung it. It would fly through the air and come at something. Today we do a lot of tricks to do that, or we use CG, but in the silent era they were unable to do that. You take that thought and you bring it forward to *Spider-Man* and you're going to see that technique. That's what Sam does. He is capable, like the great directors of today, Spielberg and the rest of them, to look at something different from the way we all do. To say that he's quirky is an understatement."

Other effects built on the progress forged by films such as *The Matrix*. A scene in the high school hallway involving tingling "spider senses" was an evolution of that movie's bullet time effect, using a still camera array, but modified to include motion control in the form of a Milo camera, and even CG. And some of it, as Nobles understands, was just good old fashioned, gimmicky camera tricks, like those Raimi has been using since the days of his super 8mm movies.

With cinematographer Don Burgess at the helm, a conventional camera was used to track past real actors, who were standing still, acting frozen. "We undercranked and shot multiple passes for extra motion blur, sharp focus passes and out of focus passes,"[30] Burgess told Magid.

HERE COMES A SPIDER-MAN

Boasting a budget of $139 million and including a deal that guaranteed Marvel Comics 7 percent of the haul,[31] Sony's *Spider-Man* became the event movie of the summer when it premiered May 3, 2002. The film opened in a field consisting of *Changing Lanes*, *Deuces Wild*, *The Scorpion King*, *Jason X*, *Ice Age* and Woody Allen's *Hollywood Ending*, but competition was obliterated by Raimi's feature, which grossed $114 million in its first weekend, opening in over 3,000 theaters nationwide.

The film broke several records, including the highest one-day haul in history, the biggest weekend grosses in history, and it was also the fastest movie to crack $100 million, vanquishing previous record holder, 1999's *Star Wars Episode I: The Phantom Menace.*[32] By the time it finished in theaters, Raimi's tenth feature film earned more than $403 million, landing it at the number five slot in the coveted top ten "highest grossing films of all time" list.

Raimi's film also silenced naysayers among the fan community who, by and large, experienced what Brian Michael Bendis, author of the *Ultimate Spider-Man* comic book, termed "a geek orgasm."[33] Fans were happy not just because the film was actually good, a bar not frequently attained by superhero flicks, but also because it was faithful to the source material they so admired. "Every time a comic book gets made into a movie, perhaps 40 to 50 percent is reverent, and Hollywood makes up the rest. This is closer to 85 to 90 percent," Marvel's editor-in-chief, Joe Quesada, reported.[34]

The critical community lavished praise on Raimi's contribution to the genre. "*Spider-Man* wraps the *Star Wars* universe in his web and completely suffocates it," wrote Joseph Szadkowski for the *Washington Times*. "It completely exceeded my expectations."[35] Ethan Alter noted that "Maguire's understated presence and Raimi's off-kilter sensibility are what make *Spider-Man* both a successful adaptation and an enjoyable film in its own right."[36]

Praised along with Raimi and Maguire, was the affecting love story. "It's that rare cartoon movie in which the villain is less involving than the love story,"[37] Kenneth Turan opined in the *Los Angeles Times*. "The best invention in David Koepp's screenplay," suggested the *Christian Century*, "is the equation of love with super heroism."[38]

There were only a few killjoys, including Gary Arnold, who felt the film overindulged in a "sappiness that weighs down the scenario as grievously as twin lead balloons."[39] Roger Ebert had praise for Maguire, but felt that the special effects were a letdown, complaining that *Spider-Man* "looks like a video game figure, not like a person having an amazing experience."[40] Bafflingly, Ebert gave the more sour, less sweet *Daredevil* a positive review when it was released nine months later.

A wild ride and a crowd-pleasing blockbuster, *Spider-Man* ended the year 2002 with another victory lap, including nominations from the Academy Awards for Sound and Visual Effects. In recognition of the axiom that imitation is the sincerest form of flattery, following *Spider-Man*'s release, audiences were treated to a gaggle of superhero films, including *Daredevil*, *X2: X-Men United*, *The Hulk*, and *The League of Extraordinary Men*, with many more to come, including *Blade 3*, *Hellboy*, *The Fantastic Four*, *Deathlok*, *Ghost Rider*, *Catwoman* and *Iron Man*.

RAIMI RAP

THE MORE THINGS CHANGE: While making final adjustments on *The Gift*, Raimi commenced work on *Spider-Man*. During this period, he was paid a visit by three dear friends — Ellen Sandweiss, Theresa Tilly and Betsy Baker, the Ladies of *The Evil Dead*. "We met him not that long ago at Sony," Tilly remembers, "where he was in prep for *Spider-Man*. He took us around and showed us all of the storyboards he'd prepared, and he made us feel that he was sharing this great experience with us."

Sandweiss also recalls the visit, and that even in the midst of work on two different films, Raimi found time to play. "We were sitting in his office just chatting and he went into this full story about the folklore around *The Evil Dead* cabin and all the things that happened to it during the time we were there, just this long, involved story. We were all listening with wide eyes, and the whole story ended up being a crock of shit. He made it up on the spot, and yet it had all of us spellbound."

SHY? Many people in the press and who have worked with Raimi observe that the director is shy. Verne Nobles has a thought on the subject. "It's the opposite from what some people may think. The man is very confident. It isn't that he's insecure and therefore shy. He's very confident, but he lives within a very creative, exciting, unique world. His personal life and family life is completely divorced from all that. When he's not being the comic book, the creator of the comic book, the creator of the visual, of the bullet-in-the-head or the guy flying through the air in *Darkman*, of any of those things, he goes home to his family because that's his security. He goes home and he's *Sam*. He's *Papa*. That's the way he prefers it. Unless he knows you very, very well and he's part of your world or you're a part of his world, he's that way. If you're on the inner circle, he's funny and clever and a little nutsy in a very wonderful way. I don't think he's shy. I think he's very private."

THE HAPPY VALLEY SPIDER: "I thought Sam made a personal film in *Spider-Man*," *Evil Dead* makeup artist Tom Sullivan reflects, detailing the thematic unity in the Raimi film canon. "Peter Parker is perfect as a 'Sad Sappy' loser who can't get a break. Not unlike bullied and powerless Happy Valley Kid."

WATCH YOUR WORDS: "With great power comes great responsibility," recites Cliff Robertson. Since *Spider-Man*'s release, those noteworthy words have boomeranged back again and again. "People quote that back to me," he laughs. "I've got to be careful what I talk about..."

MIRROR, MIRROR: "That was something we had to invent," Dafoe describes Osborn's dialogue with his twisted reflection in the mirror. "It's a very simple device, but initially we didn't know quite how that would play. We knew it was going to be two voices, but we didn't know whether I was going to play both parts by myself, have one part prerecorded, or whether I would speak in two voices. The mirror was something we came up with as a device that didn't really depend on technology and would play the split personality aspect of the character."

A BIG HAND FOR SPIDER-MAN: Comic book writer and artist Phil Jimenez saw a lifelong dream realized when he had the chance to play Spider-Man. Kind of. Jimenez's hands doubled Tobey Maguire's during the scene where Parker sketches his Spider costume. Jimenez's hand was made up to resemble Maguire's, right down to identical swollen spider bites.[41]

CAMEOS: Sam Raimi fans will recognize Ash himself, Bruce Campbell, as the wrestling announcer who appears early in *Spider-Man*. Sharp-eyed viewers will also spot Marvel Comics legend Stan Lee during the World Unity Fair. He is seen for a split second rescuing a little girl from danger. Singer Macy Gray also makes a brief appearance, as does Rob Tapert's wife, Lucy Lawless, (as a punk rocker) and Scott Spiegel (as a cop).

Perhaps the most interesting cameo of all, however, comes from the music world. Paul Francis Webster and Robert Harris' "Theme from Spider-Man," the music from the 1967 animated series, plays over the end credits well after Chad Kroeger's chart-topping hit, "Hero," finishes up. Everybody who grew up with the animated series remembers the lyrics to this beloved song: "Spider-Man, Spider-Man, does whatever a spider can..."

SUPREME SPIDER: The movie *Spider-Man* doesn't merely have legs, it has eight of 'em! More than a year after its release, its opening weekend box office tally has not been equalled, let alone surpassed, even by such heavy hitters as *The Matrix Reloaded*, *The Hulk*, *Bad Boys II*, *Finding Nemo*, *Terminator 3* and *Charlies Angels: Full Throttle*. True, *The Matrix Reloaded* nabbed a higher one-day haul ($42.5 million to Spidey's $39.4 million) in May of 2003, but it didn't climb as high as *Spider-Man*'s total weekend haul of $114 million, leaving that honor, hopefully, for *Spider-Man 2*.

WE ARE WHAT WE CHOOSE TO BE

If the dynamic, visually arresting *Evil Dead* and *Darkman* represent early Raimi, and *A Simple Plan*, *For Love of the Game* and *The Gift* symbolize a middle period in the director's career, a time when considerations such as acting and story were augmented and visuals downplayed, then *Spider-Man* represents Sam Raimi *now*, the marriage of earlier periods. Dramatic and human, yet simultaneously dazzling in revolutionary visuals, *Spider-Man* is the apex of Raimi's cinematic efforts.

Looking at the human dynamic first, *Spider-Man* dramatizes its story with a gentle touch and an acknowledgment of universal human emotions. After the opening credits, the movie commences with a voice-over narration from the protagonist, Peter. Instantly then, Raimi fosters identification by making the audience privy to the thoughts of the lead. More to the point, Parker reveals that his story, "like all stories worth telling," concerns a girl. This is a pretty major thing in a big-budgeted event film, and it is Raimi's manner of acknowledging the emotional core of *Spider-Man*'s story, that this is not the story of good versus evil. It is not about the birth of a hero, or a mad villain's plan to destroy the world. Or even vengeance. Imagine a James Bond or Batman franchise entry starting off in such intimate fashion. Though *Adaptation* (2002) warns screenwriters that voice-over is a weak device, *Spider-Man*'s opening gambit works because the audience hears in the character's voice precisely what he values. He is a teenager in love, and who can't identify with that?

When the audience first sees Peter, he is a dorky kid wearing glasses, attempting to catch a school bus. Again, we all recall the horrors of high school and the feeling that we are perpetually out-of-step with things, whether it be the bus schedule or fashion sense. We all know how it feels to be less attractive than we'd like. That Peter's best friend, Harry, is drop-dead handsome (James Franco even played James Dean in a TV-movie) augments the notion that Peter is a nebbish, not a popular kid. And the life force of Dunst is an amazing thing that ratifies why any red-blooded American male would fall in love with her. It isn't just physical beauty, but a relationship this actress shares with the camera, a joy and innocence that cannot be dissected. She's full of life, and the audience sees precisely why Peter would be attracted to her.

In developing these characters and relationships, Koepp's script and Raimi's direction metaphorically hijack superhero film conventions and launch the genre in a new and welcome direction. It is telling that the film's most talked about sequence is one of simple human connection — a kiss between Spidey and M.J. in a rainy alley. Not special effects, not explosions, nor the costumes. It is the *human* story that interests the audience.

Even the film's villain gets this so-called human treatment. "You should feel for Norman Osborn because he destroys himself not out of evil, but out of a character flaw," Willem Dafoe considers. "It's not some vague thing about world domination. It's really about a guy who is trying to be the best scientist he can be, the best father he can be, the best citizen can be. It just gets perverted. I think the Osborn character is more interesting than the Goblin, more developed from an actor's viewpoint, because it is this weird mix of comedy and tragedy. It really shifts back and forth within one scene between the two. I think the father-son relationship was very interesting, and also the fact that he prefers Peter Parker to his own son. That parallels what happens to the Goblin and Spider-Man characters. It's as if the classic good guy/bad guy face-off is colored by this understandable psychology of father and son, and mentor and student.

"What made it special," Dafoe confides, "was that Sam was able to really invest in it personally, invest it with a psychology that is very near and dear to his truth."

But if *Spider-Man* charts the relationship of father and son, and the resentments and rejections therein, the film's central metaphor involves puberty and maturity. Peter learns "with great power comes great responsibility," and frankly, that's a platitude. But is it not also a lesson men and women must learn? The film follows Peter through the equivalent of puberty, the development of his unique powers, and his emotional selfishness and obsession with M.J., which in a very real sense results in Ben's death. Finally, by the end, Peter has recognized that as an adult he must approach life with a sense of responsibility and decorum. The screenplay handles this maturation process in a witty way, particularly the scenes involving Peter discovering his powers, which reflects the puberty-like changes his body undergoes as he becomes a man, a Spider-Man.

"Certainly the smartest scene in the movie comes when, full of the joys of his spring, he leaps onto a roof and tries, for the first time, to shoot his silk into the air," writes Anthony Lane for the *New Yorker*. "'Go, web, go,' the desperate teenager cries, madly flipping his hand back and forth. Hmmm."[42]

Lane suggests that the act of Peter flipping his wrist somehow equates to, well, there's no elegant way to say it, *masturbation*. On the surface, that may be an absurd assertion, but in general terms, the puberty metaphor is carefully embedded in the film. Teenage Peter falls into bed one night, and when he awakens the next morning discovers a nocturnal ... *mutation*. His body has undergone a dramatic change. He has bulked up (as youngsters do upon entering adolescence), begun to grow hair in unexpected places (like the sharp spider stickers that emerge from his fingers as he first climbs a wall), and suddenly developed the ability to shoot a sticky white substance out of his body.

In a later scene, the camera finds Peter alone in his bedroom, "practicing" his webshooting abilities. He is distinctly embarrassed when discovered. "I'm exercising," he mumbles. "I'm not dressed, Aunt May." This scene playfully acknowledges the teenager's bedroom as a place of discovery and the fear of being caught doing something both personal and embarrassing.

The metaphor might have been deeper had a scene in the school bathroom not been cut from the film. According to Mark Cotta Vaz's *Behind the Mask of Spider-Man*, the script included another moment of Peter's unexpected web emission:

> His wrists are oozing a pearly white fluid from almost invisible slits about a quarter of an inch long. Peter pushes on the skin next to one of the slits to relieve the pressure. A dark shape, the size and color of a rose thorn, emerges from beneath the skin and shoots a jet of liquid silk straight up in the air, where it *splats* onto the ceiling and adheres there.[43]

Well, okay, that may have been a bit much, which explains why it was cut. But the details indicate that screenwriter Koepp intended to draw a comparison between sexual awakening in adolescence and Peter's dawning maturity as Spider-Man. It is not an overbearing metaphor, merely an interesting one that contributes to the story's universality. Male or female, teenager or senior citizen, everybody remembers puberty. The film benefits from the fact that Raimi plays it "as straight as possible,"[44] with just a little wink here or there.

If *Spider-Man* is remarkable in the human component, it is nothing short of spectacular in the visual arena. The film opens with an expressive title sequence that finds the audience caught inside Spidey's web, traversing it to the beat of Danny Elfman's rousing, martial score. Like Saul Bass on steroids, this engaging opening expresses the director's excitement with the material, and there are brief glimpses of Spider-Man to build anticipation. It's a fun, individualistic way to start the film, and there is a hyperactive joy to the manner in which the letters forming the talents' names join up, then separate, like strands of Peter's mutated DNA.

Later, Raimi adopts his old tool from *The Evil Dead*, the first person POV, to help audiences share in Parker's exuberance as he jumps from roof to roof. We feel exhilaration as we see, from Peter's perspective, the skyscrapers far below. The excitement is palpable.

Another familiar touch involves Raimi's use of montage, a technique seen in *Darkman*, *The Quick and the Dead* and *For Love of the Game*. Here Raimi gives us two classic collages of rapid images, the first involving Peter's designing of his costume (*Symbol? Utility belt? Needs more color...*) And the second is a rapid-fire editing of *Spider-Man*'s Manhattan exploits intercut with first-person interviews of jaded New Yorkers talking about the hero in their midst. Fast and furious, these sequences, like the opening credits, foster excitement in their aggressive editing and presentation of image over image.

Regarding *Spider-Man*'s CGI, and therefore the character's very movement, there is considerable debate. Roger Ebert felt it looked like storyboards in action, not human movement. This author, on one of his less insightful days, wrote a column for the Web-zine *Deep Outside* (now renamed *Far Sector*) entitled "Not Very Special Effects" that took on the CGI movement in Hollywood. Exhibit A was *Attack of the Clones*, and exhibit C or D was *Spider-Man*. At the time, late May 2002, the author wrote of the CGI in Raimi's film: "There is no vital connection to reality in the costumed sequences. We are watching CGI cartoons duke it out instead." I also noted that the balance "felt wrong."[45] In hindsight, these criticisms were off the mark.

CGI is not perfect, no doubt, but the effects in *Spider-Man* do not represent, in fact, the *truth* of our everyday reality, as this author expected. Just as a live-action camera can be deployed in ways that express different notions, so can digital effects express a world not necessarily strictly real. Consider, for instance, that "bullet time" in *The Matrix* is not strictly realistic. Time doesn't freeze for extended moments, like a hiccup. Even if we could view them in slow motion, bullets don't really let off little visible rings of displaced air. The effects are good, brilliant even, but not strictly reflective of reality. And don't even get started about special effects in outer-space movies. There is no sound or fire in space, which nobody would know if they watched *Star Wars* movies.

Likewise, *Spider-Man* represents what might be called "Swing Time" considering the hero's unique abilities. As depicted in the film, Spider-Man does not move the way we expect in this reality. He doesn't have to. Instead, he moves precisely as the character does in a two-dimensional comic book, down to the very stances and poses he adopts. It is not a strictly realistic interpretation of gravity and weight, as many expected, but rather an artistic expression of the comic book ethos, accomplished via computer. This was not a fact immediately obvious until the film was released on DVD and could be slowed down, reversed and frozen, shot for shot, frame for frame. But a comparison with the Spider-Man of the comics reveals a concerted effort to mimic the four-color, individual frames of the comic hero.

Spider-Man's flight through the skies of Manhattan, the coda of Raimi's *Spider-Man*, is deft in its explicit referencing of the movements of the character on the page. As though an invisible camera is documenting his flight, we see Spidey's sky dance from a variety of angles and distances, and if the film is paused, any single pose could be straight out of the comics, particularly those of the early 1970s.

The CGI effects accomplish another task, recording and expressing Peter's development. The chase involving the carjacker depicts a Parker still uncomfortable with his abilities, flying wildly from side-to-side, barely controlled. When compared with the graceful, almost ballet-like movements seen in the coda, a character point is established. Peter has learned to harness his powers, bringing with them that great responsibility he speaks about. It's fine use of a new technology and evidence that Raimi understands that even without a "camera" as it were, visuals can express *personality*.

Spider-Man is remarkable because it is a breath of fresh air in a genre on life-support. For thirty years the superhero genre in film and TV has attempted to recover from the camp *Batman*, which comic book fans felt mocked their hero. Starting with Burton's *Batman* in 1989, the shift has been too far in the opposite direction. The *Batman* films, *Spawn*, *The Crow* and now *Daredevil* are dark and gloomy, but for no real reason other than to establish that they are *serious*. These films focus on revenge, an ugly quality of humanity, as the motive behind a superhero's birth and mission. And the villains always take over the pictures, leaving the hero, like Clooney's Batman, a guest star in his own franchise.

The *Spider-Man* approach is determinedly different. It is not hatred and revenge that inspires Parker, it is love for M.J. and guilt regarding Ben, as well his sense of responsibility. The Green Goblin is not just a giggling maniac like other villains, he is a father figure who feels rejection from the boy he loved. And, *my god*, there is actually sunlight in this film, not just never-ending night and blackness. Spider-Man need not live in a warped world of poverty, freaks and evil to function as a hero. He needn't be a rich man or a being from another world, he just needs to be ... *responsible*. What a concept!

Spider-Man does not rely on unexplained plot devices to succeed. Burton's *Batman* is a pretty decent superhero film, but there were real failures in it too. For instance, near the film's end, Batman strafed the Joker with the Batplane, firing a million or so bullets at the maniac. Not one of the bullets struck the guy, not even a glancing blow. Then the Joker pulled out a long-barreled pistol, fired once, and brought down the speeding Batplane with a single shot. Even Thell Reed couldn't manage that. Some fans may insist this occurred because the Joker had his lucky deck of cards on him, but it is really a contrivance that supports a plot necessity, getting Batman on the ground so he can meet Joker face-to-face. *Spider-Man* doesn't show its plot strings to that degree and is more believable because of it.

When so many of our heroes are angst ridden and tortured by their pasts, twisted by revenge and consumed with anger, it is a relief to meet a hero who dwells in sunlight. Who admits feeling love and a connection to the people in his life, and actually seems to enjoy, at least sometimes, the fact that he has uncommon abilities.

Long live Spidey. He's the superhero template for the twenty-first century.

SPIDER-MAN 2 (2004)

A.K.A. THE AMAZING SPIDER-MAN

BY MAY 6, 2002, A SPIDER-MAN SEQUEL was a done deal, the original having already shattered box office records. It was announced soon after that weekend (like, *hours...*) that director Raimi would return to helm the follow-up, the first back-to-back sequel in his two-decade-long career (*Crimewave,* one must remember, separated *The Evil Dead* and its sequel). A few other facts were also established: producer Laura Ziskin, Tobey Maguire, and Kirsten Dunst would return to the fold, and the highly-anticipated sequel would reserve a release date in the first weekend of May, 2004.

As 2002 became 2003, gossip began circulating that things were not so certain as early announcements made seem. By March 27, 2003, *Entertainment Weekly* reported that re-shoots and delays on the Tobey Maguire horse-racing picture *Seabiscuit* had pushed back shooting on the Spider sequel, landing *The Amazing Spider-Man* in theaters late, come July 2, 2004.[1]

Then, like some Marvel Comics mutant, the story morphed again. Word on the street indicated that Maguire had injured his back on *Seabiscuit,* and the herniated disc in his back was causing pain. It was widely speculated that he might be forced to surrender the Spider-Man role, unable to perform the rigorous stunt work.

But the story wasn't done shape-shifting. By May, the press reported that Maguire was fired from the sequel after failing to report for a new full-body scanning process required for the digital effects of *The Amazing Spider-Man*.[2] Stories intimated that doe-eyed Jake Gyllenhall, Donnie Darko himself, was in line to replace Maguire. But apparently at the urging of a studio boss that also happened to be his girlfriend's father, Maguire had second thoughts, apologized to Raimi for dereliction of duty and returned to the fold. Or so went the reports.

"It's not true that I was fired," Maguire explained in late July, months into principal photography. "Basically, we had some concerns, as did the studio, because the level of stunts is so much greater on the second picture than the first, and we both wanted to make sure I could do it."[3] According to Maguire, the back injury was a pre-existing condition that troubled him for some time and had nothing to do with *Seabiscuit*. Complicating matters, the actor, who slimmed down to play the jockey in the horse movie had to buff up again for *The Amazing Spider-Man* in very little time.[4]

Such behind-the-scenes drama illustrates the hunger fans felt for news on the sequel. But beyond this gossip, few details were known about the $200 million sequel. Pulitzer prize–winning author Michael Chabon was retained to write the screenplay, but then, consequent reports indicated it was actually the duo of Alfred Gough and Miles Millar, from the WB's young Superman series *Smallville*, who would be penning. Then David Koepp apparently returned to write the first draft, with Gough and Millar waiting in the wings to polish it.[5] The story itself revolves around two nefarious villains — Dr. Octopus, a rogue scientist with mechanical tentacles, and Dr. Connors, the Lizard and Peter Parker's former employer.[6]

Cast as Doc Ock, an ex-atomic researcher, was veteran performer Alfred Molina of *Species* (1995), *Boogie Nights* (1997), *Magnolia* (1999) and *Frida* (2002). Early rumors hinted that Bruce Campbell might play the Lizard, but that story was debunked, and Campbell instead appears in a cameo as a movie theater usher. Also cast, as Parker's rival for M.J.'s affection, was young actor Daniel Gillies.[7]

As one might expect from Raimi, a few familiar hands appear in the new film, including actor Brent Briscoe. "I'm getting ready to do *Spider-Man 2* for him," he said in spring 2003. "I can tell you what I'm playing. They won't send me a script. They're going to send me my scene the week before. I'm playing a homeless guy who finds Spider-Man's suit in a dumpster. And once I find it, I take it to the newspaper guy, who is played by that great actor J.K. Simmons.

"Right now, I'm growing a beard to play this part," Briscoe laughs. "It's not until July, and I wouldn't do that for many people. But for Sam Raimi, I want it to be right."

Cliff Robertson, the late Uncle Ben himself, would be returning, even though his character died in the previous film. In fact, Robertson had just finished shooting when he was interviewed for this book. He was surprised, but happy to get the call from Raimi to re-enlist. And the pitch? "They said, 'Well, you know, Alec Guinness [in *Star Wars*] was resurrected. And we know Jesus was resurrected. How about you? Why not Cliff?' And I said, 'What do you mean?' And he [Raimi] said, 'Even though you died, we are sufficiently impressed that we might resurrect you,' and they subsequently did. So I just finished it a week ago."

When asked to reveal the nature of Ben's role in the sequel, Robertson clams up. "I couldn't do that, John," he says. "I would betray my good friend."

All right. I had to try.

One thing that *can* be reported is that, if there is to be another sequel, a *Spider-Man 3*, Robertson might return for another encore. "When we finished the other night, Sam came out and locked his arm around my head and he was very, very happy with the scene with Tobey and myself," Robertson reveals. "And then he said, 'I have to tell you now, good friend, when there is a *Spider-Man 3*, you are going to do it.' So that isn't for two years, because *Spider-Man 2* will not be released until July 2004."

The Amazing Spider-Man began shooting in New York on April 12, 2003, and a scene involving Peter Parker on a moped was lensed in Greenwich Village.[8] There were Parker sightings elsewhere, but the biggest news about the sequel was unveiled at the San Diego Comic-Con on the weekend of July 20, 2003. Raimi, an invited guest, was "stuck in bed on doctor's orders with a fever of over 100 degrees,"[9] leaving Ziskin and Avi Arad to introduce the first footage of Molina as Doctor Octopus.

The clip revealed Doc Ock's origin, as four mechanical and seemingly sentient tentacles fused to his spin. Garbed in a green trench coat and decked out with sunglasses, the evil Doctor made a splash at the Con, though a few fans complained he looked like something out of *The Matrix*.

As the months ticked closer to the film's June 30, 2004 release, primary filming completed in New York, Chicago and Los Angeles. The movie's trailer (under the title *Spider-Man 2*) was teased on the World Wide Web on December 15 through the auspices of Sony pictures, and lucky audiences finally got a good look at the film's new villain. One widely-published production still revealed a trapped Spider-Man, pinioned in the vise of Doc Ock's tentacles.

Meanwhile, Marvel Studios' Kevin Feige reported to the *Comics*

Continuum Web site that — in his opinion — the sequel would top the original in terms of quality, effects, action and romance.[10] As of this writing, details of the plot still remained sketchy, though various sites had reported rumors that comic book characters, including the doomed Gwen Stacy and even Man-Wolf, might make cameos.

This much is known (perhaps...): The film's story occurs two years after the events of *Spider-Man* and finds Peter under considerable pressure from friends, lovers and enemies alike. His friend, Harry is growing more disenfranchised with Spider-Man, and there are tensions in his relationship with Mary Jane. As before, the film reportedly stays true to Stan Lee's overarching idea of a young man "coming of age" and learning to embrace responsibility.

Another (quickly quashed) rumor about *Spider-Man 2* suggested that Raimi conducted some major re-shoots as 2003 became 2004, but it was soon learned that the additional shooting was simply to complete some of the complex effects work. The director went on the record with Mike Cotton and *Wizard Magazine* in November 2003, describing the fact that there were more "time constraints"[11] on the sequel than the original, which equates to a tougher go for the director, and a more hectic pace.

In early March 2004, more news arrived about Spider-Man movies, but oddly not about part 2, but part 3. *Variety's* Nicole LaPorte broke the news in *Variety* that *Spider-Man 3* was already in development (according to Marvel's Avi Arad) and that director Sam Raimi was already committed to the project.[12] As was Tobey Maguire. A 2007 release date is scheduled.

All the precise details regarding the web slinger's second cinematic adventure would become clear only on the film's release date, and that was always the intent of the film's stalwart director, who, as usual, had the audience's best interests at heart.

"We're trying to keep as many elements of the story as secret as possible because we really want to surprise the audience," Raimi revealed on the Internet prior to the release of *Spider-Man 2*. "I want to entertain them on the day [it opens]. I want them to come in and see the movie and not really know anything about it."[13]

Sounds like the same old Sam Raimi, doesn't it?

RAIMI RELATED

Though Sam Raimi is most widely hailed as a director of features and sometimes a screenwriter, too, his interests extend to the realms of acting and producing. This chapter is a brief survey of the *other* productions Raimi has graced throughout his career.

ACTING RAIMI

It would probably be correct to assert that Raimi began his acting career before he reached puberty, appearing in a number of his own early super 8mm films, doing Stooges schtick and so forth. But during his professional career, Raimi has also made appearances in major films.

An interested fan can find Raimi beside friend Joel Coen in a cameo during 1985's Chevy Chase movie, *Spies Like Us.* Raimi is also a recurring figure in the oeuvre of the Coen Brothers. He shows up in *Miller's Crossing*, wherein he plays a giggling hitman, and *The Hudsucker Proxy* too.

Raimi teamed with fellow horror icons Wes Craven, David Naughton (*An*

American Werewolf in London [1981]), John Agar (*Revenge of the Creature* [1955]) and Tobe Hooper in John Carpenter's 1993 Showtime E.C. Comics-style anthology, *Body Bags*. Raimi appeared with Craven in the first of three stories, a vignette called "The Gas Station" concerning night attendant Alex Datcher working through her first night on the job at an isolated filling station. Datcher encounters a serial killer (a foregone conclusion, since the gas station is located outside of a town called Haddonfield...), and Raimi played one of many corpses.

Outside the realm of cameos, Raimi had a more substantial role in Josh Becker's *Thou Shall Not Kill... Except*, also known in some quarters as *Stryker's War*. "Josh and Scott [Spiegel] had an office down the hall from Bruce and Rob [at Renaissance Pictures]," composer Joe LoDuca remembers, "and they put together their first movie."

"I think the idea is that it was *Platoon* versus the Manson family. There were military aspects to it," LoDuca explains. "There were some very weird moments with the Sam Raimi character." To wit, Raimi played the long-haired leader of a cult, the Charles Manson figure in a chilling and effectively psycho performance.

It was in 1993, however, that Raimi gave his most substantial and oft-mentioned performance. He did so in a comedy called *Indian Summer*, directed by friend Mike Binder (*Blankman* [1994] and *Londinium* [2001]). The ad-line described the picture's premise well: "A comedy about eight friends who return to the best summer of their lives." The film was an autobiographical piece for Binder because during childhood he attended a summer camp in Ontario's Algonquin Park called Camp Tamakwa, along with his friend Sam Raimi. The film concerns a reunion of former campers from the year 1972, played by Bill Paxton, Matt Craven, Diane Lane, Elizabeth Perkins, Kevin Pollak, Vincent Spano and Julie Warner. The adult campers face all manner of midlife problems, including adultery, grief, loneliness, and financial ruin, but find companionship and a sense of resolution at the tranquil camp. One obsession in the film is pulling so-called shreks, practical jokes, on fellow campers.

One of the campers in the film is obsessed with a mural painted on a cabin wall, a mural of Spider-Man. Underneath the rendering of the Marvel hero is a legend that reads "the superheroes of Tamakwa, 1972," and one is instantly reminded of Sam Raimi's personal history and childhood affection for the superhero, including the mural he had in his bedroom.

Beyond that historical footnote, *Indian Summer* remains valuable because it highlights Raimi's slapstick performance as a slow-witted maintenance man named Stick Coder. Without putting too fine a point on it, Raimi gets abused in this film the way he heaps abuse on Bruce Campbell in his own directorial work. Early on, he falls out of a boat while trying to unload luggage. Later, Alan Arkin punches him in the face — twice — during a boxing demonstration. Before the film is done, Raimi dances in most bizarre fashion with one of the film's attractive young actresses, Kimberly Williams, and has the honor of being the only performer on-screen as the end credits roll, apparently gazing at a moose.

Raimi's performance in *Indian Summer* is an accomplished physical one, often accompanied by the song "Hello Muddah, Hello Faddah." The humor is dependent largely on split-second timing, and Raimi pulls it off, particularly the balancing act on the boat. Alas, some don't agree with this perception, including Raimi's wife, Gillian. "My wife had forbidden me to act after seeing that performance," Raimi told journalist Tim Lammers. "She's afraid I'll hurt others with that acting."[1]

In addition to William Mesa's impressive work in the effects arena, the artist is also a successful director. One of his productions, the amusing *Galaxis* (originally *Terminal Force* [1995]), cast Raimi as a villain. "It was funny directing Sam Raimi," Mesa considers. "I told him he was going to be a weasly bad guy, and that we were going to end up torturing him like he tortured us all these other times. 'Whatever I can do to make the suit fit a little too tight and keep you in it, so you can't go to the bathroom, and have to say your lines over and over again....'"

And Raimi's reply? "He said, 'I knew you'd get me...'

"I miss working with Sam," Mesa says. "I ran into Sam when I was doing *Collateral Damage*. They were shooting some of *Spider-Man* on the Warner Brothers backlot and sets there, so I heard he was over there and went over to see him. Sam does these different announcements on the set, so he announced me as 'William Mesa — visual effects extraordinaire!'"

PRODUCING RAIMI

Collaborating with Rob Tapert at Renaissance Pictures, Raimi served as executive producer on a number of films, direct-to-video productions, and television series. He is widely credited with bringing John Woo to the United States for that director's first American film, 1993's *Hard Target*, by author Chuck Pfarrer and starring Lance Henriksen, Yancy Butler and Jean-Claude Van Damme. Though that film met with a studio interference, it has a cult following today and launched Woo on his Hollywood path, which eventually led the Hong Kong director to high-profile projects such as *Broken Arrow* (1996) and *Face/Off* (1997).

In 1994, Raimi executive-produced the Jean-Claude Van Damme sci-fi thriller *Timecop* and revived a hero from his own history, the amazing Darkman. *Darkman II: The Return of Durant* went straight to video; the engaging sequel sees Westlake, played by Arnold Vosloo, face off against evil Robert G. Durant (Larry Drake) for a second go round. Durant has been in a coma for 878 days(!) and seeks revenge against the man he blames for his condition. Exploiting a scientist, Dr. Brinkman, Durant utilizes a death-ray to battle the superhero, who in the years since the first film has set up a laboratory at an abandoned subway station.

1996's *Die Darkman Die* (a title that continues the horror tradition begun by *Scream, Blacula Scream*) focuses on the personal, intimate side of the disenfranchised hero. In this film, *Darkman* imitates a married gangster played by Jeff Fahey and finds that the normality of that life with a wife and child is too tempting. The film spotlights Beauty and the Beast as a metaphor to expose Westlake's more poignant, lonely side, and the sequel is filled with funny quips like Darlanne Fluegel's one-liner: "Life's a bitch, and so am I!"

On television, Renaissance Pictures has made a killing, producing nearly a decade of remarkable series. In 1994, *M.A.N.T.I.S.* aired on Fox, concerning an African American superhero played by Carl Lumbly. Lumbly's character, Dr. Miles Hawkins, is crippled and confined to a wheelchair, but as the costumed M.A.N.T.I.S. he can smash criminals thanks to a special suit.

Production of *M.A.N.T.I.S.* ran anything but smoothly, and there were extensive cast and tone changes after the pilot. For one thing, Fox ditched most of the African American cast, thereby "downplaying race."[2] "It was a horrible battle and eventually we were paid off and left," Rob Tapert reported.[3] "I did the pilot for *M.A.N.T.I.S.*," adds composer Joe LoDuca, "but I think Renaissance was not involved after the pilot. That was my recollection."

Renaissance's 1993 motion picture *Army of Darkness*, which sent a wisecracking modern man (Bruce Campbell) back in time also formed the creative gestalt for a series of TV initiatives. *Hercules: The Legendary Journeys* began as a series of TV movies in a syndicated package called "Action Pack," but quickly became a popular series starring Kevin Sorbo as the demi-god. "*Hercules* got the ball rolling," LoDuca recalls of Renaissance's total immersion in syndicated television production in the nineties. "It was definitely the cornerstone of that production run. I think the important thing to note with *Hercules* ... was at that point, my principal collaborator was Rob Tapert. He certainly was, as time went on, more and more conceptually involved with the scripts and the stories. As time went on, I think he was the creator. The musicals that we did in the *Xena* run were his idea."

Filmed in New Zealand, the humorous action series *Hercules* spawned two spin-offs, the aforementioned *Xena: Warrior Princess* starring Lucy Lawless and the short-lived *Young Hercules* (1998). This tremendous amount of work resulted in some *really* busy folks, including *Evil Dead 2*'s animator Doug Beswick, who was hired through visual effects supervisor Kevin O'Neill to work as a 3-D animator on the series. He helped design and animate some of Herc's and Xena's trademark monster foes. "I had fun on the skeletons," Beswick remembers of one show. "It was an homage to Harryhausen, to *Jason and the Argonauts*, so we had a lot of fun with that. That was very early on. We did so many shows."

"You'd work out your week so you weren't necessarily working on three shows at the same time," LoDuca describes his busy schedule scoring Renaissance fantasy programming. "One of the things I introduced early on was a talented music editor to collaborate with, so I'm not writing every minute of every show over again every week. Generally, we created an orchestral library. In other words, we'd have big-budget moments that we could use again and again."

Filled with good humor, gorgeous locations, *Jason and the Argonaut*–style effects, and involving stories, *Hercules* and *Xena* are part of the science-fiction/fantasy/horror boom of the mid-to-late 1990s, the new "golden age" that includes *The X-Files*, *Deep Space Nine*, *Babylon 5* and *Buffy the Vampire Slayer*. Available now on DVD, these two series will likely have great staying power not only because of fine production values and likable stars, but because of good stories and that less-than-serious sense of fun that dominates so many episodes.

In 2000, two further series emerged from Renaissance's stable, the Bruce Campbell spy series set in the nineteenth century, *Jack of All Trades*, and the futuristic comedy-adventure, *Cleopatra 2525* starring Victoria Pratt and Gina Torres.

There remains another Renaissance Pictures television series worthy of note. It only lasted one season, but has accumulated devoted followers, 1995's late and lamented *American Gothic*. The drama aired on CBS for one season, and concerned a small Southern town named Trinity where the Sheriff, Lucas Buck, was in league with the Devil, if not the Devil himself. One of the town's denizens was a ghost. Another was a little boy of questionable and perhaps dangerous heritage. A soap opera created by Shaun Cassidy, *American Gothic* was a seriously creepy venture.

"It was unusual and original, and a great part," Gary Cole recollects. "It wasn't any kind of bandwagon show. It wasn't a re-creation of whatever was popular at the time. It had its own flavor, and I loved everything about it."

Typical of the series' dark humor, the pilot episode featured a moment in which Lucas Buck whistled the theme to *The Andy Griffith Show*. "That was my favorite moment in the script," Cole acknowledges. "So often you see that in scripts, a piece of music or something, and then they can never afford to buy it, so when I met Shaun, I said, 'Are you really going to be able to use this theme?' And he said, 'Oh yeah, we've cleared it.'"

Raimi, who supervised post-production on the series, explained the series' premise in *Shivers* magazine:

> What we're doing is telling a story in a real town with very real characters. And in this setting, we see elements of the supernatural. We're not doing ghost stories or weird occult-type movies ... It's a story of good and evil...and evil is embodied in this very attractive, sexy, and appealing individual played by Gary Cole...[4]

Cole's affable and charming performance as Sheriff Buck was one of television's underrated gems. "You make the choice that the material is laying out the premise and the information that, yes, this guy is in fact an arm of evil and can be destructive," Cole describes. "Therefore, you get out of the way of that and don't play that at all. You let the writing take care of that. If you play the character trying to be dark and menacing to people, it's not as interesting and not as menacing. It's much more disturbing to see someone smiling and patting people on the back, knowing that he can destroy them at any moment with a smile on his face.

"Most of the character or dialogue was with Shaun," Cole notes. "He was the source of it, so he gave me a great note. It said, 'Nothing is a problem for this guy. Anytime you feel like he should be panicking, remember that nothing rattles him.' That was a good note, and he wrote the character that way; he helped me a lot."

"*American Gothic* was a personal favorite," LoDuca reveals. "I think what made it a project that I really enjoyed was the Southern locale, the Southern bad guy, and the fact that he was also the Devil. That enabled me to put certain things in the score that I could play myself. I played a lot of guitar. I played harmonica for Lucas Buck, and included these sinister textures.

"I think Shaun, in an early meeting, set the template of putting horror against the Christian elements," LoDuca considers, remembering that he worked closely with Raimi on spotting the shows. "Sam, you know, is quite musical. He understands music and how it works. He often makes suggestions, but he suggests very subtly. He pays attention. You need to get to know Sam to understand the signals. In my dealings with him, he'll always say things like, 'Your music is really going to help this scene.' The fact that he says 'your music' empowers you. Very often as a film composer, you're at the behest of another person, sometimes many, and the fact that he always reminds you that you're the one doing this is important."

Rolling Stone noted that *American Gothic* benefited from a fine cast, and that its players threw themselves into the proceedings as if it were the inspired work of collaboration "between Tennessee Williams and Stephen King,"[5] but even positive notices did not help the series stay alive. CBS played episodes out of sequence, even though the program was a serial, and dropped shows from the schedule all together, making the series difficult to follow. Despite early cancellation, the show boasts an avid cult following, even years later.

"I was walking down the street the other day," Gary Cole recounts, "and a woman driving a UPS truck just stopped the truck and said, 'Are you Lucas Buck?' And I said, 'Yes, Ma'am, I am.' She was one of those loyal fans. We didn't have a lot, but they were loyal."

FUTURE RAIMI

Shortly after the release of *Spider-Man*, Raimi and partner Tapert announced their plan to team with a German moviemaking organization, Senator Entertainment, to create a new genre label. For the first time in years, Raimi and Tapert would again dedicate themselves to low-budget horror, this time with Senator providing financing.

"With so much talent out there who we would love to work with, it's very satisfying to be in the business of bringing moviegoing thrills to mainstream audiences," Raimi told *Variety*. "Rob and I are committed to creating a business that continues to find new fans around the world."[6]

Though it is unlikely that Raimi would direct features under the new label, he and Tapert intend to produce the next generation of *Evil Dead*–style, low-budget horror initiatives. Among the films they have considered sponsoring are *30 Days of Night*, a vampire movie set in an Alaskan town that experiences around-the-clock darkness for a month.[7] Also in the offing is *The Grudge*, a remake of a popular Japanese horror film called *Ju-On*, to be directed by Takashi Shimizu.[8] Sarah Michelle Gellar (*Buffy the Vampire Slayer* [1997-2002]) and Jason Behr (*Roswell* [1999-2001]) have been cast as the leads in a film scheduled to shoot in Tokyo in January/February 2004, and which concerns a curse that spreads person-to-person like a disease. Others in the cast include *Independence Day's* (1996) Bill Pullman and Clea Duvall, fresh from her stint on HBO's Carnivale (2003). Already in production is a horror movie called *Boogeyman* that focuses on an adult reliving childhood fears. Recently, Tapert's wife, Lucy Lawless joined that cast.

On the television front, if fans are very lucky, Shaun Cassidy and Raimi may re-team on a new genre series pilot, a modern take on *Dr. Jekyll and Mr. Hyde*. "The show will be suspenseful ... and also strangely romantic,"[9] Shaun Cassidy noted in an interview for *Daily Variety*.

With so many projects on the offing, it is likely that well after *Spider-Man 2* hits theaters, fans can look forward to Raimi's name appearing on screens both large and small.

CONCLUSION

FOR LOVE OF THE GAME: A CONCLUSION TO THE FILMS OF SAM RAIMI

"HOW CAN YOU GO FROM THE SUBURBS of Detroit — Birmingham, Michigan — to being one of the most exciting directors around?" asks Raimi's old teacher, Verne Nobles. "Well it's real simple. You believe you can do it, and you believe it so much that nothing stands in your way. You learn and you study."

That prescription for success very much represents the journey of filmmaker Sam Raimi and his unique movies. Raimi practiced making his own films as a kid, applied that long period of practice in the profession, and now stands at the top of his class as one of Hollywood's most admired talents.

In the interest of total disclosure, a more appropriate title for this text might have been *For Love of the Game: The Films of Sam Raimi* because one suspects that love is the motivating factor behind the director's choice of careers. His studied homages to everything from *Jason and the Argonauts* to *The Treasure of the Sierra Madre* and the Three Stooges establish not merely the artist's knowledge of film history, but his appreciation for it.

Some reviewers may study the twenty-year span of Raimi's career and conclude that his films have somehow become less stylish, less dazzling.

That Hollywood has blunted his edge. This is a questionable assertion at best, considering the flourishes evident in *Spider-Man*. As Tom Sullivan, his makeup director from *Evil Dead* points out, *Spider-Man* is his favorite Raimi film, in part because of the adjustments Raimi has made to his distinctive style.

"He had been making super 8mm sound movies for years before I met him," Sullivan reminds us. "He had a well-rounded knowledge of films and developed a repertoire of director's schtick that he could work into his movies. That's changed today. Now he has a full cinematic vocabulary and presents full characters with depth. A far cry from the Three Stooges influence."

Indeed, the trajectory of Raimi's career reveals an entertainer who has learned the most valuable secret in the industry: that the camera is but *one* arrow in a director's quiver. Solid, human characterization (*Spider-Man*) and emotional tales about human nature and relationships (*A Simple Plan*, *The Gift*) are surely others. The Raimi of 2003 is the gentleman who not only expresses his themes with precisely the right camera angle at the right moment, but makes the audience *feel* for his characters and identify with their plights. An "apprentice to suspense" in his own words, yes. An entertainer, definitely. But also, like his idol John Huston, a director who can appreciate subtlety.

And even if his films are less overtly flashy today, Raimi boasts the gift that many of today's directors lack: the ability to jolt and surprise an audience with the most unusual of visuals. "He's in a realistic world right now of making movies for a lot of money," Nobles considers. "So he must behave himself. But that child within him, if you want to call it a child, or that genius within him that was the spark that started everything, cannot be contained. It must be let out, and when it is, it's wonderful. It comes out and you go, 'Oh my God, there it is!' You know it right away."

With *Spider-Man 2* bound for theaters and more Raimi films planned, contemporary audiences can look ahead to that moment of jaw-dropping recognition again and again.

And hopefully, *Evil Dead 4*...

APPENDIX ONE

THE SAM RAIMI MOVIEMAKING LEXICON

Raimi's films, especially his early ones, share a unique lingo. Here, those who worked behind-the-scenes explain, in their own words, the singular language of Raimi cinema.

BLANK-O-CAM: "We invented a lot of different ways to move the camera for *Evil Dead*," notes Tim Philo, photography and lighting expert on *Evil Dead*. "It's not always obvious that something weird is going on, but a blank-o-cam shot is this: you lay a blanket on the ground and the cameraman lays down facing forward (with the camera facing forward) and then gets carried, pall-bearer style, by six people." At that point, the camera would then track a character. Blank-o-cam is often employed to track somebody's feet from behind.

THE CLASSIC: Raimi's beloved automobile, that cream-colored 1973 Oldsmobile Delta 88, is often referred to in loving terms as "the Classic" by the director. The car has appeared in more Raimi films than just about any actor. It drove Ash to the cabin of the damned in *The Evil Dead*, *Evil Dead 2*, and *Army of Darkness*. It hosted a corpse in *Crimewave* and Peyton Westlake, *Darkman* himself, bounced off its hood. Parked on a snow-bound street in *A Simple Plan*, the car is rumored to have appeared (in a window reflection) in the Western *The Quick and the Dead*. And though its performance was edited out of *For Love of the Game*, the Classic experienced a career resurgence of late, co-starring with Cate Blanchett as Annie Wilson's in-need-of-repair auto in *The Gift*. The Classic was Uncle Ben's wheels in *Spider-Man* and the center of an intense chase.

"It's his signature," Cliff Robertson notes of the Classic, with whom he shared an important scene. He was unaware of its importance until "that yellow Oldsmobile appeared on the set. I was affixed to it in one scene, and I died in front of it at the Public Library.

"It will be interesting to see how he's going to put it in a futuristic movie," Robertson muses. "I'm sure he'll find a way, being the inventive creative man that he is."

COMMENCE CAPTURE: "We've gotten so entrenched in digital sequences on this film [*Spider-Man*] that Sam has created a whole new vocabulary for us," director of photography Don Burgess reported in *American Cinematographer*. "We don't roll cameras anymore, we *commence capture*."[1]

ELLIE-VATOR: A see-saw-like device used to levitate the performers playing Deadites in *Evil Dead* and *Evil Dead 2*. Used specifically for shots in which the Deadite is viewed from the front in full-shot, because the see-saw is attached to the performer's back (and usually positioned through a window). It is therefore obscured by the ghoul and hence invisible to the camera. Named after *Evil Dead*'s Ellen Sandweiss. "They just kind of made a makeshift harness and had this telephone pole in my back," Sandweiss notes of her namesake. "It was uncomfortable, but not a big deal."

FAKE SHEMPING: "Shemp was one of the Three Stooges and Shemp died after they had made three-fourths of a movie, but there were some scenes he had to be in, or they couldn't complete the movie," Phil Gillis explains. "So they got some people, who always had their backs to the camera, to play in those scenes. And if you look at *Evil Dead*'s credits, they credit me with being Fake Shemp One or Two. They had about six fake Shemps." For the record, Shemp replaced Curly in the Three Stooges team when a stroke forced Curly's retirement. Shemp himself died of a heart attack in 1955.

THE LATEX POINT: According to makeup artist Tom Sullivan, the Latex Point occurs when an actor has had "rubber pieces of makeup glued on your face so long you want to scream. But you can't because you're on the middle of making a movie and you said you'd finish it without complaining and the glue is eating into your head. 'Oh, the pain! Get it off!'" See: Bruce Campbell in *Within the Woods*.

MICKEY MOUSING: According to composer Joe LoDuca, this term "usually refers to animation scoring, where every little moment is choreographed." In the original *Evil Dead*, a certain amount of this Mickey Mousing occurred in the music. "In my own mind and probably in Sam's, I don't know that we were sophisticated enough in the process to say that this is what a sound effect is supposed to do, and this is what the music is supposed to do," remembers LoDuca. "We wanted violent reactions, so we would purposefully gang up on the action. It's really just more of a question of whether you are going to score to the point where a subtle hand gesture is drawn out [highlighted] in the music. At this point, we've probably evolved beyond that."

MOTION CONTROL: Randy Ser explains this effects technique, used in *Darkman* as well as *Evil Dead 2*. "Motion control is a camera rig where you make the camera move and the computer memorizes that move. It's a dolly track. What you have to do is multiple passes of the same shot." Examples: The revolving door shot in *Darkman*; the headless Linda dance in *Evil Dead 2*.

SAM-O-CAM: A mechanical camera rig used to torture Bruce Campbell in *Evil Dead 2*. Sort of a giant cross, to which the actor was bolted and then spun — for several takes. Used in conjunction with an undercranked camera. See the famous shot following Bruce Campbell's exit from the cabin.

SCARE SLASHES: "A little diagonal rip of light on anything you want to highlight" is a scare slash according to Tim Philo. It's also a term Philo first heard from Raimi during his interview to shoot *Evil Dead*. "Sam said, after he looked at some of the things I'd shot and directed at college, 'Well, you obviously understand lighting well enough to understand when I say I want a scare slash on the wall.' And I said, 'Yeah, okay.'"

Example? "If you look at the cabin, in the first bedroom off the living room, there were scare slashes on every surface, just a little crack of light on everything. That's what we called that, or Sam just made up the term."

SHAKY CAM: This camera rig consists of a "twenty-two inch long board with a camera mounted in the center of it," according to Philo. "It's just a two-by-four with a hole drilled up through the center to mount the camera, and you're using your two arms as stabilizing points. If you fall or you get off balance, you might smack something." For a time, the shaky cam became a heavily utilized tool in Hollywood. "I was working with Barry Sonnenfeld on a shoot a few years after *Evil Dead* and he said, 'Tim Philo! Hey, let's do a Tim Philo rig!'"

TWO-BY-FOUR: The single most essential, all-purpose, item. A necessity on any film project. Good for track-building, window punching, camera mounting and other on-the-fly requirements.

VAS-O-CAM: A variation of the shaky cam. "Basically, we just took the board of the shaky cam and mounted the camera to it," explains Philo. "We didn't have a real dolly and sometimes we were trying to do a moving shot on an uneven terrain, or up in the rafters of the cabin, or flat on the floor. We had a track made of two-by-fours. There was one two-by-four with the camera mounted on it, which fit into this track with duct tape. Then we smeared vaseline all over it, so the two-by-four with the camera would fit into this track and slide along."

APPENDIX TWO

YOU KNOW YOU'RE IN A SAM RAIMI FILM WHEN YOU SEE...

TED RAIMI

Apparently, Sam Raimi loves to torture his younger brother Ted almost as much as he loves to tourture Bruce Campbell. This brotherly love has extended to cameos in many of Raimi's films, including:

1. *The Evil Dead* (Fake Shemp)
2. *Crimewave* (Waiter)
3. *The Evil Dead 2* (Deadite Henrietta)
4. *Darkman* (Rick)
5. *Army of Darkness* (Cowardly Warrior)
6. *For Love of the Game* (Gallery Doorman)
7. *Spider-Man* (Hoffman)

BRUCE CAMPBELL

The actor with the chin that launched a thousand ships appears in many Raimi films including:

1. *The Evil Dead* (Ash)
2. *Crimewave* (The Heel, Renaldo)
3. *Evil Dead 2* (Ash)
4. *Darkman* (Climactic Shemp)
5. *Army of Darkness* (Ash)
6. *The Quick and the Dead* (Wedding Shemp; cut from picture)
7. *Spider-Man* (Ring Announcer)
8. *Spider-Man 2* (Movie Theater Usher)

J.K. SIMMONS

This experienced character actor is making a name for himself by appearing as part of Raimi's repertory company:

1. *For Love of the Game* (Frank Perry)
2. *The Gift* (Sheriff Pearl Johnson)
3. *Spider-Man* (J. Jonah Jameson)
4. *Spider-Man 2* (J. Jonah Jameson)

THE CLASSIC

Raimi's beloved car appears on-screen in the following films:

1. *The Evil Dead*
2. *Crimewave*
3. *Evil Dead 2*
4. *Darkman*
5. *Army of Darkness*
6. *A Simple Plan*
7. *The Gift*
8. *Spider-Man*

AN EARLY MIST/FOG

Smoky atmospherics — mist and fog — are the preferred Raimi image to begin a movie. Shots of billowing smoke and mist appear, sometimes very briefly, in the opening five minutes of the following films:

1. *The Evil Dead* (Mist over a swamp)
2. *Crimewave* (A foggy sky, with mist half-covering the moon)
3. *Evil Dead 2* (A fast moving smoke billows in the foreground; the background is black.)
4. *Darkman* (Gray/white mist is one of the opticals used as the opening credits begin; appears to be slow-motion mist/split-screen mist.)
5. *The Gift* (A blanket of fog blows over a Southern swamp.)
6. *Spider-Man* (Oh so briefly, there is a view of foggy smoke as the opening credits roll.)

A REFERENCE TO WES CRAVEN

Horror Maestro Wes Craven and Sam Raimi have had an interesting back-and-forth relationship. Raimi placed a torn poster of Craven's 1977 opus, *The Hills Have Eyes*, in the cabin basement in the *The Evil Dead*. In Craven's 1984 film, *A Nightmare on Elm Street*, heroine Heather Langenkamp watches *The Evil Dead* on a television in her bedroom, and in the end credits, Wes Craven offers a "special thanks" to Sam Raimi. Reportedly, Raimi returned the favor by including a shot of Freddy's trademark glove somewhere in the work-shed scene of *Evil Dead 2*.

The two men also appear in *John Carpenter Presents Body Bags* in cameo roles, Raimi as a corpse and Craven as the "Pasty Faced Man." Coincidentally, the two artists met up in New York in 1998, when they were each shooting a non-horror film. Raimi was in the city to shoot *For Love of the Game* and Craven to lense *Music of the Heart*.

Peter Deming, cinematographer of *Evil Dead 2*, also shot *Music of the Heart*. "The interesting thing is that we would frequently, like two or three times a week, run into each other at dailies," he remembers. "Either Sam would be coming out, or we'd be inside, and Sam would be waiting. It was pretty funny. They had a good laugh."

A MONTAGE OF OVERLAPPING, SUPERIMPOSED IMAGES

1. *Darkman:* As Darkman attempts to re-create his artificial skin formula, the film cuts to a montage of his work, with beakers, test tubes, and formulae superimposed over images of the scientist's labor.
2. *The Quick and the Dead:* Midway through the gunfight competition, the film cuts to a montage of the less important contests. Kevin Conway's Eugene empties both pistols into an off-screen enemy, superimposed guns flip by the camera, and all the while, a cold-eyed Herod watches...

3. *For Love of the Game:* As the film opens, old home movies of baseball player Billy Chapel are intercut with newspaper headlines announcing his triumphs. A superimposed baseball flies by the camera, from left to right.
4. *Spider-Man:* Raimi's 2002 blockbuster features two montages. The first involves Peter Parker in his bedroom designing his costume. We see false starts superimposed behind Peter, and phrases such as "utility belt?" streaming by the camera. The second montage comes as Spider-Man rescues folks in the city and it's intercut with first-person interviews from New Yorkers on the street.

AN INANIMATE OBJECT'S POV

The Point of View subjective shot is ubiquitous in Raimi cinema, but in the director's unique spin on it, the object in question need not actually have a legitimate point of view — in other words, it doesn't need to have eyes or sentience for the camera to adopt its stance.

1. *The Evil Dead*: The Unseen Force
2. *Crimewave*: A gale force, storm wind; Coddish and Crush's truck
3. *Evil Dead 2*: The flying eyeball
4. *Darkman*: Machine-gun fire; bullets
5. *Army of Darkness*: Speeding arrows

SAM RAIMI FILMOGRAPHY

AS DIRECTOR

The Evil Dead (1982): director Sam Raimi; producer Robert Tapert; writer Sam Raimi.

Crimewave (1985): director Sam Raimi; producer Robert Tapert; writers Sam Raimi, Ethan and Joel Coen.

Evil Dead 2: Dead by Dawn (1987): director Sam Raimi; producer Robert Tapert; writers Sam Raimi, Scott Spiegel.

Darkman (1990): director Sam Raimi; producer Robert Tapert; writers Chuck Pfarrer, Sam and Ivan Raimi, Joshua and Daniel Goldin.

Army of Darkness (1993): director Sam Raimi; producer Robert Tapert; writers Sam and Ivan Raimi.

The Quick and the Dead (1995): director Sam Raimi; producers Joshua Donen, Patrick Markey, Allan Shapiro; writer Simon Moore.

A Simple Plan (1998): director Sam Raimi; producers James Jacks, Adam Schroeder; writer Scott B. Smith.

For Love of the Game (1999): director Sam Raimi; producers Amy Robinson, Armyan Bernstein; writer Dana Stevens.

The Gift (2000): director Sam Raimi; producers James Jacks, Tom Rosenberg, Robert Tapert; writers Billy Bob Thornton, Tom Epperson.

Spider-Man (2002): director Sam Raimi; producers Laura Ziskin, Ian Bryce, Avi Arad; writer David Koepp.

Spider-Man 2 (2004): director Sam Raimi; producers Laura Ziskin, Avi Arad; writers Michael Chabon, Alfred Gough, David Koepp, Miles Millar, Alvin Sargent.

AS ACTOR

Spies Like Us (1985): director John Landis; producers Brian Grazer, George Folsey Jr., Sam Williams; writers Dan Aykroyd, Lowell Ganz, Babaloo Mandel, Dave Thomas.

Thou Shall Not Kill...Except (1985): director Josh Becker; producers Shirley Becker, Scott Spiegel; writers Josh Becker, Bruce Campbell, Sheldon Lettich, Scott Spiegel.

Intruder (1988): director Scott Spiegel; producer Lawrence Bender; writer Scott Spiegel.

Maniac Cop (1988): director William Lustig; producers Larry Cohen, Jef Richard; writer Larry Cohen.

Miller's Crossing (1991): directors Joel and Ethan Coen; producers Joel and Ethan Coen; writers Joel and Ethan Coen.

Innocent Blood (1992): director John Landis; producers Leslie Belzberg, Lee Rich; writer Michael Wolk.

Indian Summer (1993): director Mike Binder; producers Lynn Bigelow, Jack Binder, Jim Kouf, Robert Newmyer, Jeff Silver; writer Mike Binder.

John Carpenter Presents Body Bags: "The Gas Station" (1993): director John Carpenter; producers John Carpenter, Sandy King; writers Dan Angel, Billy Brown.

The Flintstones (1994): director Brian Levant; producer Bruce Cohen; writers Tom S. Parker, Jim Jennewein, Steven E. De Souza.

Stephen King's The Stand (1994; TV mini-series): director Mick Garris; producers Stephen King, Michael Gornick, Mitchell Galin, Richard R. Rubinstein; writer Stephen King.

Galaxis (1995): director William Mesa; producers Eung Pyo Choi, Patrick D. Choi; writer Nick Davis.

Stephen King's The Shining (1997; TV mini-series): director Mick Garris; producers Laura Gibson, Stephen King; writer Stephen King.

AS WRITER (FILM)

Easy Wheels (1989): director David O'Malley; producers Bruce Campbell, Jake Jacobson, Dimitri Villard; writers Ivan and Sam Raimi (as Celia Adams), David O'Malley.

The Nutt House (1992): director Scott Spiegel, Adam Rifkin; producer Brad Wyman; writers Ivan Raimi (as Alan Smithee Sr.), Sam Raimi (as Alan Smithee Jr.), Bruce Campbell (as R.O.C. Sandstorm), Scott Spiegel (as Peter Perkinson).

The Hudsucker Proxy (1994): directors Joel and Ethan Coen; producers Joel and Ethan Coen, Eric Fellner; writers Joel and Ethan Coen, Sam Raimi.

AS PRODUCER/EXECUTIVE PRODUCER (FILM)

Lunatics: A Love Story (1991): director Josh Becker; producer Bruce Campbell; writer Josh Becker.

Hard Target (1993): director John Woo; producers James Jacks, Sean Daniel; writer Chuck Pfarrer.

Darkman II: The Return of Durant (1994, direct-to-video): director Bradford May; producer David Roessell; writer Steve McKay.

Timecop (1994): director Peter Hyams; producer Moshe Diamant; writer Mark Verheiden.

Darkman III: Die Darkman Die! (1996, direct-to-video): director Bradford May; producer David Roessell; writers Michael Colleary, Mike Werb.

Hercules and Xena—The Animated Movie: The Battle for Mount Olympus (1998, direct-to-video): director Lynne Naylor; producer Robert Tapert; writer John Loy.

Boogeyman (2004): director Stephen T. Kay; producers Michael Kirk, Chloe Smith, Rob Tapert; writers Erick Kripke, Darren Lemke, Juliet Snowden, Stiles White.

The Grudge (2005): director Takashi Shimizu; producers Doug Davison, Nathan Kahane, Roy Lee; writers Takashi Shimizu, Stephen Susco.

AS EXECUTIVE PRODUCER (TV SERIES)

M.A.N.T.I.S. (1994–1995; Fox)

American Gothic (1995–1996; CBS)

Hercules: The Legendary Journeys (1994–1999; syndicated)

Xena: Warrior Princess (1995–2001; syndicated)

Spy Game (1997; syndicated)

Young Hercules (1998–1999; syndicated)

Cleopatra 2525 (2000–2001; syndicated)

Jack of All Trades (2000–2001; syndicated)

NOTES

INTRODUCTION

1. Mark Horowitz, "Coen Brothers A-Z: The Big Two-Headed Picture," *Film Comment*, September/October 1991, 27–28.

2. Robert Emmet Long, ed., *John Huston Interviews* (Jackson: University Press of Mississippi, 2001), 160.

3. David Denby, "Clotheshorse Country," *New York*, February 27, 1995, 110.

4. Dennis Fischer, *Horror Film Directors, 1931–1990* (McFarland and Company, 1991), 812.

5. Kevin Thomas, *Los Angeles Times*, March 13, 1987, 14.

6. S.F. Said, "Spinning a Worldwide Web," *Telegraph*, May 4, 2002, http://www.telegraph.co.uk/arts/main.jhtml?xml=/arts/2002/06/04/bfsaid04.xml.

7. Anthony Lane, "Current Cinema: Balkan Homecoming," *New Yorker*, March 13, 1995, 111.

8. David Chute, "A Simple Plan," *Film Comment*, November/December, 1998, 78.

9. Michael Atkinson, *Ghosts in the Machine: Speculating on the Dark Heart of Pop Cinema* (Limelight Editions, 1999), 187.

1. GROWING UP WITHIN THE WOODS OF MICHIGAN

1. Paul Gray, "Those Good Old Games," *Time*, January 17, 2000, 85.
2. Scott Proudfit, "Dark Man Lightens Up," *Back Stage West*, January 11, 2001, 5.
3. Brian Hiatt, "First Look: On the set of *Spider-Man 2*. Tobey Maguire, Kirsten Dunst, and new villain Alfred Molina are all on board for day one of the Columbia University shoot," *Entertainment Weekly*, April 14, 2003, http://www.ew.com/.
4. Glenn Lovell, "Cronenberg Works Out of the Mainstream," *Mercury News*, March 10, 2003, http://www.centredaily.com.
5. "Interview with Sam Raimi," *Cinema Voice*, Spring, 2002, http://www.wowow.co.jp/.
6. KJB, "Featured Filmmaker: Sam Raimi—We take a look at the career of the director of *Evil Dead, Darkman, A Simple Plan* and *Spider-Man*," *Film Force*, April 29, 2002, http://filmforce.ign.com/articles/358/358197p1.html
7. Maitland McDonagh, *Filmmaking on the Fringe: The Good, the Bad and the Deviant Directors* (Citadel Press, 1995), 139.
8. Ronald Bergan, *The Coen Brothers* (Thunder's Mouth Press, 2000), 65.
9. Mike McGrady, *Newsday*, August 16, 1986, part 2, 5.
10. *Current Biography Yearbook 2002, 63rd Annual Cumulation* (H.W. Wilson Company, 2002), 472.
11. Laurence Lerman, "Killer of Dreams," *Video Business*, August 28, 2000, 23.
12. Kevin Carr, "Bruce Campbell: Hail to a B-Movie Legend," *Film Threat*, October 22, 2002, http://www.filmthreat.com/Interviews.asp?Id=467
13. Terry Lawson, "A cult figure since *The Evil Dead*, actor leads with his chin," *Knight-Ridder/Tribune News Service*, June 20, 2001, K7979.
14. Peter Calder, "Sam Who?" *New Zealand Herald*, December 6, 1999, http://www.nzherald.co.nz.
15. Marc Savlov, "Interview with Actor Bruce Campbell—Just Your Average Stiff," *Austin Chronicle*, http://www.austinchronicle.com/issues/vol18/issue40/screens.campbell.html.
16. David Michod, "Sam Raimi on *Spider-Man*," *Inside Film*, February 4, 2002, http://www.if.com.au/interviews/spiderman-sam-raimi.html.
17. Stanley Wiater, *Dark Visions: Conversations with the Masters of the Horror Films* (Avon Books, 1992), 146.
18. Scott Proudfit, "Dark Man Lightens Up," *Back Stage West*, January 11, 2001, 4.
19. Susan Schindechette, "Up from the Dead," People Weekly, December 6, 1993, 135.

2. EVIL DEAD (1982)

1. Chris Chase, "At the Movies: Breaking into Movies by the Horror Route," *New York Times*, April 15, 1983, C10.
2. Maitland McDonagh, *Filmmaking on the Fringe: The Good, the Bad, and the Deviant Directors* (Citadel Press, 1995), 140.
3. Amy Murphy, "Inside the Head of Josh Becker," *Whoosh!* 75 (January/February, 2003), http://www.whoosh.org/issue75/ibecker2.html
4. Carolyn R. Russell, *The Films of Joel and Ethan Coen* (McFarland and Company, 2001), 5.

5. John Pym, ed., *Time Out Film Guide*, 7th ed. (Penguin Books, 1999), 214.

6. Tim Kiska, "Via computer, a local composer wins an Emmy scoring 'Xena,'" *Detroit News*, August 29, 2000, http://www.detnews.com/2000/entertainment/0008/29/c01-112017.htm.

7. "*Evil Dead* Director Returns to Cast Spider Web over Horror Again," *Business of Film*, May 18, 2002, 4.

8. Paul R. Gagne, *The Zombies that Ate Pittsburgh: The Films of George A. Romero* (Dodd, Mead & Company, 1987), 64.

9. Jeffrey M. Anderson, "Lurking with Bruce," *San Francisco Examiner*, 2001, http://www.examiner.com/.

10. Bruce Campbell, *If Chins Could Kill: Confessions of a B-Movie Actor* (St. Martins Press, 2002), 139.

11. Stephen King, "Evil Dead," *Twilight Zone Magazine* 2, no. 8 (November 1982), 20.

12. William Schoell and James Spencer, *The Nightmare Never Ends: The Official History of Freddy Krueger and the Nightmare on Elm Street Films* (Citadel Press/Carol Publishing Group, 1992), 1.

13. John Monaghan, "'Dead' and kicking: It's been 20 years, but the Detroit-made cult horror flick is hotter than ever," *Detroit Free Press*, February 18, 2002, http://www.freep.com/entertainment/movies/.

14. Kevin Thomas, *Los Angeles Times*, May 26, 1983, 4.

15. Archer Winston, *New York Post*, April 15, 1983, 33.

16. David Chute, "New Faces of 1982," *Film Comment*, January/February 1983, 18–19.

17. Kim Newman, *Monthly Film Bulletin*, November 1982, 264.

18. *People Weekly*, May 2, 1983, 12.

19. David Sterritt, *Christian Science Monitor*, May 5, 1983, 16.

20. Peter Nicholls, *The World of Fantastic Films: An Illustrated Survey* (Dodd, Mead and Company, New York, 1984), 150.

21. John Ezard, "Campaigner Mary Whitehouse Dies, Aged 91," *Guardian*, November 24, 2001, http://www.guardian.co.uk/.

22. Andrew Holmes, "Let There Be Blood," *Guardian*, July 5, 2002, http://www.guardian.co.uk/friday_review/story/0,3605,749052,00.html.

23. Martin Baker, ed., *The Video Nasties: Freedom and Censorship in the Media* (Pluto Press, 1984), 61.

24. Rebecca Mead, "Cheese Whiz," *New Yorker*, November 23, 1998, 40.

25. Serena Donadoni, "Return of the Dead: Troy-based Anchor Bay studio keeps cult horror classic alive after twenty years," *Detroit News*, February 21, 2002, http://www.detnews.com/2002/entertainment/0202/21/c01-422358.htm.

26. Elliott Stein, *Village Voice*, May 3, 1983, 54.

27. Glenn Abel, "Living Dead, Evil Dead," *Hollywood Reporter*, April 2, 2002, 18–19.

28. William Schoell and James Spencer, *The Nightmare Never Ends: The Official History of the Nightmare on Elm Street Films* (A Citadel Press Book, 1992), 31.

29. Gina McIntyre, "American Gothic," *Wicked*, Spring 2001, 24–25.

30. Jake Horsely, *The Blood Poets: A Cinema of Savagery, 1958–1999, Volume 1: American Chaos from Touch of Evil to The Terminator* (Scarecrow Press, 1999), 248.

31. Bruce Lanier Wright, *Nightwalkers: Gothic Horror Movies: The Modern Years* (Taylor Publishing, 1995), 159.

32. Nathan Anderson, "DVD Review: Modern horror can't compete with 'Dead,'" *America's Intelligence Wire*, January 29, 2002, 1.

3. CRIMEWAVE (1985)

1. Archer Winsten, *New York Post*, June 6, 1986, 26.

2. Steve Jenkins, *Monthly Film Bulletin*, April 1986, 105.

3. David Jon Wiener, "Producer and President of the Motion Picture Arts and Sciences: Robert Rehme," *Point of View Online* Empire Productions, 1998, http://www.empire-pov.com/rehme.html.

4. James Fabiano, Sean Beard, Matt Williams, Matthew Anscher (Compilers), "Embassy Limited Partners," http://www.angelfire.com/tv2/closinglogo/embassy.html

5. David Kohrman, "Hotel Tuller," *Forgotten Detroit*, November 14, 2001, http://www.forgottende-troit.com/tuller.

6. Lawrence Van Gelder, "At the Movies: Louise Lasser Trusts *Crimewave* Director," *New York Times*, June 6, 1986, C8.

7. James Mottram, *The Coen Brothers: The Life of the Mind* (Brassey's, 2000), 174.

8. Mike McGrady, *Newsday*, August 16, 1986 part 2, 5.

9. Cart, "Crimewave," *Variety*, May 22, 1985, 29.

10. Vincent Canby, "Screen: *Crimewave*, Gangster-Film Spoof," *New York Times*, June 6, 1996, C5.

11. Mike McGrady, *Newsday*, August 16, 1986, part 2, 5.

12. Jami Bernard, *New York Post*, August 15, 1986, 20.

13. David Edelstein, *Village Voice*, June 10, 1986, 56.

14. Robert Kurson, *The Official Three Stooges Encyclopedia* (Contemporary Books, 1998), 39.

15. Robert Kurson. *The Official Three Stooges Encyclopedia* (Contemporary Books, 1998), 238.

16. Peter Korte and George Seeslan, eds., Joel and Ethan Coen (Limelight Editions, 2001), 26.

4. EVIL DEAD 2: DEAD BY DAWN (1987)

1. Maitland McDonagh, *Filmmaking on the Fringe: The Good, the Bad, and the Deviant Directors* (A Citadel Press Book, 1995), 144.

2. Harry and Michael Medved, *The Golden Turkey Awards: Nominees and Winners—The Worst Achievements in Hollywood History* (Perigee Books, 1980), 113.

3. Jason Anderson, *National Post Online*, March 26, 2001, http://www.nationalpost.com/.

4. Jason Pollock, "Directoscopy: Sam Raimi," *Creature Corner* 1, http://www.creature-corner.com/columns/directoraimi1.php3.

5. Will Murray, "WHY is Bruce ("Ash") Campbell Still Alive?" *The Bloody Best of Fangoria* 7 (1988), 50.

6. William Paul, *Laughing Screaming: Modern Hollywood Horror and Comedy* (Columbia University Press, 1994), 434.
7. Jagr, "Evil Dead 2," *Variety*, March 15, 1987, 15.
8. Jack Mathews, "How *Evil Dead 2* Dodged the Kiss of Death—An X," *Los Angeles Times*, March 13, 1987, http://www.latimes.com/.
9. Caryn James, "Evil Dead 2: Dead by Dawn," *New York Times*, March 13, 1987, C18.
10. Bill Kaufman, *Newsday*, February 13, 1987, 5.
11. John Pym, ed., *The Time Out Film Guide*, 7th ed. (Penguin Books, 1999), 274.
12. Doug Brod, "Don of the Dead," *Entertainment Weekly*, March 5, 1993, 40.
13. Roger Ebert, "Evil Dead 2: Dead by Dawn," *Chicago Sun-Times*, April 10, 1987, http://www.sun-times.com/ebert/ebert_reviews/1987/04/227094.html.
14. Bruce Kawin, "After Midnight," in *The Cult Film Experience: Beyond All Reason*, edited by J.P. Telotte, (Austin: University of Texas Press, 1991), 24.

5. DARKMAN (1990)

1. Bill Warren, *Set Visits: Interviews with 32 Horror and Science Fiction Filmmakers* (McFarland and Company, 1997), 156.
2. Steve Biodrowski, "Sam Raimi—*Darkman*: The X-rated auteur of visceral shock goes Hollywood and turns to classic horror," *Cinefantastique* 21, no. 12 (September 1990), 12.
3. Bill Warren, "Darkman," *Fangoria* 90 (February 1990), 12.
4. David Scheiderer, "This Screenwriter Trained the 'Navy SEALS Way;' Movies: For Chuck Pfarrer, the same rule applies in the military and Hollywood: 'You learn to adapt and survive. Or Else,'" *Los Angeles Times*, August 6, 1990, http://www.latimes.com/.
5. Frederic G. Szebein, "Darkman 2: Durant Returns," *Cinefantastique* 25, no. 60 (December 1994), 36.
6. Stanley Wiater, *Dark Visions: Conversations with Masters of the Horror Films* (Avon Books 1993), 139.
7. Kyle Counts, "Heart of Darkness," *Starlog* 161 (December 1990), 45.
8. Michael Wilmington, *Los Angeles Times*, August 24, 1990, 10.
9. David Edelstein, *New York Post*, August 24, 1990, 21.
10. Jim Farber, "Video: Demolition Derby," *Rolling Stone*, February 21, 1991.
11. Terry Kelleher, *Newsday*, August 24, 1990, 2.
12. Terrence Rafferty, "The Current Cinema: High and Low," *New Yorker*, September 10, 1990, 103.
13. Richard Corliss, *Time Magazine*, September 17, 1990, 71.
14. Ralph Novak, *People Weekly*, September 10, 1990, 13.
15. Peter Jensen, "*Darkman* Lover," *Starlog* 158 (September 1990), 38.
16. Ronald Bergan, *The Coen Brothers* (Thunder's Mouth Press, 2000), 113.
17. Ethan Alter, "Spider-Man," *Film Journal International*, June 2002, 38–39.

6. ARMY OF DARKNESS (1993)

1. Les Paul Robley, "Mobilizing Army of Darkness Via 'Go-Animation,'" *American Cinematographer*, March 1993, 74.
2. Sue Uram, "Bruce Campbell, Horror's Rambo," *Cinefantastique* 23, no. 2/3 (October 1992), 31.
3. Steve Biodrowksi, "Sam Raimi's *Evil Dead III*," *Cinefantastique* 22, no. 5 (April 1992), 4.
4. Aimee Phan, "Childhood interest in special effects fuels kids' movie. Tony Gardner's lifelong hobby proves profitable as well as fun," *Daily Bruin*, April 29, 1997, http://www.dailybruin.ucla.edu/DB/issues/97/04.29/ae.warriors.html.
5. Sue Uram, "Sam Raimi's *Evil Dead III*," *Cinefantastique* 23, no. 2/3 (October 1992), 28.
6. Bill Warren, "Commander of Darkness," *Fangoria* 120 (March 1993), 39.
7. Jeffrey M. Anderson, "Lurking with Bruce," *San Francisco Examiner*, http://www.examiner.com/.
8. John Anderson, *Newsday*, February 19, 1993, 56.
9. Peter Rainer, *Los Angeles Times*, February 19, 1993, 8.
10. Jami Bernard, *New York Post*, February 19, 1993, 23.
11. Jonathan Romney, "Army of Darkness," *New Statesman and Society*, June 11, 1993, 36.
12. Owen Gleiberman, "Army of Darkness," *Entertainment Weekly*, March 5, 1993, 41.
13. Ralph Novak, "Army of Darkness," *People Weekly*, March 15, 1993, 17.
14. Mike Szymanski, "Bruce Campbell talks Elvis and an *Evil Dead* sequel," *Knight Ridder/Tribune News Service*, October 10, 2002, K1604.
15. Max Herzberg, *Readers Encyclopedia of Literature* (Thomas Crowell Company, 1962), 201–202.
16. Bill Warren, "Commander of Darkness," *Fangoria* 120 (March 1993), 38.
17. Ray Harryhausen, *Film Fantasy Scrapbook*, 2nd ed., rev. (A.S. Barnes and Company, 1972), 88.
18. Pauline Kael, "Apes Must Be Remembered, Charlie," *New Yorker*, February 17, 1968, 108.

7. THE QUICK AND THE DEAD (1995)

1. Bruce Newman, "On Location: Meet Six-Gun Sharon Stone. The actress dons high-plains drifter gear to dish out her own brand of frontier justice in *The Quick and the Dead*. And she really loves it," *Los Angeles Times*, January 30, 1994, http://www.latimes.com/.
2. Bill Warren, *The Evil Dead Companion* (St. Martins Press, 2000), 164–165.
3. David E. Williams, "Rootin', Tootin' Raimi: An Interview with Sam Raimi," *Film Threat*, 1995, http://www.filmthreat.com/Interviews.asp?Id=20.
4. Bart Mills, "Sharon's Showdown," *Entertainment Weekly*, March 4, 1994, 14.
5. Marc Savlov, "Austin Confidential," *Austin Chronicle*, October 20, 1997, http://www.weeklywire.com/ww/10-20-97/austin_screens_feature2.html
6. Gregg Kilday, "No. 1 with a Bullet: Thell Reed, Hollywood's Fastest Hand," *Entertainment Weekly*, February 17, 1995, 41.
7. M. Scot Skinner, "Fun *Quick and the Dead*: a Western put-on extraordinaire," *Arizona Daily Star*, February 14, 1995, Accent 1D.

8. Edward L. Cook, "Jobless receive bit roles in film, chance to work," *Arizona Daily Star*, February 7, 1994, Metro/Region 1B.
9. Alisa Wabnik, "Actress Sharon Stone helps serve meals to 1,000 at Convention Center," *Arizona Daily Star*, December 26, 1993, 6B.
10. Robert F. Green, ed., *Magill's Cinema Annual 1996* (Gale Research, 1996), 431–432.
11. Roger Ebert, "The Quick and the Dead," *Chicago Sun Times*, February 10, 1995, http://www.suntimes.com/ebert/ebert_reviews/1995/02/965027.html.
12. Jeff Giles, "The Quick and the Dead," *Newsweek*, February 20, 1995, 72.
13. Janet Maslin, *New York Times*, August 11, 1995, B14.
14. Peter Travers, "Sharon and the Wild Bunch," *Rolling Stone*, March 9, 1995, 70.
15. David Sterritt, *Christian Science Monitor*, February 13, 1995, 13.
16. Chris Nashawaty, "Out of Left Field: After years of not registering on mainstream Hollywood's moviemaking radar, *The Evil Dead* director Sam Raimi finally gets a chance to prove himself in a big-league *Game*," *Entertainment Weekly*, September 17, 1999, 44.
17. Cindy Pearlman, "Stone Cold," *Entertainment Weekly*, February 10, 1995, 12.
18. Martha McCaughey and Neal King, eds., *Reel Knock-Outs: Violent Women in the Movies*, "Sharon Stone's Aesthetic," (University of Texas Press, 2001), 135–136.
19. Kenneth Turan, *Los Angeles Times*, February 10, 1995, 1.
20. Christopher Frayling, *Sergio Leone: Something to Do with Death* (Faber and Faber, 2000), 141.
21. Ray Greene, *Hollywood Migraine: The Inside Story of a Decade in Film* (Merlin, 2000), 108–109.
22. Owen Gleiberman, "The Quick and the Dead," *Entertainment Weekly*, February 17, 1995, 40.

8. A SIMPLE PLAN (1998)

1. Tom Prince, "Fast Track, Making a Living," *New York*, August 1993, 48.
2. Tobin Harshaw, "Something Film Noirish," *New York Times*, September 19, 1993, sec. 7, 9.
3. Rosellen Brown, "Choosing Evil," *New York Times*, September 19, 1993, 9.
4. Rebecca Mead, "Cheese Whiz," *New Yorker*, November 23, 1998, 42.
5. Michiko Kakutani, "Plotter's Stupidity Saved by Stupidity of Others," *New York Times*, September 3, 1993, C21.
6. "Bill Paxton's Simple Plan," *Entertainment Tonight Online*, 1999, http://www.etonline.com/.
7. Serena Donadoni, "Stone-Cold Destiny," *Detroit Metro Times*, January 27, 1999, http://www.metrotimes.com/19/17/Features/filStone.html.
8. Peter Travers, "A Very Good Thing: *A Simple Plan*," *Rolling Stone*, December 10, 1998, 132.
9. "A Simple Plan," *Entertainment Weekly*, January 8, 1999, 50.
10. David Sterritt, *Christian Science Monitor*, December 4, 1998, 15
11. David Ansen, *Newsweek*, December 14, 1998, 79.
12. John Powers, *Vogue*, December 1998, 158.

13. Scott B. Smith, *A Simple Plan* (St. Martins Press, 1993), 129.
14. G. Blakemore Evans, ed., *The Riverside Shakespeare* (Houghton Mifflin Company, 1974), 1316.
15. S.F. Said, "Filmmakers on Film: Sam Raimi; Sam Raimi on John Huston's *The Treasure of the Sierra Madre*," *Telegraph*, June 6, 2002, http://www.telegraph.co.uk/.
16. Kathleen Murphy, "Toronto," *Film Comment*, November 1998, 47.
17. Andrew Sarris, ed., *The St. James Film Directors Encyclopedia* (Visible Ink Press, 1998), 224.

9. FOR LOVE OF THE GAME (1999)

1. Jeff Shaara, *For Love of the Game*, "Introduction," September 1996, viii–ix.
2. "Talking with Kevin Costner," *Pamela's Film and Entertainment Site*, September 1999, http://www.geocities.com/Hollywood/Chateau/5968/loveofgame/costner.html.
3. Jeanne Wolf, "Oh, Boy," *Redbook*, March 1999, 86.
4. Rick Lyman, "At the Movies: Goodbye, Fake Blood," *New York Times*, September 17, 1999, E14.
5. "Fall Movie Preview," *Entertainment Weekly*, August 20, 1999, 28.
6. Hal Erickson, *The Baseball Filmography, 1915–2001*, 2nd ed. (McFarland and Company, 2002), 208.
7. David Hochman, "The Un-Natural: Actor John C. Reilly learns to be a baseball catcher," *Esquire*, April 1999, 145.
8. Beth Laski and Annabelle Villanueva, "Holiday Movie Preview," *Cinescape*, November/December 2001, 56.
9. Timothy J. Lammers, "Co-Stars Explain *Love of the Game*," *Channel 4000*, 1999, http://www.channel4000.com/.
10. Mark Miller, "Throwing Heat: It's great to see Costner back in the ballpark. The actor opens up about women and movies—and talks bluntly about the struggle over *For Love of the Game*," *Newsweek*, September 13, 1999, 62.
11. "*Blue Streak* bats Costner flick out of the box office ballpark," *Las Vegas Sun*, September 20, 1999, http://www.lasvegassun.com/sunbin/stories/text/1999/sep/20/509327781.html.
12. Bill Higgins, "Costner Steps up to Bat," *Variety*, September 20, 1999, 106.
13. Lawrence Van Gelder, "Reaching for One Last Strike in Life's Last Inning," *New York Times*, September 17, 1999, E14.
14. Rod Dreher, *New York Post*, September 17, 1999, 43.
15. Stanley Kauffmann, "Playing Games," *New Republic*, October 18, 1999, 28.
16. Stuart Klawans, "The Boys of Summer," *Nation*, October 11, 1999, 34.
17. "A Game Full of Cheers and Tears," *Christian Science Monitor*, September 17, 1999, 15.
18. Richard Corliss, "No Hit Game: Kevin Costner strikes out in a baseball weepie," *Time Magazine*, September 20, 1999, 79.
19. Mark Morrison, "Only Kevin Knows," *In Style*, September 1, 1999, 476.
20. Stephen C. Wood and J. David Pincus, eds., *Reel Baseball: Essays and Interviews on the National Pastime, Hollywood and American Culture* (McFarland and Company, 2003), 260–262.

21. Kenneth Turan, *Los Angeles Times*, September 17, 1999.

10. THE GIFT (2000)

1. Frank Goodman, "A Conversation with Billy Bob Thornton," *Puremusic*, January 2002, http://www.puremusic.com/pdf/BBT.pdf.
2. Robert Welkos, "Odd Man Out," *F2 Network—Arts and Entertainment*, December 1, 2001, http://smh.com.au/.
3. Sean O'Hagan, "Quick on the Drawl," *Guardian Unlimited/Observer*, April 28, 2002, http://www.film.guardian.co.uk/interview/interviewpages/0,6737,706529,00.html.
4. Alex Lewin, "Raimi Gets Metaphysical," *Premiere.com*, July 2000, http:/www.premiere.com/.
5. Susan Stark, "Ferndale Native Sam Raimi has 'Gift' for Directing," *Detroit News*, January 20, 2001.
6. Dave Kehr, "At the Movies: Beyond Genre," *New York Times*, December 14, 2000, E15.
7. Gina McIntyre, "American Gothic," *Wicked*, Spring 2001, 24–25.
8. Anthony Kaufman, "Interview: Sam Raimi Opens *The Gift*, Discovers Suspense Indiewood-Style," *IndieWire*, January 16, 2001, http://www.indiewire.com/people/int_Raimi_Sam_010116.html.
9. Susan Stark, "Ferndale Native Sam Raimi has 'Gift' for Directing," *Detroit News*, January 20, 2001.
10. Merele Ginsburg, "Heaven's Cate," *WWD*, January 18, 2001, 4.
11. Steven Rea, "Familiarity certainly doesn't breed contempt for Cate Blanchett," *Knight Ridder/Tribune News Service*, January 19, 2001, K2135.
12. Bob Strauss, "Cate's Captivating Gift: In-demand actress Cate Blanchett is all work, and anything but dull, nailing characters as disparate as a psychic widow in Georgia and Tolkien's elf queen," *Globe and Mail*, January 17, 2002.
13. Bert Osborne, "Movie Interview: Keanu Reeves," *Creative Loafing*, January 20, 2001, http:/reel-time.cln.com/movies/interview.asp?ID=321.
14. "American Gothic," *Entertainment Weekly*, August 11, 2000, http://www.ew.com/.
15. Anthony C. Ferrante, "For Love of the Game," *Eon Magazine*, November 24, 2000.
16. Barry Koltnow, "*The Gift* Star Cate Blanchett's Eye Is on the Future," *Knight Ridder/Tribune News Service*, January 21, 2001, K2128.
17. Todd McCarthy, "The Gift," *Variety*, December 18, 2000, 24.
18. Peter Travers, *Rolling Stone*, February 1, 2001, 61.
19. Roger Ebert, "The Gift," *Chicago Sun Times*, January 19, 2001, http://www.suntimes.com/ebert/ebert_reviews/2001/01/011902.html.
20. Michael Betzold, *Magill's Cinema Annual* (Gale Group, 2002), 205.

11. SPIDER-MAN (2002)

1. Steve Pond, "Stan Lee's Spidey Guide: Everything You Need to Know About the Sticky-Fingered Avenger, Straight from the Man Who Ceated Him," *E! Online Features*, May 6, 2002, http://aol.eonline.com/Features/Features/Spiderman/Guide/index.html.
2. Charles Dubow, "The Amazingly Profitable Spider-Man," *Forbes.com*, May 6, 2002, http://www.forbes.com/2002/05/06/0506spidey.html.

3. Robert Friedman, "Will Cannon Boom or Bust?" *American Film*, July/August 1986, 57.

4. Tom Russo, "Swing Time: What a costume drama! All the superheroics behind *Spider-Man*'s leap to the big screen," *Entertainment Weekly*, April 26, 2002, 38.

5. James Inverne, "Hero Worship: Armed with colossal budgets and fancy special effects, Hollywood is bringing old comic book characters to the big screen. Get ready for the summer of the superheroes," *Time International*, April 15, 2002, 60.

6. Steve Hockensmith and Beth Laski, "Along Came a Spider: Cult Fave director Sam Raimi reveals his plans for the *Spider-Man* movie," *Cinescape*, November/December 2000, 16–17.

7. "Movies," *Cinescape*, September/October 1999, 21.

8. James Mottram, *BBC Film Interviews*, May 9, 2002, http://www.bbc.co.uk/films/2002/05/09/sam_raimi_spider-man_interview.shtml.

9. Gillian Flynn, "Web Casting," *Entertainment Weekly*, February 11, 2002, 9.

10. S.F. Said, "Spinning a Worldwide Web," *Telegraph*, April 6, 2002, http://www.telegraph.co.uk/arts/main.jhtml?xml=/arts/2002/06/04/bfsaid04.xml.

11. Steve Hockensmith, "Fashion Bug," *Cinescape*, March/April 2001, 16.

12. Paul Daza, "John Dykstra: There's Nothing He Can't Make," *INQ7—Inquirer News Service*, May 12, 2002, http://www.inq7.net/.

13. John Reading, "World Wide Web," *Film Review*, issue 619 (July 2002), http://www.visimag.com/filmreview/f142_feat01.htm.

14. Alfred Hermida, "Sci Tech: Bringing Digital Actors Alive," *BBC News*, October 14, 2001, http://news.bbc.co.uk/1/hi/sci/tech/1591598.stm.

15. Gillian Flynn, "Web Casting," *Entertainment Weekly*, February 11, 2000, 9.

16. Luaine Lee, "*Spider-Man* Tobey Maguire's Life Lessons," *Knight-Ridder/Tribune News Service*, April 30, 2002, K7164.

17. Jess Cagle, "Who Is that Masked Man?" *Time Magazine*, May 20, 2002, 74.

18. "Tobey's True Tale: Tobey Maguire's a big movie star. But long before he put on the *Spider-Man* outfit and fought crime on screen, he was a regular teenager in search of friends," *Scholastic Choices*, May 2002, 16–19.

19. Galina Espinoza, Jason Lynch and Sophronia Scott, "How to Get Super Fit: *Spider-Man* Tobey Maguire went from soft to solid in six months. Could you?" *People Weekly*, May 27, 2002, 82.

20. Chrissy Iley, "Call It Chemistry: Chrissy Iley on Tobey Maguire and Leo DiCaprio," *Europe Intelligence Wire*, November 2, 2002.

21. Samantha Miller, "Web Master: Tobey Maguire, Hollywood's go-to Sensitive Young Guy, pumps up his pecs, delts and career with Spider-Man," *People Weekly*, May 20, 2002, 67.

22. "Buzz Box: *Spider-Man*," *Cinescape*, January/February 2001, 22.

23. Shawna Malcom, "Along Came a *Spider-Man*," *TV Guide*, April 27, 2002, 23.

24. Michelle Tauber, "Webbed Feat: Kirsten Dunst had a nice, low-key career—then along came a $300 million spider," *People Weekly*, June 2, 2002, 73.

25. Will Forbis, "The Tangled Web of Spider-Man. An interview with Joe O'Malley of No-Organic Webshooters.com," *Acid Logic E-Zine*, http://www.acidlogic.com/no_organic_webshooters.htm.

26. Fred Topel, "Sam Raimi Talks *Spider-Man*: Interview with the director of the comic superhero film," *About Action Adventure Movies*, April 21, 2002, http://actionadventure.about/com/library/weekly/2002/aa042102.htm

27. Barry Koltnow, "*Spider-Man* director Sam Raimi responds to criticism," *Knight-Ridder/Tribune News Service*, April 29, 2002, K1632.

28. Sam Raimi, "What a Web He Weaves: One Question for...Sam Raimi," *Entertainment Weekly*, May 3, 2002, 92.

29. Ron Magid, "Crawling the Walls," *American Cinematographer*, June 2002, 50.

30. Ron Magid. "Making Spidey Sense Tingle," *American Cinematographer*, June 2002, 52.

31. Scott Brown, "Insider-Man: Meet Avi Arad, the Marvel Studios exec overseeing the big-screen invasion of Spidey and other superheroes," *Entertainment Weekly*, July 12, 2002, 28–30.

32. Bridget Byrne, "Spidey's Record Spin," *E! Online*, May 5, 2002, http://aol.eonline.com/News/Items/0,1,9903,00.html?eol.tkr.

33. Tom Russo, "Monster Ink: New deals, more superheroes—*Spider-Man* isn't the only comic-book creation going Hollywood," *Entertainment Weekly*, May 10, 2002, 38.

34. Stephen Lynch, "A new spin on superheroes: Spider-Man changed comic books," *Knight-Ridder/Tribune News Service*, April 29, 2002, K1631.

35. Joseph Szadkowski, "Lucas' Force succumbs to Raimi's Spider-Man," *Washington Times*, June 1, 2002, B02.

36. Ethan Alter, "Spider-Man," *Film Journal International*, June 2002, 38.

37. Kenneth Turan, "The Spider and the Fly Girl,'" *Los Angeles Times*, May 3, 2002, http://www.latimes.com/.

38. Steve Vineburg, "To Kiss a Spider," *Christian Century*, May 22, 2002, 48.

39. Gary Arnold, "Relationships trib up nimble *Spider-Man*," *Washington Times*, May 3, 2002, B05.

40. Roger Ebert, "Spider-Man," *Chicago Sun-Times*, May 3, 2002, http://www.suntimes.com/ebert/ebert_reviews/2002/05/050303.html.

41. Chuck Kim, "Drawn to *Spider-Man*: Out comic writer Phil Jimenez went from drawing Wonder Woman to subbing for Tobey Maguire's hands on the *Spider-Man* set," *Advocate*, May 14, 2002, 66.

42. Anthony Lane, "Tangled Webs: *Spider-Man* and *The Lady and the Duke*," *New Yorker*, May 13, 2002, 96.

43. Mark Cotta Vaz, *Behind the Mask of Spider-Man* (Del Rey/Ballantine, 2002), 195.

44. Christine Tomassini, *Magill's Cinema Annual 2003* (Gale Group/Thomson Learning, 2003), 446.

45. John Kenneth Muir, "Not Very Special Effects," *Deep Outside Science Fiction, Fantasy and Horror*, June 2002, http://outside.clocktowerfiction.com/Column/200206jm.shtml.

12. SPIDER-MAN 2 (2004)

1. Gary Susman, "Tangled Web: *Spider-Man* sequel pushed back to July 4, 2004. Production delays create a summer lineup shakeup," *Entertainment Weekly*, March 27, 2003, http://www.ew.com/.

2. "Raimi gives absent Spidey a second chance," *Guardian Unlimited Film*, May 13, 2002, http://film.guardian.co.uk./news/story/0,12589,954926,00.html.

3. "Maguire Rebuts Spidey Reports," *SciFi.com*, July 21, 2003, http://www.scifi.com/scifiwire/art-main.html?2003-07/21/11.00.film.

4. Stephen M. Silverman, "The Real Skinny (Ahem) on Tobey Maguire," *People News Daily*, June 6, 2003, http://people.aol.com/people/.

5. Michael Fleming, "Spidey scribe spins sequel: David Koepp to work on script for *Spider-Man 2*," *Daily Variety*, June 10, 2002, 16–17.

6. Mari Cartel and Brian M. Raftery, "Hanging Tough," *Entertainment Weekly*, April 29, 2002, http://www.ew.com/.

7. "Spider-Man 2," *Hollywood Reporter*, April 16, 2002, 19.

8. Andy Gallacher, "Radio 1 Exclusive: *Spider-Man 2* filming in full swing," *BBC Entertainment News*, April 23, 2003, http://www.bbc.co.uk/radio1/news/entertainment/030423_spiderman.shtml.

9. "Quint," "Holy Crap! Quint's Got Pictures of Doc Ock?? And Has Seen Some of *Spider-Man 2*!!" *Ain't It Cool News*, July 20, 2003, http://www.aintitcool.com/display.cgi?id=15699.

10. "*Spider-Man 2* Update," *Comics Continuum*, January 21, 2004, http://www.comicscontinuum.com/stories/0401/21/.

11. Mike Cotton, "The *Spider-Man 2* director swings through questions about his top secret set, the theme of the sequel, and how he chose his Doc Ock," *Wizard* 145 (November 2003), http://www.spiderman.sonypictures.com/bugle/press_releases/4.php

12. Nicole LaPorte, "Spidey Spins Web for a Third Time," *Variety*, March 2, 2004.

13 "Director Sam Raimi and Tobey Maguie Talk *Spider-Man 2*," Killer Movies.com, June 5, 2003, http://www.killermovies.com/s/spiderman2/articles/3143.html

13. RAIMI RELATED

1. Tim Lammers, "Director Raimi Has *The Gift*," *Denver's ABC 7*, *TheDenverChannel.com*, 2001, http://www.thedenverchannel.com/.

2. "New Shows: *M.A.N.T.I.S.*, *Under Suspicion*, *Friday*, Fall TV Preview," *Entertainment Weekly*, September 16, 1994, 70.

3. David Tobenkin, "MCA muscles in on action hours; on strength of *Hercules*, producers add *Xena*," *Broadcasting and Cable*, August 21, 1995, 25–26.

4. Joe Mauceri, "Unholy Trinity," *Shivers* 32 (August 1996), 9.

5. David Wild, "Television 'X'-Ploitation," *Rolling Stone*, November 30, 1995, 79.

6. Cathy Dunkley, "Raimi and Senator join in fantasy deal," *Daily Variety*, May 16, 2002, 6.

7. E. Michael Fleming and Claude Brodesser, "Heated Pic Bids Simmer," *Daily Variety*, July 15, 2002, 1.

8. Chris Gardner, "*Grudge* remake haunts fast track at Ghost House," *Hollywood Reporter*, February 21, 2003, 89.

9. Melissa Grego, "Split Personality at CBS," Daily Variety, November 11, 2002, 1.

14. THE SAM RAIMI MOVIEMAKING LEXICON

1. Jay Holben, "Spider's Strategem," *American Cinematographer* 83, no. 6 (June 2002), 45.

BIBLIOGRAPHY

BOOKS

Atkinson, Michael. *Ghosts in the Machine: Speculating on the Dark Heart of Pop Cinema*. Limelight Editions, 1999.

Baker, Martin, ed. *The Video Nasties: Freedom and Censorship in the Media*. Pluto Press, 1984.

Bergan, Ronald. *The Coen Brothers*. Thunder's Mouth Press, 2000.

Campbell, Bruce. *If Chins Could Kill: Confessions of a B Movie Actor*. LA Weekly Books/Thomas Dunne Books/St. Martins Press, 2001.

Current Biography Yearbook 2002, 63rd Annual Cumulation. H.W. Wilson Company, 2002, 472–475.

Erickson, Hal. *The Baseball Filmography*, 1915–2001, 2nd ed. McFarland and Company, 2002.

Fischer, Dennis. *Horror Film Directors*, 1931–1990. McFarland and Company, 1991.

Frayling, Christopher. *Sergio Leone: Something to Do with Death*. Faber and Faber, 2000.

Gagne, Paul R. *The Zombies That Ate Pittsburgh: The Films of George A. Romero*. Dodd, Mead and Company, 1987.

Giannetti, Louis. *Understanding Movies*, 5th ed. Prentice Hall, 1990.

Green, Roberta F., ed. *Magill's Cinema Annual 1996*. Gale Research, 1996.

Greene, Ray. *Hollywood Migraine: The Inside Story of a Decade in Film*. Merlin, 2000.

Harryhausen, Ray. *Film Fantasy Scrapbook*, 2nd ed., rev. A.S. Barnes and Company, 1972.

Herzberg, Max. *Readers Encyclopedia of Literature*. Thomas Crowell Company, 1962

Horsely, Jake. *The Blood Poets: A Cinema of Savagery, 1958–1999. Volume 1: American Chaos from Touch of Evil to The Terminator*. Scarecrow Press, 1999.

Kawin, Bruce. "After Midnight." In *The Cult Film Experience: Beyond All Reason*, edited by J.P. Telotte. Austin: University of Texas Press, 1991.

Korte, Peter and George Seeslen, eds. *Joel and Ethan Coen*. Limelight Editions, 2001.

Kurson, Robert. *The Official Three Stooges Encyclopedia*. Contemporary Books, 1998.

McCaughey, Martha and Neal King, eds. "Sharon Stone's Aesthetic." In *Reel Knock-Outs: Violent Women in the Movies*. University of Texas Press, 2001; 124–137.

Medved, Harry and Michael Medved. *The Golden Turkey Awards: Nominees and Winners—The Worst Achievements in Hollywood History*. Perigee Books, 1980.

Mottram, James. *The Coen Brothers: The Life of the Mind*. Brassey's, 2000.

Muir, John Kenneth. *The Encyclopedia of Superheroes on Film on Television*. McFarland and Company, 2003.

———. *Horror Films of the 1970s*. McFarland and Company, 2002.

———. *Terror Television: American Series, 1970–1999*. McFarland and Company, 2001.

———. *Wes Craven: The Art of Horror*. McFarland and Company, 1998.

Nicholls, Peter. *The World of Fantastic Films: An Illustrated Survey*. New York: Dodd, Mead and Company, 1984.

Paul, William. *Laughing Screaming: Modern Hollywood Horror and Comedy*. Columbia University Press, 1994.

Russell, Carolyn R. *The Films of Joel and Ethan Coen*. McFarland and Company, 2001.

Schoell, William and James Spencer. *The Nightmare Never Ends: The Official History of Freddy Krueger and the Nightmare on Elm Street Films*. Citadel Press/Carol Publishing Group, 1992.

Shaara, Michael. *For Love of the Game*. Ballantine Books, 1991.

Smith, Scott B. *A Simple Plan*. St. Martin's Press, 1993.

Stanley, John. *John Stanley's Creature Features Movie Guide Strikes Again*, 4th rev. ed. Creatures at Large Press, 1994.

Taylor, John Russell. *Great Movie Moments*. Crescent Books, 1987.

Vaz, Mark Cotta. *Behind the Mask of Spider-Man: The Secrets of the Movie*. Ballantine Books/Del Rey, 2002.

Von Gunden, Kenneth, and Stuart H. Stock. *Twenty All-Time Great Science Fiction Films*. Arlington House, 1982.

Warren, Bill. *The Evil Dead Companion*. St. Martins Press, 2000.

———. *Set Visits: Interviews with 32 Horror and Science Fiction Filmmakers*. McFarland and Company, 1997.

Wiater, Stanley. *Dark Visions: Conversations with the Masters of the Horror Films*. Avon Books, 1992.

Wood, Stephen C., and J. David Pincus, eds. *Reel Baseball: Essays and Interviews on the National Pastime, Hollywood and American Culture*. McFarland and Company, 2003.

Wright, Bruce Lanier. *Nightwalkers: Gothic Horror Movies: The Modern Years*. Taylor Publishing, 1995.

PERIODICALS

Abel, Glenn. "Living Dead, Evil Dead." *Hollywood Reporter*, April 12, 2002, 18–19.

Alter, Ethan. "Spider-Man." *Film Journal International*, June 2002, 38–39.

Anderson, Nathan. "DVD Review: modern horror can't compete with *Dead*." *America's Intelligence Wire*, January 29, 2002.

Ansen, David. "The Best Laid Plans." *Newsweek*, December 14, 1998, 79.

Biodrowski, Steve. "Sam Raimi *Darkman*: The X-rated auteur of visceral shock goes Hollywood and turns to classic horror." *Cinefantastique* 21, no. 2 (September 1990): 12–13, 61.

Brod, Don. "Don of the Dead." *Entertainment Weekly*, March 5, 1993, 40.

Brown, Rosellen. "Choosing Evil." *New York Times*, September 19, 1993, section 7, 9–11.

Cagle, Jess. "Who Is that Masked Man?" *Time Magazine*, May 20, 2002, 74.

Canby, Vincent. "Screen: *Crimewave*, Gangster-Film Spoof." *New York Times*, June 6, 1986, C5.

Cart. "*Crimewave*." *Variety*, May 22, 1985, 29.

Chase, Chris. "At the Movies: Breaking into Movies by the Horror Route." *New York Times*, April 15, 1983, C10.

Chute, David. "New Faces of 1982." *Film Comment*, January/February 1983, 19.

———. "A Simple Plan." *Film Comment*, November/December, 1998, 78–79.

Corliss Richard. "No Hit Game: Kevin Costner strikes out in baseball weepie." *Time Magazine*, September 20, 1999, 79.

———. *Time Magazine*, September 17, 1990, 71.

Counts, Kyle. "Heart of Darkness." *Starlog* 161 (December 1990): 45–58.

Cunneen, Joseph. "When you're talking dialogue, it's hard to top the Bard." *National Catholic Reporter*, January 22, 1999, 18.

Denby, David. "Clotheshorse Country." *New York*, February 27, 1995, 108–110.

Donadoni, Serena. "Return of the Dead: Troy-based Anchor Bay studio keeps cult horror classic alive after 20 years." *Detroit News*, February 21, 2002.

Dunkley, Cathy. "Raimi and Senator join in fantasy deal." *Daily Variety*, May 16, 2002, 6.

Ferrante, Anthony C. "For Love of the Game." *Eon Magazine*, November 24, 2000.

Flynn, Gillian. "Web Casting." *Entertainment Weekly*, February 11, 2000, 9.

Friedman, Robert. "Will Cannon Boom or Bus?" *American Film*, July/August 1986, 57.

Gardner, Chris. "*Grudge* remake haunts fast track at Ghost House." *Hollywood Reporter*, February 21, 2003, 89.

Giles, Jeff. "Cate Expectations: Blanchett astounds yet again—this time in the spooky thriller *The Gift*." *Newsweek*, January 15, 2001, 58.

———. "The Quick and the Dead." *Newsweek*, February 20, 1995, 72.

Ginsburg, Merele. "Heaven's Cate." *WWD*, January 18, 2001, 4.

Gleiberman, Owen. "*Army of Darkness*." *Entertainment Weekly*, March 5, 1993, 41.

Green, Jesse. "Fresh Blood: Leonardo DiCaprio." *New York Times*, February 12, 1995. sec. 6, 28.

Grego, Melissa. "Split Personality at CBS." *Daily Variety*, November 11, 2002, 1.

Harshaw, Tobin. "Something Film Noirish." *New York Times*, September 19, 1993, sec. 7, 9.

Higgins, Bill. "Costner Steps Up to Bat." *Variety*, September 20, 1999, 106.

Hockensmith, Steve, and Beth Laski. "Along Came a Spider: Cult fave director Sam Raimi reveals his plans for the *Spider-Man* movie." *Cinescape*, November/December 2000, 16–17.

Holben, Jay. "Spider's Strategem." *American Cinematographer*, June 2002, 34–45.

Horowitz, Mark. "Coen Brothers A–Z: The Big Two-Headed Picture." *Film Comment*, September/October 1991, 27–28.

Iley, Chrissy. "Call it Chemistry: Chrissy Iley on Tobey Maguire and Leo DiCaprio." *Europe Intelligence Wire*, November 2, 2002.

Inverne, James. "Hero Worship: Armed with colossal budgets and fancy special effects, Hollywood is bringing old comic book characters to the big screen. Get ready for the summer of the superheroes." *Time International*, April 15, 2002, 60.

Jagr. "*Evil Dead 2*." *Variety*, March 15, 1985, 15.

James, Caryn. "Film: *Evil Dead 2: Dead by Dawn*." *New York Times*, March 13, 1987, C18.

Jensen, Peter. "Darkman Lover." *Starlog* 158 (September 1990): 37–41.

Jones, Alan. "Sam Raimi Interview." *Starburst Magazine*, 1987.

Kakutani, Michiko. "Plotter's Stupidity Saved by Stupidity of Others." *New York Times*, September 3, 1993, C21.

Kauffman, Stanley. "Playing Games." *New Republic*, October 18, 1999, 28.

Kehr, Dave. "At the Movies—Beyond Genre." *New York Times*, December 15, 2000, E15.

Kerr, Phillip. "Day of the arachnid—Phillip Kerr watches a new superhero dangle against an old skyline." *New Statesman*, June 3, 2002, 45.

Killday, Gregg. "No. 1 with a bullet: Thell Reed, Hollywood's fastest hand." *Entertainment Weekly*, February 17, 1995, 41.

Kim, Chuck. "Drawn to *Spider-Man:* Out comic book writer Phil Jimenez went from drawing Wonder Woman to subbing for Tobey Maguire's hands on the *Spider-Man* set." *Advocate*, May 14, 2002, 66.

Klawans, Stuart. "The Boys of Summer." *Nation*, October 11, 1999, 34.

Koltnow, Barry. "*The Gift* star Cate Blanchett's eye is on the future." *Knight Ridder/Tribune News Service*, January 21, 2001, K2128.

———. "*Spider-Man* director Sam Raimi responds to criticism." *Knight-Ridder/Tribune News Service*, April 29, 2002, K1632.

Lane, Anthony. "Current Cinema: Balkan Homecoming." *New Yorker*, March 13, 1995, 111.

———. "Tangled Webs: *Spider-Man* and *The Lady and the Duke*." *New Yorker*, May 13, 2002, 96.

Laski, Beth, and Annabelle Villanueva. "Holiday Movie Review—*The Gift*." *Cinescape*, November/December 2001, 56.

Lawson, Terry. "A Cult Figure since *The Evil Dead*, actor leads with his chin." *Knight-Ridder/Tribune News Service*, June 20, 2001, K7979.

Lee, Luaine. "Spider-Man Tobey Maguire's Life Lessons." *Knight-Ridder/Tribune News Service*, April 30, 2002, K7164.

Lyman, Rick. "At the Movies." *New York Times*, September 17, 1999, E14.

Magid, Ron. "Crawling the Walls." *American Cinematographer*, June 2002, 45–57.

———. "Making Spidey Sense Tingle." *American Cinematographer*, June 2002, 52–53.

Malcom, Shawna. "Along Came a *Spider-Man*." *TV Guide*, April 27, 2002, 20–24; 55.

Mauceri, Joe. "Unholy Trinity," *Shivers* 32, August 1996, 9.

McCarthy, Todd. "The Gift." *Variety*, December 18, 2000, 24.

McDonald, Kathy A. "Laura Ziskin, self-starting *Spider-Man* producer stays real, seeks perfection." *Variety*, September 20, 2002, A6.

McIntyre, Gina. "Dark Man." *Wicked*, Spring 2001, 16–20.

Miller, Mark. "Throwing Heat—It's great to see Costner back in the ballpark. The actor opens up about women and movies—and talks bluntly about the struggle over *For Love of the Game*." *Newsweek*, September 13, 62.

Miller, Samantha. "Web Master: Tobey Maguire, Hollywood's go-to sensitive young guy, pumps up his pecs, delts and career with *Spider-Man*." *People Weekly*, May 20, 2002, 67.

Mills, Bart. "Stone's Showdown." *Entertainment Weekly*, March 4, 1994, 14.

Morrison, Mark. "Kevin Only Knows." *In Style*, September 1, 1999, 476.

Murray, Will. "WHY is Bruce ("Ash") Campbell Still Alive?" *The Bloody Best of Fangoria* 7 (1988): 50–53.

Nashawatay, Chris. "The Man with the Plan." *Entertainment Weekly*, November 20, 1998, 59.

Pearl, Cyril. "Turn the Page." *Video Business*, March 4, 2002, 15.

Pearlman, Cindy. "Stone Cold." *Entertainment Weekly*, February 10, 1995, 12.

Powers, John. *Vogue*, December 1998, 158.

Prince, Tom. "Fast Track—Making a Living." *New York*, August 30, 1993, 48.

Rafferty, Terrence. "The Current Cinema: High and Low." *New Yorker*, September 10, 1990, 103.

Raimi, Sam. "What a Web He Weaves: One Question for...Sam Raimi." *Entertainment Weekly*, May 3, 2002, 92.

Rea, Steven. "Familiarity certainly doesn't breed contempt for Cate Blanchett." *Knight-Ridder/Tribune News Service*, January 19, 2001, K2135.

Robley, Les Paul. "Mobilizing *Army of Darkness* Via 'Go-Animation.'" *American Cinematographer*, March 1993, 72–80.

Romney, Jonathan. "Army of Darkness." *New Statesman and Society*, June 11, 1993, 36.

Russo, Tom. "Swing Time: What a Costume Drama. All the superheroics behind *Spider-Man*'s leap to the big screen." *Entertainment Weekly*, April 26, 2002, 38.

Scheiderer, David. "This Screenwriter Trained the 'Navy SEALS Way.' Movies: For Chuck Pfarrer, the same rule applies in the military and Hollywood: 'You Learn to adapt and survive. Or else.'" *Los Angeles Times*, August 6, 1990.

Schickel, Richard. "Cold Comfort: A Plan goes awry. Alas the movie does the same." *Time Magazine*, December 14, 1998, 98.

Schindecehette, Susan. "Up from the dead." *People Weekly*, December 6, 1993, 135–136.

Schwartz, Robert J. "That's No Gun Twirling; It's an Antenna." *New York Times*, February 26, 1995.

Schwartzbaum, Lisa. "The Pitch is Back: Baseball has been very, very good to Kevin Costner. But in *For Love of the Game*, he could use some relief." *Entertainment Weekly*, September 24, 1999, 117.

Stein, Elliott. *Village Voice*, May 3, 1983. 54.

Sterritt, David. *Christian Science Monitor*, May 5, 1983, 16.

Strauss, Bob. "Cate's captivating gift: in-demand actress Cate Blanchett is all work, and anything but dull, nailing characters as disparate as a psychic widow in Georgia and Tolkien's elf queen." *Globe and Mail*, January 17, 2002.

Szadkowski, Joseph. "Lucas' Force succumbs to Raimi's *Spider-Man*." *Washington Times*, June 1, 2002, B02.

Szebin, Frederick C. "Darkman 2: Durant Returns." *Cinefantastique* 25, no. 6 (December 1994): 36–37.

Thomas, Kevin. *Los Angeles Times*, May 26, 1983, 4.

Tobenkin, David. "MCA muscles in on action hours; on strength of *Hercules*, producers add *Xena*." *Broadcasting and Cable*, August 21, 1995, 25–26.

Tourlette, Rob. "*Matrix Reloaded* Sets U.S. Opening Day Record." *Reuters*, May 16, 2003.

Turan, Kenneth. "The Spider and the Fly Girl." *Los Angeles Times*, May 3, 2002.

Van Gelder, Lawrence. "At the Movies: Louise Lasser Trusts *Crimewave* Director." *New York Times*, June 6, 1986, C8.

Vineburg, Steve. "To Kiss a Spider." *Christian Century*, May 22, 2002, 48.

Uram, Sue. "Bruce Campbell, Horror's Rambo." *Cinefantastiqu*e 23, no. 2/3 (October 1992): 31.

Warren, Bill. "Commander of Darkness." *Fangoria* 120 (March 1993): 38–40; 68.

Winston, Archer. *New York Post*, April 15, 1983, 33.

Wolf, Jeanne. "Oh, Boy." *Redbook*, March 1999, 86.

INTERNET

Anderson, Jeffrey M. "Lurking with Bruce." *San Francisco Examiner*. http:/www.examiner.com/.

"Bill Paxton's Simple Plan." *Entertainment Tonight Online*. http://www.etonline.com/.

Brasel, Doug. "But You Are, Blanchett." *Flaunt Magazine*, holiday, 2001.

Churchill, Bonnie. "On screen she beams but off she likes her anonymity." *Christian Science Monitor*, January 4, 2002. http://www.csmonitor.com/.

Daza, Paul. "John Dykstra: There's Nothing He Can't Make." *INQ7—Inquirer News Service*, May 12, 2002. http://www.inq7.net/.

Fabiano, James, Sean Beard, Matt Williams, Matthew Anscher (Compilers). "Embassy Limited Partners." http://www.angelfire.com/tv2/closinglogo/embassy.html

Forbis, Wil. "The Tangled Web of Spider-Man. An Interview with Joe O'Malley of No-Organic Webshooters.com." *Acid Logic E-Zine*. http://www.acidlogic.com/no_organic_webshooters.htm.

Goodman, Frank. "A Conversation with Billy Bob Thornton." *Puremusic*, January 2002. http://www.puremusic.com/pdf/BBT.pdf.

Lammers, Tim. "Director Raimi has *The Gift*." *Denver's ABC 7, Denver Channel.com*, 2001. http://www.thedenverchannel.com/.

Lee, Patrick. "Sam Raimi unwraps a decidedly different ghost story in *The Gift*." *Science Fiction Weekly*. http://www.scifi.com/sfw/issue192/interview2.html.

Lewin, Alex. "Raimi Gets Metaphysical." *Premiere.com*, July 2000. http://www.premiere.com/.

Michod, David. "Sam Raimi on *Spider-Man*." *Inside Film—Australia's Filmmaker Magazine*, February 4, 2002.

Mottram, James. *BBC Film Interviews*, May 9, 2002. http://www.bbc.co.uk/films/2002/05/09/sam_raimi_spider-man_interview.shtml.

Osborne, Bert. "Movie Interview: Keanu Reeves." *Creative Loafing*, January 20, 2001. http://reeltime.cln/com/movies/interview.asp?ID=321.

Savlov, Marc. "Austin Confidential." *Austin Chronicle*, October 20, 1997. http://www.weeklywire.com/ww/10-20-97/austin_screens_feature2.html.

———. "Interview with Actor Bruce Campbell. Just Your Average Stiff." *Austin Chronicle*. http://www.austinchronicle.com/issues/vol18/issue40/screens.campbell.html.

Topel, Fred. "Sam Raimi Talks *Spider-Man*—Interview with the director of the comic book superhero film." *About: Action Adventure Movies*. http://www.actionadventure.about.com/library/weekly/2002/aa042102.htm

Welkos, Robert. "Odd Man Out." *F2 Network—Arts and Entertainment*, Saturday, December 1, 2001. http://www.smh.com/.

Wiener, David Jon. "Producer and President of the Motion Picture Arts and Sciences: Robert Rehme." *Point of View Online*, Empire Productions, 1998. http://www.empire-pov.com/rehme.html.

Williams, David E. "Rootin' Tootin' Raimi: An Interview with Sam Raimi." *Film Threat*. http://www.filmthreat.com/Interviews.asp?Id=2

INDEX